W9-BZL-692

Early Schooling

ALSO BY DORIS R. ENTWISLE

Iconic Communication: An Annotated Bibliography
(with William H. Huggins)

Introductory Systems and Design
(with William H. Huggins)

Word Associations of Young Children

Too Great Expectations: The Academic Outlook of Young Children
(with Leslie Alec Hayduk)

The First Birth: A Family Turning Point
(with Susan G. Doering)

EARLY SCHOOLING

Cognitive and Affective Outcomes

DORIS R. ENTWISLE   LESLIE ALEC HAYDUK

WITH THE COLLABORATION OF THOMAS W. REILLY

THE JOHNS HOPKINS UNIVERSITY PRESS
Baltimore and London

Printed in the United States of America
The Johns Hopkins University Press, Baltimore, Maryland 21218
The Johns Hopkins Press Ltd., London

Library of Congress Cataloging in Publication Data

Entwisle, Doris R.
Early schooling

Bibliography: pp. 204–11
Includes index.
1. Education, Primary 2. Child psychology
3. Academic achievement. I. Hayduk, Leslie Alec.
II. Reilly, Thomas W. III. Title.
LB1511.E57 372 82-82
ISBN 0-8018-2761-2 AACR2

To George and Ann

Contents

List of Tables

List of Figures

Preface

The sociopsychological basis of schooling has challenged researchers all through this century. For one of us (DRE) it has been the most important thread running through a career—beginning with a study of placebo effects in a field experiment in 1961 and continuing through other kinds of experiments in the sixties and seventies. Hopefully the work presented here, which is based entirely on observational data, will shed some new light on early schooling.

This book has been a long time coming. Pilot work on children's expectations started in 1969. Then, in September 1971, we began to collect data systematically and we continued until June of 1977. In 1976 and 1977, one of us (DRE) held a Guggenheim fellowship and the other (LAH) was a postdoctoral research associate in the Department of Social Relations. The entire year was spent working out our modeling strategy and experimenting with various kinds of data reduction. The timely publication of LISREL III (1976) encouraged us to tinker with some rather complex structural models, and we have worked since then challenging the models in various ways and writing up the findings. After more than a decade we are finally ready to make a full report.

In an earlier book (Entwisle and Hayduk 1978a) we presented data we had collected during the first two years (1971-73) of the project. The present book takes account of that data as well as all the data collected later on. When we wrote the earlier book, methods for analyzing noisy observational data were not as well developed as they are now, nor did we have much feel for what the data might show. We saw general patterns like those reported in the present book (for example, the too-high expectations of lower-class children), but the conclusions were necessarily far fewer and much weaker. However, the earlier work led us to introduce new measures of parent variables and helped enormously in building our basic models. As a consequence, in the present book we have been ambitious: our purpose is to develop a general model for the schooling of young children.

It is truly astounding that so little sociological research directly concerns young children. By demonstrating that even first-graders can be successfully interviewed and that peer and family relations for these children reveal consistent patterns, we hope to encourage other investigators to study social phenomena early in the life cycle.

The first chapter gives some general background on schooling, including considerations of policy and of research strategy. In the next two chapters we review previous psychological and sociological research on schooling, and then, in the fourth chapter, we present a heuristic model that outlines our view of the schooling process. In later chapters, we give empirical grounds for the heuristic model and we modify it into a set of formal structural-equation models that describe the schooling process. We then use data gathered in the three schools to estimate the models. Finally, we interpret the models in the hope of shedding light on the early schooling process.

Acknowledgments

Many persons have contributed substantially to this work, but especially the staff, students, and parents of the three schools involved. For reasons of confidentiality, they must remain anonymous. However, their cooperation and their generosity have been outstanding, and we are more grateful for this than words can express. We also wish to acknowledge the support of Dr. John Crew, Superintendent of Schools in Baltimore City, and Dr. George Gabriel, Director of Research in Baltimore County, for their encouragement of a project of long duration whose outcome was not always clear.

We have enjoyed the support of many students and colleagues. John Stephens kindled our early interest in issues of schooling. We mark it a privilege to have been associated with Murray Webster in the early stages of this work. Through his own experiments and theoretical insights, he did a great deal to help us. Others who have contributed valuable suggestions and ideas are David Baker, Muriel Berkeley, Sylvia Brown, Marguerite Bryan, Ly-yun Chang, Stauros Daoutis, Ellen Dickstein, Susan Doering, Robert Gordon, Esther Greif, Robert Hogan, Willie Jasso, Anne Ricks, Cornelius Riordan, Eileen Rudert, and Michael Swafford. We are especially grateful to Karl Alexander, Andrew Cherlin and Arthur Stinchcombe for reading the penultimate version of the manuscript and for suggesting so many ways to improve it.

A very special debt is owed to Linda Olson. She served as a research assistant from 1971 through 1978. Her talents were employed at every stage, from gathering data and supervising interviewers to preparation of drawings and tables for the final manuscript. She is the person chiefly responsible for organization of the data archive. Her contributions to this research have been very substantial.

Those who have helped with manuscript preparation include Darlene Beall, Judy Kennedy, Mary Klingmyer, and Shelley Rojas. Gloria Zepp has helped in all phases of preparing the final manuscript.

We have been fortunate to obtain the financial resources to underwrite this project from government agencies and from private foundations. Early support was provided by two DHEW grants. One, from 1971 to 1974, was an Office of Education Grant (No. OEG-3-71-0122), supervised by Dr. Albert Crambert of that office. Another, from 1974 to 1978, was a National Institute for Education Grant (NIE-G-74-0029) for which Dr. Oliver Moles served as NIE project officer. A Guggenheim fellowship to Doris Entwisle in 1976–77 allowed her the uninterrupted time needed to tackle modeling issues systematically and to do a first draft of this book. In addition, a small grant from the Spencer Foundation in 1978 allowed exploration of teacher effects, and although this tack proved impossible to pursue as fully as we hoped, we nevertheless are grateful for that support.

From 1978 to date, the Center for the Social Organization of Schools at The Johns Hopkins University has provided the support needed to bring this work to a conclusion. We are grateful to Joyce Epstein, Edward McDill, and James McPartland of that Center for their loyal encouragement over the past four years.

It seems particularly appropriate here to recognize the key role that administrators of The Johns Hopkins University have played in helping us with this work. Grants with specific time boundaries are essential, and without them we could not have even started this work. On the other hand, a project like this, which spans more than a decade, and which has many ups and downs, requires the kind of commitment to individuals that only a university can make. We could not have devoted the effort to bring this project to a satisfactory conclusion without the University's consistent support, month in and month out. Over many years the University has unquestioningly provided the atmosphere we needed for research. There are relatively few places in the world where social scientists can work year after year on a project without an immediately visible "product." We would like to acknowledge here how important it has been for our work to have the kind of atmosphere that the Hopkins administration has provided. We are truly grateful.

Early Schooling

Chapter 1

Basic Questions about Schooling

Until well into the present century, Americans believed schooling was the chief remedy for inequalities in social and economic opportunity. They thought that the American dream would eventually be achieved if all children could go to equally good public schools with merit standards: in a just system of contest mobility, qualified individuals should inevitably obtain their deserts and rise to the top. However, in the last two decades, leaders and laypersons alike have become increasingly disturbed by the failure of children from low socioeconomic groups (roughly the bottom 15% of the population in terms of income) to attain an education that will boost their life chances. There seems to be some danger that this segment of the population will become a permanent "under class," consisting of persons who lack steady employment because of their low level of education and work skills, and who in many ways are not closely integrated with the remainder of society (Havighurst 1970).

Schooling is a cornerstone of stratification, although the extent to which schooling supports occupational stratification has not been determined to everyone's satisfaction. Moreover, it is not known exactly how schooling occurs, or under what conditions schooling betters or worsens children's chances for life success, even though such knowledge is essential for understanding stratification in industrial and developing societies more generally. Schooling today occupies a dominant place in children's lives, but we know less about it than we need to.

The facts as we now know them justify concern. The tendency for members of disadvantaged groups to underachieve in school is especially well documented. Whether evidence comes from large national surveys or from single classrooms, the conclusion is the same—blacks, Spanish-Americans, Chicanos, and American Indians do not profit as much from school as majority-group students do. There is also evidence that educational attainment (number of school years completed) is more closely related to social class or home background than to measured IQ. These are unsettling facts for Americans who live in a country dedicated to social equality, where society's rewards are supposed to depend more on achievement than on ascription. Fifteen years ago Coleman et al. (1966) concluded: "Schools bring little influence to bear on a child's achievement that is independent of his background and general social context (p. 325)," and "our schools have great uniformity insofar as their effect on the learning of pupils is concerned (pp. 296–97)."

Coleman's conclusions, although sharply questioned, have not been overturned, although since 1966 there has been much additional research directed at the same questions. The conclusion that most minority-group or low-socioeconomic-status children are underachievers is still valid. However, to document this underachievement over and over again is not useful. Instead, the time has come to discover *how* the schooling process works and what specific mechanisms are responsible for achievement, and to answer these questions robustly.

SCHOOLING

What is schooling? First, it is the process by which children are made able to read, to do arithmetic, and to acquire competence in the other academic subjects. However, schooling also fosters affective and social development, which are much harder to define than cognitive development. Affective outcomes of schooling could include developing a stable self-image, acquiring the means of interacting with classmates and peers, learning social customs and mores, and learning to like or dislike school. Later we develop in greater detail our ideas about some of the cognitive and affective outcomes of early schooling. Here it is enough to note that our focus is ultimately on children's achievement in reading and arithmetic as cognitive outcomes, and on their marks in conduct and expectations for their own academic success as affective outcomes.

In order to develop and test our ideas about schooling, we undertook three extensive case studies in which we followed a large number of children through the first three grades of three elementary schools. Each of these case studies focused on a particular school: a white middle-class suburban school, a lower-class urban integrated school, and lower-class black urban school. Each school is unique, yet in our view each served as an examplar of a kind of school found in many areas of the United States. Since it seems plausible that long-term cultural learning opportunities may lead to stable differences in both attainment and self-image, we hoped to gain insight into what affects young children's early school experience by seeing what happened to these children as they progressed through the first three grades in the unique atmospheres provided by these schools. We asked, among other things, whether the process of schooling depended on the social context. Our choice of variables and hypotheses was based on a number of considerations that arose from theory and from identification of particular gaps in the empirical literature in sociology and education, but was mainly motivated by our wish to understand the basic nature of the schooling process for young children.

THE LACK OF DIFFERENTIAL SECONDARY-SCHOOL EFFECTS

Sociological Studies

Perhaps more than any other, the puzzle of status attainment has captured sociologists' attention over the past decade, beginning with the Coleman et al. (1966) report and Blau and Duncan's (1967) models of status attainment. Analysis and re-analysis of several large American data sets have served to modify and elaborate Blau and Duncan's basic model, particularly with respect to the specification of variables antecedent to educational attainment. Among data sets used for such analyses, those of particular note are the Equality of Educational Opportunity data (Mosteller and Moynihan 1972), the Project Talent data (Jencks et al. 1972), several sets of data from Wisconsin (see, for example, Hauser 1971; Sewell, Haller, and Portes 1969), and a national sample procurred by the Educational Testing Service (Alexander and Ekland 1975). Without exception, these studies have led to the same conclusion: a comparatively small amount of variance in status attainment is explained (typically in the neighborhood of 30%-40%), and the contribution of school factors to this variance appears to be small or even negligible. This conclusion, based on empirical investigations in the United States, parallels that of a study of the children born in Warsaw in 1963, in which school and other factors could be clearly separated from one another (Firkowska et al. 1978). Therefore, despite increasingly sophisticated models and big and carefully measured samples, at this time one can say only that, on the basis of a large amount of evidence, differential school influences appear relatively unimportant.

Some take comfort in these statements, interpreting them as evidence of the robustness of human learning. After all, they argue, if children's learning were so frail a process as to be swayed by every environmental breeze, the human race could hardly have survived generation after generation (see, for example, Stephens 1956, p. 469).

Yet it is hard for many other people to accept the conclusion that schools make little difference. For one thing, this conclusion flies in the face of all society's myths about the "right school." People are reluctant to conclude that schools make little difference for other reasons as well, including reasons that may have more to do with the psychological make-up of human beings than with the objective evidence. Finding "no difference" is psychologically distasteful, unsettling, disconcerting, and, of course, ultimately unverifiable.

For these reasons and others, the issue of small or negligible school differentials in achievement is not likely to go away soon. Seasoned investigators, in fact, continue to cast about for alternative hypotheses, hoping to catch the differential influence that schools "should exert." Two such hypotheses have been articulated lately: 1) Dynamic models should replace the (so far) static models serving as paradigms for research on school effects because the static models may mis-specify, and therefore miss, effects that are principally dynamic in nature (see Sorenson and Hallinan 1977). 2) Differential school effects may be substantial in the early school years but gradually diminish, and since practically all sociological research on school effects has focused on the secondary school, effects present earlier may have gone unnoticed (see Alwin and Otto 1977). To our knowledge, few empirical data exist to inform either the "mis-specifications" or the "early-schooling" hypothesis. Actually, of course, both hypotheses, as well as others, are plausible. That is, schools may have a significant effect upon children mostly early in their academic careers, through a dynamic or feedback process. The functional form of models of the schooling process is certainly debatable (see Hauser 1978), but the desirability of multiwave data is not: it is very hard to study a continuing process like school learning with data that have been gathered at only one or two discrete points in time and then have been analyzed by statistical techniques suitable for cross-sectional surveys. Luecke and McGinn (1975), particularly, have faulted the use of cross-sectional data to estimate structural models of schooling, and the bias introduced in some parameters can be large enough to obscure cause-effect relations (Alexander, McPartland, and Cook 1981; Cook and Alexander 1980).

Still another hypothesis that accounts for the lack of differential school effects is the proposal that effects of education cannot be operationalized as differences among schools. Heyns (1978) tested this notion empirically and at least tentatively confirmed it. Her idea is that schools and families are complementary—and possibly competing—influences upon educational attainment. She isolated school effects by contrasting the learning achieved by a large sample of sixth- and seventh-graders over the school year, when schools are in session, to the amount of learning achieved by the same children during the summer, when schools are closed. She concluded that summer learning depends much more heavily on the family background of students than does learning accomplished while school is in session. Rates of learning were uniformly higher during the school year for all children, but, for disadvantaged and minority youth, rates dropped off precipitously in the summer. Thus, Heyns showed indirectly that school influences are substantial, and that school attenuates the influence of socioeconomic status.

Our view, like that of Heyns, is that investigators have been asking the wrong questions about schooling. Heyns points to the logical inconsistency involved when small differences between effects of schools are taken as evidence of negligible effects of schools altogether. She argues (1978, p. 9 ff.) that educational research has been seriously flawed, not only by the lack of variability in children's exposure to schooling, which in essence leads to inability to apply Mill's canon of differences, but also by the confounding of schooling and other determinants of achievement. To say that differential effects between schools are small does not imply that schools have little impact on students. Children are continuously learning, in school and out of school, and actually, since students spend much more time outside school than inside it, family or other background influences on achievement could be very strong. Heyns' points are especially well taken for young children beginning school, because their curriculum embraces topics that are frequently encountered in everyday life, and therefore learning about these topics is highly responsive to experiences outside school. This view is also consistent with Stephens's (1967) theory of spontaneous schooling.

The neglected aspect of schooling research is *process*: what occurs while pupils are in school. Or, expressed another way, what do schools do to pupils that leads pupils to achieve? The several large-scale studies mentioned above, including the Coleman report and others like it, suggest that schools themselves contribute little to differential achievement. These studies, however, do not attempt to explain the schooling process. For example, Coleman and his associates investigate library size, but they do not explicitly specify how library size, or other school facilities, could lead to pupil achievement. Although pupil background is a relatively important explanation for variance in pupil achievement in all the large-scale studies, no study directly addresses how background is converted into attainment. By contrasting pupil achievement when schools are in session with achievement when schools are closed, Heyns suggests the circumstances under which home background may be important, and how background and school may interact. She does not believe that the increasing gap that separates the economically favored children from the disadvantaged can be attributed to the fact that schools have no effects, because the distance between students narrows during the school year. She does not say so explicity, but her data invite a further conclusion—differential school effects should probably be modeled as differential interaction effects between home and school, rather than simply as differential main effects. In any case, her study underlines the dangers of concluding that schools have little effect.

Other Studies

Sociological studies are often undertaken on a large scale, and focus directly on differential school effects. Most psychological and educational studies, in contrast, are small scale, and make only oblique contributions to our understanding of differential school effects. The latter studies often focus on some small aspect of pupil-teacher relations: for example, how teachers who hold high expectations for certain students treat those students. Generally, social structure is ignored, and, partly for this reason, such studies so far have not shed much light on the schooling process either. The large- and small-scale studies are at opposite poles in many other respects as well. The large-scale studies deal with aggregate standardized achievement levels by school, and the small studies cover individual behavior and performance.

The large studies are multivariate and observational; the small often involve experiments with very few variables.

However, both large and small studies have one feature in common: they do not address the actual nature of schooling. They fail to specify how background variables and individual characteristics contribute to attainment within the social structure of the classroom. To take an example of large-scale research, the Wisconsin studies show that home background explains considerable variance in educational attainment (Sewell and Hauser 1972, 1975). The process by which background exerts its influence, however, is not altogether clear. Do fathers who are in the professions read a lot, and thereby serve as models who encourage their children to read also? Or, to take an example of small-scale research, many investigators (e. g., Brookover, Erickson, and Joiner 1967; Brookover, Patterson, and Shailer 1962; Brookover, Thomas, and Patterson 1964; Brookover et al. 1965) find that low self-image is correlated with low achievement. We do not know, however, whether low self-image is a cause or a consequence. A low self-image could discourage a child from making the effort necessary to achieve, or poor achievement could lead children to have a low opinion of themselves. The explanations are equally logical.

There is, then, little knowledge about the actual schooling process, and few studies fall in what might be termed the "mid-range"—between the macro and the individual levels of theorizing. To indicate the path that such mid-range studies can take and the promise that they hold, a few recent studies are reviewed briefly below. These studies all fall in the mid-range because they link social-structure variables to pupil attainment. A few of these studies, drawn from diverse literature sources, are discussed separately because they make clear what is meant by a "mid-range" study and the likely fruitfulness of this level of analysis.

MID-RANGE STUDIES

Pedersen, Faucher, and Eaton (1978)

In a research project of "unconventional methodology and unusually long duration" in a disadvantaged urban neighborhood, Pedersen, Faucher, and Eaton (1978) examined the influence of classroom teachers on children's later adult status. The investigators happened to notice that IQ change varied by first-grade teacher, and so they altered the original thrust of their investigation from being directed at IQ change to being directed at teacher effects. Specifically, they found a positive correlation between children's exposure to one first-grade teacher (Miss A) and their success as adults many years later.

A number of measures distinguished between the pupils of Miss A and those of other first-grade teachers even while all pupils were still in grammar school. Perhaps most noteworthy is the observation that Miss A's pupils did better in second grade, and that this superior performance was linked to higher scores on a number of personality indicators measured during the rest of elementary school. In fact, Miss A's pupils demonstrated higher achievement in all grades through the seventh, they showed a consistently higher level of effort in the first seven grades, and they received higher ratings in leadership and initiative over that period as well. Later, when Miss A's pupils were between 13 and 30 years old, they continued to surpass other pupils from the same school: for example, 57% completed ten grades or more, compared with a 42% completion rate for pupils of other teachers. Using a summative index of adult status based on six variables (type of home, rent paid, educational attainment, occupational prestige, appearance of house, and personal appearance of the respondent) as the ultimate endogenous variable, a path analysis shows a statistically significant and relatively large direct effect linking the children's first-grade teacher to their status as adults.

One plausible alternative explanation for these findings is that selective factors operated to give members of Miss A's class some unknown advantage from the start—perhaps Miss A received relatively more children from favored social backgrounds than the other teachers. However, several variables known to have high positive correlations with both socioeconomic status and IQ (number of children, father's occupational status, and whether the family was ever on welfare) were included in the path analysis, and thus both initial socioeconomic status and/or IQ were effectively controlled. Personality differences cannot be effectively dealt with.

The evidence must be weighed cautiously—the sample is small, and the particular characteristics or teaching methods of Miss A are left unspecified—but the study contradicts the idea that teachers have negligible effects, and it is provocative because it hints that research on student's earliest school days may be fruitful. The study offers the possiblity that getting students off to a flying start in first grade is critical to the remainder of their educational careers.

Murnane (1975)

In order to analyze the relations between school resources and the cognitive achievement of black inner-city children in a large urban school system (New Haven), Murnane examined reading and arithmetic performance in the second and third grades. He gathered longitudinal data from individual pupils and related the student data to detailed information on individual classroom teachers. To allow for effects of family or background factors outside the school, he included, as exogenous variables in his models, data on rental costs of students' dwellings and on whether children lived in a household with a female head. Seven teacher characteristics were studied; four were related to the teacher's training and three were based on demographics.

It turned out that, during a teacher's first few years of teaching, there were successive increments in students' achievement, and then something of a decline. Teachers with several years of experience were markedly more effective than first-year teachers, but, after about five years, additional experience did not lead to more effectiveness. Male teachers were consistently more effective than female teachers with children of both sexes. Generally, mathematics achievement responded more strongly to teacher variables than reading achievement.

Murnane's analysis provides evidence that individual teachers *do* make substantial differences in second and third-grade children's achievement. [Hanushek (1972) also finds differential school effects for second and third graders.] Because Murnane's research suggests exactly where to look, further studies employing direct observation might have a better chance of detecting the specific factors that differentiate experienced from inexperienced teachers.

Summers and Wolfe (1977)

Using randomly selected data for sixth-, eighth-, and twelfth-grade students in the Philadelphia School District, Summers and Wolfe studied composite achievement over a 3-year period. Their most interesting findings relate to teacher variables. When they studied rating of a teacher's college, years of teaching experience, and National Teacher Exam score, teacher by teacher, rather than averaged by school, each variable proved to be a significant predictor of student achievement. The same is true of class size: averaged by school, it was unimportant, but, considered teacher by teacher, it proved efficacious.

A number of Summers and Wolfe's conclusions refer particularly to low-income or minority-group students. For example, students from lower-income families benefited most from teachers who had attended higher-rated colleges. Third-grade students who were very much below grade level did best with teachers who were relatively inexperienced. Small class size helped low-achieving students but hindered high achievers. Smaller schools seemed to be generally better, but especially for blacks. All students seemed better off in racially balanced (40% to 60% black), rather than in highly segregated, schools.

Again, as in Murnane's analysis, these investigators offer strong evidence that teachers do make a difference when the unit of analysis allows those differences to emerge.

Schneider (1980)

In a study of 493 children in grades three to seven in four schools, Schneider estimates two production function models. The first is linear and measures "value added" to achievement. The second examines the reciprocal influences of children's motivation and achievement, with school and background variables controlled. Data on teachers' evaluations and peer influences (taking account of instructional grouping practices for reading and mathematics) are included, so that students are effectively nested in classrooms. Of the factors shown to contribute to achievement, some are negative, including effects of the length of teachers' experience and employment of both parents. Boys had higher mathematics gain scores than girls, and men were found to be more effective mathematics teachers than women.

Schneider also reports effects associated with student age—the older the child, the smaller the gains in achievement. She explains age effects as being attributable to the student's diminishing sense of efficacy (as students remain in school and continue to make insignificant gains in achievement, their feelings of helplessness increase) or on the basis of diminishing marginal productivity (no matter how many additional resources are allocated to the student, academic achievement begins to level off). Whatever the explanation, and there are others that we review elsewhere, Schneider's research points to the wisdom of investigating children's school achievement early in their school careers.

Summary of Mid-Range Studies

Other mid-range studies that are not discussed in detail here but that point in the same direction include those by Berkeley (1978), Brookover et al. (1978), Eder (1981), Hanushek (1972), Klitgaard and Hall (1977), Lockheed and Morgan (1979), McDermott (1977), Rist (1970), Sewell, Haller, and Straus (1959), and Wilson (1959).

The consistency of the findings in this diverse set of mid-range studies is impressive. In terms of the minimum age included in each study, the students span the whole range of elementary schoolkindergarten (Berkeley 1978; Rist 1970), first-grade (Eder 1981; Pedersen et al. 1978), second grade (Lockheed and Morgan 1979; Murnane 1975), third grade

(Schneider 1980), fourth grade (Brookover et al. 1978), and sixth grade (Summers and Wolfe 1977). The dependent variables range from success in the next grade to measures of adult status, but in general concentrate upon standarized achievement measures. The students are also a diverse lot, encompassing the range from economically disadvantaged blacks to middle-class whites.

These studies all focus on events *within* schools. Either teachers with particular characteristics are compared with other kinds of teachers or classroom interaction is analyzed in an effort to reveal differences in student achievement. The mid-range studies suggest, in contrast to the macro-studies of between-school effects by Coleman and others, that schools *do* have substantial differential effects on their clients. Moreover, these studies provide a number of clues about how such differential effects may be mediated. Significant others (teachers and peers) and affective measures of the student ("expectations" and "motivations") are repeatedly shown to be efficacious. Some of these studies are methodologically tighter than others, and some are based on much more adequate samples than others, but the overall quality of this research far exceeds most previous work on elementary school achievement. The research that employs multivariate models, in particular, brings to this work a richness and a degree of control that are not present in the earlier investigations that are reviewed in later chapters.

EARLY LIFE EVENTS

Our society is supposed to be one of contest mobility. It is important, therefore, to recognize when the contest begins. Family background affects eventual placement in the stratification system, but family background exerts effects long before a child reaches secondary school.

All the mid-range studies just reviewed focus on students in the elementary grades. Thus they employ the strategy advocated by Alwin and Otto (1977), who believe that observing children early in their school careers (before secondary school) will lead to a better understanding of the nature of school attainment. Indeed, Schneider's study provides direct evidence that gains in achievement can be more readily observed in younger children, because she found larger student gains in the third grade than in the seventh grade.

Kahn (1978) emphasizes the importance of the early years:

> students who do well in high school and go on to college have values and attitudes different from those who do poorly . . . these differentiating characteristics were with them before they entered high school. . . . For me the inference is to start earlier both for purposes of explanation and for purposes of change. (p. xiv)

Although the early days of school must have a highly significant effect on how children develop and on how they are sorted into social strata, our knowledge of this life period is fragmentary. We know, for example, that black children who attend integrated schools often question their own self-worth (Rosenberg and Simmons 1971), but we do not know the level of their self-worth when they started school. We also know that a slight cleavage in dialect between teacher and pupils is often a prelude to underachievement (Rist 1970), but, in some schools, language differences have the opposite effect (Lambert and MacNamara 1969). We even know that the effect of the school's social structure on the pupil can outweigh the consequences of individual rates of maturation—self-esteem in adolescence is more affected by the kind of school attended than by the physiological timing of pubescence (Blyth, Simmons, and Bush 1978)—but we have no catalogue of sociodevelopmental changes. Instead, schools are organized in accordance with tradition, convenience, political constraints, and financial exigencies, and students just have to fit in.

In research on the schooling process, self-contained classrooms like those in elementary schools offer obvious advantages. If a teacher's marks and the effect of these marks upon children and their families influence both the children's subsequent achievement and their ideas about that achievement, it seems likely that the first two or three teachers a child encounters are more influential than teachers encountered later on. Teachers themselves often acknowledge that they teach first or second grade because they feel they have considerable influence on children at this age. Also, in the early grades, children usually remain with a single teacher all day long. Schools are likely to be small, and students' reputations are easy to make or break. In a secondary school, however, students move from class to class and receive marks from many teachers. It would be difficult to tease out the effect of any particular teacher, because, in 36 weeks of high school, a student may see one teacher 4 periods a week, at 45 minutes a session, for a total of 108 hours in a year. This hardly compares to the 32 hours a week, for a total of 1152 hours a year, of exposure to a single teacher experienced by a child in elementary school. Moreover, the influences of home and school are likely to be more consistent in elementary schools, and parents and teachers are more likely to get together.

Folk wisdom stresses the importance of events early in the life cycle. There is more than a kernel of truth in the rhyme:

You've got to be taught
Before it's too late
Before you are six or seven or eight
© Rogers and Hammerstein, 1949

Child development theorists express the same notion less succinctly. For instance, Bloom (1964) says: "The first period of elementary school (grades 1 to 3) is probably the most crucial . . . for the development of general learning patterns . . . and all subsequent learning in the school is affected and in large part determined by what the child has learned . . . by the end of grade 3" (p. 110). Likewise, Kagan and Moss (1962) conclude that "for some children the first four years of contact with the school and peer environments . . . crystallize behavioral tendencies that are maintained through young adulthood" (p. 272). Similar reasoning is used to argue for Head Start and other preschool programs: If children are groomed so that they can do well in the first few grades, their future success is more likely. In fact, a recent study by Rosenberg and Adcock (1979) suggests that earlier pessimistic reports about preschool intervention programs (e. g., the Westinghouse study) may be open to question. In a longitudinal study of several cohorts of Maryland preschoolers followed to the end of third grade, they find persistent and dramatic differences on measures of reading success and other standardized test scores. For example, third-grade reading scores of 72% of the children who had been enrolled in preschool programs were at or above grade level, while only 4% of children not enrolled in such programs scored as well.

It is likely that by the end of the third grade most children's achievement levels are fairly stable. In other words, the quality of children's performance by that age is a good long-term indicator of school performance. In Husen's (1969) large cross-national study, for example, intelligence scores and teacher's rating in third grade were both good predictors of children's subsequent educational careers, and Kraus (1973), who followed children in New York City for over 20 years, found that the most significant predictor of adult status was the score obtained on third-grade reading achievement tests. There was a high correlation between this score and all subsequent reading, mathematics, and intelligence test scores. In a similar vein, Silverstein and Krate (1975) argue strongly that the child has made a commitment to a middle- or lower-class life style by 8 or 9 years of age.

> Middle-class behavior and reading readiness become inextricably intertwined in kindergarten or first grade, mutually reinforcing each other and determining a child's class placement. If the child in kindergarten or first grade shows signs that he is ready to read, he stands a chance of going to the best or second-best class in the grade, where his peer contacts and his teacher are likely to influence him to become more adult-oriented and a better reader. If the child shows little reading readiness in kindergarten or first grade (as was true, we found, of peer-oriented children), his chances for academic success are virtually nil, for he will almost certainly be streamed into a class below the top two on grade, where he will associate mostly with other children who suffer the double jeopardy of a strong peer orientation and little readiness to read. Thus, by the time the child is eight or nine years old his ability (or lack of ability) to read and his adult (or peer) orientation have usually mutually reinforced each other through a sorting process that the school directs. (p. 230)

There are, however, few long-term longitudinal studies of young children, and none, to our knowledge, that employs a representative sample.

Why should early events be so important? For one reason, because of a self-fulfilling prophecy: children's expectations for their own performances shape that performance, and then the performance is evaluated, and subsequently feeds back to modify expectations. Once in motion, this cycle may be hard to break. If children's first report cards rate them low on reading, their initial high expectations may be shattered or their low expectations confirmed. They may then make little effort or be given little opportunity to prove themselves. One evaluation, in this case a first mark that happened to be low, could cause children to treat themselves in a way that impedes learning in the future. Then the kind of treatment they come to expect is altered, and their performance keeps pace. The low reading marks may have had no "real" basis. The teacher may have given the marks merely because she was required to issue a certain percentage of low marks. Such early events, however unrelated they might be to children's actual potential, could nevertheless have profound implications for an academic career, since they may trigger a vicious circle of later events.

Another reason that early experience is crucial is that future gains in achievement are proportional to present levels of achievement (Fishman 1964; Sarason and Gladwin 1958). Children who know the most when they begin school are the ones who learn the most during the year. Coleman et al. (1966) termed this "fan-spread" to emphasize that initially disparate groups become increasingly so—they fan out—over time. The extent of fan-spread is not widely appreciated. By the time children leave sixth grade, their basic reading and mathematics skills commonly range from first-grade competence to tenth-grade competence, a range of over 9 years. Some seventh-graders do as well on SAT tests as the most talented eleventh or twelfth graders (see Stanley 1976). Clearly, it would be advantageous to begin research on schooling early, when the spread among social groups is just beginning to emerge.

What could explain widening differences in achievement over time? One explanation is that children who learn the most in the beginning, say the first semester of first grade, have the capacity, personal style, motivational set, or whatever it takes, to be good students, and that these personal qualities will continue to ease their path in subsequent semesters. This argument is weakened, however, by Gottfredson's (1980) analysis of the Youth in Transition data. She finds that school achievement is a cause of personality characteristics, rather than the reverse. Another explanation is that the high achievers have already acquired better skills than the moderate or low achievers, so their future mastery of related tasks is made easier. For example, children who read better or more efficiently can look up words in a dictionary when necessary. Superior readers can also read arithmetic problems better, which makes success at arithmetic more likely. Rarely does a child who fails reading early in school have a bright future.

Still another reason why early achievers surpass their age-mates by wider and wider margins is children's accumulated experience in the system. If children have spent several discouraging years in school, they are not receptive to most remedial efforts. Gottfredson's finding that poor achievement produces affective or motivational decrements has already been cited. Teachers and laymen alike comment on the alienation or malaise that poor students suffer. Whereas a particularly good teacher or good method of teaching might have some chance to boost student learning early in school, older children may resist even the best efforts. Schneider (1980) points to a similar phenomenon, a student's reduced sense of efficacy with increased time in the system.

Whatever its cause, the pivotal nature of early attainment, especially in reading, is clear. The school curriculum hinges on reading. It is the first topic of instruction and occupies the largest fraction of school time in the first three grades. In addition, since the effect of instruction in higher grades is largely conditioned by reading ability, a poor reader will have a hard time, even if talented in other respects. A mathematics problem in seventh grade might be easy for all children who have sixth- or seventh-grade reading ability, but it will be obscure to children with poorer reading abilities even though their mathematical aptitude is average or better.

The crux of the matter may not be so much what happens in the elementary school, as what does not happen. If sons of blue-collar workers themselves become blue-collar workers, it may be less a consequence of the oppressive price tag on a college degree than of the fact that their educational background, by the time they reach choice points in the system, permits them no alternatives (Silverstein and Krate's point). Children who attend an elementary school in a poor urban neighborhood, for example, usually will not do well if they transfer to a place like the Phillips-Exeter Academy. Children not instructed in foreign languages, music appreciation, or reading for pleasure in the elementary school may find it very hard to compete later with those who have been so instructed. In addition, emotional or affective support may be lacking. Without role models at home, children will not learn habits of mind, such as considering many alternatives before solving a problem, or even the joys of building and maintaining a personal library. By high school, children whose early schooling is weak may be essentially eliminated from further competition.

OVERVIEW

In reviewing both what is known and what remains to be discovered about causes of children's school achievement, we have reached two major conclusions. The first is that, although the social stratification system in America is presumed to respond to schooling variables, so far it is not clear by what means it does respond or to what extent it could respond. We lack knowledge about the actual process of schooling. Second, several investigators have lately voiced the opinion that it might be fruitful to study the schooling process in primary age children (a group curiously neglected by sociological researchers). Several recent studies point to the wisdom of this strategy. The available data suggest that children tend to locate themselves in achievement trajectories early in their academic careers and also that social-structure variables are critical in this sorting process. What needs to be determined is how social structure and the schooling process interact.

In an effort to understand the nature of early schooling, we undertook the research reported in this book. Part of the task consisted of rethinking the major strategic problems affecting research on schooling. Some of these problems have already been mentioned: for example, the unit of analysis may obscure or elucidate schooling phenomena, and children of one age may be more suitable candidates for study than those of another. Another part of the task consisted of drawing upon existing work to put together a reasonable model of the schooling process for young children.

The time is ripe for models of elementary schooling that incorporate both social and psychological components. Schooling is a two-sided process. Pupils achieve as individuals, but they do so in response to demands placed upon them—by others and by themselves—largely as a consequence of their positions in a social network. The network includes both a "sociocultural context" and the persons who are "significant others."

All influences on pupil achievement must be mediated by the individual student—students learn because they hear, see, feel, touch, and respond. If the socioeconomic context in which students live affects school achievement, it must do so by affecting something about pupils, their attitudes (they think adults are entitled to supervise children), their cognitive abilities (they learn a dialect at home that is different from the teacher's), their values (they think that an education is worthwhile), and so on. Socioeconomic context can be measured in many ways, and sometimes it has been measured, e.g., in terms of the number of books in the home. However, to extend this example, books in the home by themselves obviously do not cause achievement. Somehow, what is in the books, or the fact that there are books there, and so books are seen as "important," or the children's observation of parents reading books, causes pupils to change. [In calling for this kind of specification, we follow Whiting (1975) in her plea for an "unpackaging" of social class. Social class of itself causes nothing; however, it implies certain activities or certain outlooks that could serve as causes.] In addition, if significant others affect achievement, they do so through some form of interaction with the student. Students learn because their parents importune them to learn or because their peers expect them to. They learn things mainly to please people, including themselves.

The schooling process involves the child in a series of complicated and interrelated events. The child comes to school with attitudes about the self, expectations about school, ways of dealing with authority figures, and certain rudimentary cognitive skills—for example, the child may know color names and letters of the alphabet. Once in school, children try to master the topics of the elementary curriculum, the most important being reading and arithmetic. Along with their classmates, they are instructed in these matters daily. Children also spend part of each day at home, and some schooling occurs there. At home, children may even receive explicit instruction in academic subjects: they may complete homework assignments, they may play "school" or "library," they may amuse themselves with academic puzzles and games, or their parents may insist that they watch educational TV. Most events of this kind have both social and psychological components.

In this book we focus on two major outcomes of schooling: 1) achievement outcomes, represented by proficiency in reading and arithmetic, and 2) affective outcomes, including the child's academic self-image with reference to particular school subjects and the child's ability to "get along" with teacher and peers (school deportment). In doing so, we pay careful attention to the child's social context. Prior work in both psychology and sociology provided some guideposts, and we review that work before proposing our models. In the next two chapters we turn to the literature review.

Chapter 2

The Psychological Perspective

Common bridges from psychological and sociological concepts to schooling are weak. On the sociological side, although models explaining variance in educational attainment are numerous and empirically well grounded, we do not know whether the structural properties of schools affect achievement of individual students, or even if schools have any differential effects. On the psychological side, abundant evidence testifies that individual-level variables, such as sex or race, are strongly correlated with achievement, but the exact links between a pupil's sex or race and achievement are sketchily understood at best. Significant others are presumed to shape educational attainment because they react to an individual's characteristics and achievements—if first-grade teachers believe girls learn to read more easily than boys, it often turns out that girls in their classes *do* learn to read better than boys. However, with the possible exception of Bandura, psychologists do not usually concern themselves with explaining why or how psychological processes are affected by social context.

There is also very little research showing how the interplay between teacher and student affects achievement over a semester or a school year, except for recent studies like those by Lockheed and Morgan (1979) or Clifton (1980). The course of children's affective/social development over a span of time is also unclear. Children's self-esteem, vocational aspirations, and feelings of efficacy must emerge gradually out of earlier tendencies or vague attitudes, but psychologists usually study these traits only after they have been well developed.

We cannot point out all the gaps and conceptual deficiencies in research on the psychological basis of schooling, but in this chapter we try to clarify how variables in the models we propose, especially students' self-expectations, relate to earlier psychological research.

Social approval must lie at the base of teachers' expectations and rewards for students, but very little is known about the dynamics of social rewards. We have little insight into how rewards (or punishments) affect classroom learning. If a teacher holds high expectations, the implication is that she expects eventually to approve of the student. In the meantime, she will interpret student behavior in the light of her expectations and alter her probability of indicating approval. It is hard to say, though, at any given moment, whether approval is made more or less likely by the teacher's expectations. A student for whom the teacher holds high expectations for performance of a given caliber may be less likely to be rewarded (held to higher standards) or may be more likely to be rewarded (evaluated more leniently so as to agree with the teacher's prior conceptions). The conditions leading to either outcome cannot be set down a priori.

As even these simple examples illustrate, relations between expectations, performance, and rewards are complex, and conditioned by the social context in which they occur. An added complexity is that all students witness the interaction between the teacher and any single student, so other students may be rewarded or punished vicariously. All students are vicarious participants in *any* teacher-student interaction.

At the present stage of knowledge, because of the complexity and ambiguity of moment-by-moment behaviors mentioned above, it may be impossible to test seriously a micro-model that links teachers' expectations and student performance. For a mid-range model, however, we need only assume that teachers' expectations and evaluations add up over time and have some *net* effect, along with the effects of parents and peers. A mid-range model can also account for social-structure effects—how race, socioeconomic status, or gender affects the interactions between student and teacher—because again we can study cumulative effects. In any short series of interactions involving a few students with a teacher, it may be impossible to detect the effects of ascriptive variables, but in large samples their effects may be detectable (Clifton 1980).

For clarity, this chapter concentrates on previous research with psychological variables, and the next chapter concentrates on the sociological.

PSYCHOLOGICAL VIEWS OF SCHOOLING

Early schooling coincides with a period in the life cycle that we term the "school-child stage," when the child acquires a new role set and a more elaborate self-image. After the child begins school, the overall self-image is presumably elaborated to incorporate an academic self-image. We see the academic self-image both as an important outcome of the educational process and as an important determinant of it. Taking this view offers several advantages, one being that it ties together the individual-level (self-image) and the social-level (role set) variables involved in schooling, and another being that it gives a useful perspective on a large body of psychological research related to schooling.

Most psychological research related to schooling is of two types: 1) the small experimental study evaluating a method of instruction, a curricular change, a particular grouping of pupils, and similar issues, or 2) the shotgun study evaluating whether a measure of some psychological characteristic—locus of control, curiosity, self-concept, or the like—is related to school achievement. Much of both kinds of research is conceptually barren, and despite its volume, has done little to clarify the nature of schooling. Occasionally, a clever approach yields a glimmer of insight, as, for example, when the early Pygmalion studies suggested how teachers' "demand characteristics" could influence pupil behavior. However, even such exceptionally insightful studies have failed to pin down the mechanisms by which schooling effects are produced.

A major conceptual stumbling block for psychological studies of schooling is that most formal models of learning, as psychologists present them, place the individual learner in a social vacuum (Estes 1970). The only notable exceptions are Bandura's (1977) social learning theory and Stephens's (1967) theory of spontaneous schooling. Many learning theories emphasize reinforcement or reward, but the social nature of rewards in schools, or their effective range with schoolchildren, is generally ignored. For example, how does a child's race affect the rewards he or she receives in school? Empirical work shows that "rewards" given some black children by white adults are interpreted by the children as denigrating their status (Massey, Scott, and Dornbusch 1975). Under other circumstances, however, white adults can be as effective as blacks in dispensing rewards (Entwisle and Webster 1973) and it is next to impossible to predict when one outcome or the other will occur. We do not have a typology of reward or reward systems. We sense that social approval promotes learning, yet we have no systematic understanding of what social approval is or how it varies.

Bandura's social learning theory (1973, 1977) emphasizes the social context of learning. Bandura (1973) believes that most new behavior is acquired vicariously through the observation of models of behavior and their consequences: "Man's capacity to learn by observation enables him to acquire complex patterns of behavior by watching the performances of exemplary models" (p. 44). Children in a classroom, for example, could learn to reward themselves for good performances by watching the teacher reward other students. Once learned, this behavior could carry over to situations outside the classroom. In its most recent version, Bandura's theory also emphasizes *self-efficacy*, an idea closely related to the child's academic self-image.

Self-efficacy is a concept that is specifically formulated to incorporate cognitive processes into Bandura's theory. From a cognitive viewpoint, learning from one's own trials and errors become a special case of observational learning. The child's conception of the appropriate behavior is gradually constructed from observing the effects of his or her own actions rather than from examples provided by others.

A principal assumption underlying the idea of self-efficacy is that all kinds of events or interactions between persons can serve to create and strengthen expectations of personal efficacy. One major source of expectations is "performance accomplishments," the child's own achievement history. Such expectations govern the initial attempts that a person will make to try to learn a particular thing and also a person's persistence at the task. However, Bandura does not mean to imply that expectations are the sole determinants of behavior. Rather, "given appropriate skills and adequate incentives . . . expectations are a major determinant of people's choice of activities, how much effort they will expend, and of how long they will sustain effort" (p. 174).

Bandura is interested in general learning rather than in schooling per se, but his perspective provides a psychological model looking outward toward significant others. It thus offers some of the conceptual building blocks required for a mid-range model of schooling.

LIFE STAGES

Research along rather different lines incorporates developmental changes or life-cycle transitions as key concepts. Indeed, the notion of "developmental stages" underlies much thinking about human behavior (Erickson 1950). As part of each developmental stage, the self is redefined; the person's role set is revised in a major way by some non-familial authority (see Elder 1968, p. 4). Furthermore, a person's social relations, more than attainment of some chronological age or physical status, seem to govern life stages and how transitions are managed (see Blyth, Simmons, and Bush 1978).

Curiously, one developmental stage in the life cycle when many new kinds of social relations begin, although universal in modern industrial societies, has no generally accepted name.[1] Perhaps, for this reason, its significance has attracted little attention. It is the school-child stage, marked by the transition from "home child" to "school child." When children begin formal schooling, they add an important new role set. They are now students, with a new set of supervisors (teachers, principals, other school personnel), a new set of peers (fellow students), and a new set of role obligations. As Finn (1972) notes: "in school [the child] first discovers that not all students receive the same reactions from the teacher, the principal or from others. At this age, the reactions to him are not colored by his achievement record so much perhaps, as by his sex, color, physical appearance, or his exhibiting proper—that is, docile—behavior " (p. 395). School forces children to expand and to refine their concepts of themselves and their relations with other people. The early days of school, in fact, provide an ideal "looking glass" for the development of the self, as outlined by Cooley, Mead, and others (Sullivan 1947). The well-known theorizing about the looking-glass self is largely devoid of empirical data, however.

Recognizing an explicit school-child stage directs attention to the looking glass and identity formation. Children, once they start school, think of themselves as pupils, and their "work" is schoolwork. However, even though they usually do not know it, when they begin school they are almost immediately stratified along lines that will separate them into various occupations when they become adults.

What happens to children when they go to school? First, there is an end to complete dependence on the family. The child takes some responsibility for his or her own welfare. Next, the schoolchild has some limited mobility—going to school means traveling to and from school with other children, on foot or by bus. Typically, 7 to 8 hours a day are spent away from home. Perhaps the most critical change is that the basis of rewards changes. As children emerge from the protective circle of the family, they find themselves rated according to how well they do *compared to others*, whereas before they were evaluated in terms only of how well they did with respect to their own past record. Children are accepted by their parents and loved for who they are; at school, they are accepted or rejected by teacher and peers according to *what they can do*.

In school the child's success is supposed to depend on activities like reading and arithmetic, but children soon discover that they are rated on their ability to please the teacher, to impress peers, and to forecast others' reactions, as well as on purely cognitive performance. They get feedback from many sources—teachers, principals, and classmates—much of it evaluative. They must learn to differentiate carefully among these persons, according to age and rank, if they are to be successful. Once in school, whether children find it pleasant or painful, their rewards depend on attention to school activities and school personnel. Success is no longer guaranteed. Children can no longer concentrate on only the things at which they excel: Even if they cannot tell one note from another, they are urged to sing, and even if they would rather stand than sit, they must sit. The compulsory nature of the grade-school curriculum has profound significance, because it means that children cannot guarantee themselves success. Adults are free to move—from one house to another, one job to another, one spouse to another, or one hobby to another. One consequence of this freedom is that adults can improve their odds of being successful. If promotion at the present job is refused, they can try another job. In fact, adults' most frequent response to failure is to move. Elementary-school children do not have that luxury. They are harnessed into a job they must stick with, like it or not. They are legally compelled to attend school, and they usually have no option about which school they go to.

It is easy to overlook how overwhelming the change from home to school can be. When schooling begins, children quickly learn that they are being evaluated, but they do not always learn how it is being done. Frequently, they get marks in topics like "language" without knowing exactly what "language" is supposed

[1] Interestingly, in considering moral education, Durkheim (1973) emphasized this developmental stage: "One can distinguish two stages in childhood: The first taking place almost entirely within the family . . . the second, in elementary school, when the child . . . is initiated into a larger environment" (pp. 17–18).

to be. They also may find out that they are in the "second reading group" or even the "third," and be profoundly puzzled about how reading groups are chosen. For the first time, many children feel seriously threatened and fear failure. Only one child in a class can be "best" in reading, so with thirty children in a class, twenty-nine are bound to suffer some loss of reward. The possibility of an unfavorable comparison, furthermore, is outside children's control, because it depends on who their classmates happen to be. Because elementary schools enroll students who tend to be much alike, small differences among the children are often magnified. The absolute differences among the top fifteen students in arithmetic may be small, but these differences are large in the eyes of the children. The early days of school plunge children into what must be a confusing and frightening new environment of social comparisons, but the net residue of these comparisons shapes the child's self-evaluation, what is variously termed the self-concept, self-image, or self-esteem.

We, along with many others, suspect that children's self-images are a crucial component in their academic development, because their views of themselves will filter, color, and even determine their experiences. If they think they will do well, they will be glad to try. If they think they will do poorly, however, they are apt to hang back and to avoid doing the very things that will help learning.

THE SELF-IMAGE

Concepts related to the self, whether called the self-image, self-concept, self-esteem, or some other term, bear on schooling for two main reasons. First, a child's self-regard can be seen as an *outcome* of schooling. Second, the child's self-regard influences other outcomes, especially achievement: positive attitudes toward the self enhance learning (see Brookover, Thomas, and Patterson 1964; Wattenberg and Clifford 1964). Although not always clearly drawn, this distinction between self-concept as outcome and self-concept as mediator of schooling has long been implicit in the literature. Clark (1963), for example, saw the fostering of positive self-images in children as one of the school's major tasks. In the long run, affective outcomes of schooling could be even more important than cognitive outcomes because children with positive attitudes toward school may remain in school longer, may try to learn on their own outside of school, and may even be disposed to continue learning for the rest of their lives.

Aside from humanitarian or ideological reasons for advocating development of a healthy self-image in children, there are grounds for believing that self-regard is an important educational outcome. Students may not fully employ their talents unless their self-image is positive. Davis (1966), for example, in his well-known frog-pond study, found that students who attended highly selective colleges (like Princeton) and received B's were less likely to apply for graduate school than students who attended less selective colleges and got A's, even though, by objective criteria (Graduate Record Examination scores), the Princeton graduates were better qualified. Self-comparison with stiffer competition had eroded the B student's academic self-image. We know of no parallel study of young children, but similar events must occur, and perhaps the young child is even more vulnerable to negative evaluation.

The self-image[2] has been measured in many different ways. Unfortunately, the measures are weak, both conceptually and psychometrically. A noticeable conceptual weakness is lack of a developmental context, even though interactionist notions are generally used to account for the individual's development of a self-image (Kinch 1960). To our knowledge, no one has explicitly traced how a child develops a self-image in empirical terms.[3] A few sociologists (see Parsons 1955) address themselves to the genesis of notions about the self in early childhood [see Denzin (1972) for other citations], but their discussions pivot on revisions of the Mead-Cooley theoretical perspective rather than on empirical analysis. We therefore can assemble from the literature an intuitively appealing range of propositions purporting to describe how the self evolves, but very little data that would inform a developmental theory.

The lack of understanding of exactly how self-image develops is troubling for two reasons. First, most investigators apparently agree that learning is a prime source of individual differences in self-image—the self-image, being a product of experience, must follow learning experiences that should be identifiable. Second, the self-image is sometimes designated as a target for change, but to change the self-image implies knowing something about how it is formed in the first place. To say that minority groups have a lower (or higher) self-image compared to majority groups is not useful unless one can modify or "further the redevelopment" of these self-images. A few sociological papers (see Cohen and Roper 1972; Entwisle and Webster 1972, 1973, 1974a, 1974b, 1978), which we review later, address the modification issue, but to our

[2]From now on, the term "self-image" is used to cover self-concept, self-esteem, and all other similar variables.

[3]Engel (1959), who demonstrated stability of the self-concept over a 2-year period in adolescence, and Morse (1964), who showed a decrease in favorableness of self-perception between the third and fifth grades, are mild exceptions.

knowledge the literature is completely silent on the initial development issue.

Academic Self-Image

At this point it is fruitful to review the research on self-image fairly systematically. We follow Epstein (1973) in seeing the self-image as one part of a theory that individuals unwittingly construct for themselves about themselves, that is part of a broader theory that individuals hold with respect to their entire range of significant experiences. Individuals make and test hypotheses about their "self" and revise their concepts accordingly. The purpose of a self-theory is to optimize the individual's pleasure/pain balance; a self-theory facilitates the maintenance of self-esteem and organizes the data of experience to promote effective coping.

The elaboration of a self-image, we believe, is one of the developmental tasks of the school-child stage. When children are separated from their families, they have the opportunity—indeed they are forced—to develop a more elaborated view of themselves. They are evaluated along a new set of dimensions: citizenship, social maturity, athletic prowess, academic competence, musical and artistic talent, and so on. Accordingly, as children progress through the early days of school and as they experience a new range of opportunities, they are evaluated in *relative* terms (see Rosenberg 1965).

Some propositions in an individual's self-theory consist of expectations for performance in particular academic areas, for example, how competent children believe themselves to be in reading and arithmetic. This part of the overall self-image is of particular interest to us. We assume, in line with interactionist theories, that children's estimates of their competence at these academic tasks are based on their assessments of the quality of their previous performances at these tasks, which is usually, if not largely, conveyed by the evaluations received from significant others.

In our research, we operationalized the concept of "academic self-image" by measuring children's expectations for their marks on their next report card: we asked children to guess what marks they would get on their next report card in reading, arithmetic, and conduct. We inferred from a child's reply what his or her self-image in these three areas was.[4]

A number of questions immediately follow. Do children have any concept of their own academic ability when they start school? To what degree is performance shaped by the child's own self-perceptions? Is the academic self-image relatively stable over the first 3 years of school? These are all important questions, especially for trying to define the role the self-image may play in mediating educational attainment.

Minority-group children who start school with low self-images that interfere with early school performance present quite a different case from minority children who lower initially high self-images as a consequence of receiving low evaluations from first-grade teachers. In the past, poor achievement of minority-group children has often been attributed to their low self-images, which presumably reflect the low opinions society holds of their group as a whole. Impaired self-images could then cause poor performance (see Poussaint and Atkinson 1968, 1970; Rosenberg and Simmons 1971, p. 1). A closely related explanation is that lower-class black children identify with lower-class black adults (use them as role models) and, seeing the adults' lack of prestige, then develop low aspirations for their own future achievement that lead to poor school performance (Henderson 1967). A different explanation for low self-images hinges on low evaluations teachers give minority-group children, either because the quality of the children's performance is low or because the teacher expected, and thereby encouraged, poor performance (see Massey, Scott, and Dornbusch 1975). In this case, children capable of satisfactory achievement are rated low, and they internalize the low evaluation.

The main difference between the two ideas about how low self-images develop is that the first hinges on a "low evaluation" accorded by society, and which therefore would apply to children no matter what their particular school experience, while the second sees day-to-day school experience with a particular teacher and peers as the critical factor.

Our models address these ideas explicitly because they separate out the influence of social background and teacher evaluation. By studying children when they start school, we can infer whether their self-images are well formed at that time, and, if so, how images of minority-group or lower-class children compare with those of middle-class children. As the children progress through the early grades, we can examine the relative contribution of teachers' evaluations to self-expectations, and, as schooling continues, we can assess the impact of self-expectations on attainment.

Most of the literature that deals with the self-concept in relation to schooling is not directly concerned with the causal role of the self-concept in the schooling process as outlined above. Instead, this lit-

[4] While, in general, one would think that a specific academic self-image is highly correlated with stated expectations, the correspondence may not be perfect, as when a child thinks the teacher is an "easy marker," so she will give a better mark than is deserved, or, conversely, when a child feels the teacher is "unfair" because she marks down for some reason other than the inferior quality of performance.

erature consists mainly of correlational studies showing that children's self-concepts vary with their positions in the social stratification system.[5]

Rosenberg and Simmons's (1971) large-scale study of Baltimore children is probably the best demonstration of the critical nature of the social environment. They found that black children's self-esteem may be lower than, the same as, or higher than white children's, depending on whether the black children take as reference groups children who are better off, as well off, or not as well off as they are. Beers (1973) draws similar conclusions. Black children from father-absent homes, for example, may not experience a diminution in self-regard if they attend a school where most of the other children are also black and from broken homes. On the other hand, children from broken homes attending a school where most other children came from intact families might suffer a loss in self-esteem. Social contexts can protect self-esteem or erode it. The context, however, must be the child's—the world of the elementary-school child is not the adult world. Children apparently do not use the society at large as a comparison group. Rather, the evidence is that they use their home, neighborhood, and school as reference groups.

The hidden agenda of many of the correlational studies of self-image and achievement is to explain the low school attainment of blacks or other minority groups, and most studies do not directly test the link between self-concept and achievement. Fortunately, however, the link has been verified in other studies, which are scattered from the kindergarten level (Lamy 1965, Wattenberg and Clifford 1964), through grade school (Brookover, Thomas, and Patterson 1964; Campbell 1965; Caplin 1966; Gustafson and Owen 1971; Hirsch and Costello 1970; Reeder 1955), high school (Brookover, Erickson, and Joiner 1967; Epps 1969), and college (Stevens 1956), and which even consider separately black and/or disadvantaged students (Epps 1969; Frerichs 1970; Paschal 1968).

The major use we can make of the extensive literature on self-concepts as related to schooling is to assume that self-regard and achievement are consistently associated. Except for establishing this linkage, the psychological literature on self-concept and schooling is weak in every respect. Nevertheless, for the models of the schooling process that we develop, this is a key linkage: educational expectations apparently can be both a cause and an effect of achievement. Also, children's expectations (their academic self-images) represent affective outcomes of schooling. While rarely measured, affective outcomes are important and perhaps even more important than strictly cognitive outcomes, for reasons mentioned earlier. Our models examine these outcomes.

EXPECTANCY

Expectations are a key concept in our models of the early schooling process, but two other key concepts, evaluation and reward, are also pivotal because they tie expectations to schooling. Reward or non-reward is conditional upon evaluation, because the same response can be rewarded at one time and not rewarded at another. For example, a child who reads a paragraph in halting fashion on one day may be positively evaluated by the teacher, but a similar performance the next day may be negatively evaluated. The child is held to stricter standards of performance the second day, and is not rewarded for the same quality of performance. Furthermore, evaluation depends on the teacher's expectation. A halting performance by a child for whom the teacher holds high expectations may be negatively evaluated even on the first day. The teacher carries out her evaluations using her expectations as a reference point.

The picture is even more complicated because a success in the teacher's eyes need not be a success in the student's eyes. The child may not be satisfied on the first day with a halting performance even though the teacher is. The student's definition of success also depends on expectations. A student who gets a B may be rewarded (if he or she expected a C) or punished (if he or she expected an A). The child also has expectations about the likelihood of reward, and they operate to interpret the teacher's reaction. Thus, non-response of the teacher can be rewarding, neutral, or punishing depending on the child's expectancy. If a child has been rewarded previously, non-response may be punishing (Adelman 1969). Psychological research on children's expectancy is largely experimental, and to our knowledge none of it is tied to long-term school performance.

[5] Although very early it was assumed that self-images of schoolchildren match the status groupings of society, and that more modest self-estimates of ability occur in girls as compared to boys, in blacks as compared to whites, and in children from low-status homes as compared to those from more affluent homes, even the earliest empirical studies suggested that matters may not be so simple. Controlling for IQ and socioeconomic level, Wylie (1963) found no racial differences in children's estimates of their ability for college, and her conclusions about the relative self-regard of the two sexes are equivocal. More recent studies of the same type suggest that, if anything, self-concepts of low-status or black elementary school children equal those of high-status or white children (Carpenter and Busse 1969; Coleman et al. 1966; Gibby and Gabler 1967; Henderson, Goffeney, and Butler 1969; McDaniel 1967; Scott 1969; Yeatts 1967), or even that self-concepts of low-status or black children are higher (Clark and Trowbridge 1971; DeBlaissie and Healy 1970; Green and Rohwer 1971; Hodgkins and Stakenas 1969; Hunt and Hardt 1969; Phillips 1972; Soares and Soares 1969a, 1969b, 1970a, 1970b, 1970c; Trowbridge 1969, 1970a, 1970b, 1972; Zirkel and Moses 1971; Wilson 1967). However, in many cases the findings are not clear-cut, and it is puzzling that the majority of earlier studies (for example, Deutsch 1960; Keller 1963; Radke-Yarrow 1965) found that whites have higher self-concepts than blacks, while later studies found the reverse.

The interrelationships among expectation, evaluation, and reward can be made clear from a diagram (Figure 2.1). Evaluation implies a *comparison of behavior with expectations*. The determination of whether there is agreement between behavior and expectations leads to rewards or non-rewards. Both teachers and students can react to any one student behavior. If agreement occurs between the quality of the student's behavior and the teacher's expectation, and both are high, then she will decide "success" and give a reward. If both are low, no reward will be given. Similarly, agreement between the quality of behavior and student's self-expectation will lead to satisfaction, a "self- reward." Teacher and student evaluations can agree or disagree. That is, both may give a positive evaluation, both may give a negative evaluation, or one may give a positive evaluation while the other gives a negative evaluation.

One kind of disagreement between the reactions of teachers and children is particularly interesting: the teacher rewards (she perceives performance in excess of her low expectations) but the student's evaluation is negative, because the behavior is perceived as below his or her expectations. This case exemplifies what has lately been pointed to as "institutional racism," i.e., teachers reward poor pupil performance by blacks because they judge them incapable of a better performance (see Massey, Scott, and Dornbusch 1975). These ideas are more fully addressed in the sociological literature discussed in the next chapter.

The explicit micro-model linking expectations, evaluations, and rewards (Figure 2.1) is meant to supplement the heuristic model of the schooling process presented in Chapter 4. The micro-model here outlines in detail the nature of the interaction between the child and significant others (mainly the teacher) that occurs in the classroom. The heuristic model postulates only that teacher expectations and evaluations can affect children's expectations and performance, *not* how the intricacies of the process are structured. In other words, in the heuristic model, the *net* effect of teachers' evaluations is estimated, but not the relationship among teachers' expectations and evaluations. The micro-model is given only to make clear that effects of

Figure 2.1

Model of How Evaluation May Affect Students' Behavior

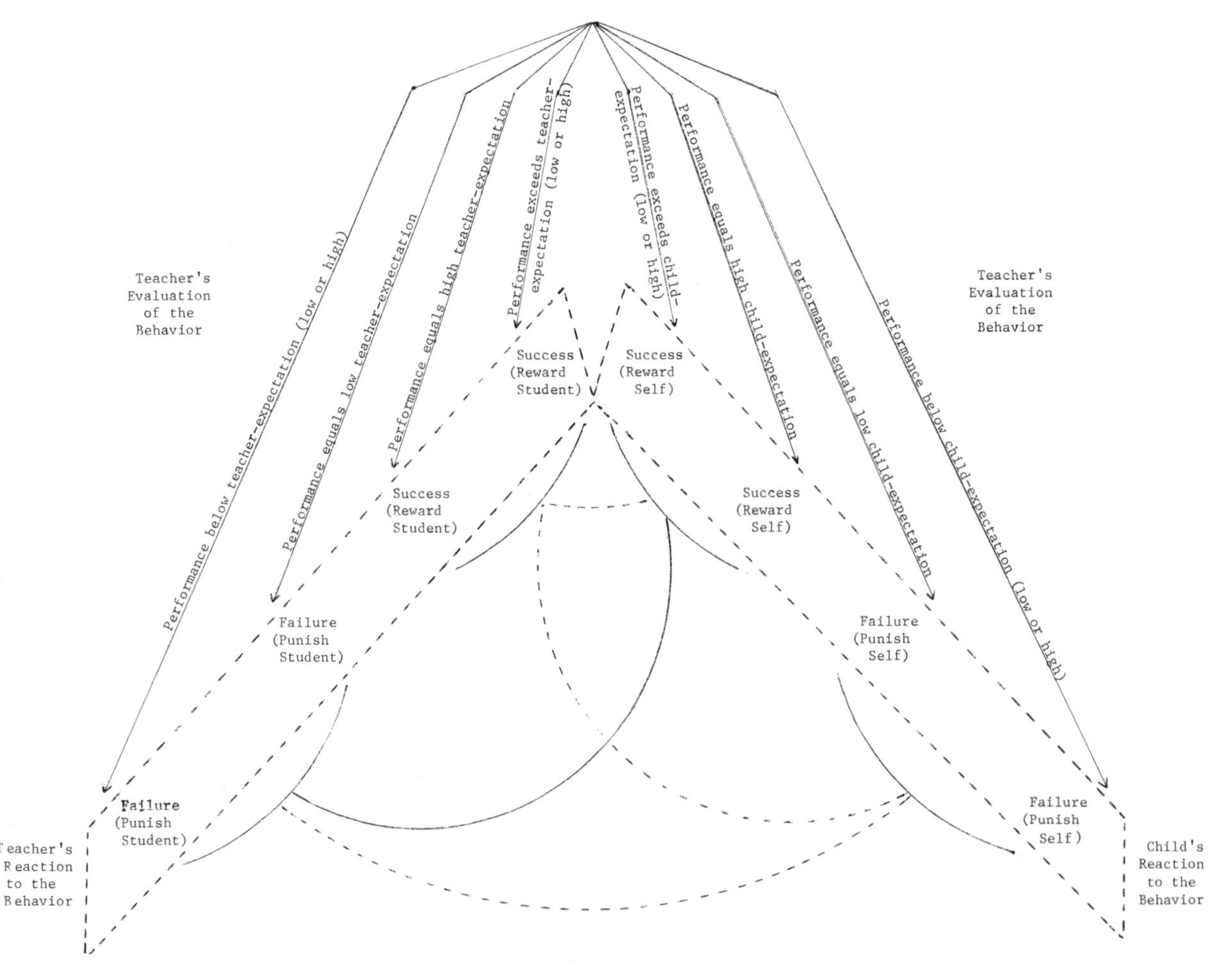

teachers' expectations and evaluations depend on children's own expectations and evaluations. We see its empirical verification as beyond our present capabilities.

Teacher Expectation

The literature on teacher expectations is extensive, its content is fairly well known, and by now it has been thoroughly reviewed on several occasions (Baker and Crist 1971; Braun 1976; Brophy and Good 1974; Finn 1972; Rosenthal 1972; West and Anderson 1974). Although expectancy effects are by no means uniformly found (for exceptions, see Claiborn 1969; Fleming and Anttonen 1970; Goldsmith 1970; Jose and Cody 1971; Mendels and Flanders 1973), the phenomenon of teacher expectancy has sufficient psychological credibility that failures to find it are not necessarily interpreted as proof of its non-existence. However, the research on teacher expectations, which now encompasses scores of articles, is not as directly useful in formulating mid-range models of schooling as one might think. It can be classified along two main lines—experimental studies, in which teachers' expectations are manipulated and then the consequences observed, or studies in natural settings, where teachers' expectations are assessed and then their classroom behavior is observed to see if, and how, their expectations are expressed in their behavior. The early Pygmalion-in-the-classroom work (Rosenthal and Jacobson 1968) is an example of the former: children identified to teachers as "early bloomers" at the beginning of the school year supposedly gained more on IQ tests over the ensuing year than did other children, who were not labeled early bloomers. An example of the latter type of study is Brophy and Good's work—they find that students for whom teachers hold high expectations are held to stricter standards, are called upon more, and are more often pressed for answers (Brophy and Good 1974). In a nutshell, the early studies showed that students could react to teachers' expectations, while the more recent studies inquired into how these effects come about. In this work, children's own expectations have mostly been ignored, and for that reason such studies do not help us much.

On the other hand, there are hints that very young students are particularly susceptible to teacher-expectations effects (see Brophy and Good 1974; Mendels and Flanders 1973; Rosenthal and Jacobson 1968; Seaver 1973), and this evidence supports our decision to study young children. Children just starting school have no basis on which to judge teachers, so their teachers' expectations may be more potent then than later. In fact, this may be one reason for the difference in findings from one teacher-expectations study to another. So far, children's age in relation to teacher expectations has been studied only incidentally, but to the extent that teachers' expectations do have effects, one would expect these effects to be greatest with young children.

In one respect these studies are particularly murky: they do not clarify how praise and reward are related to teachers' expectations. Generally, teachers' patterns of praise do not mimic their expectations, but these are extremely subtle matters. Probably, as Silberman (1969) suggests, teachers consciously try not to play favorites. Also, most teachers today are aware of children's need for positive reinforcement: they know that children who are never praised will probably cease trying. However there are exceptions (Brophy and Good 1970; Kranz et al. 1970), seen particularly in Rubovits and Maehr's studies (1970, 1973) of gifted students. The investigators found that gifted students generally received more praise than regular students, and that white gifted students received extra praise denied black gifted students. Finally, the quality of teacher-pupil interaction can reflect subtle aspects of praise and reward, even when the amount of praise is constant. Kranz et al. (1970) found that students for whom teachers hold low expectations are the targets of more "managerial" teacher behavior.

Some of the most imaginative studies in naturalistic settings are those seeking to explain how teachers' expectations arise. Seaver (1973), for example, found that teachers held high expectations for first-graders whose siblings had done well earlier, and teachers held low expectations for first-graders whose siblings had done poorly. (Perhaps as a consequence, the achievement scores of the high-expectation first-graders exceeded those of low-expectation first-graders.) Other student characteristics that shape teachers' expectations are names and dialect: Harari (1973) found that children with unusual names are labeled losers, and a number of studies (e.g., Clifton 1980; Rist 1970) show that children's speech influences teachers' expectations.

One reason that the extensive literature on teachers' expectations is so weak is that status characteristics have not been included in many teacher-expectations studies, although when pupils are white, of high IQ, or of relatively high socioeconomic status, teachers are likely to form high expectations (Cooper, Baron, and Lowe 1975; Cooper and Lowe 1977). The general lack of attention to race effects on teachers' expectations is surprising in view of the well-known "experimenter effects" attributable to race in experimentation, testing, interviewing, and psychotherapy (see Sattler 1970). In addition, an entirely different line of work—research on the correlates of school achievement of disadvantaged or minority-group children—emphasized the cultural differences in how status characteristics affect classroom interactions. Middle-class children, for example, are more receptive to verbal rewards or smiles from adults than lower-class children, and middle-class children have a sociolinguistic competence different from that of lower-class children. These facts have not diffused into work on teachers' expectations. However, in our research we examine the influence of a pupil's race and sex on teachers' evaluations, and we also try to estimate how much of a teacher's mark reflects achievement, as measured by objective tests, and how much reflects subjective factors.

In our formal models we have no explicit variable labeled "teacher expectations." Rather, to ensure a naturalistic observational context, we had to rely on marks as the closest available proxy for teacher expectations. We assumed that teacher evaluations (marks) are one consequence of teacher expectations, but, to anticipate our findings, we made some supplementary study of teachers' expectations as measured at the end of the school year, and we found that, by including teachers' marks in the models, we had effectively taken account of teachers' expectations as well.

Several heuristic models recently proposed by psychologists [see expecially Finn (1972) and Braun (1976)] aim to account for the effect of teachers' expectations on pupils' expectations and achievement. These models draw heavily upon many of the ideas discussed in this chapter—that teachers' expectations influence achievement, that race or socioeconomic status may affect expectations, that the child's expectations (self-image) are correlated with achievement, and so on. Although the models include social elements—race, parents' expectations, peer expectations—they merely acknowledge that social structure must influence the process of schooling. They do not suggest how a testable model that includes social structure might be formulated. Another major element missing from these models is evaluation, either by the teacher or by the student; therefore, what drives the process is left unspecified. In these models the child's self-image is not mentioned as an explicit outcome of schooling: as is the case with most sociological research on schooling, achievement outcomes are the focus of attention. The weaknesses that we have identified in these models are also pointed to by Scheirer and Kraut (1979), who, in a review of educational interventions designed to improve the self-concept, note that the child's self-concept cannot be altered "in isolation from his social networks of interaction in his everyday life" (p. 142) and that "self-concept change is likely to be an outcome . . . rather than an intervening variable" (p. 144).

SUMMARY

The research reviewed in this chapter underscores the piecemeal nature of psychological research related to schooling. Despite recent emphasis of life-span developmental perspectives, the school-child stage of development has been glossed over. The child's acquisition of a new set of roles and children's reactions to the new social structure provided in the elementary school may be keys to understanding the process of schooling, because children achieve mainly in response to social incentives.

The new social relations that the school child becomes involved in, particularly in respect to *relative* evaluations, appear critical for construction of the child's self-image. Some aspects of the self-image have been shown to pertain specifically to current academic performance, but the self-image is an important outcome in itself, and may be even more important for long-term learning than cognitive variables.

Links between research on children's expectations and teacher expectations are weak or absent, and generally the research designs in most teacher-expectation studies omit race and other background factors. Feedback or circular effects, while acknowledged to be likely, are not directly investigated. In addition, almost no attention is given to marking practices or to how evaluation relates to expectations, despite the importance of marks and report cards in schools.

Thus we are left with little solid knowledge about how children develop their self-image or how teachers' actions impinge on the process. The wealth of information on teachers' expectations—what prompts them and how they are expressed—is counterbalanced by a dearth of information on the overall effects, if any, that expectations have on schooling. Despite the obvious relation between teachers' expectations and their evaluations, evaluations per se have not been explicitly investigated.

Chapter 3

The Sociological Perspective

Educators and developmental psychologists have dominated the research on early schooling. The preceding chapter reveals how complete this monopoly has been, since aside from a few recent papers that take limited notice of race or social status, most previous research on elementary schooling is blind to the social context in which students function. However, concepts such as teachers' expectations or children's self-esteem cannot be truly meaningful without taking into account the social setting in which they occur.

For secondary schooling the picture is different. At this level there has been a great deal of attention to students' social background. In fact, sociologists first inquired into secondary and post-secondary schooling because they wished to explain social stratification (Blau and Duncan 1967). After it was found that educational attainment mediated nearly all the effects of background on occupational attainment, sociologists took on the explanation of educational attainment as a goal in itself. Thus schooling, which is now seen as the major link between background resources and socioeconomic achievement in the early career period (Sewell and Hauser 1976), became an object of sociological inquiry partly by default.

Being able to explain almost three times as much variance in educational attainment as in occupational attainment has been a strong stimulus to sociological research. As Jencks et al. (1972) state, "Research on the relationship between a high school's socioeconomic composition and its students' college plans became a minor sociological industry during the 1960's" (pp. 151-152). This preoccupation continued during the seventies, with re-analyses of previous studies (see Mosteller and Moynihan 1972), examination of differences associated with race and gender (DeBord, Griffin, and Clark 1977; Kerckhoff and Campbell 1977), and assessment of the impact of extracurricular activities (Otto 1976; Spady 1970).

Nevertheless, and perhaps because of their oblique approach to research on schooling, sociologists have ignored developmental issues. If an explanation of secondary schooling had been their initial objective, they probably would have conceptualized later schooling as strongly dependent on earlier schooling from the start, because it has long been known that the best single predictor of achievement at any given level in school is a student's achievement in the immediately prior level. In addition, the forces that shape achievement must be much the same at any age—a student generally has the same parents and similar peers throughout his or her school career. These significant others would be expected to affect younger students just as much as older students, or perhaps more, although the balance of power between parents and peers may shift as students develop. At any rate, some sociologists now conjecture that elementary schools may display differential school effects, even though secondary schools apparently do not (Alexander, McPartland, and Cook 1981; Alwin and Otto 1977). Partly for this reason, their attention has turned to elementary schools.

Research on secondary schooling is the primary link between our research and prior work in sociology, but other strands of sociological investigation are also relevant. One strand is experimental work on expectations and evaluation. A second draws upon theory and research in formal organizations. A third is represented by sociologists' work on self-esteem and the academic self-image. This work, unlike the psychological research on these topics, includes socioeconomic and/or ethnic variables and is based on large or random samples of respondents. Heyns's (1978) longitudinal study of sixth- and seventh-graders in Atlanta actually comes closer than any other previous research to both the style and purpose of our research, since Heyns contrasts the learning process when schools are open to that prevailing when schools are closed for the summer. This chapter examines these several strands of previous sociological research in turn.

THE SELF-IMAGE

Following Coleman's (1961) pioneering inquiry into effects of the social system on adolescents' psychological status, several major sociological studies addressed the possible relationship between children's self-image and their school performance. One set of these studies defines the self-image globally [e.g., "How happy are you with the kind of person you are?" (Rosenberg and Simmons 1971); or "I do not have much to be proud of" (Portes and Wilson 1976)]. The other group of studies defines self-image more specifically, in terms of the *academic* self-image ["How do you rate yourself in school ability compared with your close friends?" (Brookover et al. 1967)] (See also Bachman, O'Malley, and Johnston 1978; Coleman et al. 1966; Wilson and Portes 1975). This distinction appears to be critical if self-image is taken as a predictor of school achievement; Brookover et al., as well as Bachman et al., found that measures of the academic self-image predicted school performance better than measures of overall self-esteem. Consistent with this, Rosenberg and Simmons found no relation between self-esteem as they measured it (globally) and school performance at the elementary level, and they found only weak relationships at the secondary level. Similarly, Rubin, Maruyama, and Kingsbury (1979), in a careful longitudinal analysis, found no evidence of relationships between self-esteem and achievement of 15-year-olds. In light of these findings, although a measure of generalized self-esteem was originally included in our research, we were not surprised when it failed to pass muster as a predictor, and it was eliminated from the final version of our models.

Brookover et al.'s (1962, 1964, 1965, 1967) basic postulates, like ours, are derived from a symbolic interactionist perspective. Their findings were that the expectations that students perceived parents, friends, and teachers to hold for them considerably correlated with the students' self-concept of academic ability (correlations ranging from 0.50 to 0.77), and that changes in perceived evaluation were significantly related to changes in self-concept of ability. Self-concept of ability apparently intervened between perceived evaluations and achievement.[1]

[1] In a tandem study, Morse (1967) found that, for black students, the academic self-concept accounted for more variance in school achievement than did IQ.

The interpretation of the Rosenberg and Simmons and the Brookover studies is limited by the crudeness of models available. In particular, the regression and other analyses then available did not do justice to the full multivariate picture. Similarly, in Bachman et al.'s (1978) more recent study, the stepwise regression analysis does not allow the specification of the role of self-regard in the achievement process. However, net of background factors, school achievement consistently correlated with *specific* aspects of the self-image, as was borne out by Brookover's later work tying the educational plans of elementary school children to their self-concept of ability (Brookover et al. 1973; Brookover and Schneider 1975).

Recently, research employing self-concept measures with older children has been criticized on the grounds that measuring children's self-perception of academic ability is tantamount to collecting self-reported data on academic achievement, a criticism supported by evidence that the correlation between self-concept and academic attainment is primarily due to the dependence of each on academic ability (see Gottfredson 1980). This criticism cannot be leveled at research on the academic self-image of children in the first or second grade, however, because these children have not yet established a level of academic achievement. In addition, our analysis shows that the academic self-image early in life can influence achievement, *net* of ability.

EXPECTATION STATES

A separate line of sociological research deals with expectation states. Unlike other research so far discussed, this research includes a carefully worked-out statement of theory that guided work in the laboratory and in the field from the start. Expectation-states theory (see Berger et al. 1974, 1977) includes the basic expectation assumption: the structure of expectations held by members of a group will determine the power and prestige structure of the group. The theory also includes the concept of a "source": an actor is a source if his or her evaluations are accepted and used by others in the group as the basis of the expectations they hold for their own and each other's performance. Considerable laboratory research testifies to the validity of the basic expectation assumption and the usefulness of the source concept.

A series of field experiments by Entwisle and Webster (1972, 1973, 1974a, 1974b, 1978; Webster and Entwisle 1976) extended the scope of the laboratory experiments in expectation-states theory to elementary-school children. These studies showed that young children's expectations for their own performance responded to evaluations given by teacher-like adults. Another series of experiments by Cohen and her associates (Cohen 1968; Cohen et al. 1970; Cohen and Roper 1971, 1972) tried to discover how expectations held by children could be modified. Both of these sets of field experiments inquire how children's expectations are affected by status characteristics (race), and they explicitly incorporate evaluation as a major experimental maneuver. Hence, they address directly an important issue neglected by psychological studies of expectations, namely, the relation between children's expectations and evaluations. For schooling, which consists of repeated evaluations and grading, the link between expectations and evaluation is of paramount importance.

The series of experiments by Entwisle and Webster sheds light on the schooling process mainly because children's expectations, a topic receiving relatively little attention elsewhere in the literature, is the pivotal concept. Teachers' expectations have often been investigated, but children's expectations are usually passed over despite the fact that *children's* achievement is at issue. The experiments with children are also useful because they suggest how status may affect responses to teachers' evaluations. In a laboratory, subjects can be forced to attend to evaluations, but, in real life, evaluations are often ignored. The experiments suggest that a black child, for example, may not even process the evaluation of a white middle-class teacher.

Experiments by Cohen and her associates (see Cohen and Roper 1972) suggest that evaluations may respond much more strongly to status characteristics than to evidence of competence, and they point to the critical nature of children's expectations for their own and other children's performance. It seems that racially based expectations may be very resistant to change, and that evaluation may be exquisitely sensitive to non-performance-based criteria.

The Cohen experiments led us to inquire into children's everyday experience. What causes children to develop high or low expectations for themselves? Obviously, the children in the Cohen experiments had very well-defined expectations for members of the two races when the experiments began. What is it about a child's social milieu that leads some blacks (or others) to develop low expectations for themselves? What kinds of everyday events, such as evaluations from teachers, can cause children's expectations to change? In fact, the experimental findings caused us to rechart the direction of our research, because the range of children's initial expectations in the Entwisle and Webster studies and the refractoriness of children's expectations discovered by Cohen et al. suggested that observational study of children's expectations in natural settings was a more immediately productive line of inquiry than further experiments.

Apparently, the only other research that examines the relation between young children's expectations and their achievement in natural settings is that by Lockheed and Morgan (1979) and by Lockheed (1976). This work also springs from an expectation-states-theory perspective. In the 1979 study, the classes of 41 second-grade and 54 fifth-grade teachers were selected from school districts representative of the state of California, and students' achievement was found to be the strongest single predictor of teacher expectations. Achievement accounted for more variance in expectations than all other demographic variables combined (ethnic group, race, sex, socioeconomic status, and others). Furthermore, teacher expectations were significantly correlated with students' own expectations (as measured by the student's perception of his or her own abilities). Although there is some question about the causal direction of this relation, students' expectations were taken as determinants of teachers' expectations for reading and mathematics performance, and the relative predictive power of universalistic criteria (student achievement) vs. particularistic criteria (sex, status, and so on) was tested. High teacher expectations were estimated to increase the academic growth of the average student as much as one standard deviation, when it was compared to the academic growth of similar students for whom teachers held low expectations.

EVALUATION IN FORMAL ORGANIZATIONS

Our field experiments showed that positive evaluations by a credible source can lead to a rise in children's expectations. The evaluations themselves were not the major thrust of these experiments, however. Fortunately, Stinchcombe (1964) and Dornbusch and Scott (1975) focus specifically on evaluation and how it can lead to alienation from the social system. Their research helps fill part of the conceptual void noted earlier, which leaves the explicit relation among expectations, evaluations, and rewards unclear.

Dornbusch and Scott believe that the clarity of the evaluation criteria in the eyes of the person being evaluated is keyed to the person's satisfaction with his or her work organization. Also, they maintain that non-performance criteria are often used in formulating evaluations in work settings. Their ideas about "incompatibility" are especially insightful. One type of incompatibility occurs when an evaluation is below the acceptance level of the person being evaluated. For example, a teacher may demand less of a student than the student demands of him or herself. Incompatibility leads to instability, or personal dissatisfaction with the organization. If a teacher rewards a student for behavior that the student denigrates, then the teacher's status is undercut. Such dissatisfaction may be registered by acts of non-compliance (rebellion, disorder) as well as by changes in attitude (alienation, disaffection). In their analysis of the properties of evaluations, Dornbusch and Scott point to several ordinarily neglected factors in schooling research that must have enormous influence on how young children react to their marks early in school. The several incompatibilities they mention all ring true as sources of breakdown in classroom learning:

1. Contradictory evaluations. Children are often rewarded and punished for the same behavior. Also, frequently one child is rewarded or punished for behavior that is ignored in others. (This point was made earlier in discussion of the leakage in reward systems. When all students in a class witness the rewards or punishment given any one student, they then can compare this with how they themselves have been treated.)

2. Uncontrollable evaluation. To the extent that socioeconomic status or gender influence evaluation, the student is not in control. Other dimensions of control related to the compulsory and non-elective nature of the elementary school curriculum are mentioned in Chapter 1.

3. Unpredictable evaluations. The pupil often does not know what marking standards are in force or what behaviors are being judged. A particularly perplexing aspect of unpredictability for some students, mentioned earlier, is that the standards are constantly moving. Also, standards are multiple: for example, students' oral reading proficiency depends on accuracy of decoding, on speed of decoding, on "expression" in tone of voice, and so on.

4. Unattainable evaluations. For some children unattainable evaluations are closely related to unpredictability. Other children may be unable to attain an A in reading because the teacher decided not to give any A's. Further reasons for unattainable evaluations are children's being absent, having visual or hearing disorders, or being immature for their age.

All these incompatibilities lead to pressure for change. For young schoolchildren such pressures have no natural outlet because they cannot change classrooms or schools, nor can they revise the curriculum or the marking system. Since changing their environment is impossible, the children themselves must change. One option is for pupils to change by ignoring the standards (by skipping school or by not paying attention). Another way to change is to say that school goals are unimportant and therefore the evaluations are irrelevant. However, if evaluation of current performance is not processed, achievement is hampered.

Dornbusch and Scott do not discuss young schoolchildren, but their conceptualization of authority and its relation to evaluation helps fill out all the literature so far reviewed. For instance, teachers' expectations are often expressed as part of an evaluation process, and all psychological theories of learning see evaluation as critical either in terms of reinforcement (affect) or information (cognition); in addition, children's relative positions in the classroom are determined by the evaluations they receive. Large-scale studies of schooling neglect the role of the teacher as evaluator.

Massey, Scott, and Dornbusch (1975) also illustrate how critical evaluation is for understanding schooling. They point to a distorted evaluation system in an urban school district as one explanation for the poor school performance of minority students. Black high-school students surveyed in San Francisco in 1974 did not consider their teachers' evaluations to be soundly based. About half the students believed that, even if they did poor work or did not try, they would not get poor marks. Furthermore, low achievers perceived teachers as giving more praise to them than to high achievers. These observations led Massey et al. to see faulty evaluation as a major cause of the poor performance of black students, and to underscore the need for research that examines expectations, evaluations, and social structure jointly.

Researchers have not linked the structure of evaluation to students' achievement in elementary schools in a causal way. Theories of school learning (see Bossert 1978) traditionally treat the school at two extremes, either as a "black box," or as a highly individualized and fragmented system of social exchanges. In either case, evaluation is missing as an analytical element, even though patterns of evaluation are probably critical in establishing early achievement levels. Basically, evaluation provides feedback to guide performance. Unless children know how they are doing, they cannot judge how to modify their actions. Young children also need to learn how to evaluate themselves. In fact, most of the time, self-evaluation is the only kind available. Obviously, there is an almost unlimited scope for important research in evaluation that involves social approval. School systems sometimes question their grading policies, but it would be more pertinent to investigate how effectively evaluations are communicated and if students understand what is being evaluated.

SOCIOLOGICAL RESEARCH ON SECONDARY SCHOOLING

Substance

Sociological research on secondary schooling is too extensive to allow a comprehensive review here. Rather, in this section we highlight the similarities and differences between our research and previous sociological research on secondary schooling.

The reader should be careful not to jump to the conclusion that our research is just another example of "typical" sociological research on educational attainment. Although our modeling style owes much to studies of educational attainment at the secondary level, our research has a unique purpose and strategy. The similarity between our models and previous models is more apparent than real. In the first place, we are attempting to describe schooling per se. Second, both affective and cognitive outcomes are considered. Third, processes, rather than outcomes, are the major focus. Fourth, assumptions about significant others' influence, although reminiscent of what is seen in models for secondary students, differ in conceptual formulation and in the way that influence is measured. Finally, data were collected over a long time, in order to measure variables repeatedly at times corresponding exactly with assumptions about the causal processes affecting young children in the first three grades. We did not start this research by adapting any existing sociological model. Rather, we started from a heuristic psychological model (presented in the next chapter) linking children's expectations to their achievement, and then stretched that model out over time. The basic model, which incorporated a number of assumptions about how psychological and sociological variables impinge upon early school performance, was conceived in dynamic terms in order to allow feedback from prior performance to affect the subsequent schooling process.

Sociological research on secondary schools is guided by three questions (Sewell and Hauser 1975, p. 7): 1) To what degree does achievement depend on factors not under the individual's control? 2) What are the organizational and social psychological mechanisms of this dependence? 3) To what extent do ability, aspiration, and effort depend on factors other than the individual's own experiences and prior achievement? In short, what educational rewards accrue to a person by virtue of his or her social role? Or, put another way, what forces limit students' prospects for adult success, even though these forces may be beyond the students' control, and may even carry implications the students cannot fully appreciate?

Our research aims to develop models by which to address similar questions for elementary students. That is, one aim is to discover the extent to which children's achievement in reading and arithmetic in the early grades responds to parents' expectations, peers' expectations, the evaluation process, and/or the cultural context of the school. A closely related objective is to specify the structural relation linking, say, reading achievement, with expectations of significant others or with self-expectations (aspirations). By following the same individuals through the early grades (tracing their individual histories) and contrasting what happens to children in three prototypical schools, we hoped to draw at least limited conclusions about how students may respond to social factors and to their own personal achievement histories.

The particular conceptualization of the secondary schooling process advanced by the Wisconsin group (Sewell and Hauser 1972, 1975) is broadly representative of most such research, and therefore will serve in what follows as a backdrop for discussion of the process of elementary schooling. The Wisconsin model includes social, economic, and psychological information. Educational attainment is attributed to intellectual ability, academic performance, social influences stemming from parents, peers, and teachers, and to the student's aspirations for schooling and job. Specifically, the Wisconsin model (Sewell and Hauser 1975, p. 92; or Sewell and Hauser 1976, p. 16) takes as predetermined: father's education, mother's education, father's occupational status, and parents' average income. Successive endogenous variables are: student's mental ability, high-school marks, encouragement of significant others (friends, teachers, parents), student's aspirations (for college and job), and, finally, educational attainment after high school as well as later occupational achievement. The data for estimating the model consist of a probability sample of Wisconsin high-school seniors who were questioned in 1957 about their socioeconomic origins, educational experiences, and educational and occupational aspirations, and who were requestioned at intervals since then. It turned out that family socioeconomic status and the social-psychological factors accounted for 54% of the variance in years of schooling (Sewell and Hauser 1976).

Understanding schooling for elementary children requires a different approach. First-graders cannot write answers to questionnaires. They cannot respond to questions about family background. Their aspirations have a different meaning from aspirations of secondary-school students. For example, they may hope to get good marks in reading or arithmetic but their aspirations about college or jobs are largely fantasy. In addition, expectations of significant others for young children relate to more immediate goals, and are not equivalent to "encouragement to attend college." Parents' encouragement is manifest by the parents' making sure the child gets to school on time, or the parents' expecting the child to do well in school. Although the social-psychological forces affecting students in elementary school are reminiscent of those in the Wisconsin model, the actual variables that can be measured are considerably different. A quick overview will help show how the present research differs from the Wisconsin work.

1. Elementary schools usually serve neighborhoods that are homogeneous with respect to social class, income, and parents' education. Hence, in the present research the school that children attend is a proxy for socioeconomic background.

2. The influence of significant others is represented by guesses of parents and peers about how well the child will do in reading, or in other school subjects, on a forthcoming report card.

3. Students' educational expectations are represented by their guesses about what a forthcoming report card will show in terms of marks for reading, arithmetic, and conduct.

4. "Educational attainment" is taken as achievement in reading and arithmetic and is measured mainly by school marks (or standardized tests).

Much of the flavor of the Wisconsin model is present in our work, but the review just given emphasizes how the variables and their definitions differ importantly from those of the Wisconsin model.

Another key point is that there are pronounced differences in social structure between elementary and secondary schools. Elementary schools are parochial neighborhood institutions, even in large cities. Elementary schools enroll children for a long time—typically 1 year of kindergarten plus 6 or 8 years of grade school—and classrooms are self-contained. Parents, although rarely seen in higher-level schools, are often in close touch with the neighborhood elementary school. Furthermore, school and parent influences may be mutually reinforcing, because the school and neighborhood are the same on many important dimensions. School effects, then, if they exist, should be more pronounced in the elementary school than in the secondary school, because school influence is exerted over a longer period, in more concentrated form, and is consistent with "neighborhood" influences.

It bears repeating that the process of elementary schooling is the focus of attention in this work rather than the level of attainment. Both affective and achievement outcomes are of interest in the models that are developed. Early in the child's school career, the major tasks are learning how to behave in school and learning how to read and do arithmetic. Along the way, the children develop ideas about their own competence.

Method

Most sociological research on secondary schooling conceptualizes the process of educational attainment as occurring over some period of time, even when the data are cross-sectional. For purposes of modeling, students are asked to recall information pegged to prior events. (In the Wisconsin sample, students reported on father's education, family income, and the like). Thus, the data, although procured at a single time, may be used to estimate a longitudinal model. True panel studies, with students actually queried on successive occasions, are less common, although there are some (see references cited in Cook and Alexander 1980). Information procured from students and other persons on several occasions in a time frame matched to the structural dependencies of the model (the strategy used in the present research), so far as we know, is a strategy not yet used with secondary students. Obviously, however, for studying the schooling process, it is desirable to measure students at several points in their school careers. For one thing, outcomes are probably exaggerated without earlier "control" levels. For another, without a sequence of measurements, it may be impossible to specify unambiguously the direction of causal influences. A low self-image, for example, may cause a student's poor school performance, or, on the other hand, a poor performance may lead to a low self-image. If these variables are measured in sequence, it may help in specifying the direction of causal influence.

In conclusion, the present research adopted its general style of modeling and parameter estimation from previous studies of secondary-school attainment, but the design and execution of this research is different from any prior study. The elementary schooling process is conceptualized as a time-dependent continuous process, where students are nested in a set of significant others and respond to the expectations and evaluations of others as well as to their own. The research uses a series of overlapping panels, where the endogenous variables of one panel are the exogenous variables of the next panel. (Children's expectations at the end of first grade are an outcome of the first-grade schooling process but also serve as input variables in the second-grade model). In addition, the different variables within each panel are measured at times consistent with assumptions of causal priority. For example, within the first panel, parents are queried before children, because it is assumed that parents' expectations are a cause of children's expectations when the children start school. Later on, allowance is made for the possible influence of children's expectations upon parents' expectations. Generally, respondents were questioned at times closely corresponding to hypotheses about the causal processes presumed to be operating.

SUMMARY

In Chapter 1 we briefly review large-scale studies of schooling (Alexander and Eckland 1975; Coleman et al 1966; Hauser 1971; Jencks 1972; Sewell, Haller, and Portes 1969) and conclude that differences among schools have generally turned out to be small. However, as Heyns's (1978) research on summer learning makes clear, this conclusion does not necessarily imply that effects of schooling are small. Some clues suggest that a macro unit of analysis may obscure the schooling process or even veil schools' differential contributions to attainment. In addition, we observed that the period in life when schooling effects may be largest—the time that the child begins school—is the one so far least studied by sociologists.

Differential schooling effects may, in fact, occur early and fade out after only a few years in school, but previous research on elementary schooling does not adopt an analytic framework geared to the task of estimating early school effects. With the notable exception of Heyns's recent work, heuristic models for elementary schooling are the limit of what has so far been proposed. Such models are useful, but are not explicit enough to guide multivariate research.

Fortunately, the analytic models developed by sociologists for understanding secondary-school attainment point the way toward modeling of the early attainment process. The established body of cumulative work on secondary attainment is also a rich source of clues about the key variables. "Mother's encouragement" in the Wisconsin model, for example, is closely related to "parents' expectations" in Braun's heuristic psychological model. On the other hand, for both theoretical and practical reasons, the paradigms used so successfully with secondary students cannot be adopted willy-nilly. The nature of the schooling process and the possibilities for measuring variables are different at the elementary level.

Other kinds of sociological research contribute less directly to the understanding of schooling, but offer significant insight into the nature and role of self-image and evaluation, and the effect of status upon both. This work ties children's self-expectations to their performance level via evaluations.

Chapter 4

A Heuristic Model of Schooling

Causal models, although widely used in sociology and economics, are not yet very common in other branches of social science. However, ideas about such models are beginning to filter into child development (Ambron and Rogosa 1975) and education (Anderson 1978), where they could be especially useful, since in those disciplines so many problems can be addressed only with non-experimental data. Our use of structural equation models with data gathered from elementary-school children is novel. Apparently, except for Heyns (1978) and Lockheed and Morgan (1979), only Walberg and Marjoribanks (1976), who estimated a series of models with British data taken from the Plowden report, have previously used comprehensive models with young children to address issues of schooling.

In this chapter a heuristic model of the schooling process is proposed. This model helps to organize what follows and to provide links to what has gone before. Drawing upon the intuitions gleaned from the literature review in the previous chapters, the model provides a springboard for the later presentation of a series of cyclic structural-equation models that we actually try to estimate. The heuristic model is an idealized conception of the schooling process unfettered by practical considerations of availability of data or measurement problems. It is often helpful to attack a problem by temporarily ignoring practical constraints and outlining what one would do to solve the problem if unlimited resources were at hand. The heuristic model is intended to focus discussion in order to make clear our own research aims while it informs the reader about prior research that bears on our own.

ELEMENTS OF THE MODEL

Cultural Setting

The dependence of the schooling process upon its cultural context and the fact that elementary schools are almost always neighborhood institutions argue for two environmental influences in any model of the schooling process: 1) an overarching variable describing the neighborhood and school setting (the cultural context of the school) and 2) a set of home environment variables placed within the neighborhood context. For example, the school reflects the composition of the neighborhood by being integrated or segregated, while the home provides (or does not provide) help with homework independent of any neighborhood context.

In our research, cultural setting has been attended to in several ways. Most important, we studied children in three schools that were picked to represent different settings in order to model possible effects of segregated vs. integrated schools and middle-class vs. lower-class neighborhoods. (Several "family" factors differed among the schools, notably the socioeconomic and educational status of parents.) We studied children who attended an all-white suburban school in a middle-class residential area, children who attended an integrated school in a lower-class urban area, and children who attended a segregated black school also in a lower-class urban area.

The cultural context could bring into play a large set of influences that may "explain" socioeconomic differences in school achievement, but we made no effort to investigate them explicitly. [The list of influences might include dialect cleavages (Baratz 1970) or language barriers (Lambert and MacNamara 1969), sociolinguistic customs (Bernstein 1970), attitudes toward adults (H. F. Wolcott, cited by Havighurst 1970), cultural differences in authority relations (Wax 1969), ability to defer gratification (Hess 1970), feelings of efficacy or control (Coleman et al. 1966), problem-solving styles (Hess and Shipman 1965), the appeal of tangible vs. intangible rewards (Zigler and de Labry 1962), and whether ego or others mediate rewards (for a critical review, see Havighurst 1970).]

One particular contextual influence, brought sharply to our attention in the course of this study, may be of critical importance: informal school achievement norms. Preliminary work (Entwisle and Hayduk 1978a) suggested that, for children of comparable ability levels who are starting school, achievement norms can be vastly different according to the school they attend. In the integrated school we studied, 40% of the children received D's as a first mark in reading, while in the middle-class school a mark of D was an exceedingly rare event at any age. In addition, in the integrated school, parents did not expect their children to receive marks as high as those expected by middle-class parents. The difference in tested IQ level between these two schools was not large enough when children began school (just over 10 points on average) to account for such a huge difference in initial performance, and school facilities were similar. Therefore, we began to suspect that the social climate, particularly informal norms, partly accounted for the widely different levels of proficiency of children in the two different cultural milieux.

A major way for cultural context to exert an effect on schooling is through beliefs and values about what is proper, and, as a consequence, through people's readiness to tolerate certain outcomes. It is often stated that minority-group members see themselves as pawns of fate, powerless to confront institutions like schools. One consequence of this view is that, if minority-group children receive low marks, their parents do not protest. We did observe, informally, strong differences among the schools in accountability of teachers to parents. In the middle-class school especially, the principal was very sensitive to parent demands.

Other cultural factors may act to encourage or discourage communications between parents and teachers, and thereby alter the influence of parents on achievement. Hess (1970) points out that members of the lower class avoid verbal interaction with members of the middle-class, and such avoidance was certainly manifest in lower-class parents' relations with school in our study. Lower-class parents were much less likely than middle-class parents to be in close touch with the school. The cultural context can thus not only discourage achievement by routinely providing harsh evaluations, but also prevent the exchange of information necessary to promote achievement.

Failure to appreciate school norms or the social distance between parents and school should not lead to the conclusion that lower-class parents are indifferent to middle-class values. For example, in a survey of lower-class black mothers in Philadelphia that asked what they believed to be most important for a man to get ahead in his job, 82% of the women selected the response "hard work and ambition" (Bell 1975). Thus, middle-class values are not necessarily eschewed by lower-class parents. Rather, for lower-class parents, the ways to achieve goals are not clear—the parents in our study did not seem to be aware that pressure from parents could change school marking norms or that a visit to the child's teacher might lead the teacher to rate the child more leniently.

Individual Characteristics

The perceived characteristics of the individual—race, gender, and possibly tested IQ scores—may have both direct and indirect effects on schooling. The heuristic models shows these characteristics as a set of exogenous variables separate from cultural context. The child's race and sex are visible characteristics and could exert effects in several ways. For example, a child's race may affect teacher's marks directly because a white teacher may hold blacks to lower standards. A child's gender could also affect marks directly because some teachers hold boys to different standards of conduct, or to lower standards of reading than they hold girls.

Similarly, race and gender could have indirect effects on teachers' marks by several routes, for example, by affecting peers' expectations (white classmates may have low expectations for blacks that cause blacks to avoid action opportunities), by affecting parents' expectations (black parents may be pessimistic about the likelihood of their children's academic success and therefore not encourage their children to do extra work at home), or by affecting pupils' expectations for themselves (a black child may have high self-esteem in an all-black school and reflect this by seizing all learning opportunities offered).

Considerable evidence in prior chapters supports the kinds of conjectures just listed. In addition, significant gender effects have been found in marks assigned [girls get higher marks than their twin brothers (Doma, citied by Finn 1972), girls do better than boys in early reading (Averch et al. 1972), and girls score higher on teachers' ratings of children's behavior in the first three grades (Alberti 1971)]. Boys are also expected to do worse than girls in reading (Palardy 1969) and are more often the targets of criticism and disapproval in first grade (Brophy and Good

1970). Many of the studies indicating that race affects children's expectations were cited in Chapter 2, and, while findings on this topic are far from unitary, they bob up often enough to suggest that race (or ethnicity) should be in a heuristic model if only to check on the absence of such effects.

Significant Others

Whether at home or at school, the child is part of a group, and the group consists of "significant others" in the Mead-Cooley sense (Cooley 1922; Mead 1934). There must be important effects on children when they exhibit their elementary skills in the presence of significant others. Children's self-regard and psychological well-being are intimately linked to the reactions they sense in those who care about them. The child whose parents praise early attempts to read or to count, for example, learns many things besides how to read or to do arithmetic. He or she learns how to win favor from the parents, and the kinds of activities that adults generally value.

By the same token, in the classroom, where the teacher is the adult significant other, the child is being continuously evaluated. Children shape their activities according to the kind of feedback they get. The teacher informs the child about the caliber of performance she expects, and her evaluations contribute to the child's self-evaluations. If the child's behavior is approved, he or she learns the proper response and at the same time is pleased or gratified. Cognitive and affective rewards go hand in hand.

There is every reason to think reciprocal causation is the general rule. For example, the teacher's expectations for the child could affect the child's expectations, and then the child's expectations could in turn affect the teacher's expectations. For example, the child who expects to do well impresses the teacher with his or her self-confidence, perhaps because the teacher thinks the self-confidence must have some basis.

Several researchers (see Breland 1970; Braun 1976; Finn 1970, 1972) present heuristic models that depict the net of expectations surrounding elementary school students in much the way that it is being described here. Our heuristic model (Figure 4.1) is much like one presented by Finn (1972), which he adapted from Finn (1970) and Breland (1970). Finn, however, did not emphasize the model's dynamic nature explicitly nor did he develop the model beyond a heuristic stage. In particular, Finn did not go on to test his model.

Braun (1976), following Finn's lead, developed a "micro-model" for teacher expectations in which all inputs to teacher expectations are individual-level variables, and where teacher expectations can then lead to actions directed at a particular pupil (for example,

Figure 4.1

A Heuristic Model for Schooling

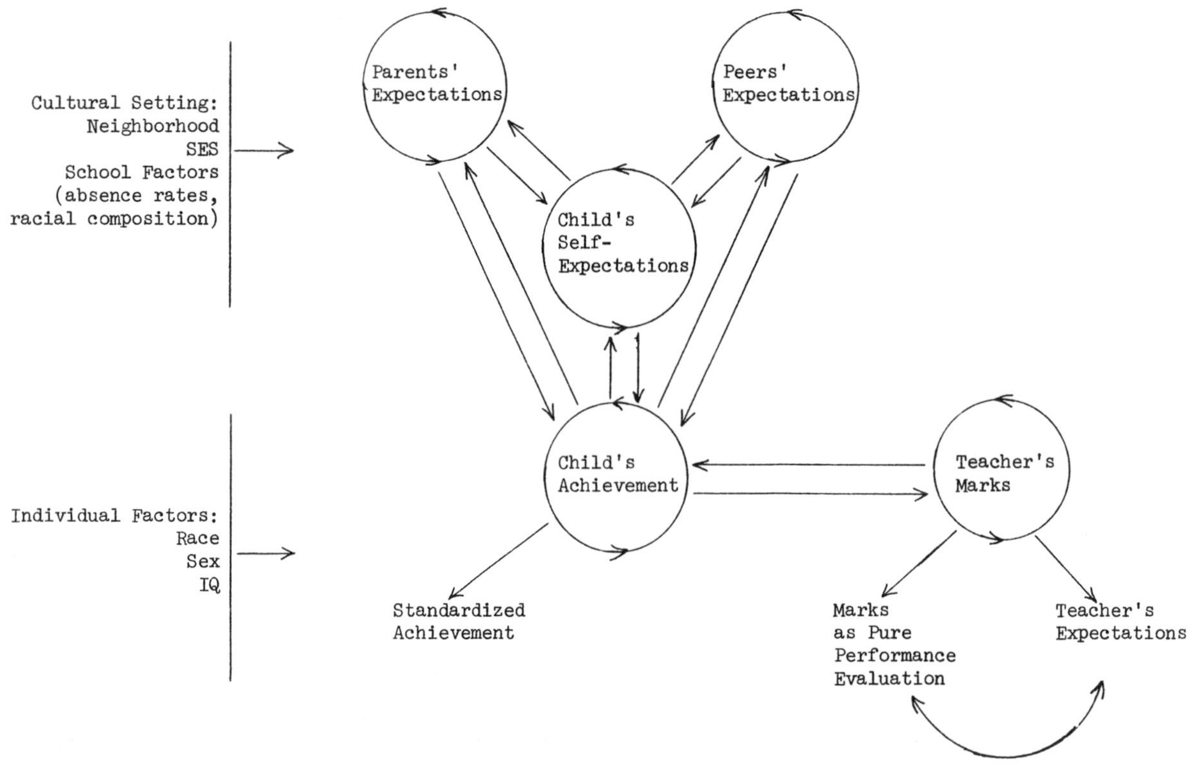

the teacher's using an expectant voice or prompting). For Braun, actions directed at the pupil and mediated through pupil self-expectations lead to output, whereas Finn seems to allow for direct effects of the cultural milieu apart from their mediation through the network of significant others. Braun apparently does not intend to allow for indirect effects. The dyadic nature of Braun's model poses some drawbacks: for example, teachers are not the only significant others. Furthermore, we would argue for a direct effect of gender on pupils' self-expectations, as well as for other direct effects from cultural context.

Perhaps the chief difference between our heuristic model and its conceptual predecessors is its purpose. Previous models were developed mainly to account for influence of teachers' expectations on "achievement" (Finn 1972) or to elucidate the process by which teachers' expectations exert their effects (Braun 1976). Our purpose is broader. We wish to model attainment over the first 3 years of school in two distinct areas, the cognitive and the affective-social. In addition, teachers' expectations can be dealt with only indirectly, because teachers' expectations could not be measured directly in our research while it was in progress without jeopardizing the observational process. We were afraid that, if we asked teachers their expectations directly, we would alter the schooling process, because teachers might try to make marks consistent across areas or otherwise be prompted to act in ways different from their normal actions. They would react to being observed, in other words.

It is critical to note that the model proposed here (Figure 4.1) could turn into a *different* model in different cultural contexts. That is, in a lower-class setting, peers' expectation may be important, while the contrary is true in a middle-class setting. Thus, certain variables could be causally connected in one cultural setting but not in another. In fact, our heuristic model presages a set of structural-equation models estimated in different social settings. In addition, to take account of feedback parameters, the model is estimated using a set of multiwave data.

STRUCTURE OF THE MODEL

With figure 4.1 as a guide, the various links in the model are now discussed.

Cultural Setting

Farthest in the background is cultural setting, which includes the neighborhood and family environmental factors implied by socioeconomic status, and whether the school the child attends is integrated or segregated. The student's cultural context could exert effects on the schooling process in several ways, both directly and indirectly. Direct effects could occur because achievement norms might differ from one place to another, as already mentioned. The average evaluation in one place may be lower than in another, with all else controlled. Indirect effects could occur because children in lower-class schools may feel achievement is unimportant (Stendler 1951), and this could lead them to ignore feedback from teachers. Their schooling could thus hinge mainly on peers' reactions rather than on teachers' reactions. In contrast, children in middle-class settings may pay little attention to peers. Actually, the literature on socioeconomic differences in school achievement suggests a multitude of causes, many of which already have been briefly reviewed.

Parents

Parents set the style of family life, and "family" effects appear at two levels in the model. First, parents' socioeconomic status and occupation are, without exception, shown to be a significant source of variance in the many studies of status attainment of secondary school students, and, although similar data on primary-school children are scarce, all the available evidence also points to strong parent effects (see Weikart et al. 1978). Relations with parents could also be important for school performance because of their contribution to the overall cultural context. They are *part* of the cultural context.

Second, parents are implicated in the role of the significant others. By their sanctions they could shape the child's early self-concept or achievement. Parents' influence is documented in many studies (see Kaminski et al. 1976; Mosteller and Moynihan 1972 p. 40). To represent parents' specific influence on reading and arithmetic achievement as different from family background, parents' expectations for their children's performance—how well they expect the child to perform in a particular subject—appear as explicit variables in our models.

Peers

We assume that informal relations among pupils, particularly peer-popularity, affect students' performance. Inclusion of peers in the model rests mainly on theoretical grounds that support the existence of relationships between peer-popularity and pupil attitudes and achievement. Achievement is partly conditioned by the pupils' self-concept *as peer*, and a pupil's self-regard is predicted in part by peer-popularity (Coopersmith 1959; Horowitz 1962).

Several studies demonstrate empirical associations between interpersonal processes of school peer groups, the psychological processes of individual pupils, and pupil behavior in the classroom (Sewell et al. 1959; Wilson 1959) or show that, in elementary-school children, low peer-popularity leads to a low utilization of academic abilities (Echelberger 1959; Lippitt and Gold 1959; Schmuck 1962, 1963; Van Egmond 1960). However, with very young children, peer effects are sometimes absent (Bushwell, cited in Hoffman and Hoffman 1966, p. 245) and one would certainly expect peer influences in elementary school to be smaller than those in high school.

Children's Expectations

We include the child's self-expectations as both an antecedent and a consequence. The child develops a set of expectations based on how others react to him or her. Some of the clearest evidence for a link between self-concept of ability and attainment is contained in a study by Brookover et al. (1967, p. 77) that shows that, over a 6 year period, correlations between the self-concept of ability and grade-point average ranged between 0.48 and 0.63. These correlations were virtually unaffected when IQ and socioeconomic status were partialled out.

Reciprocal Causation

As Figure 4.1 indicates, we see possible reciprocal causation between every pair of endogenous variables in this heuristic model. For example, if the child does well, we anticipate that self-expectations will rise to reflect this. Also, if the child has high self-expectations, we see this as a cause for parents and peers to hold higher expectations.

Obviously, a child's race and sex cannot be changed, so these variables are not the targets of reverse causation. IQ measures could be affected by a child's expectations or attainment, but, because we lacked the data to inform such a model, we measured achievement by teachers' marks and standardized tests and made no attempt to use IQ as an endogenous variable. We use it only as an exogenous variable.

The heuristic model is intended to be general—that is, to explain educational attainment of elementary-school children irrespective of the school they attend and no matter what their personal characteristics or social background. Looking for school effects on learning processes as well as on achievement outcomes, however, leads to difficult problems in defining a model's parameters (see McPartland and Karweit 1978). We eventually address this issue by using similar but distinct models for each of three schools. That is, we posit the same models (patterned after that shown in Figure 4.1) for each school, but in no way force the parameters to be the same in each of the three contexts. It is entirely possible that a parameter will be zero in one school and not in another. In fact, one way to detect school differences, if they exist, is by differences in parameter size.

Time in the Model

A principal difference between our style of modeling and all previous models of school attainment is in its conceptualization of time. In an effort to elucidate the schooling process and to disentangle some of the reciprocal effects posited in the heuristic model, we stretched the heuristic model out along a time continuum that matches the schooling process. Structural-equation models proposed in Chapter 5 are isomorphic with cycles of time. In order to procure data to estimate the models, we followed children from before they started first grade until the end of third grade. In the heuristic model, no time indicators are included, except that the two sets of exogenous variables (cultural and individual) are taken as prior to the endogenous variables. In order to disentangle complicated effects, however, it was helpful to match closely the timing of some measurements with the time frame governing some of the variables affecting schooling. We could then estimate the causal effect of one variable on other variables that follow it in time. Also, we could study variables in "time-series." For example, we could study what happens to a child's expectations for reading over time. The reciprocal causal influences depicted in the heuristic model are translated into dependencies between successive time cycles. Children's expectations were obtained before the first marks were issued; therefore, initial expectations were assumed to affect first marks. After the first mark has been issued, we allowed for self-expectations to respond. In the structural models we therefore show a causal path from children's initial expectations to their first marks, and then another path from first marks to expectations obtained later, in the latter half of first grade. Peers' expectations appear as an exogenous variable introduced late in first grade because it takes time for peers to form expectations. Parents' expectations, however, are present when the child starts school, so they precede children's expectations.

As pointed out earlier, our heuristic model implies a kind of dynamic omitted from Finn's model and others like it: each set of expectations is enclosed in a circle. On the circumference of each circle there are arrowheads, which suggest that each of these variables is rolling along through time and is not static. The earlier models of Finn and Braun probably did not mean to imply that expectations remained fixed at any one level, but they did not allow for self-loops, expectations affecting expectations or marks affecting marks, and we wish to allow explicitly for persistence or change in both. There is good reason to expect that the first marks assigned to a child may directly influence later marks. Furthermore, such self-loops are appropriate for expectations.

The model in Figure 4.1 is elaborated further in Chapter 5, and eventually a separate set of models is estimated for each school. Why not model the process with school setting as an exogenous variable? That is, "school" could be entered at the outset as a dummy variable, along with race and sex. One problem is that this style of modeling would assume a common metric for achievement. Considerable evidence suggests that the metric, especially teachers' marks, may not be the same from school to school. A more serious problem is that such a modeling style would make it difficult to describe differential processes within schools. As is shown, one important finding is that marks are more stable in the lower-class schools than in the middle-class school. Using dummy variables, such a finding would turn up as an interaction between marks and schools, and where schools cannot be ranked along any particular continuum and where the metric for the interaction is arbitrary, it did not seem useful to us to couch findings in "interaction" terms.

SUMMARY

This chapter presents a heuristic model, adapted from previous models, that is the conceptual basis for explicit structural models developed in the next chapter. Eventually, the structural-equation models are estimated for three separate schools. The heuristic model depicts relations among variables as suggested by previous research in psychology, sociology, and education. In addition, the heuristic model explicitly incorporates evaluations (teachers' marks) and self-loops, as well as feedback loops.

Chapter 5

Schooling Variables and Their Measurement

For the elementary-school child, one of the most important consequences of schooling is success in mastering the basic skills: how well and how quickly he or she learns to read and to do simple arithmetic. Another consequence of schooling is the ideas children forge about their own competence. We strongly suspect that eventual status attainment, or even short-run attainment on the next rung of the education ladder, depends on both children's absolute level of achievement and their conceptions of their own ability. These notions, dealt with at length in earlier chapters, led to formulation of a heuristic model in the last chapter. In this chapter we make our ideas about schooling even more explicit and state them in a form susceptible to empirical test. We propose a set of cyclic structural-equation models adapted from the heuristic model.

The basic conceptual scheme underneath the structural models is that, as children mature and pass through educational institutions, schooling comes about through social interaction between the child and significant others. This interaction occurs in a definite time frame, and this frame determined when our measurements were taken.

The exact timing of the various measurements is shown in Figure 5.1. Parents were questioned early in the fall of each year. Children were interviewed later each year to determine their expectations. Measurement of parents' *and* children's expectations preceded the appearance of report cards. Later, around April or May of each school year, peer ratings were obtained. Near the end of the school year, children were interviewed again, to obtain their expectations for marks on the final report card of the school year. Finally, after school closed for the summer, absence figures and final marks were obtained. The six time periods indicated on the figure, T1 to T6, correspond roughly to school semesters. Data were collected on all these separate occasions in a way that corresponded exactly with causal assumptions about effects.

Although schooling outcomes are numerous, we concentrate on two, operationalized as the variable M (marks given by teachers) and E (the child's expectations).

The child's marks in reading and arithmetic are taken as two "cognitive" outcomes. Marks in reading and arithmetic form the heart of the elementary-school curriculum, particularly in the first three grades.

Children's expectations for their own performance in reading, arithmetic, and conduct are taken as three "affective" outcomes and reflect the children's attitudes about their own capabilities. The conduct mark can be taken as an indicator of the level of the child's social development relative to other children of the same age, and we see it as a further affective outcome of schooling. Furthermore, since children's behavior in school may help or hinder their performance in reading and arithmetic, the marks the teacher gives the child in conduct are useful in estimating the portion of the child's reading or arithmetic mark that may be attributable to non-academic factors.

The basic list of variables that appear is: RACE, the child's race; SEX, the child's sex; IQ, IQ as measured on any one of several standardized tests given by the school system; ABIL, parent's estimate of the child's ability to do schoolwork; PE, the parent's (usually the mother's) expectations for the child's performance; E, the child's expectations for his or her own performance; M, the marks given by the child's

Figure 5.1

The Timing of Data Collection

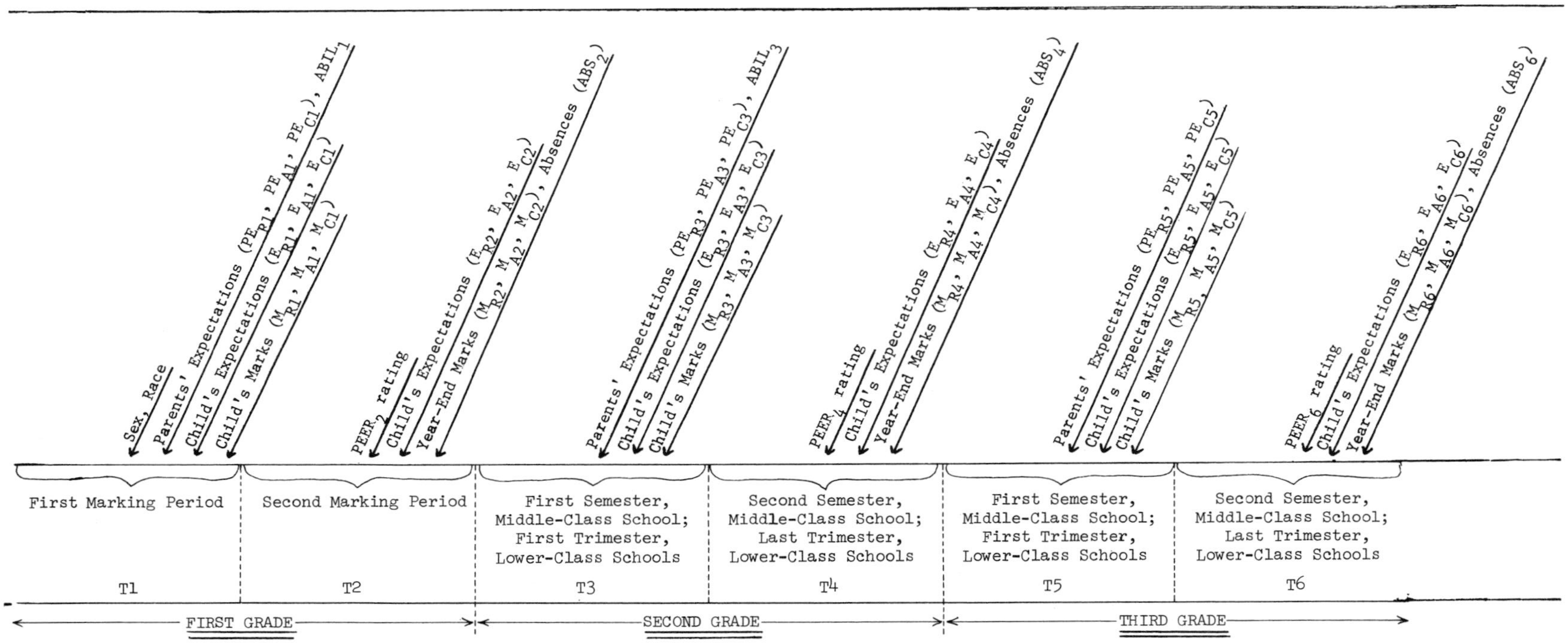

Sex, Race
Parents' Expectations (PE_{R1}, PE_{A1}, PE_{C1}), $ABIL_1$
Child's Expectations (E_{R1}, E_{A1}, E_{C1})
Child's Marks (M_{R1}, M_{A1}, M_{C1})

$PEER_2$ rating
Child's Expectations (E_{R2}, E_{A2}, E_{C2})
Year-End Marks (M_{R2}, M_{A2}, M_{C2}), Absences (ABS_2)

Parents' Expectations (PE_{R3}, PE_{A3}, PE_{C3}), $ABIL_3$
Child's Expectations (E_{R3}, E_{A3}, E_{C3})
Child's Marks (M_{R3}, M_{A3}, M_{C3})

$PEER_4$ rating
Child's Expectations (E_{R4}, E_{A4}, E_{C4})
Year-End Marks (M_{R4}, M_{A4}, M_{C4}), Absences (ABS_4)

Parents' Expectations (PE_{R5}, PE_{A5}, PE_{C5})
Child's Expectations (E_{R5}, E_{A5}, E_{C5})
Child's Marks (M_{R5}, M_{A5}, M_{C5})

$PEER_6$ rating
Child's Expectations (E_{R6}, E_{A6}, E_{C6})
Year-End Marks (M_{R6}, M_{A6}, M_{C6}), Absences (ABS_6)

First Marking Period	Second Marking Period	First Semester, Middle-Class School; First Trimester, Lower-Class Schools	Second Semester, Middle-Class School; Last Trimester, Lower-Class Schools	First Semester, Middle-Class School; First Trimester, Lower-Class Schools	Second Semester, Middle-Class School; Last Trimester, Lower-Class Schools
T1	T2	T3	T4	T5	T6
FIRST GRADE		SECOND GRADE		THIRD GRADE	

teacher; PEER, the peer-popularity rating of children in terms of rank within classroom; and ABS, the number of days absent in one school year.

Precisely because teachers are likely to be influenced by a child's appearance and demeanor and because teachers vary in the marking standards they apply, school systems routinely evaluate children's reading and arithmetic skills with standardized tests by the end of third grade. Later, in Chapter 7, we demonstrate that children's marks in reading and arithmetic as given by the teachers included in this study did predict the children's performance on standardized achievement tests and that the structure of the models is invariant whether teachers' marks *or* standardized test scores are taken as the ultimate endogenous variables. In the basic models presented here and in Chapter 6, however, we consider teachers' marks in reading and arithmetic as the main achievement criteria.[1]

Since we are concerned with marks in three areas, we are also concerned with expectations in those same three areas. Specifically, shortly before report cards were issued, we asked what marks children expected their forthcoming report cards would show in these three subjects. Similarly, we asked parents about expectations for their child's performance in each of the same three areas before the reports appeared.

Some variables used in preliminary work were later eliminated. For example, a three-factor test of self-esteem (Dickstein 1972), especially developed for use with young children, was included but later dropped. We thought that this test of self-esteem might be better than previously developed tests because it was based on a carefully worked-out theory and it had three separate factor scores for boys and three for girls. Nevertheless, it did not have predictive validity for children's marks or self-expectations and its erratic patterns of relationships with other variables prompted misgivings about its construct validity. A number of other variables, such as total number of years of schooling parents expected their children to attain, whether parents intended to help with homework, how many of their children's friends parents knew, how often the family ate dinner together, and family patterns of verbal interaction, were also put on trial and later eliminated for the same kinds of reasons. Kindergarten-teacher forecasts for reading and arithmetic performance in first grade also proved relatively ineffective as predictors. The impotence of such variables is of some interest in itself, of course.

[1] In pilot work, marks in two other academic areas, spelling and language, were included. They were eventually dropped because neither teachers nor students had clear ideas about exactly what was being evaluated under these rubrics. By examining reading and arithmetic marks, then, we believe we are covering *all* the important academic information available for first-graders.

Racial identity, peer-popularity ratings, gender, IQ, and absences, all of which are exogenous variables, are thoroughly discussed. Although the child's race had effects we judge to be negligible, the important role this variable has played in the recent literature, and theoretical concerns, prompted our inclusion of race in all models for the integrated school.

DESCRIPTION OF VARIABLES

A brief description of variables used in the models is now given. (See also Appendix A, and Appendix B, "Issues of Measurement.")

RACE

Race was coded 1 for white, 2 for black. The few Orientals and Hispanics were classed as white (1).

SEX

Sex was coded 1 for boys, 2 for girls.

IQ

IQ scores were taken from a variety of tests given in the different schools at various times. A summary of the nature of these tests and the time of their administration is given in the notes to Table B.1.

ABIL, Parents' General Ability Estimate

A parent of each child (usually the mother) was asked, "How do you rate your child in school ability compared with other children in this school?" (check one):

(✓) Among the best
( ) Above average
( ) Average
( ) Below average
( ) Among the poorest

The responses were coded from 1 (among the best) to 5 (among the poorest).

PE, Parents' Expectations

The parents of each child were presumed to have expectations for how well their child would perform in reading, arithmetic, and conduct. Parents were asked to fill out a questionnaire indicating their expectations (or, if necessary, they were queried by an interviewer who filled out the questionnaire for them). Figure 5.2 reproduces the part of the questionnaire that tapped parents' expectations. When necessary, interviewers

Figure 5.2

JOHNS HOPKINS UNIVERSITY
PARENT OPINIONNAIRE--Confidential

Name of Student ______________________ Room ________

Parent filling out questionnaire:

_____ Mother

_____ Father

This student has ___ older brothers

___ older sisters

___ younger brothers

___ younger sisters

(Please enter a number in <u>each</u> blank space above.)

Below is part of a report card like the one your child will bring home before long. Please fill in the boxes with marks (A, B, C, D, U, or 1, 2, 3) to show <u>what you guess your child's next report card will look like</u>.

For <u>reading</u> and <u>arithmetic</u> enter one of the following marks:

A - outstanding, very good

B - good

C - satisfactory

D - poor

U - unsatisfactory

For <u>conduct</u> enter one of the following marks:

1 - good

2 - satisfactory

3 - unsatisfactory

Please guess the marks your child will receive as accurately as you can.

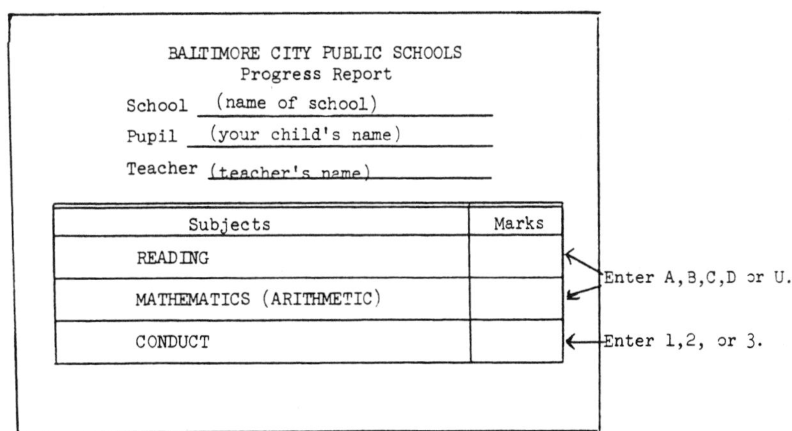

BALTIMORE CITY PUBLIC SCHOOLS
Progress Report

School (name of school)

Pupil (your child's name)

Teacher (teacher's name)

Subjects	Marks
READING	
MATHEMATICS (ARITHMETIC)	
CONDUCT	

Enter A, B, C, D or U.

Enter 1, 2, or 3.

interpreted the marking standards used by the school and answered questions parents asked.

Data were gathered only once a year from parents, shortly before report cards were issued in the fall, by interviewers whose race usually matched that of the parent. Data from parent interviews were procured during the first cycle in each grade (T1, T3, and T5) with the exact timing depending on the timing of report-card issuance as discussed below. Parents' interviews preceded children's interviews when the two were obtained within a single time cycle. (Children were interviewed twice during each grade, parents once.) Parents' expectations were coded from 1 (high) to 4 (low).

E, Children's Expectations

Just before their earliest report cards were issued in first grade, children were queried about their own expectations for their forthcoming marks in reading, arithmetic, and conduct. Children were presumed to have some notion of how well they would perform in each area. A trained interviewer, whose race usually matched that of the child, conducted an individual interview with each child. Using a large, stylized plastic replica of a report card and cardboard squares containing large numerals, the interviewer explained to the child what report cards are, what marks are, how marks are coded, and, if necessary, the meanings of reading, arithmetic, and conduct. She then asked each child to "play a game" in which the child tried to guess what marks the forthcoming report card should show in reading (E_R), in arithmetic (E_A), and in conduct (E_C). The child indicated a guess by placing the cardboard squares on the big "report card." Great care was taken that the children understood the task and understood the meaning of both marks and report cards. This interview provided the Time 1 (T1) measure of children's expectations. Children's expectations were coded in the same manner as parents'—from 1 (high, or A), to 4 (low, or D).

Later in first grade, just before the year-end report card was issued, children were interviewed a second time in an identical manner and asked to make guesses concerning the marks they expected to receive on the last report card of that school year. The second interview provided the Time 2 (T2) measure of children's expectations. The same kind of individual interview yielded data for children's expectations—E_R, E_A, E_C—at subsequent time points, T3 and T4 for second grade, and T5 and T6 for third grade. For convenience, subscripts indicate both the kinds of expectations and the times they were procured. For example, E_{R2} is the child's reading expectation procured in the second cycle (T2), while E_{C6} is the child's conduct expectation measured in the sixth cycle (T6).

Expectations were always procured shortly before the relevant report cards were issued. The large plastic report-card replica was used only as long as necessary, consistently for initial expectations (T1), infrequently at the end of first grade (T2), and never beyond first grade.

M, Marks

Children's marks in reading, arithmetic, and conduct were ascertained from school records.

Marks on the *first* report card in first grade are T1 marks. Marks on the last report card in first grade are T2 marks. During the second and third grades, marks were again recorded in the middle of the year and at the end of the year. The mid-year marks were recorded either one-third or one-half of the way through the year, depending on whether the school used three (integrated and black schools) or four (white school) marking periods per year.[2]

One systematic way the schools differed was in marking policies. In the two lower-class schools, which were both in Baltimore City, the children's performance was supposed to be evaluated in relation to the performance considered average for that grade level, while in the middle-class school, in Baltimore County, marks were supposed to indicate the child's effort independent of actual ability. Actual implementation of these policies, however, differed greatly, even between teachers in the same system. We believe marking policies as actually carried out differed somewhat between schools in the first grade, but not as markedly as the policies suggest. After school closed for the summer each year, we obtained written statements from teachers describing their marking criteria. From reading these statements, we believe that teachers' standards for evaluating students were very similar across schools, especially as the children reached higher grades, despite the differences in official policy.

All marks, like expectations, were recorded on a scale from 1 to 4, with 1 high. The subscripts again indicate the subject area and timing. M_{A1}, for example, is the mark in arithmetic at T1.

PEER, Peer-Popularity Ratings

The average rating of a child's popularity with classmates was obtained in several different ways over the course of the study. Mainly it was procured by noting the order in which children chose up sides "to play a reading game." Two captains, a boy and a girl, were first selected by the teacher according to whom she judged best in the class in reading and social maturity. Captains then took turns picking people to be on their team to play a relay game that, they were forewarned, called for reading skills. The rating thus probably is a mixture of popularity and peers' estimates of the child's reading ability.

This variable was scored separately for each classroom as follows. First, all children were ranked in the order in which they were chosen. There were pairs of ranks because of the two teams. That is, the two captains were ranked 1.5, the two children chosen first by each captain were ranked 3.5, and so on. Then, each child's rank was normalized to lie between 0 and 1, with the highest ranks scored 0, the lowest scored 1, and the others located at equal intervals between. In a class with twenty-two students, two would receive 0, two would receive 1, and the eighteen lying within the extremes would receive scores of 0.10, 0.20, 0.30, and so on.[3]

[2]The white school skipped the usual first reporting period for first-graders, making the first marks these children received (T1 marks) comparable in time to the marks they received in the middle of the second and third grades (times T3 and T5, respectively).

[3]In the first two cohorts in the middle-class school, a more complicated procedure was used in which each child chose six classmates on two rounds. Then the same procedure for scaling was used. In the last two cohorts in all schools, peer-popularity scores were obtained by similar scaling of the number of children who chose any particular child as their best or second-best friend. The "friend" data are presented in Chapter 7.

ABS, Absence

The total number of absences for the entire school year was taken from the year-end report card.

SOCIAL CONTEXT

An important part of our conceptual scheme is an assumption that the child's social milieu—the race and socioeconomic composition of the school and neighborhood—may affect the schooling process. Specifically, we wished to allow for the possibility that the schooling process is different in different social contexts. Middle-class children might be very responsive to parents' expectations, for example, and lower-class children less so, or absences may impair performance in a lower-class school but not in a middle-class school. Whatever the case, to get some idea about possible effects of race and socioeconomic status, models were estimated separately for data collected from three different schools: an all-white middle-class suburban school, an integrated lower-class urban school, and an all-black lower-class urban school. Characteristics of the three schools and their clienteles, given in the top portion of Table 5.1, were obtained from an accountability summary required of all schools by the Maryland Department of Education for 1973 to 1976 inclusive.

All data on *school facilities* point to reasonable comparability among schools. Enrollment, pupil-staff ratios, and teachers' qualifications are highly similar from one school to another. In contrast, all data pertaining to *students or their families* point to close comparability between the two urban schools, but to lack of comparability between them and the all-white suburban school. The suburban school significantly outranks its urban counterparts on mother's median education and median family income, and has fewer disadvantaged students.

Summary data for pupils [non-verbal ability test (SAS), grade equivalent (GE) scores on vocabulary, reading comprehension, and mathematics] in the lower portion of Table 5.1 also show that the two urban schools are similar but that the suburban school is considerably higher on all pupil-test measures. The differences between the suburban and the urban schools in accountability data are greater in the third grade than differences in IQ noted in first grade between the middle-class and integrated schools. (Compare values in Table 5.1 and with those in Table 5.2.)

The three schools were deliberately chosen to be as different as possible, but they represent types of schools commonly found in the United States: first, a suburban all-white elementary school in an affluent neighborhood where parents take an active role in school affairs; second, a school in an urban fringe area where members of the two races are of approximately equal status, which represents the situation for integrated schools not affected by busing; and third, an all-black inner-city school that is in a black ghetto neighborhood.

AVERAGE VALUES OF VARIABLES

Children's expectations in reading and arithmetic are remarkably similar by the end of the third grade in all three schools, and the slight differences in level that exist are in the direction of more conservative expectations for middle-class children (see Table 5.2). In each school, the trend from first to third grade is mildly downward, but less so in the middle-class school. The expectations of children in both lower-class schools were at a higher level to start with, however. Their expectations on the average dropped a little more, especially in the integrated school. In each school, conduct expectations tend to be highest, reading expectations next highest, and arithmetic expectations lowest, except that, for middle-class children, reading and conduct are about the same. These trends are consistent with findings that expectations of older children are lower (Parsons and Ruble 1977; Morse 1964) and that there is progressively less overestimation of expectations from first through fifth grades (Rahe and Blaess 1975).

Expectations differed little by race in the integrated school; at the start, they were almost identical for the two races. Small differences, at most 12% of a grade-point, favored whites at the end of the third grade.

Middle-class children's first-grade average *marks* in reading, arithmetic, and conduct are almost identical at mid-year (somewhat over a B). All marks rose a little—from 0.15 to 0.20 grade-points—between the middle and end of the year, so that again at the end of the year marks in the three areas are practically identical. At the start of second grade, marks in reading and arithmetic were slightly lower than at the start of first grade—very close to a B—but conduct remained close to the level noted at the end of first grade. Over second grade, marks generally rose once more, but the increases vary by area. In reading, there was a gain of 0.28 grade-points, while in arithmetic and conduct the gains were considerably smaller, 0.12 and 0.05, respectively. In third grade, once again, marks returned to the initial baseline found in the earlier grades—just over a B—and then over the year all marks rose a little (0.13 to 0.16). The standard deviations are relatively constant over the period—from one-half to two-thirds of a grade-point—with the largest standard deviations associated with conduct.

Two conclusions may be drawn. First, in each year,

Table 5.1

Maryland Accountability Program Report Statistics

School and Family Data

	School Enroll-ment	Pupil Staff Ratio	Average Daily Attend-ance (%)	Average Experience of Teachers (Years)	Staff Masters Degree or Above (%)	% Disad-vantaged	Mother's Median Education	Median Family Income
1973-1974								
White Middle-Class School	659	20.7	97.1	10.1	28.3	2.2	12.5	$14,869
Integrated Lower-Class School	784	24.9	88.8	11.1	28.6	29.3	10.0	$7,435
Black Lower-Class School	776	25.0	92.3	14.1	19.3	26.8	10.0	$7,952
1974-1975								
White Middle-Class School	644	21.6	96.4	11.4	26.8	2.1	12.4	$14,868
Integrated Lower-Class School	742	22.8	87.5	9.4	18.5	29.4	9.9	$7,434
Black Lower-Class School	720	22.1	91.7	14.0	24.5	26.8	10.0	$7,951

Student Data

		Vocabulary		Reading Comprehension		Mathematics	
	SAS (non-verbal IQ)	Grade Equivalent	Predicted G.E.[a]	Grade Equivalent	Predicted G.E.[a]	Grade Equivalent	Predicted G.E.[a]
1973-1974							
White Middle-Class Sch.	113.1	4.50	4.38	4.60	4.47	4.30	4.35
Integrated Lower-Class Sch.	90.4	2.40	2.90	2.73	2.94	2.93	3.10
Black Lower-Class Sch.	86.7	2.61	2.70	2.82	2.71	2.89	2.91
1974-1975							
White Middle-Class Sch.	110.7	4.70	4.22	4.80	4.32	4.60	4.23
Integrated Lower-Class Sch.	89.5	2.74	2.86	2.76	2.89	3.04	3.00
Black Lower-Class Sch.	87.4	2.40	2.72	2.56	2.75	2.80	2.88
1975-1976							
White Middle-Class Sch.	113.6	4.62	4.45	4.71	4.54	4.63	4.44
Integrated Lower-Class Sch.	89.6	2.67	2.92	2.75	2.96	2.84	3.03
Black Lower-Class Sch.	90.6	2.69	2.98	2.76	3.02	2.77	3.09

[a]Predicted G.E. (grade equivalent) norm derived by regressing non-verbal IQ (SAS) on G.E.

marks in the middle-class school started from almost the same relatively high point and then rose a little. With annual improvements, a ceiling would soon be reached, however, so evidently each teacher in successive years retreats to a baseline slightly above a B in all three areas. Second, some mild distinctions appear among the three areas in grades two and three, but patterns are mixed.

In the integrated lower-class school, children's first marks in reading and arithmetic are about a C, with reading slightly lower. Conduct marks are better, averaging above a B. There are improvements over the year in all three areas—over half a grade-point in reading, over a quarter of a grade-point in arithmetic, and a trifle in conduct. In second and third grades, the picture looks much the same at the start of the year—reading and arithmetic marks average close to a C, with conduct about one grade-point higher. Improvements within the second and third-grade years, however, are relatively larger for arithmetic—0.35 in second grade and 0.26 in third grade. Improvements in reading are slight or nil. In second grade, the gain for reading is 0.15, and there is a small decline in third grade (-0.06). Conduct stays at roughly the same high level throughout. Standard deviations are larger than in the middle-class school—0.68 to 1.02 units.

In the black lower-class school, the average marks in reading and arithmetic are close to a C throughout, and there are no within-year or between-year changes of any note, with the exception that first-grade arithmetic marks rise about one-quarter of a grade-point. Average marks in conduct are close to a B in grade one, and above a B in grades two and three, with no noticeable change over the year. Standard deviations are about the same size as those in the lower-class integrated school.

Table 5.2

Means and Standard Deviations of the Basic Variables for all Schools

White Middle-Class School

	T1 (Gr. 1--Midyear)			T2 (Gr. 1--Year End)			T3 (Gr. 2--Midyear)			T4 (Gr. 2--Year End)			T5 (Gr. 3--Midyear)			T6 (Gr. 3--Year End)		
	N	Mean	S.D.	N	Mean	S.D.	N	Mean	S.D.	N	Mean	S.D.	N	Mean	S.D.	N	Mean	S.D.
Marks																		
Reading	380	1.82	0.56	387	1.67	0.62	332	1.89	0.57	335	1.61	0.56	259	1.80	0.52	269	1.66	0.52
Arithmetic	380	1.85	0.51	387	1.65	0.59	338	1.97	0.50	341	1.85	0.57	268	1.88	0.51	276	1.75	0.55
Conduct	380	1.80	0.66	384	1.65	0.69	337	1.63	0.67	341	1.58	0.65	268	1.96	0.57	276	1.80	0.65
Child's Expectations																		
Reading	408	1.60	0.77	385	1.55	0.63	344	1.65	0.59	330	1.71	0.61	270	1.78	0.52	256	1.74	0.60
Arithmetic	408	1.79	0.78	385	1.69	0.76	344	1.69	0.73	330	1.74	0.70	270	1.81	0.64	256	1.89	0.73
Conduct	408	1.71	0.86	386	1.58	0.65	344	1.73	0.72	330	1.65	0.58	270	1.74	0.61	256	1.79	0.54
Parent's Expectations																		
Reading	348	1.78	0.63				271	1.71	0.61				222	1.68	0.57			
Arithmetic	348	1.80	0.63				270	1.86	0.62				223	1.81	0.50			
Conduct	343	1.78	0.61				271	1.77	0.62				223	1.76	0.59			
Peer Rating	364	0.49	0.30				332	0.57	0.31				271	0.63	0.30			
Absence	302	8.64	5.94				336	8.04	6.17				271	9.56	7.62			
IQ	237	113	11.07				102	104	11.47				176	112	14.09			

Table 5.2 (Continued)
Integrated Lower-Class School

	T1 (Gr. 1--Midyear)			T2 (Gr. 1--Year End)			T3 (Gr. 2--Midyear)			T4 (Gr. 2--Year End)			T5 (Gr. 3--Midyear)			T6 (Gr. 3--Year End)		
	N	Mean	S.D.	N	Mean	S.D.	N	Mean	S.D.	N	Mean	S.D.	N	Mean	S.D.	N	Mean	S.D.
Marks																		
Reading	341	3.31	0.77	404	2.76	1.02	242	3.11	0.85	297	2.96	0.95	156	3.02	0.90	214	3.08	0.83
Arithmetic	397	3.00	0.72	408	2.71	0.89	287	3.14	0.69	302	2.79	0.84	204	2.94	0.82	209	2.68	0.99
Conduct	393	1.87	0.68	411	1.76	0.69	288	2.05	0.73	301	1.86	0.81	205	1.91	0.59	211	1.91	0.65
Child's Expectations																		
Reading	364	1.46	0.76	350	1.48	0.75	286	1.46	0.75	245	1.66	0.75	211	1.70	0.78	151	1.74	0.79
Arithmetic	365	1.70	0.72	351	1.70	0.82	284	1.72	0.78	245	1.81	0.78	212	1.86	0.85	151	1.85	0.84
Conduct	365	1.16	0.38	352	1.37	0.56	285	1.45	0.63	245	1.43	0.58	212	1.48	0.55	151	1.66	0.60
Parent's Expectations																		
Reading	348	2.44	0.76				257	2.39	0.74				170	2.33	0.81			
Arithmetic	349	2.36	0.74				259	2.41	0.68				170	2.39	0.73			
Conduct	348	1.70	0.66				260	1.78	0.70				171	1.81	0.63			
Peer Rating	327	0.49	0.30				211	0.61	0.31				162	0.64	0.29			
Absence	422	21.42	18.83				307	20.98	17.55				214	22.28	20.42			
IQ	281	97	16.01				177	83	13.04				164	90	13.09			

Table 5.2 (Continued)

Black Lower-Class School

	T1 (Gr. 1--Midyear)			T2 (Gr. 1--Year End)			T3 (Gr. 2--Midyear)			T4 (Gr. 2--Year End)			T5 (Gr. 3--Midyear)			T6 (Gr. 3--Year End)		
	N	Mean	S.D.	N	Mean	S.D.	N	Mean	S.D.	N	Mean	S.D.	N	Mean	S.D.	N	Mean	S.D.
Marks																		
Reading	220	2.96	0.87	239	2.97	0.78	105	2.86	0.86	129	2.88	0.86	105	2.89	0.61	166	2.84	0.78
Arithmetic	231	3.01	0.66	250	2.75	0.93	173	3.08	0.59	178	3.01	0.74	165	2.98	0.66	171	2.88	0.82
Conduct	243	2.12	0.61	262	2.04	0.72	174	1.77	0.57	177	1.69	0.63	165	1.79	0.68	172	1.72	0.71
Child's Expectations																		
Reading	260	1.53	0.82	191	1.52	0.79	183	1.48	0.75	126	1.63	0.74	158	1.68	0.73	130	1.67	0.72
Arithmetic	260	1.78	0.84	191	1.77	0.84	183	1.80	0.85	126	1.78	0.86	158	1.71	0.82	130	1.93	0.86
Conduct	260	1.33	0.57	191	1.30	0.54	183	1.27	0.52	126	1.37	0.55	158	1.44	0.53	130	1.57	0.56
Parent's Expectations																		
Reading	90	2.39	0.77				79	2.54	0.78				114	2.46	0.88			
Arithmetic	88	2.39	0.70				79	2.48	0.71				113	2.51	0.75			
Conduct	92	1.78	0.75				79	1.92	0.66				114	1.72	0.63			
Peer Rating	238	0.50	0.30				160	0.67	0.30				150	0.65	0.31			
Absence	265	20.68	15.28				189	18.17	14.84				175	13.78	13.84			
IQ	187	90	14.41				64	91	14.76				70	91	10.87			

The overall picture is for marks in reading and arithmetic to be lower in the black and integrated schools when compared with the white school. Conduct marks are nearly uniform across the schools—being higher than reading and arithmetic marks in the black and integrated schools and comparable to the academic marks in the white school.

Expectations in Relation to Marks

Expectations in the middle-class school are *slightly* above the average marks awarded, while those in the other two schools are about one full marking point too high in both reading and arithmetic. Over time, children's expectations in the two lower-class schools decline somewhat, but there still is a considerable gap between marks and expectations at the end of grade three. For example, between grade one and grade three, in the integrated school the gap between reading expectations and marks declines from 1.85 to 1.34 and that in arithmetic from 1.30 to 0.83. Gaps between expectations and marks in the two lower-class schools at the end of grade three far exceed the size of gaps noted in the middle-class school.

The most obvious differences among schools are that, all through the first three grades, average marks in reading and arithmetic are considerably higher in the middle-class school, and, in this school, within each grade there is a slight improvement over the year in both subjects. In the other two schools, the average marks in both academic areas are lower throughout (around a C) and patterns of over-year improvement are weaker, especially in reading. The integrated school does manifest consistent, small within-year gains in arithmetic, and a relatively large gain in reading in first grade, but the initial mark in reading in this school was very low (between a C and a D).

On balance, the aggregate feedback given the average child in the middle-class school is considerably more positive than that given children in the two lower-class schools. The marks in reading and arithmetic are a full grade-point higher, and within each year there are increases. Individual trajectories need not mimic the average, of course, but both the upward trends within years and the consistency of the patterns between years in the middle-class school must provide encouragement.

Racial Comparison within the Integrated School

In first grade in the integrated school, children's marks in reading were almost identical for both races for both marking periods. In second grade, there were some small differences in reading that favored whites, but by third grade differences were negligible.

For whites, first-grade marks were slightly better in arithmetic (up to 0.17 grade-points) and in conduct (up to 0.21 grade-points). In fact, whites consistently exceeded blacks in arithmetic in all three grades, and the gap is larger in second and third grades than in first. Children of both races improved consistently in arithmetic within each year however.

For conduct, whites had better marks in every grade, with average differences as large as one-third of a grade-point in some instances. However, as is shown in Chapter 6, these average differences by race can be explained on the basis of other variables, because, with two mild exceptions, race itself has no significant links to performance. In other words, the small differences by race are mostly the consequence of other uncontrolled influences. Furthermore, the overall picture for this school holds for each race separately—that is, after a first-grade improvement in reading, levels of reading marks remain constant thereafter; arithmetic is the only subject that registers consistent within-year improvements; and conduct is higher than reading or arithmetic and remains so throughout the three grades.

Parents' Expectations

Parents' expectations in the middle-class school were approximately equal (at just above a B) for reading, arithmetic, and conduct, and did not vary much by grade. Parents' expectations in the integrated and lower-class schools were also fairly constant across grades, but expectations for reading and arithmetic (midway between a B and a C) were lower than expectations of middle-class parents, and expectations for reading and arithmetic were lower than for conduct.

Parents' expectations for conduct were approximately equivalent in all three schools. Parents' expectations in the middle-class school were slightly higher than children's marks at the beginning of third grade, but approximately equal to their year-end marks in third grade. In the other two schools, parents' expectations, like children's expectations, remained consistently higher than reading and arithmetic marks, even though the parents' expectations were considerably more modest than children's. Black parents in the integrated school had slightly lower expectations for arithmetic and conduct than white parents in that school, but the average differences were small—0.15 grade-points in arithmetic, 0.16 grade-points in conduct.

That parents' expectations are closer to reality than children's is in line with previous work. Marks (1951) found that 9- to 12-year-old children overestimate their grades.

As far as homework is concerned, mothers from all three schools indicated they would help their children with homework. In the middle-class school, about 80% of fathers were also reported to be willing to help. Fewer fathers (50% or less) in either lower-class school were reported available for help with homework. The number of father-absent families in both lower-class schools could not be exactly determined. School records are not accurate on this topic, and, for reasons of privacy, we were not permitted to query parents on this point directly. We suspect, however, that *most* of the negative answers to father's helping came from women who are solo parents.

There were differences between schools in parents' ratings of their children's ability. Despite the fact that all parents rated their children with respect to others in the same school, middle-class parents saw their children as considerably above average, parents in the integrated school saw their children as slightly above average, and parents in the all-black school saw their children as average. These parental opinions about their children's relative ability are congruent with parents' expectations for reading and arithmetic marks, since parents in the middle-class school expected more than a B, while parents in the other two schools expected between a C and a B. Not surprisingly, the middle-class parents expected their children to come close to finishing college, whereas the lower-class parents expected their children to finish high school and perhaps attend college for 1–2 years.

SAMPLING DESIGN

The sampling plan for this research is not easy to describe because it does not fit neatly under any commonly used rubric. It is "longitudinal" in more than one sense of that term, and to complicate matters further, data pertaining to each child have been gathered from several different respondents and sources.

This research is unusual in terms of both the length and nature of its sampling frame. Data for most micro-level school research is gathered over short periods—a few days or a week or two. Data for macro-level school research is often procured by sampling at two widely separated points in time: for example, in high school and then again several years later. In contrast, data in this research were gathered over a 3-year time span (a long interval), but were obtained from many interviews sprinkled throughout that period. Furthermore, several respondents were queried, not just students. Parents, teachers, and peers were all interviewed separately, and in every instance interviews occurred at points matched to the causal frame of reference. For example, parents were asked how they expected their children to perform in the fall of the first grade before teachers gave any formal evaluation. We asked the parents to make forecasts *before* their forecasts could be altered by what children actually did. We also asked for the forecast at a time when presumably it would be most accurately stated. Thus, the data collection is longitudinal, with data collection periods corresponding to the hypothesized causal effects in the model (see Figure 5.1).

Much sociological research that is labeled longitudinal is longitudinal mainly by virtue of the assumption that certain effects have occurred in the past in a particular sequence, but the actual measurement of variables linked to those effects is not time-sequenced. For example, father's education can be seen as a determinant of father's occupation, although both are measured simultaneously when students fill out a single questionnaire. In such cases the validity of the "longitudinal" assumption can be questioned (Cook and Alexander 1980). Our study is at the other extreme: almost every measure is taken at a different time according to a carefully worked-out scheme about the causal relations among variables.

The second way in which this research is longitudinal is that the same children were followed over a minimum of one or two semesters and up to a maximum of six semesters. Actually, the sample is a succession of overlapping two-wave panel designs, where the majority, but not all, of the persons included in one panel are present in the next. Usually, the criterion for including a child in the study was that at least the child's expectations or marks could be obtained for two consecutive semesters. A few children were present in only the first semester of first grade, and a few others were included for whom there were parental but not child expectations. Thus, a child could drop out of the study after first grade, or enter as late as the beginning of third grade.

Table 5.3 summarizes entry and departure of students separately by school. In each school the within-year changes from semester to semester are noticeably fewer than the between-year changes. Changes are most numerous in the integrated school. The catchment areas for these schools were periodically revised while the research was in progress, and these catchment changes are responsible for some entries and departures.

Of the 1,567 children who provided at least some data for this study, 557 attended the white middle-class school, 604 attended the integrated lower-class school, and 406 attended the black lower-class school. For these schools, 34%, 23%, and 23%, respectively, of the children were included in the study for a full three years (192, 140, and 95 cases), while a further 97, 79, and 30 were available for study in the first two grades, and 102, 151, and 130 were available only throughout the first grade. *The procedure of adding a new first-grade cohort of children with each successive year is the major reason for differences in children's*

Table 5.3

Number of Students Entering and Departing from Study[a]

	Time Interval				
	T1-T2	T2-T3	T3-T4	T4-T5	T5-T6
White Middle-Class School					
Enter	423	8	56	8	46
Depart	13	35	9	20	1
Integrated Lower-Class School					
Enter	438	33	65	22	30
Depart	22	65	24	49	17
Black Lower-Class School					
Enter	285	19	49	6	38
Depart	11	33	10	32	6

[a]In this table, the total numbers of children entering the schools are slightly smaller than the totals in Table 5.8 because Table 5.8 includes all children (no matter what information was available for them) while this table is based primarily on children for whom expectations were available at some time.

longevity in the study. Proportionately fewer children reached the higher grades in the lower-class schools simply because these schools joined the study later. Too little time was available for most of the children in these schools to reach third grade. Children arriving at the beginning of second grade and at the beginning of third grade account for most of the remaining cases. For about 10% of the children in each school, however, information on marks or children's expectations was available for only a single time period.

The coverage provided by the sample is incomplete in that students who were in any school less than one semester were often missed. Not many were missed for other reasons. For instance, a child who was absent when expectations were measured was the target of several call-backs. Interviewers returned to schools at least three times to interview children for expectations, and efforts to locate parents were equally intense. Only an illness that kept a child away from school for several weeks would lead to failure to obtain a measure of that child's expectations, and even such a chronic illness would lead merely to a missing value on that particular variable, not to exclusion of the child from the panel.

Occasionally, a student was too shy to respond to the interviewer. In such a case, the interviewer did not press the child but tried an interview at some later date. In a miniscule number of cases, probably no more than three in any school over the entire period of the research, a value is missing on the child's expectations variable for this reason. The child remained part of the sample, however, because marks and the other information could be obtained.

The major reason for exclusion of some children after September 1974 was failure to obtain informed consent from parents. Pilot work for this research started in 1969, and from then until June 1974 it was necessary to secure approval from school authorities, but not from individual parents, for a child to be included in the research. In the schools selected for this study, there were no teachers who declined to participate, and therefore all children in appropriate grades were in the sample. Starting in the fall of 1974, when it became necessary to obtain informed written consent from every child's parent or guardian, in all schools there was some reduction in the sample. This reduction was mainly because we had difficulty in reaching parents, rather than because of refusals. In 1974–75, percentages of children included ranged from 71% to 97%, and in 1975–76 from 63% to 89%.

The population in any school is, of course, a moving target. Children are entering and leaving all during the year. A two-wave panel design for any pair of successive semesters will reflect attrition from the earlier to the later semester. This kind of attrition in the present sample is much smaller than might be thought, however, because if children entered at any time in a semester up until two or three weeks before the relevant report card was issued, they would be included from then up until they departed. The question of how representative the sample is then becomes: how different are children who are present for only a fraction of a semester (either for only the first two months of a grade or the last month of a grade) from those present for periods longer than one semester? Because of the relatively short time periods involved, we do not think the composition of even more closely spaced cross-sections would be very different from our "half-year" panels.[4] (See Appendix A for further discussion of sampling limitations.)

Cohorts

In order to procure samples of a size sufficient to support the analysis and at the same time to keep the data as homogeneous as possible, we aggregated data over several years for different cohorts in the three schools. Research was begun in the white middle-class school in 1971, in the integrated school in 1972, and in the black school in 1973. All children in first grade in each school were studied beginning in those years. Then in the following years (1972, 1973, and 1974) all the children entering first grade were added to the study, and the children observed in previous years were followed. By the last year of the study (1975–76), in the middle-class school five cohorts of children had been picked up and followed through first grade, four cohorts were followed for two grades, and three cohorts for all three grades. In the integrated school, four cohorts passed through first grade, three through second grade, and two cohorts completed third grade. In the black school, three cohorts passed through first grade and two cohorts passed through both grades two and three. The cohort that reached third grade in the black school in 1976–77 was followed for an "extra" year in order to provide a minimum of two cohorts in all grades in all schools. Each of these cohorts is comprised of several classrooms of children.

In aggregating cohorts, we assume that inter-cohort differences are small compared to other differences. For example, comparisons between schools based on aggregated data are blind to any differences caused by the fact that data collection in the middle-class school lasted from 1971 to 1976 compared to a 1972–76 duration or a 1973–76 duration in the two lower-class schools. Obviously, there are other differences in cohorts that we also ignore—some cohorts had different teacher from others. When very young children are studied, there has to be a trade-off between "independent" units and validity or completeness of response. To get permission to observe or to interview at various times and sites, and to collect data in the proper sequence over a five-year period, is no small undertaking. In fact, some parts of the data collection, such as playing a game with a class to get peer ratings, imply that the same clustering that has the disadvantage of lack of independence in sampling units also has the advantage that another important variable can be assessed.

In most surveys, data are obtained from one respondent, and in typical studies of status attainment, students report on father's education and employment, and on other similar variables (see Sewell and Hauser 1975). The validity of variables measured by this single-respondent approach can vary, and accuracy of students' report generally varies with the objectivity of the information—age of parents is more reliable than reports of parents' aspirations for the child, for example. In our study, the children were too young to provide written information and they could hardly be expected to furnish dependable information on their parents' or peers' expectations in any case. Consequently, both parents and peers were directly questioned. In addition to presumably increasing the validity of the measures, this practice should cause disturbance terms associated with various expectation variables to be nearly independent.

THE MODELING STRATEGY

We propose to estimate six basic models (Figures 5.3 to 5.8) to represent the schooling process over a child's early school career. The first two models (Figures 5.3 and 5.4 for T1 and T2) cover the first-grade year. The third and fourth models, for grade two (Figure 5.5 and 5.6 for T3 and T4), are identical to the fifth and sixth models, for grade three (Figures 5.7 and 5.8 for T5 and T6). They are given separately for each grade to make the notation clear.

In the middle-class school, each model covers one semester. In the other two schools there were three marking periods each year with the first ending in late November or early December. The first model of each year for the latter two schools covers the first marking period and the second covers the remainder of the year.

Rationale for Sequencing of Variables

The models are divided into two cycles per year mainly for convenience in presentation and computation. All outputs of the first-cycle model in any year are inputs to the second-cycle model for that same year. In first grade, for example, all the endogenous variables in the first model (Figure 5.3) are taken as exogenous variables for the second model (Figure 5.4). The time sequencing of every variable in the models shown in Figures 5.3 and 5.4 (with four exceptions: IQ, $ABIL_1$,

[4] Cook and Alexander (1980) offer evidence that parameters estimated via successive cross-sections are not very biased compared to parameters estimated with panel data for which the panel duration was longer (2 years) and therefore more problematic in terms of representativeness.

Figure 5.3
Cycle 1, First Grade[a]
(T1)

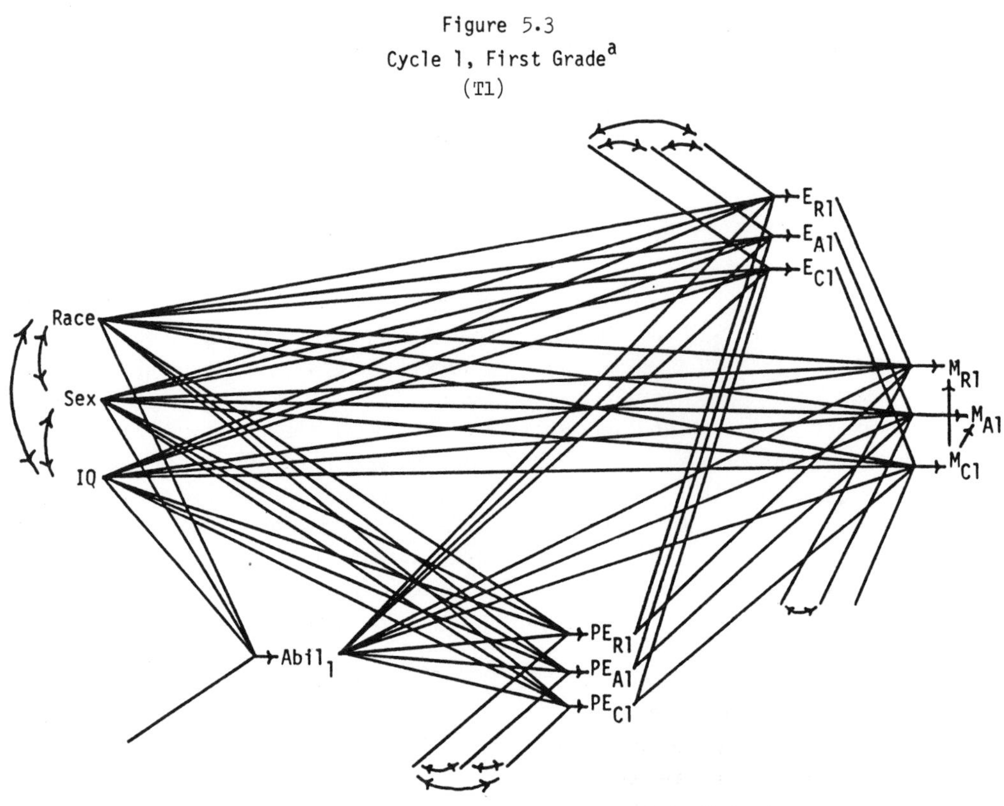

[a]Only in the integrated lower-class school was Race included as an exogenous variable.

Figure 5.4
Cycle 2, First Grade[a]
(T2)

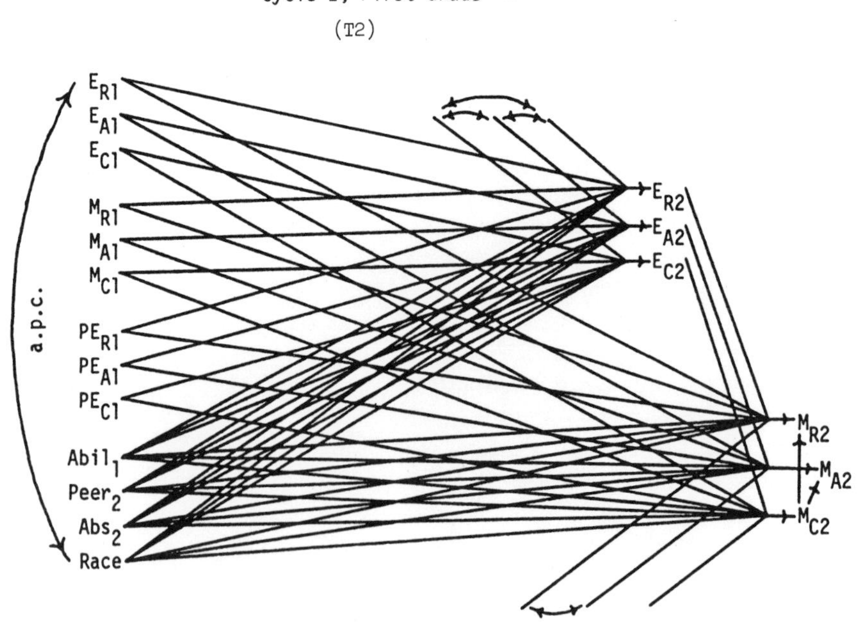

[a]Only in the integrated lower-class school was Race included as an exogenous variable.

a.p.c. denotes the inclusion of all the possible correlations between these variables.

Figure 5.5

Cycle 3, Second Grade[a]

(T3)

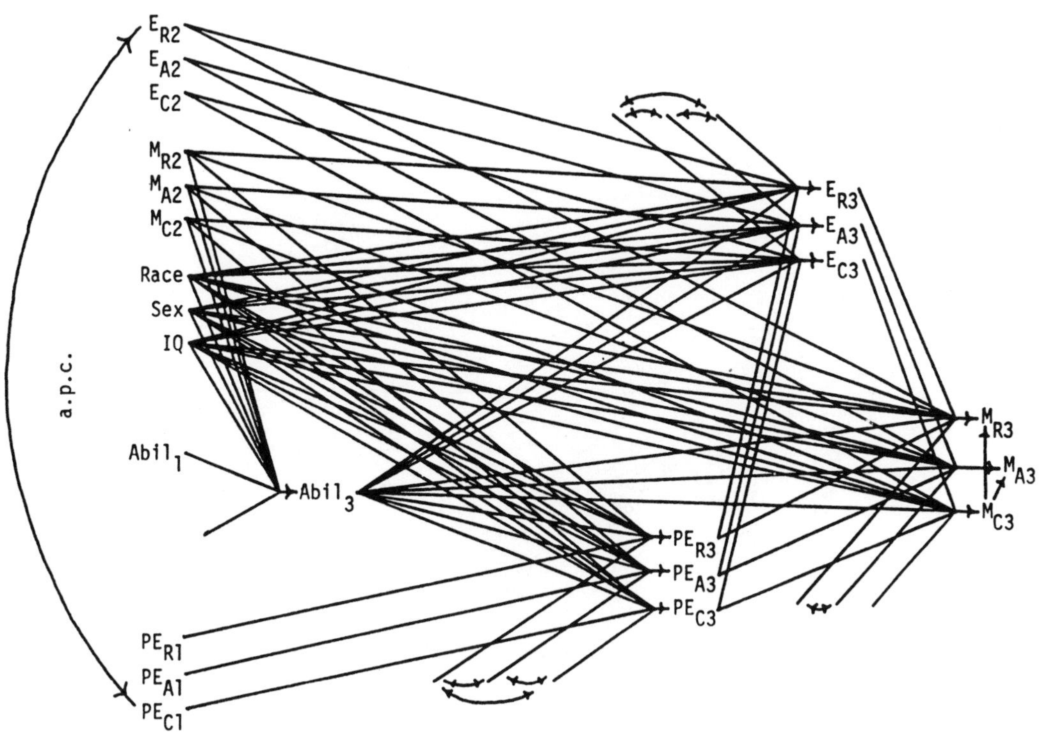

[a]Only in the integrated lower-class School was Race included as an exogenous variable. a.p.c. denotes the inclusion of all the possible correlations between these variables.

Figure 5.6

Cycle 4, Second Grade[a]

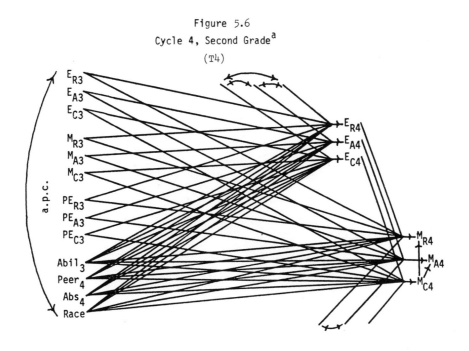

(T4)

E_{R3}
E_{A3}
E_{C3}
M_{R3}
M_{A3}
M_{C3}
PE_{R3}
PE_{A3}
PE_{C3}
$Abil_3$
$Peer_4$
Abs_4
Race
a.p.c.
E_{R4}
E_{A4}
E_{C4}
M_{R4}
M_{A4}
M_{C4}

[a]Only in the integrated lower-class school was Race included as an exogenous variable.
a.p.c. denotes the inclusion of all the possible correlations between these variables.

Figure 5.7
Cycle 5, Third Grade[a]
(T5)

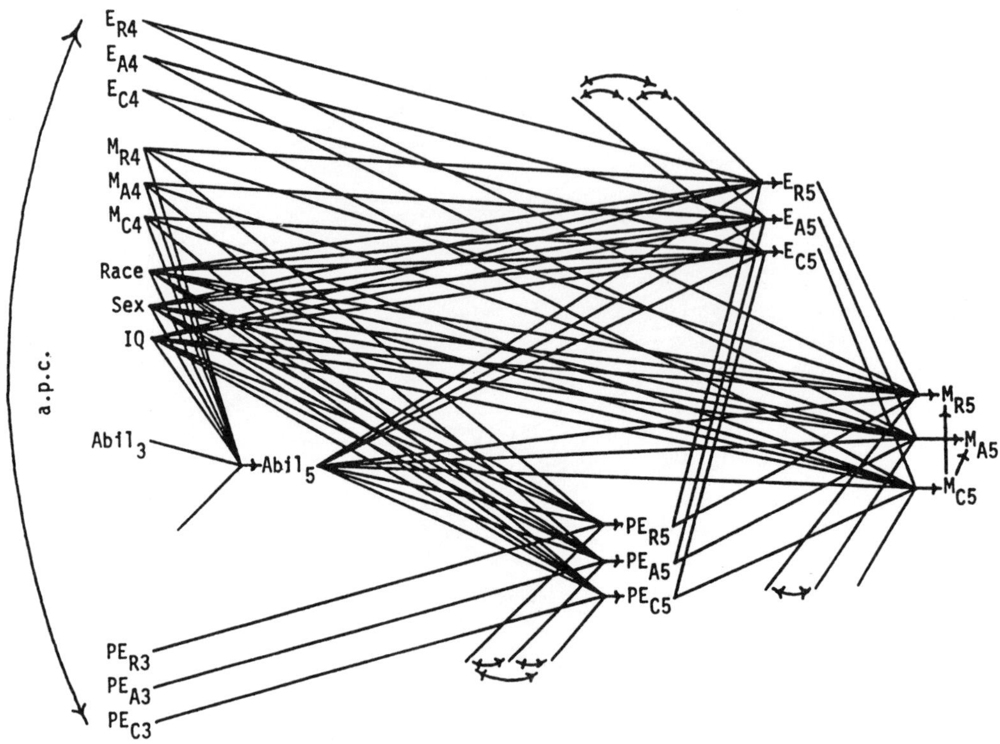

Figure 5.8
Cycle 6, Third Grade[a]
(T6)

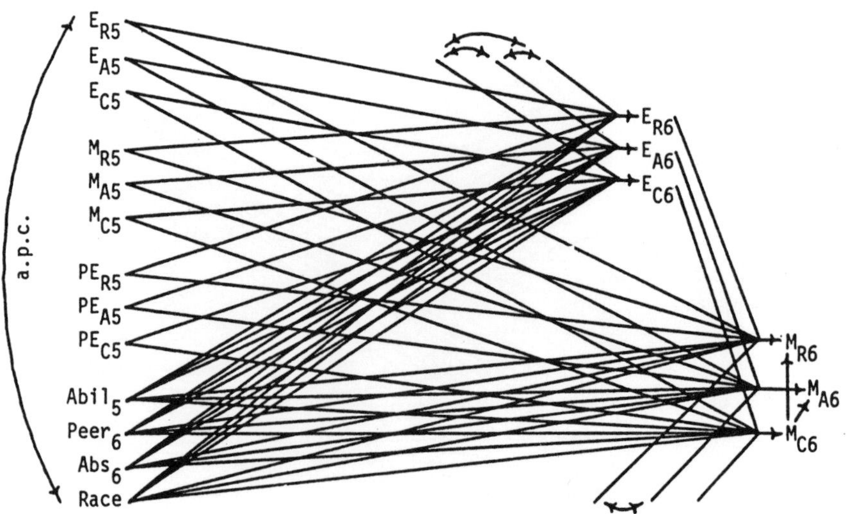

[a]Only in the integrated lower-class school was Race included as an exogenous variable.
a.p.c. denotes the inclusion of all the possible correlations between these variables.

M_{C1}, M_{C2}) strictly corresponds with the actual point in the school year when the variable was measured. That is, the child's sex and race are ascriptive characteristics present at the start of school. Parents' expectations were measured before children's expectations and before children's marks. Children's expectations were measured before marks were issued. Peer ratings were measured in the second semester, after children had spent the better part of the school year associating with one another in class, but before either end-of-year expectations or marks were obtained.

The four exceptions to actual timing of measurements compared to their placement in the model are explained in the following paragraphs.

IQ was measured whenever the school's testing schedule decreed. Its time of measurement was therefore different for different children. Usually, however, it was measured around the middle of the second semester of first grade and remeasured in later grades. Our justification for placing it as an exogenous variable in Figure 5.3 is that a child's tested general ability to do schoolwork, which is our working definition of scores derived from IQ tests, is shaped by many factors prior to the time the child starts school. In addition, some related test scores, for example, those derived from reading readiness tests, were often available to teachers before, or near, the beginning of first grade.

The parent's estimate of the child's ability to do schoolwork, $ABIL_1$, was derived from the same parent questionnaire that was used to measure the parent's expectations for the child's performance in reading, arithmetic, and conduct. We placed it ahead of parents' expectations in the model, however, because we believe parents form *general* estimates of their children's "true" ability to do schoolwork before the child starts school, and that these general ability estimates are one kind of information parents consider in forming particular expectations for a child's performance in specific areas like reading and arithmetic.

The child's conduct marks in first grade, M_{C1} and M_{C2}, appeared on the same report card with marks for the same marking period in reading and arithmetic. The reason for placing conduct marks ahead of the other two marks is our belief that the child's deportment in an important sense *causes* performance in reading and arithmetic. We see children's deportment as a determinant of both how much they may actually learn—if they are talking with other children or moving around they are not attending to the lesson—and also of how their performance is evaluated by the teacher—the teacher may be biased in her evaluations of reading and arithmetic competence if the child misbehaves. (In Appendix C a variety of evidence is assembled that supports the causal priority of conduct.) Our major reason for measuring marks in conduct as well as marks in the two core academic subjects was to get some idea of how performance in reading and arithmetic is affected by non-cognitive factors like deportment in the early days of school. In every model M_C appears ahead of M_R and M_A, and the child's conduct is therefore seen as one predictor of reading and arithmetic achievement.

Review of Overall Model Structure

There are two models for each grade: one model is a transition into the year, covering the period until the first or second[5] report card is issued, and the other covers the remainder of the school year. As already mentioned, the models for the second and third grades are structurally identical. Subscripts are used to distinguish between the same variable measured at the various times. That is, $ABIL_3$ refers to the parental ability estimate obtained during the third cycle, or the first part of grade two. $ABIL_5$ refers to the fifth cycle, or the first part of grade three. The model covering the second cycle for first grade has the same structure as models covering the latter parts of second and third grades. The "start-up" model in first grade is the only one that contains no inputs based on children's prior marks or prior expectations.

Parent Variables

We assume the parent's estimate of the child's ability to do school work ($ABIL_1$) is a possible source of parent expectations (PE_{R1}, PE_{A1}, PE_{C1}) as well as a direct source of the child's initial expectations (E_{R1}, E_{A1}, E_{C1} and initial marks (M_{R1}, M_{A1}, M_{C1}). The parent has many opportunities to convey expectations to the child before the child starts school. Rosenberg (1965) found that parental effects appeared whether the parent's involvement was pleasant or unpleasant from the child's perspective. Parents' expectations could affect the child's marks because the parent may coach the child outside school or because the parent may place demands directly on the teacher in conferences or other face-to-face meetings.

The parent's estimate of the child's general ability to do schoolwork is also a possible determinant of the marks children receive, because parents can determine whether home conditions are suitable for completing assignments. In addition, overall ability estimates may act as a continuing force upon the child during the entire school year, and so there are links

[5] As noted earlier, because of differences in marking periods, in the middle-class school the first model in each year covers the first semester. The first report card in first grade was issued at the end of the first semester. In the second and third grades, the report card issued at the end of the first semester was the second issued in any year.

from this variable to both children's expectations and their marks measured at the end of grade one. The parent's general ability estimate may directly alter the child's expectation later in the year (E_{R2}, E_{A2}, E_{C2}), for example, because the child might become increasingly aware of the parent's ability assessment in carrying out first-grade assignments at home. The ability estimate could act as a direct determinant of children's marks later in the year as well (M_{R2}, M_{A2}, M_{C2}): a teacher may become better and better acquainted with a parent during the school year, and therefore the parent's opinion could directly influence the marks the teacher gives at the end of the year. The same arguments can be put forward about the immediate and more distant consequences of parents' specific expectations in the three performance areas (PE_{R1}, PE_{A1}, PE_{C1}).

Children's Expectations

One of the major reasons for undertaking this research was to determine the role that young children's own expectations play in the schooling process. We have already discussed how children's expectations are both influences upon schooling and outcomes of schooling. Furthermore, children's expectations are a key variable from several theoretical perspectives. Expectation-states theory sees self-expectations as the cognitive states that determine performance. The research on teacher expectations assumes (usually implicitly) that teacher expectations affect children's expectations, and much of the research on disadvantaged or minority-group children posits that their relatively low levels of achievement are a consequence of their relatively low expectations for themselves (the self-fulfilling prophecy). In line with these notions, our models are cyclic, so that expectations impinge on evaluations, but then evaluations (marks) in turn impinge on expectations.

Children's initial expectations (E_{R1}, E_{A1}, E_{C1}), which were obtained before children received their first report cards, may depend on race, sex, and measured IQ level. Black children, for example, may draw different conclusions from those drawn by white children from experiences prior to entering first grade about their own ability to learn to read or do arithmetic. Similarly, there is reason to suppose that gender may affect children's estimates of their own probable success in reading, arithmetic, or conduct. Sex-role expectations for boys and girls are very different long before children start school. In addition, once school starts, boys are the target of more teacher disapproval than girl (Meyer and Thompson 1956; Perry 1975).

Measured IQ could affect children's expectations because IQ tests are geared to predict ability to do various kinds of schoolwork, and children could make inferences from their own experience that are the same as those implied by the test score.

The links between children's expectations and their performance are a critical feature of the model. Children's notions about their own competence, we argue, could be critical determinants of their performance, especially early in their school careers. In previous chapters we reviewed evidence suggesting that children's expectations shape specific behaviors related to learning, such as hand-raising, or more general behaviors, such as the amount they participate in group problem-solving sessions. Without repeating all of the contentions of expectation-states theory, we accept its basic premise: a person's expectation state could affect many variables, among them actual behavior, attitude toward that behavior, how a person is evaluated by others, and the interpretation of evaluations made by others. Therefore, we place children's expectations prior to first marks (performance) in the model shown in Figure 5.6[6] and we take children's initial expectations as a possible cause of the first formal evaluations they receive in school.

Evaluation, as we state above, should affect expectations, and vice versa. To portray this mutual dependence, children are presumed to have expectations for their own performance that affect both the nature of the performance and how that performance is evaluated (marks). It is also assumed that evaluations (marks) affect later expectations. For this reason the model for the latter part of first grade includes as part of its input marks received earlier in the year, and there are direct paths from these marks (M_{R1}, M_{A1}, M_{C1}) to the appropriate expectations (E_{R2}, E_{A2}, E_{C2}). These paths allow for feedback from marks to affect expectations.

Children's expectations may persist, drift up or down as a consequence of maturation, or decay over time. These possibilities are represented by the connection between children's expectations obtained early in first grade and those obtained near the end of the school year (the direct paths from E_{R1} to E_{R2}, E_{A1} to E_{A2}, E_{C1} to E_{C2}). How could such links be accounted for? First, children's expectations could persist because, having once expressed them verbally to an interested adult, the child could be made consciously aware of what those expectations are and cling to them. Also, unless the forces determining the initial expectations changed, the child might find little reason to alter expectations. Alternatively, some children's expectations could drift up as they grew older, while other children's self-images may actually decrease over time. Therefore, we posit direct paths between children's expectations early in the year and

[6]This means that we are assuming children's expectations cause first marks, rather than the reverse. More extensive justification for this assumption appears in the next section and in Chapter 7.

their expectations later in the same year so that the direct effect of expectations at one time on those at subsequent times—their persistence—can be assessed. In both practical and theoretical terms, the stability of children's expectations and the question of whether or not children's expectations crystallize early are important. From a theoretical standpoint, if expectations are very stable starting at the time of the first measurement, one conclusion would be that home and parents, rather than the school, are primarily responsible for children's ideas of their own capabilities, or, alternatively, that a child's earliest school experiences are very potent. From a practical standpoint, if children's expectations turn out to be stable, the conclusion would be that it would be hard to devise artificial procedures that would raise (or lower) children's expectations with the aim of improving children's performance.

It also seems reasonable to assume that a teacher's initial evaluations (M_{R1}, M_{A1}, M_{C1}) will influence her later evaluations (M_{R2}, M_{A2}, M_{C2}). Performance at one time may be a good barometer of performance at subsequent times. These assumptions are embodied in direct paths from marks early in the year to marks later in the year.

Departure from Complete Recursivity

The principal structural features remaining to be discussed are the connections from marks in conduct to marks in reading and arithmetic and the other features of the models that lead them to be only partially recursive. To aid in the discussion of the partial recursivity, the assumption of one-way causation should first be explored.

There are no reciprocal paths or backward paths in any model. Although it might be thought that marks on the first report card (M_{R1}, M_{A1}, M_{C1}) could influence children's earliest expectations (E_{R1}, E_{A1}, E_{C1}) because teachers evaluate the child in class long before the first report cards are issued, tests of models incorporating this assumption showed that such backward paths had very small parameters associated with them.[7] Further justification for this order is that our measurements were taken in the time frame indicated by the model—that is, initial expectations were measured *before* the first report cards were issued.

The departures from complete recursivity, now to be discussed, are of several varieties.

At first we explored the possibility of treating marks in all three areas in an identical manner by estimating a block recursive model with M_R, M_A, and M_C in a single block. However, upon reflection we decided to place M_C ahead of M_R and M_A, even though all three were measured simultaneously. It hardly needs to be said that teachers' marks are fallible indicators of children's proficiency. As noted before, teachers may give higher marks to children with pleasing manners or pleasing appearances, or base their marks on many other criteria unrelated to objective standards of performance. For example, if teachers do not call upon a child often enough, if the child is shy, misses school, or is often late, or even if the child happens to be placed in a class with other children who are either much better or worse, the assigned mark may not reflect the caliber of the child's absolute performance. One way to model marks in reading and arithmetic in order to reflect other-than-objective performance in these subjects is to assume that the same non-cognitive components are the chief determinants of the conduct mark. In evaluating the child's conduct the teacher is likely to be swayed by appearance and attendance, and, in fact, the conduct mark *should* reflect manners and deportment. If the conduct mark is seen as a cause of the marks in reading and arithmetic, then that portion of the variance in reading and arithmetic marks *not* accounted for by conduct or accidental factors can be allocated as a pure measure of proficiency. From such a point of view, reading and arithmetic competence are taken as what remains of marks after variance attributable to accidental factors and to conduct is subtracted. All models therefore show conduct marks as determinants of marks in reading and marks in arithmetic.[8]

Another way the models fail to be completely recursive is that paths from the various expectations to the various marks are area-specific: expectations in conduct affect only conduct marks, expectations in reading affect only reading, and expectations in arithmetic affect only arithmetic. This area-specificity is true for both parents' and children's expectations. The clustering of triplicate expectation variables and the clustering of reading and arithmetic marks, both with correlated disturbances, makes the models almost block recursive within cycles—the exception caused by placing conduct ahead of the other two marks. The reader should note carefully that children's conduct expectations do not directly affect children's reading and arithmetic marks, and the expectations for reading and arithmetic marks do not affect the conduct mark. In addition, children's expectations do not causally influence one another. The consequence of this area-

[7]Two other kinds of evidence also indicate that such paths are probably inappropriate. One is the consistently small size of the partial derivatives of the likelihood function (LISREL III) with respect to parameters associated with such paths, suggesting that even large changes in these parameters would not improve the fit of the model. The other is the small amount of variance in children's expectations that can be accounted for by marks (the impact of M_{R1} on E_{R2}, for example) when the causal order is unambiguously specified.

[8]Models with reciprocal paths between conduct and the other two marks proved unattractive. These are discussed in Appendix C.

specificity, from a modeling perspective, is that the causal sequencing of some variables is unspecified (e.g., E_{R1}, E_{A1}, E_{C1}) making some parts of the model block recursive only.[9]

Another kind of departure from full recursivity occurs between cycles in any one year. Sex and IQ in any one year appear as inputs only to the first cycle. This is equivalent to assuming that gender and IQ are direct determinants of parents' ability estimates and parents' expectations, as well as of children's initial expectations and marks in any year, but that after the first cycle is complete, further effects of gender and IQ during the year are brought about indirectly, through mediating variables. We thus took the position that gender and IQ affect initial judgments of parents, children, and teachers at the start of each year, but that, from then on in that year, their effects are indirect. It is hard to argue that a sex bias of parent or teacher will change over the year, or that children's responses to biases they perceive will change much within one year. (Models that have gender and IQ introduced again at mid-year were estimated and are discussed in Appendix C. It turned out that differences were minor.)

At the start of second and third grades, however, sex and IQ appear again. This is to allow for potential changes in the contribution of these variables when children move from first grade to second, or from second grade to third. The new environment created when a child changes grade may introduce direct effects from these variables on marks, parents' ability estimates, parents' expectations, and children's expectations. Boys and girls might evaluate themselves differently as a consequence of no longer being the youngest in the school, and real abilities may play an increasingly important role in the formation of children's expectations. The parent may find out IQ test scores between the beginning of first grade and the beginning of second grade, or new test results may become available. Also, parents may react to teacher, or "school," sex biases, if they are present in first grade, by lowering their expectations for boys' reading performance or for boys' ability to do schoolwork.

Similar reasoning applies to the introduction of peer-popularity ratings and the absence variable, which appear as inputs only to the second cycle for each year. Each year the child's classroom has different members, and the importance of these peers may fluctuate. Since it takes a while for children to get to know and to evaluate one another's capabilities, the peer rating is introduced anew in the second semester of each year. Absence patterns may also differ from year to year, and different subject materials may change the importance of absences from year to year. Peer rating and absences are introduced only as exogenous variables because we are not interested in explaining them.

Random Replications

All modifications of the model's structure that were based on exploration of our data were derived from data *on cases with odd ID numbers*. Only after the models were available in the form presented in Figures 5.3 to 5.8 (from study of the odd-numbered cases) were parameters separately estimated using the data derived from the even-numbered cases. Thus, judgments of whether to include paths or variables, whether the ordering of variables was appropriate, or whether the fit of an entire model suggested structural changes, were first based on observation of one (random) half of the data set. *All of the models in Figures 5.3 to 5.8 were decided upon before the second half of the data was explored.* Parameter estimates for final models were derived by estimating parameters using the full data set, but the parameters for the even and odd divisions are also available in Chapter 6. We later use the odd-even split-half data to judge the importance of having used part of our data to determine the model's structure.

The even-odd strategy offers a number of advantages, although obviously it carries costs as well. The costs involve greatly increased computation expense and more work interpreting output. Starting with the basic covariance matrices, all computation had to be carried out in triplicate, once for the data based on odd-numbered cases, once for the data based on even-numbered cases, and once for the entire data set.[10]

The most important advantage was in overcoming the pitfalls of exploratory work in which there are many opportunities for the vagaries of a particular data set to influence the form of the model. Structural coefficients are, of course, subject to sampling variability, and there is a high probability, when so many coefficients are estimated, that some particular coefficient will lie outside its two-standard-error boundary strictly because of the vagaries of sampling. Particularly in research such as this, where sampling procedure cannot justify assumptions about random error, being able to examine the consistency of a parameter

[9]Examination of the partial derivatives of the likelihood function (LISREL III) for all the models estimated with the full data sets, in all the schools, turned up no systematic evidence questioning our routine deletion of the following types of paths—the effects of children's expectations on later parental expectations, the effects of parent's prior expectations (for reading, arithmetic, and conduct) on their later ability estimates, and the numerous cross-area paths both within or between the clusters of variables indexed with reading, arithmetic, and conduct.

[10]The models were estimated a fourth way—the odd-even data was "stacked" in LISREL IV and the parameters of the replicates constrained to be equal. The results of this fourth procedure are summarized and discussed in Chapter 6.

from one subsample to another, helps to guard against such pitfalls.[11]

Exactly how to divide up a data set, particularly when so many variables are being estimated, is not well understood (see McCarthy 1976, and references cited therein). If the model is large and multivariate, repeated estimates on fractions of the data set (like jackknifing) are ruled out for many reasons, including expense. Therefore, we took the simpler approach of developing the models using only the odd-numbered case data. With six cycles and three schools, there was considerable redundancy as well as subsample replication to serve as guides in trimming models. In the final analysis, where estimates based on even and odd data as well as the full set are available, precise structural tests can be applied. In the discussion we pay attention mainly to *patterning* in the parameters, rather than to any particular parameter's absolute size.

Omitted Variables

From a modeling perspective, some of the most crucial decisions are those concerning paths or relations to be omitted. These decisions determine the fit of the model even more strongly than the paths that are included, because an included path can receive a coefficient of zero, indicating it could have been omitted, whereas an omitted path is unalterable. Some reasons for the omission of paths are obvious. When sex and race are taken as exogenous variables, for example, they receive no causal inputs. Or, when absences and peer ratings are introduced in the second half of the year, it is because we do not wish to explain absences.

Other paths are omitted because of timing. All of the successive expectations and mark variables influence one another in a temporal sequence. An expectation in the second semester cannot affect an expectation in the first semester, and since parental expectations were recorded prior to issuance of marks, the only possible causal impact is from parental expectations to marks, and not the reverse. Other omitted paths, such as from children's expectations to parents' expectations, are omitted for several reasons, one being that it is reasonable to assume that parents exert unilateral influence on young children at the beginning of first grade.

In addition, paths among variables with correlated disturbances were omitted. Since no obvious causal ordering exists among the triplicate variables (reading, arithmetic, conduct) within clusters of children's or parents' expectations or between reading and arithmetic marks, and since triple or double sets of reciprocal causes could not have been estimated, we did not try to decompose this aspect of the causal structure. Instead, we let the correlated structural-disturbance terms absorb all these possible causal relations. Correlated disturbance terms could arise because greater consistency is expected between areas than can be accounted for by the exogenous variables. For example, the set of expectations of each actor might be made more homogeneous by internalized demands for psychological consistency. Additionally, since the clustered variables were measured at a single time, the correlated disturbance terms might reflect consistency produced by the measurement context.

Although our basic model allows marks at any one time to influence subsequent children's expectations, it omits effects of marks on children's expectations within any time period. While this is consistent with the timing of the collection of expectations prior to mark issuance, informal feedback from teachers to students could carry the essence of the formal mark prior to the actual handing out of report cards. This objection is discussed further in Appendix C.

The largest remaining type of excluded paths concerns the absence of paths between different substantive areas—arithmetic expectations do not influence reading marks, for example.

Except for the causal priority assigned the conduct mark over marks in reading and arithmetic, there are no "across-area" paths. The triplicate paths leading from the exogenous variables to parental expectations, for example, provide for the development of three distinct expectations, and the parallel paths arising from parental expectations maintain the distinct causal efficacy of these separate expectations. This distinct-area assumption is maintained throughout all the models for all expectation and mark variables, with the exception of forward paths from conduct to the other two marks.

Judging the Models

As we worked with the data and tried to understand their implications, we estimated many models and tried other modes of data reduction. This cut-and-try activity was extensive, and it is impossible to give an accurate account of the whole course of our thinking over a period encompassing several years. On the

[11] A clear example of how data can be misleading occurred in the preliminary analysis of first-grade data for the middle-class school. In that analysis, the kindergarten teacher's forecast (a variable later eliminated) was a predictor variable whose significance appeared to outstrip that of several others. Its effect was in a counter-intuitive direction, however, leading us to regard it with some suspicion and to postpone judgment about its true role. As odd-numbered case data for other schools were studied, the kindergarten teacher's forecast was much less useful, so the variable was eventually dropped. Not surprisingly, in the second random replicate ultimately analyzed for the middle-class school, which was based on even-numbered cases, the parameters associated with the kindergarten teacher's forecast were generally small and in the opposite direction from those obtained in the first replicate, clearly suggesting that the first estimates reflected a rather extreme case of sampling fluctuation.

other hand, as mentioned, we were careful to preserve a random "fresh" half of the data to fit with the models we ultimately decided upon. In Chapter 6, the various fits are presented. In Chapter 7 and Appendix C some alternative models are estimated. After examining a number of more elaborate models, we are convinced that those shown in Figures 5.3 to 5.8 are optimal in several respects:

1. The models are relatively simple, although they take account of the major background factors almost anyone would wish to evaluate (race, sex, IQ) and the major interpersonal forces known to affect school achievement (parents, peers).

2. The models allow expectations and marks to influence each other in a way that seems isomorphic with the life events affecting children. Furthermore, they allow for repeated feedback over time between expectations and evaluations.

3. The models are almost homogeneous in terms of the variables included over all three schools, with the obvious exception of race, which applies only to the integrated school. For example, we did not find, in our exploratory analyses, that in one school parents' knowledge of their children's friends seemed important while in another it was not important. The number of friends known by parents did differ from one school to another, but parents' knowledge of their children's friends did not seem to affect children's expectations or performance in any of the schools. The variables eliminated seemed unimportant in all schools, whether in terms of causal efficacy or in terms of increasing the amount of variance explained.

4. The models are relatively simple partly because they are area-specific—parents and children are presumed to have distinct expectations in reading, arithmetic, and conduct. This clustering greatly reduces the number of free parameters to be estimated, while at the same time it acknowledges the interdependencies among the triplicate variables, modeled by the covarying disturbance terms.

5. In most cases, the models, which have similar structure from year to year and from school to school, fit the data surprisingly well. Table 6.1 summarizes the likelihood-ratio χ^2 goodness-of-fit statistics for each of the three schools based on all cases, and for odd- and even-case subdivisions of the white and integrated schools. Where the fit is less acceptable (third grade) the poor fit occurs in every case. Chi-square tests of the differences in fits between the random replicates are never significant, and are discussed in Chapter 6.

In this chapter and in Appendixes A and B, the structure of the models, the rationale supporting inclusion of particular variables, and measurement assumptions are covered. The next chapter deals with the process of estimating the structural coefficients in the various models and some of the implications of these estimates.

Chapter 6

Estimating the Models

Actual estimation of the models (Figures 5.3 and 5.8) proceeded in two steps, the first being the selection of this particular set of six models from among many alternatives, and the second being estimation of the structural parameters for the final models selected. Parameter estimation, and discussion of the estimates, are the main topics of this chapter. To make clear what our overall research strategy has been, however, we need to back up a little and discuss the winnowing process that led to selection of this particular set of models.

SELECTION OF THE MODELS

Figures 5.3 to 5.8 are basically a start-up model for the first semester of first grade, plus models cycling through first grade, into second grade, through second grade, into third grade, and, finally, through third grade. In arriving at these models, we relied mainly on theory, but we let the data offer some guidance as well. The theory is discussed in earlier chapters. We now review how the data guided us.

It cannot be overemphasized that all decisions about model structure in which data guided us were based on only one-half of the sample—the odd-numbered cases. We first divided the data into random odd-even halves, altered all the odd-case models for the middle-class and integrated schools on the basis of goodness-of-fit, consistency from one model to the next, the information value of the models, and judgment based on other explorations of the data, and then proposed the models in Figures 5.3 to 5.8. This allowed us to obtain separate estimates of parameters based on both the odd-numbered and fresh even-numbered cases. Finally, parameters were estimated using the full data base.

There were too few cases to do an odd-even split for the black lower-class school. Fortunately, the prunings suggested by estimating the models with all the data for this school were nearly identical to those suggested by the models for odd cases for the other two schools. The overall result is almost as if the models from the other schools were simply used with this data set also. There was no real conditioning of tests of significance by prior prunings, so significance levels for the black lower-class school are "honest," even though the odd-even strategy could not be used.

Odd-even replication helps in overcoming some of the limitations inherent in the sampling design. As Finifter (1972, p. 115) says, this kind of replication is at its best advantage in research like ours "in those frustrating situations . . . . where standard procedures are compromised and feasible alternatives do not yet exist." In particular, estimates based on random subsamples provide clues about the size and relative stability of model parameters. Our data do not constitute a probability sample. There is even some lack of independence between students by virtue of the fact that some shared the same classroom. Without a probability sample, standard errors of estimate cannot carry their ordinary meaning. On the other hand, we still need some way to infer which parameters are relatively large. The fluctuations in parameter estimates between random halves of the data provide just such information. Parameter sampling variability is further taken into account by the separate χ^2 fits of the model for each subsample replicate. That is, a model tried on a fresh set of data usually fits less well than it fits the data on which it was developed. Therefore, a satisfactory fit on a fresh set of data is evidence that the joint sampling variability of parameters is within acceptable limits.

The random subsample replications helped in another way by providing information on parameter sensitivity (see Green 1977). In exploratory work perhaps the most critical question is whether structural coefficients are significantly different from zero. Our assessment of parameter size is properly gross. A prime concern is to decide merely whether a particular parameter contributes to the model. In addition to the size of the parameter relative to its standard error, the consistency of the parameter estimates across replications guided our assessments. We could first judge whether a parameter was large enough to meet our arbitrary size criterion, and then examine whether that parameter was consistent in sign in the two random replicates. (The criterion based on consistency of sign led to questioning only four connections in the twelve models, with twenty to thirty significant paths per model.[1])

Only the same causal structure that was developed for the odd half of the data, and not specific parameter values, was carried over to the even half. This use of random replicates is considerably cruder than other uses, where, for example, actual regression coefficients estimated from the first half of a data set are used in assessing the fit to the second half (see McCarthy 1976). Such uses are concerned with relatively small differences in magnitude among the coefficients. Our interest is in gross structure, not in small differences among parameters. We are concerned with the implications of using the basic causal structure developed from theory and modified in light of the odd data to account for covariance patterns in the "fresh" data derived from even-numbered cases.

Space prohibits our giving a full account of all the variables eliminated in the pruning process. The major variables eliminated were: the child's general self-esteem (three factor scores for boys and three for girls); a number of parent variables Rosenberg (1965) had found related to generalized self-esteem (number of times the family ate dinner together in the preceding week, the number of "interesting" dinner conversations involving the student that the mother recalled for the past week, the number of the child's friends known by the parent); a number of other variables related to home atmosphere (whether parents intended to help the child with homework, how far the child was expected ultimately to go in school); and forecasts of the kindergarten teacher concerning how well she believed the child would perform in first grade.

In removing variables from models, we placed a good deal of emphasis on our theoretical analysis and on consistency across models. This implies much more than allegience to any particular χ^2 value. Occasionally, however, purely statistical considerations also led to rejection of models. For example, we eliminated models giving negative error variances although we did not eliminate models where a negative coefficient was occasionally observed for a link involving marks or expectations. In fact, with as many models as we estimate, one would expect some less-than-perfect fits.

Fortunately, there were many types of comparisons on which to base our judgments of consistency. The models can be viewed as replicates across the three schools, as replicates across the six time cycles, as replicates between the odd and even halves, or even as partial replications of more elaborate models as they are pruned to simpler models.[2] Although we expected differences across schools, the process cannot be altogether different from school to school. We expect, for example, that children will pay some attention to their significant others irrespective of the kind of school they find themselves in. By the same token, human development is a continuous process, and children in third grade are much like those in second or first. Thus, we expected that there would be some consistency in the models across cycles, and that later models should display only gradual transitions away from the general structure noted in first grade. We would be suspicious, for example, if IQ exerted positive effects in one cycle and negative effects in the next cycle. Also, we would be suspicious if the variables in our models become less determinate with time, because children's behavior should become more predictable with advancing age. We must again emphasize, however, that only examination of the odd-numbered cases was used for such data-induced alterations of the models.

To recapitulate, then, in deciding which variables to eliminate, our sturdiest criterion was judgment—the patterns among variables should make sense. We could expect some consistency cycle by cycle, or from school to school. Using cut-and-try procedures on one-half of the data offered further guidance. Fit was only one of several pieces of information we weighed in judging a model, and it ranked far down in our list of concerns. Even when fit was good, pruning was often undertaken to eliminate superfluous variables—those involving only small coefficients. We tried to hold fast to our major theoretical guidelines and resisted altering a single model to improve fit if such alteration would have led to a model differing

[1] All the questioned paths are in the integrated school, and are: ABS_2 to E_{A2}, ABS_4 to M_{A4}, PE_{A5} to M_{A5}, and PE_{R5} to E_{R6}.

[2] Replications by cohort do not involve enough cases to support model estimations.

from all the other models. Even in the cases where fit is poor, therefore, the coefficients are reported because they are the best available summary of the implications of our theoretical stance and the data at hand.

OTHER COMMENTS ON MODELING

We say relatively little about "indirect effects," and we never try to track down the ultimate source of all the variation in any endogenous variable. Our knowledge is too limited and we have too many relationships to exhaustively pursue the strategy proposed by Alwin and Hauser (1975). (Anyone interested in particular combinations of variables can pursue them in detail by using the information provided in Tables 6.3 to 6.21, and alternative models can be estimated using the data in Tables D.1 to D.18.) In an exploratory study, the best one can hope for is to point to variables that are probably important or unimportant as causal antecedents of others. Our models do not have a high degree of precision. Their basic structure is the main object of our inquiry. [See Duncan's (1975, p. 65) comments on explanatory power.]

Another point needs emphasis: teachers' marks in reading and arithmetic are the two main cognitive outcomes. In Chapter 7 we show that teachers' marks predict scores on standardized tests, but for the models estimated in this chapter, marks are the ultimate endogenous variables. Since each child interacts mainly with one teacher over any one grade, his or her marks are tied to a single classroom. Peers' popularity ratings are also tied to a particular classroom. The unit of analysis is therefore the child nested in a particular classroom environment. For this reason, although "classroom" effects per se are not analyzed, our models are mid-range models of the kind described in Chapter 1. Our strategy combines the approaches taken by previous investigators in that the unit of analysis is "child-in-classroom." [Like Pedersen et al. (1978), Rist (1970), and similar studies, our study has outcomes that may depend on "classroom," but like Murnane's (1975) study, our study includes many teachers, so the findings rest on a broad base.] This allows study of *very early* school achievement, prior to the time when standardized tests are given, but, more importantly, it means the ongoing schooling process, and not merely its outcomes, is being modeled.

Note particularly that to combine models over schools would be inappropriate. The metrics for marks (means and standard deviations) differ between schools. Also, the schooling process, to the extent it differs between schools, might be obscured if all the data were pooled. Unfortunately, classroom populations are too small to avoid pooling classes.

PARAMETER ESTIMATION

We used the LISREL program (Jöreskog and Sörbom 1976) to obtain full-information-maximum-likelihood (FIML) parameter estimates for all models. The LISREL strategy permits measurement error to be directly and easily incorporated into the model structure. This is a notable advantage. Structure, as represented by parameter size, can be sensitive to measurement assumptions, as recognized early by psychometricians (see Jöreskog 1970) and others (Borhnstedt and Carter 1971; Hauser and Goldberger 1971; Wiley 1973.)

LISREL offered other advantages as well. While one-way causation proved sufficient in these models, in exploratory work and in later elaborations of the models (Appendix C) we posited reciprocal causation. We also evaluated models with more than one indicator of an unmeasured construct. The program thus offered a versatile means of estimating alternative structures.

Still a further advantage of LISREL turned up as work progressed. Some time after we used LISREL III (the 1976 version) to estimate models based on odd- and even-numbered cases, a fourth version of LISREL appeared (Jöreskog and Sörbom 1978) that allows two models to be stacked together. By first estimating a baseline stacked model that contains both the odd and even data sets, and then estimating another stacked model in which all the structural parameters in the odd and even portions are constrained to be equal to each other, one can obtain the difference between the constrained and baseline χ^2's.[3] This difference is a χ^2 test of the equality constraints and has degrees of freedom equal to the number of equality constraints in the constrained model. An insignificant χ^2 indicates that the constraints do not significantly impair the fit of the model and hence that the estimates from the odd and even data sets do not differ significantly.

We thought initially that log-linear models would be useful in the analysis, but this did not prove to be true. Such models were not useful even as a supplement to a cross-tabular analysis of our data.[4]

[3] χ^2 for the unconstrained stacked model is the sum of the χ^2's for the odd and even models run separately, and the parameters estimated in the stacked run are identical to those obtained from the separate odd-even runs.

[4] It is instructive to review our experience with models of this genre. Most published data analyzed in light of log-linear models consist of dichotomous variables. In such cases there is a direct correspondence between terms in the model and cells in the data matrix. For example, failure to fit a 2 × 2 table using only the marginal splits is equivalent to a first-order interaction. Similarly, in

THE MODELS

The major task is to estimate the six models presented in Figures 5.3 to 5.8 with several data sets: the odd, even, and full data for both the white middle-class school and for the integrated lower-class school. In the black lower-class school there were insufficient cases to permit odd-even replication, so only models with the full data bases were estimated. In addition, the model for the first half of second grade in the black school could not be estimated at all because the covariance matrix was singular.[5]

The measurement structure built into the LISREL runs is summarized in Table B.1 and the input covariance matrices are presented in Tables D.1 to D.18 for the six time cycles for the full data set in each of the schools. Correlation coefficients and pairwise present sample sizes (*N*'s) are also given in these tables.

Parameter estimates for the models appear in Tables 6.3 to 6.20. Metric coefficients for the odd, even, and full data sets are presented in the upper portion of these tables. The standardized coefficients for the full data set appear in the lower portion of the tables, along with the complement of the standardized disturbance term variance for each endogenous variable—an analogue of R^2.[6] In these tables the causal variables appear along the top of the table and the effect variables are listed down the left side. The ordering of the variables along the top of the tables does not always correspond exactly to the ordering in the figures because variables are regrouped for ease of discussion.

To communicate the mass of information in the tables, we prepared several types of summaries. The first summaries review the fit and explanatory power of the models. Next, other summaries focus on the longitudinal structure of the models, school by school. Finally, a third set of summaries is organized according to the structural coefficients associated with any particular variable. For example, one discussion summarizes all the structural parameters concerning gender in the successive cycles, another concerns all the information with respect to race, and so on. These summaries are necessarily somewhat redundant, but each focuses on a different set of issues.

Fit

The overall fit for models over the six cycles was good, except for the third grade. In Table 6.1, χ^2 values far enough from the associated number of degrees of freedom to occur only 5% of the time by random sampling are denoted by asterisks.[7] The models for the fifth cycle (entry into third grade) fit poorly for five of the seven data sets, and those for the sixth cycle (the transition through third grade) fit poorly for two of the seven data sets. It is reassuring that the final models (T5–T6) fit well in two of the three schools and there is at least one acceptable fit (for the odd cases) in the remaining school.

Models for the white middle-class school fit the best, and even the three instances where models for this school do not fit well are instructive. Although precisely the same model for the transition into grade two (T2–T3) was run for the even, odd, and full data sets, the even and odd sets each indicated the model was unacceptable, although for the two sets together the fit was very acceptable. Table 6.5 indicates that there were several modest differences between the parameter estimates for the odd and even halves, but over all the parameters seem similar. It seems much more reasonable to attribute these poor fits for the subsamples to minor perturbations in the covariance matrices for the odd and even halves, rather than to claim that either is any real challenge to the model. A similar conclusion holds for the even-case model for the transition into third grade (T4–T5). The even model fits poorly—it is the poorest of any of the fits—but there are only relatively minor differences between the parameter estimates based on odd or even data (Table 6.7). Furthermore, combining this disruptive even data with the reasonably well-behaved odd data provides an acceptable fit. Again, we cannot view the poor fit of the even data as a challenge to the basic model, and we attribute it to sampling fluctuations.

The fits for the integrated lower-class school are highly acceptable until third grade. The poor fits for

---

fitting higher order tables, say a 2 × 2 × 2 table, there are eight terms in the saturated equation and eight cells in the table, so each term is identified with a clear pattern in the data. When variables have three or more categories, however, interactions can arise in one or several cells and the interpretation of interaction terms then becomes dependent upon "ransacking" the cells. When variables have four categories, as expectations and marks in this research have, log-linear models are hard to interpret and impose a frame for analysis (matrices of 4 × 4 × 4 = 64 cells) that soon exhausts even a data set as large as ours. With the number of variables we must consider (sex, IQ, race, etc.), the cells in any table quickly become more numerous than the number of observations. Log-linear models are unsuitable in other respects as well. Only recursive models are possible and there is no calculus to estimate the strength of indirect effects.

[5] The pairwise nature of our variance-covariance data matrices exacerbates the usual problems encountered in obtaining matrix inversions.

[6] This is the proportion of the variance in the conceptual variable that is accounted for by all the causally prior variables in the model, and is equivalent to the "determinacy" of the variable.

[7] The precise interpretation of a "significant" χ^2 value is that the observed variance-covariance (data) matrix differs from the variance-covariance matrix implied by the model structure and parameter estimates to such an extent that it is unlikely (less than a 5% chance) that a matrix like the data matrix would appear if one repeatedly sampled from a population with the implied variance-covariance matrix.

Table 6.1

Fit of Models According to Likelihood Ratio Statistics

	T1		T1-T2		T2-T3		T3-T4		T4-T5		T5-T6	
	Figure 5.6		Figure 5.7		Figure 5.8		Figure 5.9		Figure 5.10		Figure 5.11	
	d.f.	χ^2	d.f.	χ^2	d.f.	χ^2	d.f.	χ^2	d.f.	χ^2	d.f.	χ^2
White Middle-Class School												
Odd Cases	18	12.5	42	37.6	96	151.4*	42	50.9	96	111.5	42	50.8
Even Cases	18	23.6	42	30.8	96	151.1*	42	40.1	96	248.3*	42	52.0
All Cases	18	23.5	42	31.2	96	85.2	42	49.5	96	101.1	42	50.3
Integrated Lower-Class School												
Odd Cases	18	20.3	42	30.9	96	116.5	42	45.2	96	189.2*	38	43.2[c]
Even Cases	18	15.8	42	42.5	96	74.5	42	36.4	87	171.7*,[b]	38	59.0*,[c]
All Cases	18	22.6	42	41.3	96	88.7	42	40.2	96	170.0*	38	73.0*,[c]
Black Lower-Class School												
All Cases	18	6.7	42	38.6	--	--[a]	42	78.9*	96	178.6*	42	44.6

*χ^2 values with asterisks denote values where $P(\chi^2) < .05$.

[a]The data matrix for this model was singular and could not be improved without deleting too many variables to justifiably allow inclusion of a modified model.

[b]$ABIL_3$ was deleted for the even cases model to make the data matrix positive definite.

[c] M_{R5} was deleted. A model including M_{R5} provided an acceptable χ^2 for the full data set but it provided an impossible (negative) error variance.

the transition into grade three (T4-T5) in this school and in the black lower-class school occur at points where the data sets are weakest. For these schools, data are available on fewer cohorts than for the middle-class school, and the relatively high mobility and high absenteeism of pupils in these schools made it especially difficult to follow children from grade two into grade three.

The fit of the models for the black lower-class school is worst. Two of the five models give poor fits. However, one nice feature is that both the earliest and latest models fit well. The doubtful models are therefore bracketed with earlier and later models that fit well. Thus we have successfully modeled both the initiation and outcomes of the schooling process, although some of the developmental aspects may be lost.

Of course, a good fit was not our primary objective. Several of the models with poor fits could have been improved by deleting ineffective paths or even ineffective variables. While this would have improved the fit of the models, it would have undercut the goals of developing models as consistent as possible for all schools and all time periods. Such ad hoc pruning could also have constrained our ability to draw some important conclusions, for example, that the child's race did not appear to be a variable that consistently affected expectations or marks.

Given the difficulty of studying very young children, we are pleased that poor fits occur late rather than early. Models that fit poorly are not without value. On the other hand, they must be approached with caution and with an eye to overall patterns of effects.

In addition to testing fits based on the full sample for each cycle, we tested the fit between random subsample replications by using a stacked model in the eleven instances where data for the same model were available from odd- and even-numbered cases (six models each in the white and integrated schools, except for T4-T5 in the integrated school, which included different sets of variables and so could not be stacked).

All eleven tests of the odd-even constraints produced non-significant χ^2's. This demonstrates that the odd and even models are similar except for random fluctuations. It also increases our confidence that the pairwise nature of the data matrices did not produce anomalous odd-even fluctuations, and suggests that pruning the odd models to obtain the list of variables included in all our further modeling probably did not cause us to capitalize on chance.

The structural coefficients estimated by the constrained runs were very similar to those obtained for the full case base. While there were many numerical changes in parameter values, the magnitudes of parameters, their significance, and the patterns involving parameters were surprisingly similar to those for the full case base.[8]

Explanatory Power

Table 6.2 summarizes the determinacy of children's expectations and marks, and of parents' expectations and ability estimates, over the first 3 years of school.

During the first year—cycles T1 and T2—children's expectations are least well determined. The variables in our models are thus unable to predict which children have initially lower expectations in contrast to the generally high initial expectations held by the majority of the children in all the schools. There is, however, a slight improvement in determinacy of children's expectations over the first-grade year, so that by the end of the year approximately 15% of the variance in expectations of all areas (reading, arithmetic, and conduct) in all three schools is accounted for.[9]

From first grade on, there is a continued drift toward higher predictability of children's expectations, with perhaps 20% a median for the second year and 25% a median for the third year. School differences are not clear-cut. The higher levels of predictability for middle-class children at the end of third grade are balanced by higher levels of predictability for children in the other schools at earlier times. All in all, it seems fair to say that insofar as these schools typify the effect of different social milieux on children's expectations, one milieu does not lead to more predictable expectations than another, and that children's expectations in all three schools responded increasingly with time to the hypothesized causal structures.

The predictability of children's marks is far higher, and the differences in mark determinacy by school are consistent and large, especially for marks in reading and arithmetic. In twenty of twenty-two possible comparisons, children's marks in reading and arithmetic are better determined in the two lower-class schools than in the middle-class school. The high level of determinacy for marks in the lower-class schools is striking—in eighteen out of twenty-two instances, determinacy in reading and arithmetic exceeds 50%, with some values as high as 85% or 89%, while in the middle-class school, in only two of twelve instances do values exceed 50%. Clearly, one of our later tasks must be to determine which particular variables provide this substantial predictability.

Levels of determinacy in marks do not show the continuous year-to-year growth noted for expectations. At the start of each year in the middle-class school there are drops, and then substantial and consistent increases over the remainder of the year in all three marking areas. In the other two schools, there is more carry-over between school years. Thus, a change of teachers disrupts our ability to predict marks in the middle-class school more than in the lower-class schools. The reasons for this become clearer below.

A major conclusion is that, starting with the child's first report card, marks in the two lower-class schools are highly predictable. This high level of early predictability indicates that lower-class children's marks *are* responsive to ascriptive factors (sex, IQ) or to parent (ABIL, PE) and teacher (M) influences. The children are confronted with a system in which there is little slack. Most of the variance is accounted for by a set of substantial and identifiable forces already in operation. If these children themselves are to be effective, they will have to either replace some force already operating or develop the internal strength required to make their own independent contribution in a world already filled with potent actors. We think this finding may turn out to be one of the most important to come from this research.

In contrast, there is a degree of looseness in the middle-class school—each year teachers seem to start almost from a clean slate in forming their evaluations, and by the end of third grade, marks are not much more determinate than at the end of first grade. In other words, there is room for the child to exert some force in the system, a kind of looseness lacking in the other two schools.

Is it possible, on the other hand, that the middle-class school offers too little constraint? That is, it may provide an unstable and inconsistent environment conducive to confusion and uncertainty. While lack of

[8]One advantage of the full-case-base runs over the stacked odd-even runs is that a single estimate of the error variances appears for each endogenous concept in the full case runs, while two such estimates appear in the stacked runs—one for each of the odd and even stacked data sets. The meaning of these separate error estimates is unclear, given that only random differences should appear between the odd and even data halves. The single error variance estimates from the full data runs avoid this complication. Also, the standardized solution in the version of LISREL IV available to us did not work, so obtaining the standardized parameters and error variances would have involved extensive hand calculations.

[9]The degree of determinacy (analogous to R^2) equals 1.0 minus the latent variable's error variance in the standardized model solution (where the variances of all the latent variables are scaled to be 1.0). This determinacy, like R^2, is the proportion of variance explained for the variables, but it refers to the conceptual variables (after measurement error is adjusted for) rather than to the observed variables.

Table 6.2

Coefficients of Determination[a,d]

	T1			T2			T3			T4			T5			T6		
	Read.	Arith.	Cond.	Read.	Arith.	Cond.	Read.	Arith.	Cond.	Read.	Arith.	Cond.	Read.	Arith.	Cond.	Read.	Arith.	Cond.
ildren's Expectations (E)																		
White Middle-Class School	5	9	6	13	16	14	11	29	21	17	14	18	19	35	29	36	29	22
Integrated Lower-Class School	6	6	2	13	15	17	21	37	30	18	24	17	20	13	31[b]	8	13	28[b]
Black Lower-Class School	3	14	6	27	11	23		c		19	12	31[b]	29	12	10[b]	18	25	29
rks (M)																		
White Middle-Class School	18	20	31	37	44	57	43	37	31	52	56	59	38	22	20	48	40	48
Integrated Lower-Class School	58	35	24	76	64	64	89	52	53	57	70	65	78	48	36[b]	45	59	55[b]
Black Lower-Class School	24	63	18	34	57	64		c		86	74	53[b]	63	51	7[b]	85	74	63
rents' Expectations (PE)																		
White Middle-Class School	57	55	20				50	44	49				64	48	40			
Integrated Lower-Class School	35	36	5				40	23	30				34	35	33[b]			
Black Lower-Class School	36	25	26					c					53	55	22[b]			
	Ability in General						Ability in General						Ability in General					
rents' Ability Estimate (ABIL)																		
White Middle-Class School	--	39	--				--	69	--				--	72	--			
Integrated Lower-Class School		22						45						27[b]				
Black Lower-Class School		14						c						53[b]				

[a]Each determinacy coefficient equals 1.0 minus the variable's error variance in the standardized model solution here the variances of all the variables are scaled to be 1.0), all multiplied by 100 to provide a percentage.

[b]The reading, arithmetic and conduct parameters for this school at this time are from a model that did not provide satisfactory χ^2.

[c]Model could not be estimated because covariance matrix was singular.

[d]Tables summarizing information relevant to the structural disturbance terms are available from the authors upon request. e disturbance terms in the models for all cases reveal several patterns worth noting. In the integrated school the error rms for parents' expectations in reading and arithmetic are modestly correlated at all pertinent time periods. In the black hool the T1 model shows a strong positive correlation between these disturbances and the T4-T5 model shows a smaller but zeable positive association. Except for the T4-T5 model, the white school also shows a modest positive association between ese disturbance terms. Overall, it appears that the factors which are omitted from our prediction of parental expectations reading and arithmetic are positively associated.

This pattern does not emerge, however, for correlations involving the disturbance terms for parental expectations in conduct. the white and integrated schools the correlations between the disturbance terms related to parents' expectations in reading d conduct are consistently small. The most sizeable correlations between these disturbances occur in the black school but en these are modest in size. In all three schools the correlations between disturbances for parents' expectations in arithmetic d conduct are small.

For children's expectations there is a general absence of association among disturbance terms. In every school the rrelations between disturbances of reading and arithmetic are small. Except for modest positive associations in the T1 model r the black school and the T1 and T2-T3 models for the integrated school, correlations between the disturbances of pectations in reading and conduct are also small. Further, except for modest positive associations in the T1-T2 models the integrated and black schools, correlations involving expectations in arithmetic and conduct are consistently small. nerally the disturbance terms for children's expectations are unrelated in our models.

The disturbance terms for marks in reading and arithmetic show a consistent positive association in every school. As was e case for parents' expectations, the pattern is least pronounced in the white school. In this school the pattern is positive ross all time periods but the magnitude of the correlations is modest. Again, it is reasonable that factors impinging on rks in reading and arithmetic which are left out of our models are positively related.

In three models the covariances between the errors impinging on marks in reading and arithmetic imply correlations greater an one. The three models were T3-T4 in the black school, the T4-T5 model for the even cases in the integrated school, and e T5-T6 model in the black school. Re-estimating these models with the same error variances but with the error covariances xed at a value providing a correlation of .95 provided solutions with practically identical coefficients, patterns of gnificance, and χ^2 fits. The single exception was that in the T3-T4 model in the black school, χ^2 went from 79 to 92 with d.f. (both being unacceptable fits) despite only minor other changes.

Re-estimation of the California Achievement Test standardized achievement model (Chapter 7) for the integrated school hich had an extreme reading-arithmetic error correlation) also provided a practically identical solution.

The covariances of error terms involving marks in conduct were fixed to be 0.0 by model specifications.

determinacy might operate this way, we doubt that it does, because of the superior academic performance of the middle-class children.

Table 6.2 also shows that, in the middle-class school, parents' expectations for reading, arithmetic, and conduct and their overall ability estimates are much better explained initially than those in either of the two lower-class schools. By third grade, our ability to predict parental expectations and ability estimates in the integrated school lags considerably behind the other two schools. One would expect determinacy in parents' expectations to increase as time passes, but there is no clear-cut trend of this kind.

LONGITUDINAL SUMMARIES BY SCHOOL

Cultural context does not appear explicitly in our models. Each model, however, is estimated separately for each of the three schools, so differences across schools within any cycle, or differences in school patterns over the 3-year interval, may be attributable to cultural context.

Our intention is not to make detailed comparisons across schools. The exploratory character of this research hardly supports a comparison of structural coefficients parameter by parameter. Rather, we look at the models in a broad perspective and concentrate on overall patterns, as we did above in examining differences in determinacy by school. Patterns among a number of variables that make sense in terms of other knowledge are unlikely to arise by chance, particularly if they are replicated in the even-odd estimates. Accordingly, we include all models in the following discussion, regardless of the model's fit as discussed above.

The following sections of this chapter are organized around estimates of the six models presented in Figures 5.3 to 5.8 for each of the three schools. Six new figures are drawn for each school. They are Figures 6.1W to 6.6W for the *white* middle-class school, Figures 6.1I to 6.6I for the *integrated* lower-class school, and Figures 6.1B to 6.6B for the *black* lower-class school. *These figures depict only the significant coefficients for the full data sets.* Dashed lines indicate coefficients between 1.50 and 1.99 times their standard error, and solid lines indicate coefficients 2.00 or more times their standard error. If two variables in these figures are not connected, even though they were connected in the corresponding figure in Chapter 5, this indicates the coefficient associated with that path was less than 1.5 times its standard error.

The complete set of model coefficients for the odd, even, and full data sets appears in Tables 6.3 to 6.8 for the white middle-class school, Tables 6.9 to 6.14 for the lower-class integrated school, and Tables 6.15 to 6.20 for the black school.[10] All variables except IQ and absence (ABS) are scaled in a fairly homogeneous range. All expectations lie between 1 (high) and 4 (low), race is 1 (white) or 2 (black), sex is 1 (male) or 2 (female), and peer ratings lie between 0 (high) and 1 (low). This causes most coefficients in the diagrams, except for IQ and absence, to lie generally between 0 and 1. Because of this rough comparability in the relative range of most variables, the metric coefficients within any one figure tend to be interpretable much like relative beta weights (although certainly not strictly so). The much larger range of the IQ and absence variables means numerically smaller coefficients can become significant for those variables. The signs of *all* coefficients capturing the impact of IQ on expectations, marks, and parents' ability estimates have been reversed, so that the coefficients are in the intuitively correct direction—a positive coefficient means a high IQ score is associated with superior performance or with high expectations.[11]

Middle-Class School

Figures 6.1W to 6.6W reveal that many variables are potent—there are many links with coefficients large enough to warrant inclusion. We abstract and summarize only highlights of most of the middle-class models. However, to help the reader interpret the information contained in each model, we discuss in detail Figure 6.1W and Table 6.3, which cover the middle-class children's entry into school.

The First Cycle: Figure 6.1W and Table 6.3

IQ affects parents' general ability estimates, and these, in turn, determine parents' particular expectations for children's performance in reading, arithmetic, and conduct. IQ also contributes directly to parent expectations for reading and arithmetic but not to expectations in conduct. In this school, IQ is the only exogenous variable that contributes directly or indirectly to parents' expectations for the academic subjects. Gender does not influence parents' ability conceptions, but consistent although insignificant coefficients appear for two other common sex stereotypes—expecting girls to do better in reading and boys to do better in arithmetic. Parents' expectations in conduct are affected by the child's gender (girls are expected to be better behaved).

The relationships among variables for parents and children are surprising: there are two negative coefficients linking parents' general ability conceptions with childrens's expectations. Even though no such links are visible in the second or third grades, for several reasons it seems unlikely that these negative relationships are attributable to chance. The explanation for them may be that, if parents are very confident that a child has high general ability to do schoolwork at the time when the child begins school, the child may sense this and become somewhat anxious—a lot is being expected. Parents' *specific* expectations, on the other hand, seem to have mildly positive although not significant effects.

Gender and IQ both affect children's expectations—girls' expectations for conduct marks are higher than boys', and children of high IQ expect to do better in arithmetic than children of low IQ. The most noteworthy structural feature of Figure 6.1W is the lack of connections between children's own expec-

[10] The variances and covariances for the disturbance terms of the metric coefficients are available from the authors upon request. Table 6.2 presents information on error variances, and a note to Table 6.2 summarizes patterns in the error covariances.

[11] The association of numerically large (high) IQ's with numerically small (good) marks provides negative coefficients without this sign reversal.

FIGURE 6.1W

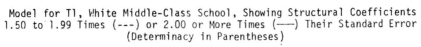

Model for T1, White Middle-Class School, Showing Structural Coefficients 1.50 to 1.99 Times (---) or 2.00 or More Times (——) Their Standard Error (Determinacy in Parentheses)

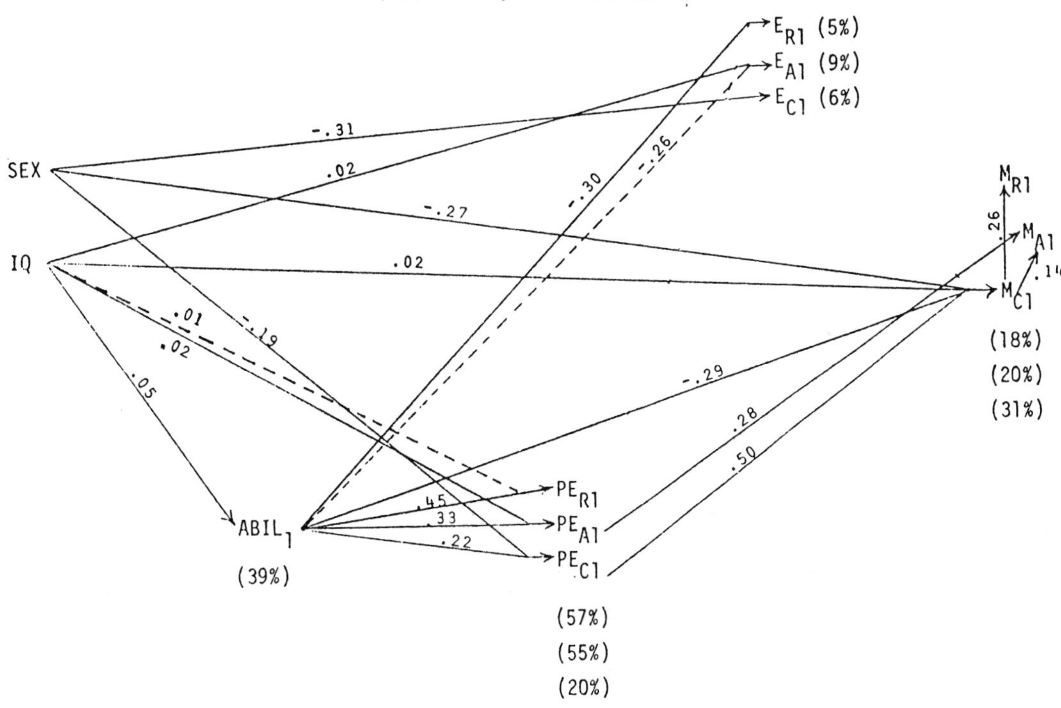

FIGURE 6.2W

Model for T2, White Middle-Class School, Showing Structural Coefficients 1.50 to 1.99 Times (---) or 2.00 or More Times (——) Their Standard Error (Determinacy in Parentheses)

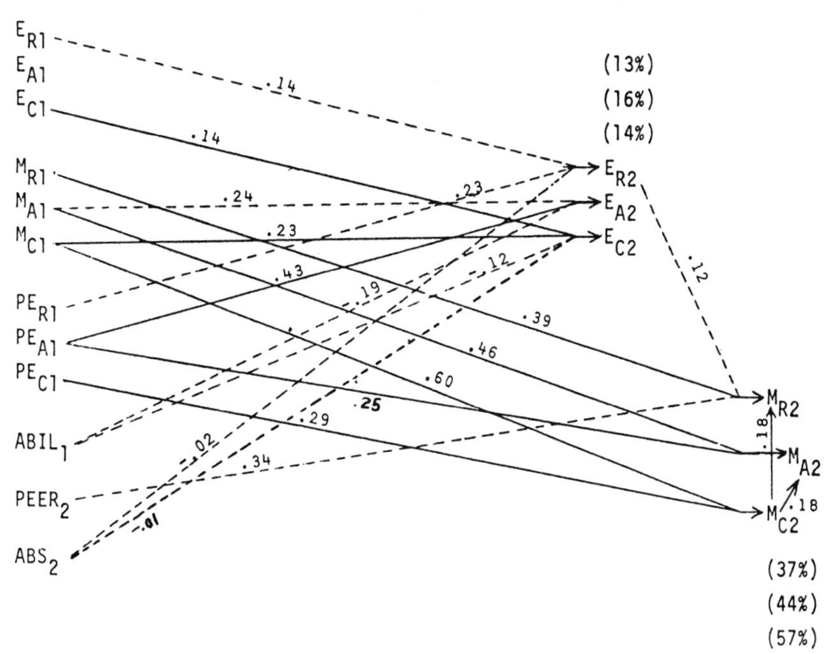

FIGURE 6.3W

Model for T3, White Middle-Class School, Showing Structural Coefficients 1.50 to 1.99 Times (---) or 2.00 or More Times (——) Their Standard Error (Determinacy in Parentheses)

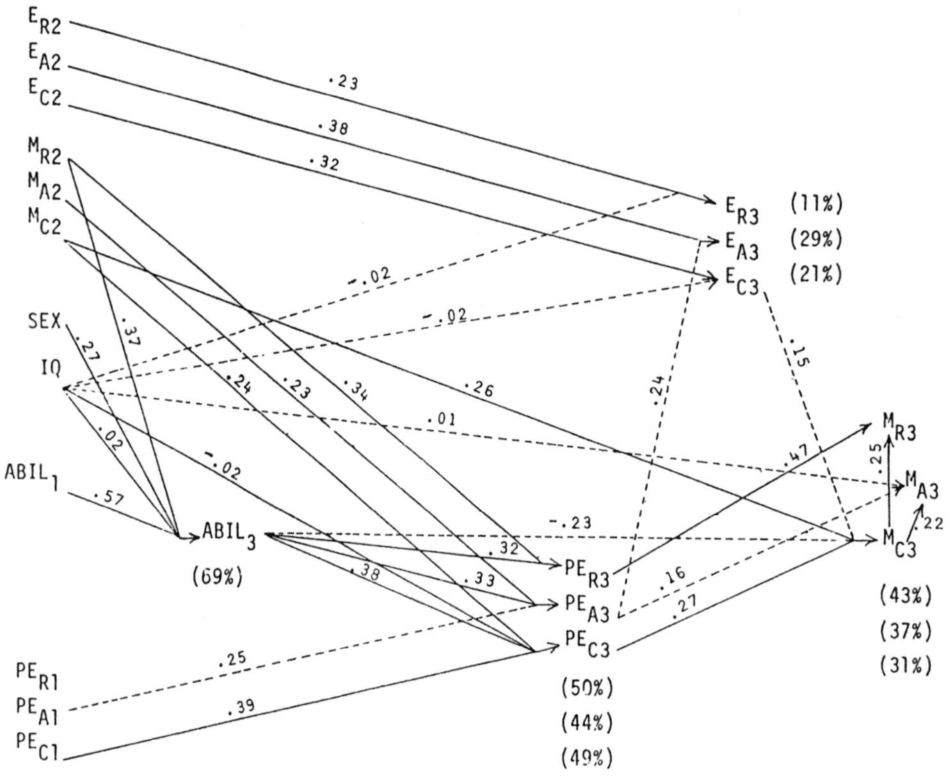

FIGURE 6.4W

Model for T4, White Middle-Class School, Showing Structural Coefficients 1.50 to 1.99 Times (---) or 2.00 or More Times (——) Their Standard Error (Determinacy in Parentheses)

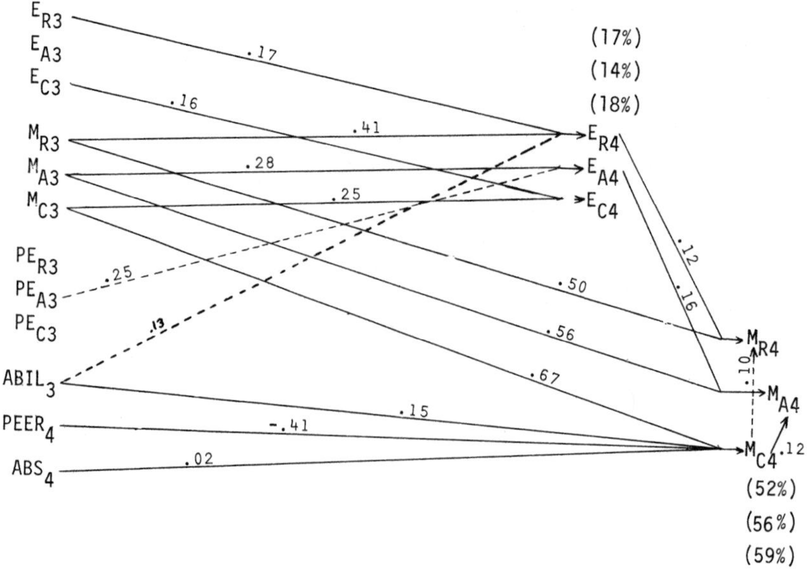

FIGURE 6.5W

Model for T5, White Middle-Class School, Showing Structural Coefficients 1.50 to 1.99 Times (---) or 2.00 or More Times (—) Their Standard Error (Determinacy in Parentheses)

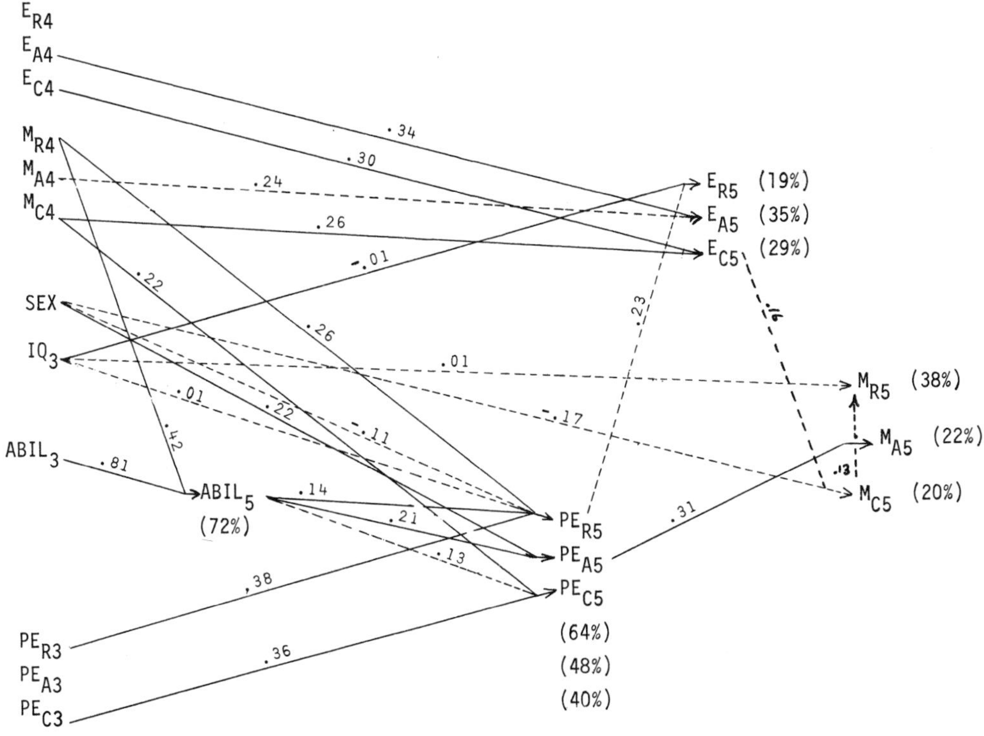

FIGURE 6.6W

Model for T6, White Middle-Class School, Showing Structural Coefficients 1.50 to 1.99 Times (---) or 2.00 or More Times (—) Their Standard Error (Determinacy in Parentheses)

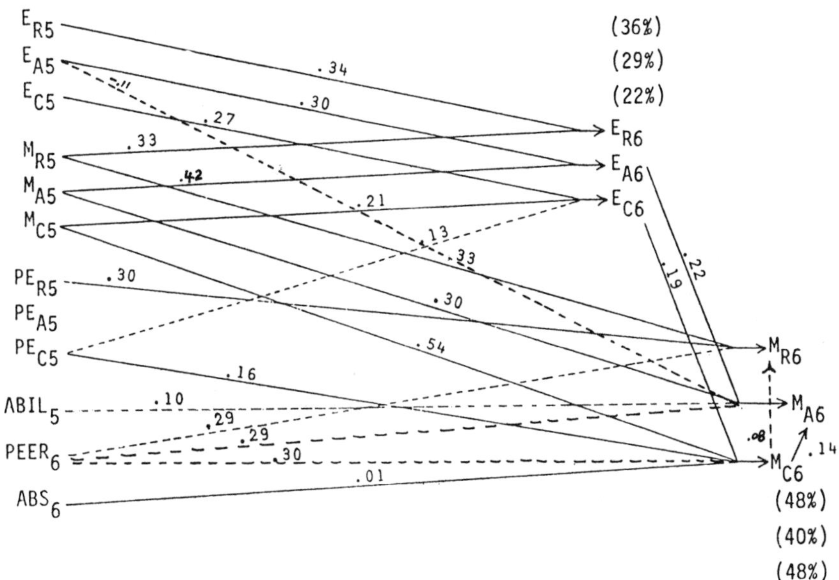

Table 6.3

Summary of Coefficients for Structural Models in Figures 5.3 and 6.1W for the White Middle-Class School:[a] Metric Coefficients in Upper Half of Table, Standardized Coefficients in Lower Half, and Degree of Determinacy

	IQ	SEX	$ABIL_1$	PE_{R1}	PE_{A1}	PE_{C1}	E_{R1}	E_{A1}	E_{C1}	M_{C1}	M_{R1}	M_{A1}	R^2
$ABIL_1$	.0492* .0509* .0500*	-.0983 -.1109 -.1002											
PE_{R1}	.0099 .0098 .0107+	-.1101 -.0473 -.0812	.4610* .4598* .4539*										
PE_{A1}	.0252* .0202* .0223*	.1206 .0675 .0951	.3063* .3341* .3264*										
PE_{C1}	.0027 .0124 .0071	-.2615* -.1318 -.1948*	.3226* .1168 .2238*										
E_{R1}	.0030 .0204+ .0103	-.0232 -.0284 -.0158	-.1732 -.5027* -.3017*	.3755 .2706 .2938									
E_{A1}	.0213 .0253+ .0224*	.0975 -.0620 .0322	-.1338 -.4078* -.2556+		.1383 .2081 .1651								
E_{C1}	-.0155 -.0010 -.0094	-.2913+ -.3343+ -.3053*	.3094+ -.0122 .1568			-.0781 .1225 .0409							
M_{C1}	.0160+ .0172+ .0161*	-.3613* -.1939+ -.2658*	-.2544+ -.3342* -.2878*			.5288* .4665* .4975*			.2198* -.0184 .0984				
M_{R1}	.0066 -.0047 .0011	-.0000 .0586 .0130	.0623 .1942 .1378	.0224 .1901 .0929			-.0299 .0777 .0034			.3705* .1515+ .2577*			
M_{A1}	.0013 .0143 .0082	.0949 .0395 .0516	-.0724 -.1558 -.1096		.2855+ .3076+ .2810*			.0259 .0694 .0583		.2131* .0524 .1379*			
$ABIL_1$	.6217*	-.0647											.3889
PE_{R1}	.1823+	-.0717	.6207*										.5680
PE_{A1}	.3775*	.0837	.4444*										.5528
PE_{C1}	.1241	-.1768*	.3143*										.1985
E_{R1}	.1423	-.0113	-.3346*	.2383									.0509
E_{A1}	.3061*	.0228	-.2804+		.1330								.0885
E_{C1}	-.1165	-.1964*	.1562			.0290							.0626
M_{C1}	.2486*	-.2138*	-.3582*			.4410*			.1231				.3142
M_{R1}	.0208	.0123	.2012	.0992			.0044			.3023*			.1842
M_{A1}	.1651	.0537	-.1764		.3323*			.0856		.1783*			.2037

[a]Metric coefficients are for odd-numbered, even-numbered, and all cases respectively. Standardized coefficients and determinacy are only for all cases. The degree of determinacy, labeled R^2, equals 1.0 minus the "latent" variable's error variance in the standardized model solution (where the variances of all the latent variables are scaled to be 1.0). Thus R^2 is the proportion of explained variance in the latent variables (concepts). The latent variables are related to the observed variables by the measurement structure detailed in Table B.1.

*Coefficient is more than twice its standard error.

+Coefficient is more than 1.5 times its standard error.

Table 6.4

Summary of Coefficients for Structural Models in Figures 5.4 and 6.2W for the White Middle-Class School:[a] Metric Coefficients in Upper Half of Table, Standardized Coefficients in Lower Half, and Degree of Determinacy

	$ABIL_1$	PE_{R1}	PE_{A1}	PE_{C1}	E_{R1}	E_{A1}	E_{C1}	M_{R1}	M_{A1}	M_{C1}	$PEER_2$	ABS_2	E_{R2}	E_{A2}	E_{C2}	M_{C2}	M_{R2}	M_{A2}	R^2
E_{R2}	-.2299+	.3605+			.0230			.1340			.1837	-.0209+							
	.0214	.1157			.2864*			.1443			-.0159	-.0170+							
	-.1199	.2277+			.1372+			.1452			.1230	-.0165+							
E_{A2}	-.0831		.4121+			.1023			.3871*		-.0219	-.0136							
	-.2901+		.3796+			.0767			.1492		-.0652	-.0105							
	-.1933+		.4305*			.1027			.2429+		-.1374	-.0111							
E_{C2}	-.2001+			.1636			.1581+			.1527*	-.0351	-.0223+							
	-.0399			-.0868			.1279			.3078*	-.0019	-.0054+							
	-.1178+			.0365			.1372*			.2272*	-.0273	-.0141+							
M_{C2}	-.0385			.4388*			.0771			.6141*	.0817	.0151			-.0112				
	.0867			.2070			.0831			.5800*	-.0840	.0035			.0918				
	.0421			.2892*			.0671			.6026*	-.0207	.0078			.0527				
M_{R2}	.1683	-.1265			.0685			.3959*			.2100	.0080	.2419+			.1520+			
	.0088	.1607			-.0819			.3825*			.4336	.0114	.0819			.2218*			
	.0766	.0541			-.0074			.3929*			.3372+	.0087	.1218+			.1761*			
M_{A2}	.0311		.2465+			.0716			.4821*		.0163	.0021		-.0171		.2177*			
	-.1791+		.3168+			.0723			.4500*		.3232	.0009		-.0138		.0909			
	-.0536		.2526*			.0684			.4647*		.1521	.0023		.0051		.1772*			
E_{R2}	-.1639	.2279+			.1689+			.1363			.0558	-.1645+							.1273
E_{A2}	-.2184+		.3576*			.1059			.1707+		-.0515	-.0915							.1583
E_{C2}	-.1565+			.0346			.1835*			.2431*	-.0120	-.1368+							.1446
M_{C2}	.0499			.2444*			.0799			.5746*	-.0082	.0678			.0470				.5732
M_{R2}	.1029	.0532			-.0090			.3621*			.1501+	.0850	.1196+			.1996*			.3738
M_{A2}	-.0756		.2617*			.0880			.4072*		.0711	.0241		.0064		.2108*			.4425

[a]Metric coefficients are for odd-numbered, even numbered, and all cases respectively. Standardized coefficients and determinacy are only for all cases. The degree of determinacy, labeled R^2, equals 1.0 minus the "latent" variable's error variance in the standardized model solution (where the variances of all the latent variables are scaled to be 1.0). Thus R^2 is the proportion of explained variance in the latent variables (concepts). The latent variables are related to the observed variables by the measurement structure detailed in Table B.1.

*Coefficient is more than twice its standard error.

+Coefficient is more than 1.5 times its standard error.

Table 6.5

Summary of Coefficients for Structural Models in Figures 5.5 and 6.3W for the White Middle-Class School:[a] Metric Coefficients in Upper Half of Table, Standardized Coefficients in Lower Half, and Degree of Determinacy

	IQ	SEX	$ABIL_1$	PE_{R1}	PE_{A1}	PE_{C1}	E_{R2}	E_{A2}	E_{C2}	M_{R2}	M_{A2}	M_{C2}	$ABIL_3$	PE_{R3}	PE_{A3}	PE_{C3}	E_{R3}	E_{A3}	E_{C3}	M_{C3}	M_{R3}	M_{A3}	R^2
$ABIL_3$	.0225+	.2672+	.6236*							.2497	-.2407	.0360											
	.0253+	.3131*	.4689*							.5344*	-.0814	-.0614											
	.0211*	.2737*	.5743*							.3665*	-.1272	-.0102											
PE_{R3}	-.0108	-.0585		.1462						.4171*			.3622*										
	.0099	.0742		-.0067						.2724+			.2831+										
	-.0013	-.0038		.0932						.3375*			.3240*										
PE_{A3}	-.0148	-.0914			.2215						.3406*		.4233*										
	-.0014	.1689			.2589+						.1868		.2696*										
	-.0058	.0303			.2510+						.2345*		.3269*										
PE_{C3}	-.0136	-.0497				.5470*						.1863	.2784*										
	-.0323*	-.0084				.2982+						.1854	.4986*										
	-.0229*	.0045				.3947*						.2390*	.3803*										
E_{R3}	-.0022	-.0003					.1180			-.0560			-.2168	.4518*									
	-.0243+	-.1848					.3280*			.0739			.4178*	-.2986									
	-.0157+	-.0927					.2275*			.0858			.1085	.0603									
E_{A3}	.0044	-.0844						.4751*			.0161		.1230		.0225								
	-.0071	.1516						.3447*			.2359		.0705		.3854+								
	.0012	.0677						.3831*			.0995		.0624		.2384+								
E_{C3}	-.0259+	.0041							.3167+			.1932	.1640			.0799							
	-.0128	-.1549							.3388+			.1171	.0170			.3297							
	-.0185+	-.0781							.3227*			.1579	.0988			.1532							
M_{C3}	.0175	-.0176							.1947			.3656*	-.2901+			.2508+			.0408				
	.0177	-.0039							.0189			.1486	-.2221			.2823			.2528+				
	.0156	-.0590							.0874			.2558*	-.2310+			.2728*			.1472+				
M_{R3}	.0206+	-.0507					.0319			.0156			-.2253+	.4338*			-.1217			.2708*			
	-.0007	-.0958					-.1513			.0288			.0143	.5938*			.0085			.2281*			
	.0095	-.0559					-.0890			.0658			-.0986	.4710*			-.0564			.2506*			
M_{A3}	.0235*	.1351						-.1463			.0125		-.1413		.2155+			.1876+		.1651+			
	.0015	.0187						-.0216			.0698		.1618		.2099			.0049		.2439*			
	.0126+	.0795						-.0721			.0381		.0369		.1556+			.0909		.2174*			
$ABIL_3$	.2532*	.1705*	.5530*							.2665*	-.0879	-.0083											.6933
PE_{R3}	-.0208	-.0032		.0906						.3386*			.4470*										.5046
PE_{A3}	-.0948	.0258			.2427+						.2216*		.4467*										.4441
PE_{C3}	-.3710*	.0038				.3662*						.2623*	.5136*										.4874
E_{R3}	-.2719+	-.0832					.2306*			.0899			.1563	.0630									.1132
E_{A3}	.0162	.0491						.3805*			.0802		.0728		.2033+								.2869
E_{C3}	-.2617+	-.0575							.2754*			.1516	.1167			.1340							.2130
M_{C3}	.2377	-.0468							.0803			.2645*	-.2939+			.2570*			.1585+				.3102
M_{R3}	.1725	-.0528					-.0950			.0725			-.1496	.5180*			-.0594			.2988*			.4334
M_{A3}	.2588+	.0852						-.1056			.0453		.0634		.1957+			.1340		.2937*			.3701

[a] Metric coefficients are for odd-numbered, even-numbered, and all cases respectively. Standardized coefficients and determinacy are only for all cases. The degree of determinacy, labeled R^2, equals 1.0 minus the "latent" variable's error variance in the standardized model solution (where the variances of all the latent variables are scaled to be 1.0). Thus R^2 is the proportion of explained variance in the latent variables (concepts). The latent variables are related to the observed variables by the measurement structure detailed in Table B.1.

* Coefficient is more than twice its standard error.

\+ Coefficient is more than 1.5 times its standard error.

Table 6.6

Summary of Coefficients for Structural Models in Figures 5.6 and 6.4W for the White Middle-Class School:[a] Metric Coefficients in Upper Half of Table, Standardized Coefficients in Lower Half, and Degree of Determinacy

	$ABIL_3$	PE_{R3}	PE_{A3}	PE_{C3}	E_{R3}	E_{A3}	E_{C3}	M_{R3}	M_{A3}	M_{C3}	$PEER_4$	ABS_4	E_{R4}	E_{A4}	E_{C4}	M_{C4}	M_{R4}	M_{A4}	R^2
E_{R4}	.2114+ .0725 .1305+	-.2211 .0140 -.1194			.2131+ .2181+ .1687*			.5995* .1323 .4066*			-.4191 .2007 -.1348	-.0044 .0032 -.0015							
E_{A4}	-.0282 -.1138 -.0628		.2216 .2686+ .2483+			-.0477 .2628* .1079			.3054+ .3047+ .2829*		-.2091 .2084 -.0007	-.0004 -.0060 -.0021							
E_{C4}	-.0548 -.0568 -.0606			-.0119 -.0481 -.0124			.1911* .1468+ .1596*			.2075+ .2940* .2452*	.3025 -.2937 -.0066	.0122 .0103 .0108							
M_{C4}	.1959* .1050 .1478*			.1217 -.0259 .0644			-.0155 .0419 .0254			.6279* .7348* .6692*	-.6487* -.1406* -.4120*	.0289* .0096 .0181*			.1608+ .0754 .1112				
M_{R4}	.1027 -.0594 .0136	-.0553 .2100+ .0946			.0932 .1041 .0470			.5445* .4884* .4981*			-.0436 .2089 .0929	.0103 .0016 .0050	.1441+ .0784 .1233*			.0845 .1197+ .0981+			
M_{A4}	.0469 .1140 .0753		.0506 .1339 .0735			-.0016 -.0292 -.0069			.6727* .3776* .5589*		.2205 .1291 .1835	-.0045 .0003 -.0011		.1840* .1677+ .1629*		.0818 .1820* .1172*			
E_{R4}	.1797+	-.1194			.1614*			.3779*			-.0603	-.0153							.1689
E_{A4}	-.0765		.2203+			.1133			.2018*		-.0003	-.0185							.1414
E_{C4}	-.0888			-.0135			.1993*			.2833*	-.0032	.1154							.1779
M_{C4}	.1912*			.0616			.0280			.6819*	-.1731*	.1707*			.0981				.5899
M_{R4}	.0208	.1049			.0499			.5140*			.0461	.0555	.1369*			.1160+			.5244
M_{A4}	.1117		.0795			-.0088			.4858*		.0884	-.0123		.1984*		.1344*			.5554

[a]Metric coefficients are for odd-numbered, even-numbered, and all cases respectively. Standardized coefficients and determinacy are only for all cases. The degree of determinacy, labeled R^2, equals 1.0 minus the "latent" variable's error variance in the standardized model solution (where the variances of all the latent variables are scaled to be 1.0). Thus R^2 is the proportion of explained variance in the latent variables (concepts). The latent variables are related to the observed variables by the measurement structure detailed in Table B.1.

*Coefficient is more than twice its standard error.

+Coefficient is more than 1.5 times its standard error.

Table 6.7

Summary of Coefficients for Structural Models in Figures 5.7 and 6.5W for the White Middle-Class School:[a] Metric Coefficients in Upper Half of Table, Standardized Coefficients in Lower Half, and Degree of Determinacy

	IQ	SEX	$ABIL_3$	PE_{R3}	PE_{A3}	PE_{C3}	E_{R4}	E_{A4}	E_{C4}	M_{R4}	M_{A4}	M_{C4}	$ABIL_5$	PE_{R5}	PE_{A5}	PE_{C5}	E_{R5}	E_{A5}	E_{C5}	M_{C5}	M_{R5}	M_{A5}	R^2
$ABIL_5$	-.0157+ .0062 -.0018	.1943 -.3464* -.1112	.8399* .8391* .8132*							.6021* .2520 .4225*	.0398 -.1542 -.0679	.0818 .0686 .0526											
PE_{R5}	.0064 .0009 .0056+	-.0240 -.1399 -.1137+		.4999* .2715+ .3770*						.3321* .3073* .2649*			.0487 .1989* .1389*										
PE_{A5}	.0065 .0034 .0060	.2824* .1129 .2154*			.0599 .1928 .1242						.1497 .0865 .1161		.2867* .1504+ .2109*										
PE_{C5}	.0048 -.0021 .0026	.1459 -.0282 .0276				.3476* .3961* .3619*						.3102* .1779 .2238*	.0449 .1928* .1273+										
E_{R5}	-.0145* -.0047 -.0109*	-.0431 -.0183 -.0517					.1404 .1054 .1027			.1127 -.0658 .0676			.0162 .0809 .0658	.1392 .3820 .2339+									
E_{A5}	-.0064 .0044 .0001	.2534+ .0277 .1146						.4384* .2890* .3384*			.3111+ .1285 .2368+		-.1739 .0669 -.0318		.3328 .1724 .2207								
E_{C5}	-.0019 -.0066 -.0071	.0790 -.0676 .0084							.3262* .2979+ .2989*			.3390* .2139 .2639*	.0420 .0384 .0680			.0423 .2285 .1453							
M_{C5}	.0032 .0076 .0062	-.0329 -.2409 -.1742+							.1919 -.0120 .0807			.1110 .0253 .0385	.0600 .0839 .0723			.1380 .0325 .1065			.0031 .2921+ .1636+				
M_{R5}	.0043 .0050 .0068+	-.0170 -.0317 -.0200					.0076 .0976 .0749			.1608 .2380 .1358			.0603 .1754+ .0878	.3137+ -.1519 .1445			.1197 .1248 .1200			.2383+ .0264 .1283+			
M_{A5}	-.0051 .0021 -.0012	-.0990 -.0637 -.0480						-.1009 .0259 -.0343			.0838 .2260 .1586		-.0397 -.0043 .0014		.6243* .0587 .3116*			.0394 .0787 .0650		.1490 .1097 .1319			
$ABIL_5$	-.0258	-.0650	.7628*							.2612*	-.0431	.0382											.7246
PE_{R5}	.1269+	-.1050+		.4057*						.2588*			.2195*										.6444
PE_{A5}	.1579	.2303*			.1551						.1348		.3855*										.4786
PE_{C5}	.0575	.0245				.3805*						.2463*	.1931+										.4020
E_{R5}	-.2697*	-.0520					.1204			.0719			.1133	.2549+									.1934
E_{A5}	.0027	.0950						.3708*			.2132+		-.0451		.1711								.3499
E_{C5}	-.1484	.0072							.2808*			.2811*	.0998			.1407							.2904
M_{C5}	.1404	-.1620+							.0821			.0444	.1149			.1117			.1771+				.1994
M_{R5}	.1694+	-.0203					.0885			.1456			.1522	.1586			.1209			.1399+			.3796
M_{A5}	-.0313	-.0502						-.0473			.1800		.0024		.3045*			.0819		.1483			.2220

[a]Metric coefficients are for odd-numbered, even-numbered, and all cases respectively. Standardized coefficients and determinacy are only for all cases. The degree of determinacy, labeled R^2, equals 1.0 minus the "latent" variable's error variance in the standardized model solution (where the variances of all the latent variables are scaled to be 1.0). Thus R^2 is the proportion of explained variance in the latent variables (concepts). The latent variables are related to the observed variables by the measurement structure detailed in Table B.1.

*Coefficient is more than twice its standard error.

+Coefficient is more than 1.5 times its standard error.

Table 6.8

Summary of Coefficients for Structural Models in Figures 5.8 and 6.6W for the White Middle-Class School:[a] Metric Coefficients in Upper Half of Table, Standardized Coefficients in Lower Half, and Degree of Determinacy

	$ABIL_5$	PE_{R5}	PE_{A5}	PE_{C5}	E_{R5}	E_{A5}	E_{C5}	M_{R5}	M_{A5}	M_{C5}	$PEER_6$	ABS_6	E_{R6}	E_{A6}	E_{C6}	M_{C6}	M_{R6}	M_{A6}	R^2
E_{R6}	.0240 .1166 .0491	.1698 .0055 .1323			.2417* .4263* .3414*			.4608* .1423* .3267*			-.0357 .2648 .0909	-.0014 .0093 .0038							
E_{A6}	.0455 .0760 .0485		-.0565 .3052+ .1164			.4221* .1443* .3019*			.4388* .5108* .4187*		.1931 .4175 .2938	.0000 .0005 -.0015							
E_{C6}	.0529 -.0770 -.0184			.2305* .0869+ .1294+			.3192* .2277* .2670*			.1501* .2386* .2091	-.5262* .1219 -.1578	.0011 .0012 -.0001							
M_{C6}	.0392 -.0341 .0095			.2168+ .1234* .1608*			.0336 .0214 .0353			.4428* .6515* .5444*	.1467 .4099+ .2987+	.0173* .0105* .0136*			.3021* .0580* .1920*				
M_{R6}	.0099 -.0416 -.0029	.3977* .3099* .2959*			.0459 -.0578 .0089			.2615* .3659* .3335*			.3041+ .1751+ .2929+	.0108* -.0041 .0029	.0715 .0423 .0232			-.0656* .2048* .0838+			
M_{A6}	.1703* .0545* .0992*		.0237 -.1207 -.0319			-.1026 -.1219 -.1079+			.2144+ .3775* .3029*		.1559 .4371+ .2856+	.0071 .0023 .0048		.2979* .1489* .2184*		.0277* .2432* .1416*			
E_{R6}	.0743	.1272			.3006*			.2858*			.0402	.0483							.3550
E_{A6}	.0593		.0785			.2615*			.2891*		.1054	-.0153							.2941
E_{C6}	-.0311			.1422+			.3070*			.2216*	-.0780	-.0019							.2244
M_{C6}	.0132			.1449*			.0333			.4730*	.1211+	.1597*			.1574*				.4824
M_{R6}	-.0050	.3281*			.0090			.3364*			.1495+	.0426	.0267			.1056+			.4789
M_{A6}	.1628*		-.0288			-.1253+			.2802*		.1372+	.0671		.2927*		.1679*			.3991

[a]Metric coefficients are for odd-numbered, even-numbered, and all cases respectively. Standardized coefficients and determinacy are only for all cases. The degree of determinacy, labeled R^2, equals 1.0 minus the "latent" variable's error variance in the standardized model solution (where the variances of all the latent variables are scaled to be 1.0). Thus R^2 is the proportion of explained variance in the latent variables (concepts). The latent variables are related to the observed variables by the measurement structure detailed in Table B.1.

*Coefficient is more than twice its standard error.

+Coefficient is more than 1.5 times its standard error.

tations and their marks. These children appear to be poor judges of the quality of their own academic performance when they start first grade. Parents' expectations, on the other hand, affect marks in both arithmetic and conduct. Parents could know the school marking norms in these subjects and/or provide learning opportunities at home to improve their children's performance. They could also influence the teacher directly.

Children's marks in conduct on the first report card are much better explained than their marks in the two academic areas, even though the conduct mark is an "extra" predictor of the other two marks. Marks in conduct are significantly responsive to every prior variable that could exert an effect, except the children's own conduct expectations. It is noteworthy that IQ affects conduct marks directly but not the other marks.

Conduct affects both reading and arithmetic, and to anticipate a little, the rest of the figures for the middle-class usually also show connections from conduct to marks in the two academic areas. The child's conduct is apparently an important determinant of academic performance early in the game. Furthermore, IQ "determines" conduct, but this may be because the children who are able to sit still, follow directions, and attend to what they are supposed to be doing are the ones who score high on IQ tests. The link, therefore, could be more associational than causal. The central role of conduct in this earliest model of the school achievement process, however, points to the importance of deportment in early schooling.

Summary of Figures 6.1W to 6.6W (White Middle-Class School)

Several basic conclusions emerge for the white middle-class school. One is that parents' expectations for reading, arithmetic, and conduct are rather well accounted for right from the beginning. Another is that parents' estimates of their children's overall ability provide a substantial and consistent foundation for their expectations in the particular areas (all nine coefficients are significant).

Middle-class parents' expectations significantly affected their children's expectations for reading or arithmetic (or both) in four of the six models covering the first 3 years of schooling. Although the magnitude of these effects is modest, all but two of the eighteen coefficients are positive. Parents' expectations show a slightly more substantial influence on the actual marks their children receive (ten of eighteen coefficients are significant and all but one are positive). Of the six marking periods considered, marks in reading responded to parents' expectations twice, arithmetic marks responded four times, and conduct marks responded four times. While teachers may award marks to please or appease parents, it is also possible that parents may simply be good judges of their children's abilities and it is the child's actual behavior that provokes an evaluation by the teacher that corresponds to the parent's expectations. Our preferred explanation, however, remains that, if parents hold high expectations, there are various ways they can improve performance, including supervision of homework or informing children about appropriate classroom behavior.

Gender has inconsistent effects on parental ability estimates (being significantly positive in second grade and slightly negative in the other years) but gender effects on particular expectations are more consistent. Both the parents and the children themselves display stereotyped sex effects in that they hold expectations that favor girls in reading and boys in arithmetic throughout the first three grades. (Only the effects on third-graders' parents attain significance beyond the 5% level.) Both children's and parents' conduct expectations significantly favor girls in first grade but not later. Academic marks display no particular sex bias in any grade, but conduct marks consistently, and significantly in two of three cases, favor girls.

Conduct marks play an active role in the models. They respond to gender and to early IQ and transmit effects of these variables through to marks in reading and arithmetic (eleven of twelve coefficients are significant). Both the special importance of the initial deportment mark and the modest direct effects of IQ on academic marks (two of six coefficients are significant—one each in second and third grade) mesh well with a marking standard based on effort. Good conduct and high academic effort seem to be inseparable in the earliest grades.

The models depicting the transitions between years yield somewhat different findings from models depicting within-year processes. Within years, children's expectations modestly influence marks (five of nine coefficients are of at least borderline significance), and they consistently respond to prior marks (eight of nine possible cases). Even the earliest feedback these children receive shapes their academic self-image. Marks consistently show strong within-year persistence (nine of nine possible cases).

Between years (including the initial model for first grade) the pattern is slightly different. Children's expectations show weaker effects on marks—two weak effects appear (of nine possible) and both are in the area of conduct, where the child has the most direct, although not necessarily the easiest, control. Between years, children's expectations do respond to prior marks (two of six possible cases) but not as strongly as within years. Marks show little persistence between years (one of six instances). There are no links between first- and second-grade, or second- and third-grade marks in the academic subjects. At first thought, the lack of such connections seems odd, and it must be confusing to the children, but it may have a beneficial effect in that each year children start off with something of clean slate. Children's expectations, in contrast, do persist both within and between years (twelve of fifteen instances).

In short, *there is a feedback cycle between marks and children's expectations and it is much stronger within years than between years*. Children's expectations in one grade are resilient enough to show some persistence to the middle of the next grade but they show little effect on later marks. The first consistent and unequivocal links between children's expectations and their marks in the two academic areas appear in second grade. By the end of the second grade, children's expectations have some influence on performance, although the influence is weak compared to the persistence of prior performance levels. Yet clearly the children's ideas about their own capabilities exert separate and noticeable effects. Furthermore, it is the children's current expectations that are effective. The expectations the children held during the prior time period had essentially null effects (a single borderline significant effect is in a counterintuitive direction).

Parental ability conceptions are very stable between years, and their specific expectations display modest stability (four of six coefficients are significant). The weaker persistence of specific parental expectations was unanticipated, but it makes sense in retrospect. Apparently, parents do not radically alter their overall impressions of their child's scholastic ability, but they do alter their ideas about levels of performance in the academic subjects. Parental expectations and ability estimates are apparently formed largely on the basis of early IQ, and expectations are modified on the basis of new information gleaned from marks (five of six coefficients). Ability estimates are also modified by mark feedback, but it is noteworthy that reading marks are the only marks these parents used in revising their ability conceptions. The effects of parents are not sharply divided between and within years.

All in all, the models paint a picture of consistent, responsive, and efficacious children and parents in this school. Teachers' marks are consistent within years but are inconsistent between years. This seems to reshuffle or loosen the system rather than totally disrupt it.

Lower-Class Integrated School

Figures 6.1I to 6.6I and Tables 6.9 to 6.14 refer to models for the integrated school (approximately 60% black). The generally poor fits that characterize the third-grade models in this school (Table 6.1) require that we treat the coefficients for these models with caution.

Numerous patterns appearing in the first- and second-grade models continue to appear in these third-grade models, despite the poor fits. Also, this school, because it is integrated, offers the only opportunity to examine the effect of a child's race unconfounded by between-school factors. In previous exploratory analyses (Entwisle and Hayduk 1978a) we found little variance attributable to race, even in cross-race comparisons involving teachers of the two races marking children of the two races. In these models, too, there are few effects attributable to race. Over the entire 3-year period there are only five structural coefficients associated with race that reach even the minimum size criterion (1.5 times the associated standard error)—only minimally more than one would expect by chance. Two occur in the first cycle, one in the second, and the others in the third. Otherwise, there are no effects attributable directly to race, even though race was introduced as an exogenous variable in each model and could have affected a total of forty-eight endogenous variables.

Again, we discuss the first model in some detail before providing a summary of all six models for this school.

The First Cycle: Figure 6.1I and Table 6.9

As first grade begins, race has two significant effects. White parents have higher expectations for conduct than black parents; however, only a small percentage of the parents' conduct expectations is determined (5%), so this effect of race requires little attention.

The effect of race on first marks in reading, with sex and IQ effectively controlled, is another matter. It appears from the −0.21 coefficient (blacks coded 2, whites coded 1) that, compared to whites, blacks receive an extra boost of about one-fifth of a grade-point in reading marks on their first report cards. The coefficients for the odd and even replicates are both negative, and hence the negative link is probably not a sampling fluke. There are only very small differences between the average first marks in reading that blacks and whites receive, however, and this holds for both the odd and even replications. Two possible explanations are that teachers hold lower expectations for black children or that the dialects of black children and other subcultural differences persuade teachers to mark blacks more leniently. We are not very happy with these explanations because it is unclear why this is the only place an effect of this kind appears in all the models for this school. Even the coefficient associated with race and year-end reading marks is near zero, and the coefficients in the even-odd replication are opposite in sign. Thus, whatever explains the impact of race on initial reading marks is unlikely to be operative later in the same year. The coefficients for the effects of race on arithmetic and conduct marks

FIGURE 6.1I

Model for T1, Integrated Lower-Class School, Showing Structural Coefficients 1.50 to 1.99 Times (---) or 2.00 or More Times (——) Their Standard Error (Determinacy in Parentheses)

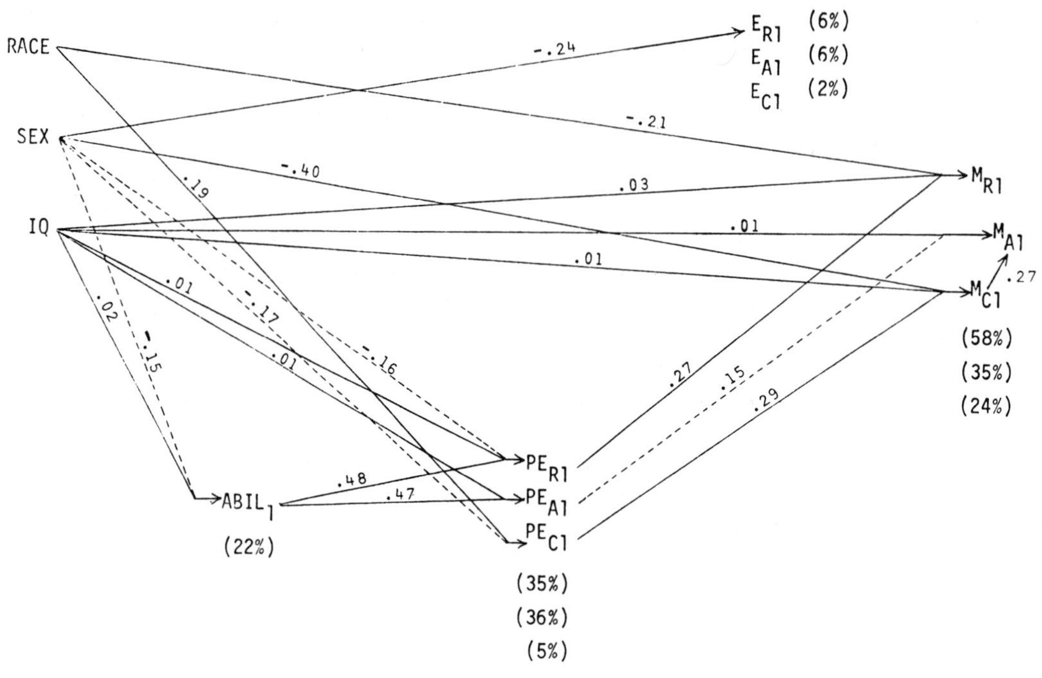

FIGURE 6.2I

Model for T2, Integrated Lower-Class School, Showing Structural Coefficients 1.50 to 1.99 Times (---) or 2.00 or More Times (——) Their Standard Error (Determinacy in Parentheses)

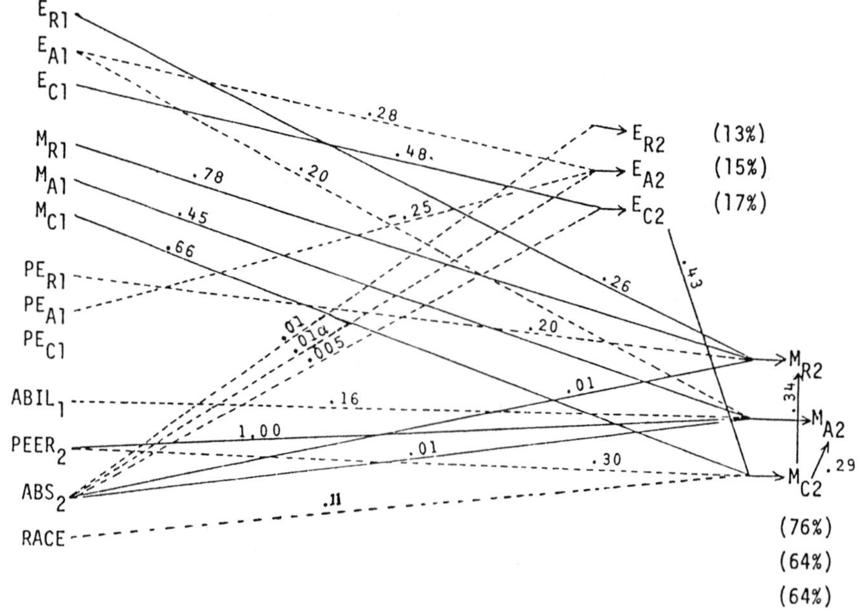

[a]In subsample replications the sign of this coefficient was inconsistent.

FIGURE 6.3I

Model for T3, Integrated Lower-Class School, Showing Structural Coefficients 1.50 to 1.99 Times (---) or 2.00 or More Times (——) Their Standard Error (Determinacy in Parentheses)

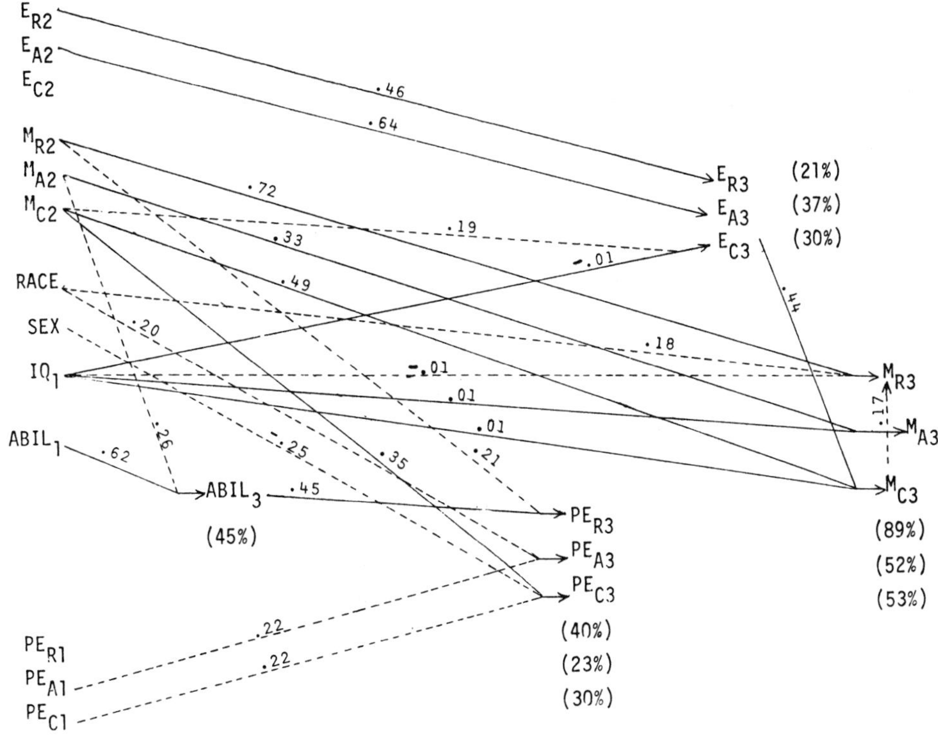

FIGURE 6.4I

Model for T4, Integrated Lower-Class School, Showing Structural Coefficients 1.50 to 1.99 Times (---) or 2.00 or More Times (——) Their Standard Error (Determinacy in Parentheses)

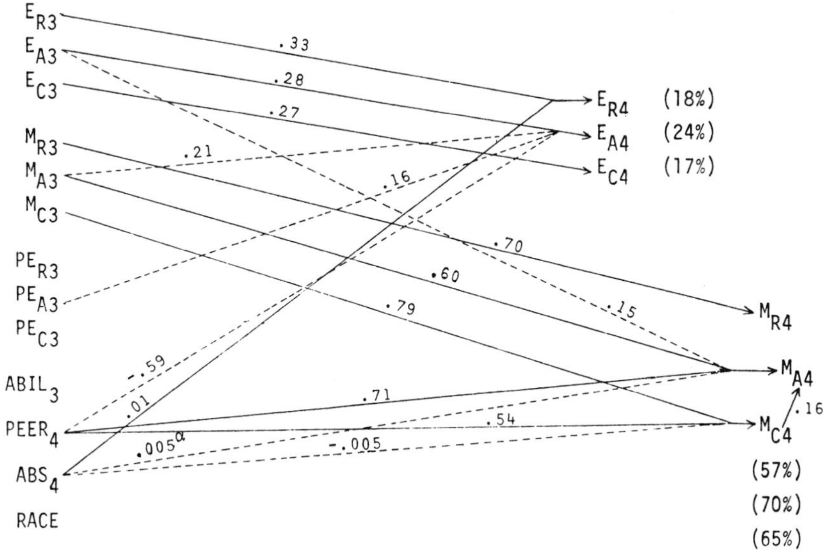

αIn subsample replications the sign of this coefficient was inconsistent.

FIGURE 6.5I

Model for T5, Integrated Lower-Class School, Showing Structural Coefficients 1.50 to 1.99 Times (---) or 2.00 or More Times (——) Their Standard Error (Determinacy in Parentheses)

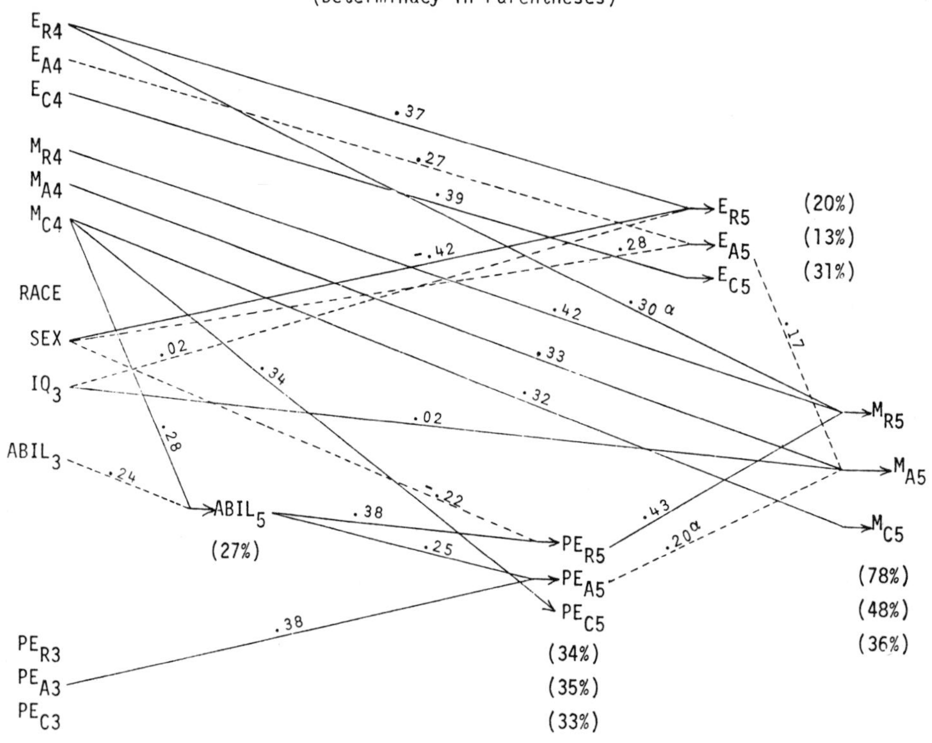

αIn subsample replications the sign of this coefficient was inconsistent.

FIGURE 6.6I

Model for T6, Integrated Lower-Class School, Showing Structural Coefficients 1.50 to 1.99 Times (---) or 2.00 or More Times (——) Their Standard Error (Determinacy in Parentheses)

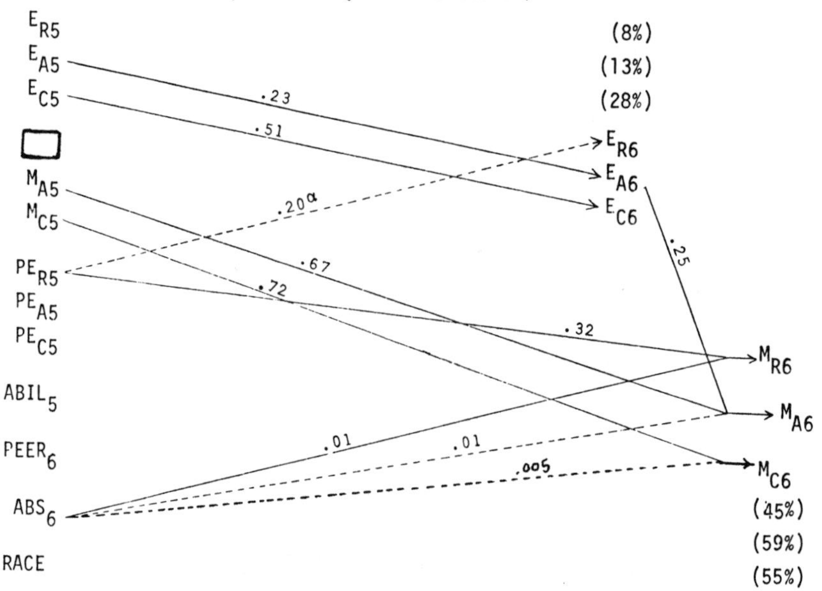

αIn subsample replications the sign of this coefficient was inconsistent.

NOTE: M_{R5} had to be deleted to avoid negative error variances.

Table 6.9

Summary of Coefficients for Structural Models in Figures 5.3 and 6.1I for the Integrated Lower-Class School:[a] Metric Coefficients in Upper Half of Table, Standardized Coefficients in Lower Half, and Degree of Determinacy

	RACE	IQ	SEX	$ABIL_1$	PE_{R1}	PE_{A1}	PE_{C1}	E_{R1}	E_{A1}	E_{C1}	M_{C1}	M_{R1}	M_{A1}	R^2
$ABIL_1$	-.1016	.0270*	-.1274											
	.0999	.0153*	-.1448											
	-.0053	.0217*	-.1462+											
PE_{R1}	-.1029	.0168*	-.1445	.3127*										
	-.1438	.0075	-.1569	.6450*										
	-.0895	.0106*	-.1617+	.4844*										
PE_{A1}	-.0554	.0113+	-.1320	.4791*										
	.0522	.0102+	-.1196	.4508*										
	.0010	.0111*	-.1259	.4672*										
PE_{C1}	.2325+	.0017	-.1729	-.0563										
	.1670	-.0030	-.1481	.1234										
	.1867*	.0005	-.1656+	.0304										
E_{R1}	.1203	.0015	-.3164*	.1166	.0266									
	-.1214	.0029	-.1249	.0467	-.1248									
	-.0025	.0036	-.2364*	.0676	-.0576									
E_{A1}	-.1535	.0084	-.0384	-.1698		.2261								
	.0647	.0064	-.0304	.0244		.0344								
	-.0408	.0060	-.0243	-.0318		.1214								
E_{C1}	.0347	.0003	-.0338	-.0541			-.0030							
	.0515	.0009	-.0787	.0630			-.0435							
	.0408	.0005	-.0503	.0065			-.0176							
M_{C1}	-.0721	.0071	-.3671*	.1311			.3039*			.3355				
	.0348	.0158*	-.4300*	-.0864			.3352*			-.1588				
	.0040	.0115*	-.4040*	-.0091			.2879*			.0005				
M_{R1}	-.2788*	.0375*	.1129	.0458	.2153*			-.1269			.0728			
	-.1490	.0264*	-.1254	-.0189	.3149*			-.0499			-.0169			
	-.2061*	.0300*	-.0174	.0261	.2717*			-.0808			.0265			
M_{A1}	-.1004	.0106+	.0812	.2888+		.0510			.1988		.3038*			
	-.0083	.0183*	-.0549	.0236		.2001+			.0144		.2211+			
	-.0695	.0146*	.0267	.1358		.1461+			.1013		.2705*			
$ABIL_1$	-.0040	.4671*	-.1133+											.2206
PE_{R1}	-.0644	.2149*	-.1177+	.4550*										.3526
PE_{A1}	.0007	.2302*	-.0941	.4504*										.3615
PE_{C1}	.1557*	.0118	-.1398+	.0332										.0472
E_{R1}	-.0024	.0945	-.2239*	.0827	-.0750									.0604
E_{A1}	-.0399	.1657	-.0241	-.0406		.1608								.0629
E_{C1}	.0752	.0279	-.0938	.0157			-.0390							.0160
M_{C1}	.0030	.2458*	-.3112*	-.0090			.2628*			.0002				.2391
M_{R1}	-.1469*	.6028*	-.0126	.0243	.2692*			-.0616			.0248			.5754
M_{A1}	-.0501	.2973*	.0195	.1279		.1427+			.0747		.2562*			.3515

[a]Metric coefficients are for odd-numbered, even-numbered, and all cases respectively. Standardized coefficients and determinacy are only for all cases. The degree of determinacy, labeled R^2, equals 1.0 minus the "latent" variable's error variance in the standardized model solution (where the variances of all the latent variables are scaled to be 1.0). Thus R^2 is the proportion of explained variance in the latent variables (concepts). The latent variables are related to the observed variables by the measurement structure detailed in Table B.1.

*Coefficient is more than twice its standard error.

+Coefficient is more than 1.5 times its standard error.

are not large enough to suggest any effect early in the first-grade year.

Gender has a number of effects. Girls generally have higher expectations for reading than boys, and parents tend to view girls as being generally more able to do schoolwork, and specifically expect them to be superior in both reading and conduct. In fact, in this school girls do receive substantially better conduct marks than boys.

First marks in reading are well determined (58%), largely due to the substantial influence of IQ. IQ has effects on marks in arithmetic and conduct as well, but smaller than for reading. The coefficient associating IQ with reading marks is 0.60 in the standardized solution (Table 6.9) and is by far the largest so far observed. IQ strongly affects parents' estimates of children's ability to do schoolwork and also parents' specific expectations for reading and arithmetic.

Table 6.10

Summary of Coefficients for Structural Models in Figures 5.4 and 6.2I for the Integrated Lower-Class School:[a] Metric Coefficients in Upper Half of Table, Standardized Coefficients in Lower Half, and Degree of Determinacy

	RACE	$ABIL_1$	PE_{R1}	PE_{A1}	PE_{C1}	E_{R1}	E_{A1}	E_{C1}	M_{R1}	M_{A1}	M_{C1}	$PEER_2$	ABS_2	E_{R2}	E_{A2}	E_{C2}	M_{C2}	M_{R2}	M_{A2}	R^2
E_{R2}	-.1278 .0193 -.0675	.1750 -.0166 .0443	.0849 .0709 .0961			.2071 .1665 .1950			-.3490 -.0255 -.1637			.8488 .0126 .3522	.0104+ .0008 .0061+							
E_{A2}	.2390 -.0849 .0532	.3121 .1328 .1664		-.5088* -.0944 -.2456+			.3186 .1770 .2843+			-.2579 .1536 -.0209		1.0766+ .0373 .4299	.0191* -.0051 .0075+							
E_{C2}	-.0086 -.0541 -.0293	-.0088 .1152 .0355			.0218 .0629 .0457			.5665+ .3462 .4757*			.0396 .0601 .0620	-.0338 .1014 -.0060	.0061+ .0022 .0046+							
M_{C2}	.1750+ .0875 .1122+	.0750 .0613 .0770			.0575 .0806 .0826			.2586 -.2801 -.1154			.6660* .6662* .6610*	.2824 .2641 .3016+	.0002 -.0045 -.0030			.2154* .5358* .4261*				
M_{R2}	-.2835+ .2328+ -.0191	-.2370 -.2570 -.1136	.0658 .4626* .2048+			.2646 .3273+ .2620*			1.1154* .7055* .7795*			-.7846 .5517 .1462	.0044 .0054 .0077*	.3033 .0522 .1256			.3746* .2999* .3431*			
M_{A2}	-.0573 .1862 .1049	.0226 .2441+ .1638+		.0940 -.0518 -.0469			.1573 .2023 .2027+			.4563* .5003* .4486*		.8712+ .8099+ .9997*	.0024 .0098 .0073*		.2825+ .0019 .1264		.3307* .2676* .2854*			
E_{R2}	-.0634	.0543	.1253			.1964			-.2165			.1617	.1970+							.1250
E_{A2}	.0457	.1868		-.2859+			.2494+			-.0249		.1807	.2197+							.1505
E_{C2}	-.0366	.0579			.0684			.3223*			.1017	-.0036	.1947+							.1662
M_{C2}	.0841+	.0754			.0742			-.0469			.6506*	.1105+	-.0771			.2557*				.6421
M_{R2}	-.0104	-.0810	.1553+			.1535*			.5999*			.0391	.1439*	.0731			.2502*			.7648
M_{A2}	.0615	.1254+		-.0372			.1213+			.3635*		.2865*	.1470*		.0862		.2232*			.6436

[a]Metric coefficients are for odd-numbered, even-numbered, and all cases respectively. Standardized coefficients and determinacy are only for all cases. The degree of determinacy, labeled R^2, equals 1.0 minus the "latent" variable's error variance in the standardized model solution (where the variances of all the latent variables are scaled to be 1.0). Thus R^2 is the proportion of explained variance in the latent variables (concepts). The latent variables are related to the observed variables by the measurement structure detailed in Table B.1.

*Coefficient is more than twice its standard error.

+Coefficient is more than 1.5 times its standard error.

Table 6.11

Summary of Coefficients for Structural Models in Figures 5.5 and 6.3I for the Integrated Lower-Class School:[a] Metric Coefficients in Upper Half of Table, Standardized Coefficients in Lower Half, and Degree of Determinacy

	RACE	IQ	SEX	$ABIL_1$	PE_{R1}	PE_{A1}	PE_{C1}	E_{R2}	E_{A2}	E_{C2}	M_{R2}	M_{A2}	M_{C2}	$ABIL_3$	PE_{R3}	PE_{A3}	PE_{C3}	E_{R3}	E_{A3}	E_{C3}	M_{C3}	M_{R3}	M_{A3}	R^2
$ABIL_3$	.1839	-.0095	.2330	.7505*							-.3027	.6385*	-.0635											
	-.0472	-.0012	-.0149	.5692*							.0742	.1439+	.0259											
	.0649	-.0083	.1409	.6248*							.0349	.2599+	.0476											
PE_{R3}	.0907	-.0127	-.1753		.2053						.2254+			.3596*										
	.1598	-.0035	-.0207		-.1973						.3149+			.5514*										
	.1059	-.0040	-.1099		.0402						.2058+			.4455*										
PE_{A3}	.3679+	-.0151	.0712			.4358*						.2918*		-.0772										
	.1631	.0105	-.0054			.0669						.0807		.2497+										
	.2025+	.0004	.0173			.2151+						.1363		.1295										
PE_{C3}	.1077	.0043	-.3146				.1621						.3214*	.1093										
	-.0361	-.0114	-.1127				.2874+						.4349*	-.0350										
	.0490	-.0030	-.2510+				.2157+						.3482*	.0371										
E_{R3}	-.0072	-.0085	-.0731					.5679*			.0418			.1255	-.0446									
	.1623	-.0089	-.0120					.0546			.1730			-.1698	.0299									
	.1045	-.0097	.0215					.4591*			.1458			-.0514	-.0249									
E_{A3}	-.2799	.0065	.0700						.4819*			.0140		-.2013		.1735								
	.0384	-.0239+	.1322						.9526*			.2263		.0252		.1350								
	-.1127	-.0042	.0375						.6435*			.0419		-.0731		.1489								
E_{C3}	.0743	-.0135+	.0088							.3993+			.2427+	.0351			.0814							
	-.1699	-.0158	-.0110							.2445			.1202	-.0601			.1974							
	-.0576	-.0148*	.0047							.2989			.1926+	-.0084			.1304							
M_{C3}	.2068	.0120	.1140							-.4221			.4219*	-.0886			.2040			.4215+				
	-.0264	.0166	.0034							-.2663			.5881*	.0090			.0632			.5363+				
	.0846	.0135*	.0275							-.2831			.4881*	-.0327			.1465			.4351*				
M_{R3}	.2181	-.0052	-.2177+					.0426			.6680*			.1740	.0933			-.0170			.1312			
	.1163	-.0223+	.2711					.0580			.7881*			.1410	.1496			-.0814			.2406			
	.1769+	-.0107+	-.0300					.0189			.7190*			.1248	.1127			-.0541			.1674+			
M_{A3}	.1475	.0101	-.1480						-.1137			.3758*		-.0089		.0797			.2924+		.1631			
	.0761	.0181	.1225						-.3317			.2956+		.0207		-.0023			.1256		.0738			
	.1137	.0131*	-.0132						-.1582			.3337*		-.0078		.0832			.1543		.1040			
$ABIL_3$	.0436	-.1570	.0958	.5486*							.0436	.3000+	.0426											.4470
PE_{R3}	.0752	-.0795	-.0789		.0396						.2711+			.4703*										.3978
PE_{A3}	.1560+	.0088	.0135			.2245+						.1802		.1484										.2273
PE_{C3}	.0366	-.0626	-.1898+				.1933+						.3468*	.0412										.2977
E_{R3}	.0866	-.2267	.0181					.4049*			.2241			-.0633	-.0290									.2070
E_{A3}	-.0884	-.0928	.0297						.5883*			.0564		-.0853		.1516								.3703
E_{C3}	-.0567	-.4096*	.0047							.2332			.2526+	-.0123			.1717							.2993
M_{C3}	.0602	.2706*	.0198							-.1599			.4633*	-.0346			.1396			.3148*				.5254
M_{R3}	.1158+	-.1981+	-.0199					.0132			.8733*			.1215	.1039			-.0428			.1538+			.8881
M_{A3}	.0856	.2776*	-.0100						-.1388			.4311*		-.0088		.0813			.1480		.1100			.5155

[a]Metric coefficients are for odd-numbered, even-numbered, and all cases respectively. Standardized coefficients and determinacy are only for all cases. The degree of determinacy, labeled R^2, equals 1.0 minus the "latent" variable's error variance in the standardized model solution (where the variances of all the latent variables are scaled to be 1.0). Thus R^2 is the proportion of explained variance in the latent variables (concepts). The latent variables are related to the observed variables by the measurement structure detailed in Table B.1.

*Coefficient is more than twice its standard error.

+Coefficient is more than 1.5 times its standard error.

Table 6.12

Summary of Coefficients for Structural Models in Figures 5.6 and 6.4I for the Integrated Lower-Class School:[a] Metric Coefficients in Upper Half of Table, Standardized Coefficients in Lower Half, and Degree of Determinacy

	RACE	$ABIL_3$	PE_{R3}	PE_{A3}	PE_{C3}	E_{R3}	E_{A3}	E_{C3}	M_{R3}	M_{A3}	M_{C3}	$PEER_4$	ABS_4	E_{R4}	E_{A4}	E_{C4}	M_{C4}	M_{R4}	M_{A4}	R^2
E_{R4}	-.0283 .0237 .0088	-.2352* .1518 -.0793	-.1130 -.2041 -.0764			.2551+ .4630* .3285*			.1059 .0849 .0268			.0789 .4207 .4335	.0110* .0072 .0083*							
E_{A4}	.0068 .0044 .0151	.1502 .0900 .1093		.2049+ .1263 .1602+			.3084+ .2811+ .2772*			.1418 .3504* .2129+		-.6396+ -.7064+ -.5883+	.0049 -.0055 -.0000							
E_{C4}	.2311+ .0880 .1080	-.0967 .0237 -.0632			-.0619 .0392 .0021			.1146 .4702* .2732*			-.0290 .1651+ .0907	-.3655 .1163 -.0927	.0037 -.0038 .0012							
M_{C4}	.2126+ .0221 .1128	-.1015 .1629 .0379			-.0055 .1136 .0575			.0797 -.1117 -.0308			.8466* .7055* .7932*	.9388* .2197 .5366*	-.0090* -.0023 -.0050+			.0052 .3033+ .1556				
M_{R4}	-.0103 -.0481 -.0435	-.0335 -.0560 -.0066	.0401 .1017 .0655			.0084 -.1379 -.0413			.7545* .6760* .7006*			.3583 .5737+ .3460	-.0026 .0059 .0019	.0145 -.0285 -.0110			.0528 .1032 .0967			
M_{A4}	.0440 .1580 .0833	.1483 -.0534 .0887		.0394 .2115+ .1160			.1208 .2460+ .1516+			.6524* .5214* .6049*		.8924* .6559+ .7104*	-.0031 .0154* .0054+		.1207 .0560 .0638		.0900 .2429* .1572*			
E_{R4}	.0073	-.0975	-.0896			.3264*			.0342			.1809	.2190*							.1831
E_{A4}	.0119	.1292		.1662+			.2775*			.2238+		-.2360+	-.0005							.2410
E_{C4}	.1147	-.1003			.0030			.2954*			.1353	-.0500	.0406							.1660
M_{C4}	.0725	.0365			.0496			-.0202			.7163*	.1752*	-.1032+			.0942				.6484
M_{R4}	-.0253	-.0058	.0544			-.0291			.6328*			.1022	.0351	-.0078			.0875			.5657
M_{A4}	.0512	.0815		.0937			.1181+			.4952*		.2219*	.1057+		.0497		.1504*			.6981

[a]Metric coefficients are for odd-numbered, even-numbered, and all cases respectively. Standardized coefficients and determinacy are only for all cases. The degree of determinacy, labeled R^2, equals 1.0 minus the "latent" variable's error variance in the standardized model solution (where the variances of all the latent variables are scaled to be 1.0). Thus R^2 is the proportion of explained variance in the latent variables (concepts). The latent variables are related to the observed variables by the measurement structure detailed in Table B.1.

*Coefficient is more than twice its standard error.

+Coefficient is more than 1.5 times its standard error.

Table 6.13

Summary of Coefficients for Structural Models in Figures 5.7 and 6.5I for the Integrated Lower-Class School:[a] Metric Coefficients in Upper Half of Table, Standardized Coefficients in Lower Half, and Degree of Determinacy

	RACE	IQ	SEX	$ABIL_3$	PE_{R3}	PE_{A3}	PE_{C3}	E_{R4}	E_{A4}	E_{C4}	M_{R4}	M_{A4}	M_{C4}	$ABIL_5$	PE_{R5}	PE_{A5}	PE_{C5}	E_{R5}	E_{A5}	E_{C5}	M_{C5}	M_{R5}	M_{A5}	R^2
$ABIL_5$	-.2597 .0920 -.1206	.0048 -.0065 .0013	.0136 .1865 .0771	-.0770 b .2393+							-.0061 .3557+ .1427	.3759+ -.0781 .0391	.2303 .3354+ .2791*											
PE_{R5}	.0703 -.4724* -.1750	-.0010 .0352* .0099	-.1006 -.3232+ -.2214+		.0557 .2849+ .1153						.1620 -.2250 .0970			.5043* .2676* .3779*										
PE_{A5}	-.0486 -.2331+ -.1228	.0006 .0266* .0095	-.1877 -.0009 -.1066			.4306* .5942* .3806*						.0085 -.0715 .0663		.5217* .0029 .2490*										
PE_{C5}	-.0083 -.0923 -.0145	-.0001 .0121 .0048	-.1426 -.0152 -.0696				-.0230 .1621 .0768						.5341* .1924 .3412*	.0468 .0670 .0717										
E_{R5}	-.0793 -.2388 -.0991	.0166 .0200 .0183+	-.3689 -.5083* -.4183*					.2531 .4153* .3685*			-.1854 -.0957 -.1867			-.1384 .3807* .1735	.0578 -.2780 -.0798									
E_{A5}	-.3714+ .0132 -.1802	.0001 -.0093 -.0060	.2122 .2769 .2811+						.2276 .2481 .2736+			-.0441 .1694 .1217		.3500 .1640 .1920		-.1594 .0623 -.0612								
E_{C5}	-.1020 -.0134 -.0494	.0040 .0032 .0010	-.0413 -.1794 -.0848							.3058* .5259* .3899*			.2143 -.0573 .1208	-.0411 .0356 -.0144			.0538 .2102+ .1349							
M_{C5}	-.0163 -.0646 .0094	.0079 .0103 .0068	-.0681 .0524 -.0114							.2160 .0930 .0735			.4050* .2509+ .3182*	-.0436 .0882 .0127			.0226 -.0044 .0496			.1006 .0374 .0877				
M_{R5}	-.3359+ .4508* -.0157	-.0050 -.0076 .0075	.0236 .0818 .0300					-.0507 .2696+ .3019*			.4655* .5096* .4165*			.2615 -.1248 .0468	.2287 .7972* .4275*			-.0327 .1676 .0223			.2589+ .0662 .1807			
M_{A5}	.1566 -.0245 .0638	.0340* .0049 .0199*	.0827 .0381 .0638						-.3525+ .0393 -.1641			.3440* .3594* .3279*		-.1114 .0108 -.0475		.3649* -.0398 .1984+			.1212 .1903+ .1664+		.0076 .3187+ .1548			
$ABIL_5$	-.0801	.0199	.0518	.2376+							.1637	.0421	.2880*											.2735
PE_{R5}	-.1125	.1461	-.1439+		.1057						.1076			.3657*										.3434
PE_{A5}	-.0874	.1564	-.0768			.3557*						.0765		.2669*										.3472
PE_{C5}	-.0120	.0924	-.0584				.0855						.4395*	.0895										.3335
E_{R5}	-.0698	.2968+	-.2982*					.3150*			-.2271			.1840	-.0874									.2021
E_{A5}	-.1161	-.0895	.1833+						.2233+			.1273		.1864		-.0554								.1335
E_{C5}	-.0493	.0220	-.0856							.3649*			.1872	-.0217			.1622							.3100
M_{C5}	.0083	.1378	-.0102							.0608			.4354*	.0168			.0527			.0775				.3552
M_{R5}	-.0097	.1064	.0188					.2262*			.4442*			.0435	.4108*			.0195			.1267			.7783
M_{A5}	.0412	.2953*	.0417						-.1342			.3434*		-.0462		.1800+			.1667+		.1135			.4816

[a]Metric coefficients are for odd-numbered, even-numbered, and all cases respectively. Standardized coefficients and determinacy are only for all cases. The degree of determinacy, labeled R^2, equals 1.0 minus the "latent" variable's error variance in the standardized model solution (where the variances of all the latent variables are scaled to be 1.0). Thus R^2 is the proportion of explained variance in the latent variables (concepts). The latent variables are related to the observed variables by the measurement structure detailed in Table B.1.

[b]In order to invert the data matrix, we had to delete $ABIL_3$ from the model for the even-numbered cases.

*Coefficient is more than twice its standard error.

+Coefficient is more than 1.5 times its standard error.

Table 6.14

Summary of Coefficients for Structural Models in Figures 5.8 and 6.6I for the Integrated Lower-Class School:[a] Metric Coefficients in Upper Half of Table, Standardized Coefficients in Lower Half, and Degree of Determinacy

	RACE	$ABIL_5$	PE_{R5}	PE_{A5}	PE_{C5}	E_{R5}	E_{A5}	E_{C5}	M_{R5}[b]	M_{A5}	M_{C5}	$PEER_6$	ABS_6	E_{R6}	E_{A6}	E_{C6}	M_{C6}	M_{R6}	M_{A6}	R^2
E_{R6}	-.1712 .3648+ .1584	-.2695 -.0881 -.1028	.4867* -.0078 .2012+			-.1124* .3419 .1285						-.8377 -.1718 -.3923	.0007 .0102+ .0050							
E_{A6}	.2327 -.0536 .0413	-.1422 -.2058 -.1726		.2155 .0120 .1211			.2579 .1901* .2328			-.1036 .2487 .1771		.0873 .4262 -.1284	.0018 .0023 .0024							
E_{C6}	.0958 -.0459 .0092	.0159 .0818 .0359			.0177 -.0202 .0153			.4215* .6144* .5051*			-.0123 .1889 .0587	-.3894 -.7256 -.3641	.0056 -.0006 .0018							
M_{C6}	.1957 .0644 .1019	.1061 -.0786 .0046			.0746 .0297 .0562			.2744 -.1257 .0320			.5520* .8519* .7232*	.6316 -.1018 .1374	.0011 .0057 .0046+			-.1111 .1602 .0423				
M_{R6}	-.0608 .3623+ .1530	.3247+ .0039 .1584	.2492* .4757* .3218*			-.0427 .1338 .0597						.6119 -.0660 .2319	.0042* .0145* .0115	-.2121 .1148 -.0159			.0874 .1910 .1641			
M_{A6}	-.0712 .2181 .0242	.4797* -.1421 .0349		-.0990 .2408 .0732			-.2263 .0040 -.0580			.4587* .6487* .6662*		1.4619* -.3812 .1475	.0013 .0084+ .0072+		.3011* .2153+ .2508*		-.0427 .0712 .0759			

E_{R6}	.1108	-.1084	.2178+			.1281						-.1307	.1305							.0762
E_{A6}	.0272	-.1712		.1121			.2374*			.1827		-.0402	.0594							.1268
E_{C6}	.0085	.0498			.0170			.4689*			.0613	-.1595	.0626							.2758
M_{C6}	.0816	.0056			.0542			.0259			.6583*	.0524	.1377+			.0368				.5509
M_{R6}	.1015	.1585	.3303*			.0564						.0733	.2844*	-.0151			.1359			.4451
M_{A6}	.0132	.0287		.0563			-.0491			.5710*		.0384	.1452+		.2083*		.0518			.5910

[a]Metric coefficients are for odd-numbered, even-numbered, and all cases respectively. Standardized coefficients and determinacy are only for all cases. The degree of determinacy, labeled R^2, equals 1.0 minus the "latent" variable's error variance in the standardized model solution (where the variances of all the latent variables are scaled to be 1.0). Thus R^2 is the proportion of explained variance in the latent variables (concepts). The latent variables are related to the observed variables by the measurement structure detailed in Table B.1.

[b]M_{R5} had to be deleted from these models to avoid negative error variances.

*Coefficient is more than twice its standard error.

+Coefficient is more than 1.5 times its standard error.

Parents' academic expectations, although not particulary well determined, seem to be a compound of an overall ability estimate modulated by considerations relevant to performance in the specific area. As in the middle-class school, parents seem to hold some overall opinion about their child's "true ability," which they modify in attempting to predict how well the child will do in any specific area.

Parents' expectations have no measurable impact on their children's expectations, but they do influence children's marks in all three areas.

In this school, as already noted, IQ is very important in determining reading marks. Discounting the effect of race on reading performance for reasons discussed earlier, we see that reading responds somewhat to parents' expectations but more strongly to IQ. Since a large coefficient of determination (58%) characterizes the first mark in reading, a major conclusion is that the skills that are tapped by IQ tests and which the child possesses before starting school are the major determinants of the distribution of first reading marks around their relatively low means. Arithmetic performance is also substantially affected by IQ. Conduct affects arithmetic performance, but not reading.

Over all, this model suggests that the exogenous variables, particularly IQ, have considerable effect. Children's expectations are not well accounted for, and they are completely independent of both the child's ability and parental expectations. In addition, children's expectations are completely ineffective. First reading marks are surprisingly well accounted for.

Summary of Figures 6.1I to 6.6I (Integrated Lower-Class School)

Several general conclusions emerge from this set of models. First, there is an almost complete lack of effects associated with race. Some effects early in the first and second grades, but these sometimes favor blacks and at other times favor whites. Next, the effect of IQ on marks is repeatedly manifest, making it a chief contributor to the high degree of determinacy in marks in this school. IQ influences initial marks in all three areas and continues to exert new direct effects even as late as grade three (arithmetic). Marks have a strong tendency to persist during each year, and, unlike marks in the middle-class school, they also persist between years (all fourteen coefficients are highly significant and substantial).

The occasional contributions of absences, IQ, and gender to children's expectations stand in bold relief to the almost complete insulation of these children's expectations from their prior marks. In this school, where marks are very stable and predictable, children's expectations are generally unresponsive to prior marks (except for borderline effects of conduct in the third cycle and arithmetic in the fourth cycle), while in the middle-class school, where marks are less predictable (especially between years), children's expectations frequently respond to prior marks (ten out of fifteen possible instances).

All the significant effects of gender on parents' and children's expectations are consistent with the usual sex stereotypes of girls' excelling in reading (two of three coefficients significant for both parents and children), boys' excelling in arithmetic (one of three significant for children, none for parents), girls' excelling in conduct (two of three for parents, none for children). Actual marks, however, are almost sex-blind. The single significant coefficient (of the nine possible) favors girls in initial conduct marks.

Children's expectations affect their conduct marks in two of the six cycles (at the end of first grade and the beginning of second grade.) In only two of twelve cases, however, do children's expectations affect marks in the academic areas (children's third-grade arithmetic expectations influence their arithmetic marks at both mid-year and year-end). All the coefficients for arithmetic and conduct are in the expected direction, while those for reading are mixed in sign and not significant.

Four lagged effects of children's academic expectations appear, however, unlike anything seen in the middle-class schools. In the integrated school, children's initial reading and arithmetic expectations influenced their marks at the end of first grade. Similarly, their arithmetic expectations at the beginning of second grade influenced their year-end second-grade arithmetic marks, and reading expectations at the end of second grade determined reading marks in third grade. The lagged effects that are not significant are mixed in sign.

It is unclear why it should take several months and possibly a change of teacher for these children's expectations to become effective. There is no obvious way that expectations might be "stored" that would not imply strong immediate effects as well. Whatever the reason, however, if we combine the effects of lagged and current expectations, two effects appear for reading, four for arithmetic, and two for conduct, for a total of eight mark responses to children's expectations, compared to seven current effects (plus one lagged effect of reversed sign) in the middle-class school.

The influence of the child's deportment on proficiency in the academic areas appears substantial. As in the middle-class school, academic marks consistently respond to classroom conduct, but only five of the twelve coefficients are significant. Since earlier conduct marks responded to gender and IQ, and since later conduct marks responded to earlier conduct marks, sex and IQ are involved in the effect of conduct on reading and arithmetic. Females and those with higher IQ's are judged to be better behaved, and those who are better behaved are judged to be better in reading and arithmetic.

Since few of the many opportunities for prior marks to influence children's expectations appear (two coefficients of only borderline significance out of fourteen possible), we must conclude that these children block out much of the evaluative information available to them. This "information block" may actually be an "information shield," protecting the children from the "bad news" implied by the low marks frequently issued by this school. While these children's initial expectations look almost random (with 6%, 6%, and 2% determinacy), their later expectations display considerable persistence (twelve of fifteen significant), respond sporadically to background factors, and influence their marks to some extent.

Parents' initial ability estimates and expectations for reading and arithmetic respond to IQ, but IQ effects on parents are unimportant thereafter. Parents base reading and arithmetic expectations on their overall ability estimates (five of six significant), but, unlike the case in the middle-class school, parents' conduct expectations are oblivious to ability considerations (none of three significant).

All twelve coefficients linking mark feedback to parents' views are positive, with three of the five significant effects being responses to conduct marks (two modify conduct expectations and one modifies third-grade ability estimates). These parents clearly attend to classroom conduct and adjust themselves to conduct reports. Second-grade parental reading expectations reflected first-grade marks and second-grade ability estimates reflected prior arithmetic marks. However, unlike the middle-class parents, who used reading performance as the *exclusive* relevant type of mark feedback for altering ability estimates, the lower-class parents never adjusted their ability estimates on the basis of reading, and they used arithmetic and conduct marks only intermittently.

Parental ability estimates persisted strongly between first and second grades, and more weakly (yet significantly) between second and third grades. Their expectations for arithmetic and conduct displayed significant persistence in three of four instances, although reading expectations never persisted to a significant extent.

Parents' expectations in the integrated school seldom affected their children's expectations (three of eighteen significant) and both the significant and insignificant effects are inconsistent in sign. Parental ability estimates are similarly ineffective as far as children's expectations are concerned (none of eighteen coefficients is significant, and signs are mixed). These parents' expectations are clearly not having much impact on their children's expectations. These same parents, however, *are* effective at influencing assigned marks (seven of fifteen significant, six of these in reading and arithmetic). All three coefficients are significant in the first cycle.

Frequent absences tend to depress reading and arithmetic marks in this school (five of six significant), but further information is required to disentangle the causal process (possible explanations include lost learning time, cognitive interference due to missed lessons, lengthy medical problems, or disruptive and discouraging home environments). Frequent absences also slightly depress the children's earliest expectations (all first-grade coefficients are significant, while only one of six is significant in later grades).

Lower-Class Black School

Figures 6.1B to 6.6B and Tables 6.15 to 6.20 refer to the lower-class black school. The data base for this school was not large enough to permit even-odd replication analyses, so the findings for this school are weak in two respects: they cannot be scrutinized in terms of internal consistency, and, with data for a smaller number of persons, the parameters are slightly less well determined. In particular, Type II errors may be more likely here. Also, a singular covariance matrix precluded estimating the third cycle (T2–T3) model for this school (Figure 6.3B) and two of the models (the end of second and beginning of third grade) do not fit well. With all these qualifications, it is fortunate that both the first-grade models and the final third-grade model fit well and can assist in identifying overall patterns.

As noted, the third-cycle model for this school could not be estimated. Therefore Figure 6.3B and the corresponding Table 6.17 are lacking. To avoid confusion and to keep the correspondence among schools by cycle as clear as possible, we have omitted this figure and its corresponding table but have *not* renumbered the following tables and figures. For example, Figures 6.4B, 6.5B, and 6.6B refer to the fourth, fifth, and sixth cycles, respectively.

Summary of Figures 6.1B to 6.6B (Black Lower-Class School)

By the end of grade three, several familiar structures appear in the models. First, there is some persistence in expectations. All the persistence coefficients are positive, but only four of the twelve are significant. Over all, the persistence of expectations in this school is much weaker than in the other schools. Marks are well determined and persist strongly within years (eight of nine coefficients are significant). The situation between years is unclear, since one between-year

FIGURE 6.1B

Model for T1, Black Lower-Class School, Showing Structural Coefficients 1.50 to 1.99 Times (---) or 2.00 or More Times (——) Their Standard Error (Determinacy in Parentheses)

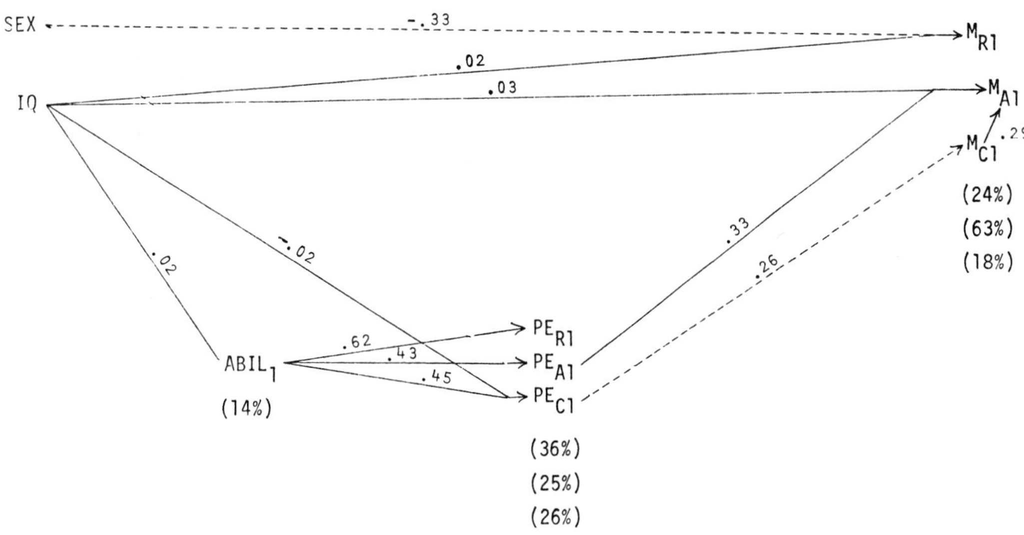

FIGURE 6.2B

Model for T2, Black Lower-Class School, Showing Structural Coefficients 1.50 to 1.99 Times (---) or 2.00 or More Times (——) Their Standard Error (Determinacy in Parentheses)

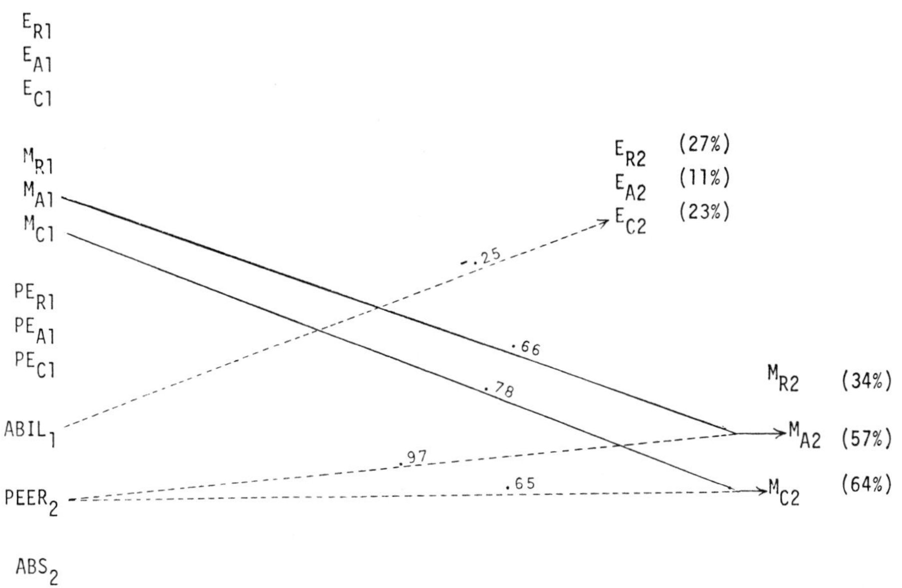

FIGURE 6.4B

Model for T4, Black Lower-Class School, Showing Structural Coefficients 1.50 to 1.99 Times (---) or 2.00 or More Times (——) Their Standard Error (Determinacy in Parentheses)

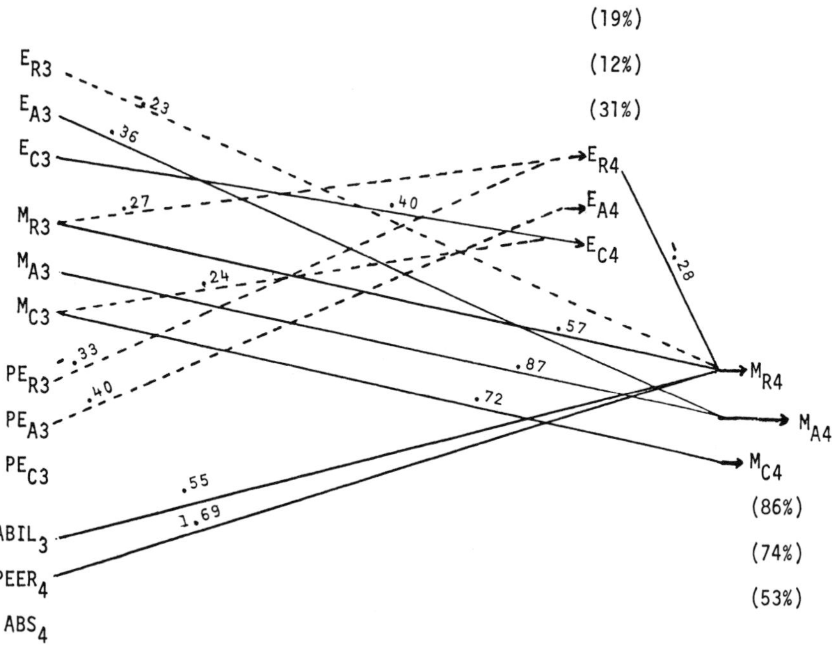

FIGURE 6.5B

Model for T5, Black Lower-Class School, Showing Structural Coefficients 1.50 to 1.99 Times (---) or 2.00 or More Times (——) Their Standard Error (Determinacy in Parentheses)

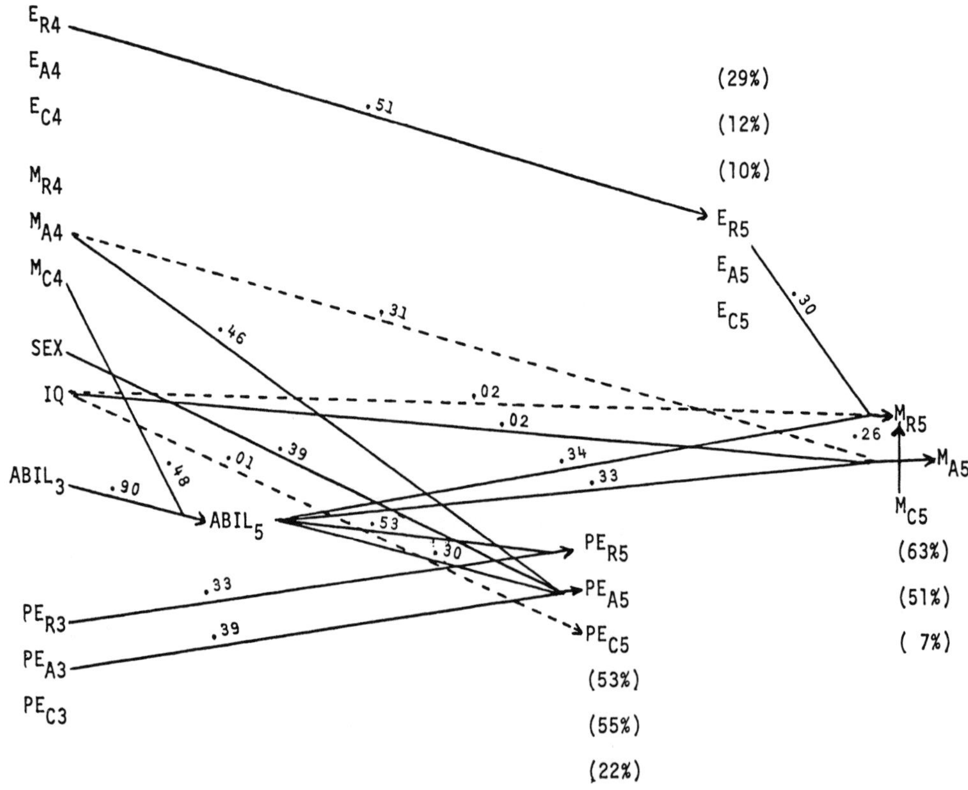

FIGURE 6.6B

Model for T6, Black Lower-Class School, Showing Structural Coefficients 2.00 or More Times Their Standard Error (Determinacy in Parentheses)

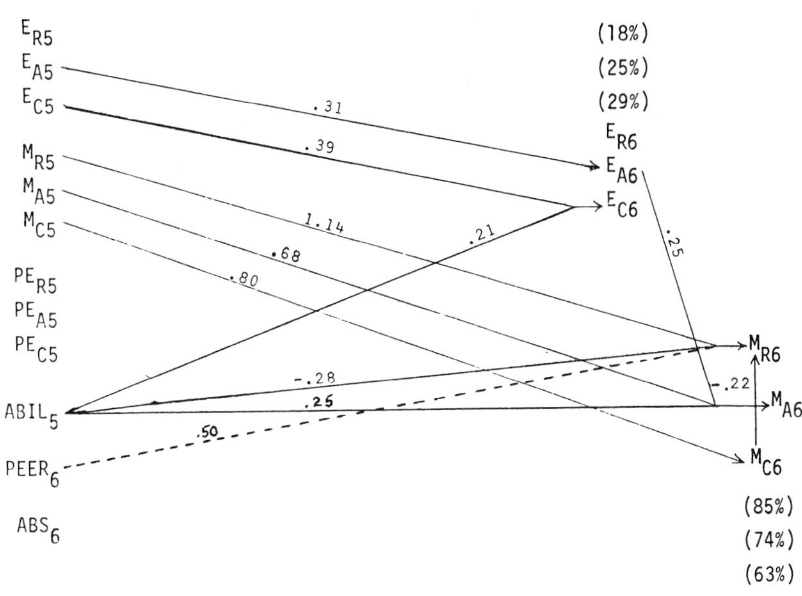

model could not be estimated and the other fits poorly and provides mixed results. Children's initial expectations are remarkably detached from the rest of the model, making them structurally unresponsive and inconsequential. Only one significant path ties children's expectations to the other variables in the entire first grade (two models). It is therefore not surprising that children's initial expectations are poorly determined.

The single significant contribution of gender to parental or children's expectations is consistent with the usual sex stereotyping—boys are expected to excel in arithmetic (parents' third-grade expectations). Seven of the eleven remaining insignificant coefficients are consistent with usual stereotypes. The single contribution of sex to marks in this school (first-grade reading) is also stereotype-consistent.

Parental ability estimates do not respond to gender, do respond substantially to IQ, and persist strongly in the single model where this persistence can be estimated. Little can be said with confidence about the contribution of IQ to parents' specific expectations. All three initial parental expectations display negative coefficients (high ability results in low parental expectations), with only that for conduct being significant. This contrasts with the sole significant contribution of IQ being a *positive* effect for conduct in third grade. No significant contributions to children's expectations arise from IQ, although marks in reading and arithmetic strongly reflect IQ (all four coefficients are highly significant). The corresponding coefficients linking IQ and conduct are positive but insignificant.

These children are very unresponsive to prior marking histories (the only two significant coefficients appear in a poorly fitting model). The children also seem insulated from their parents' views. The only two significant effects parents' expectations have on their children's expectations are mixed in sign and appear in a poorly fitting model. The responsiveness of parental expectations to mark feedback is difficult to judge, since estimates for only one model are available and only one of the three coefficients is significant, although all are positive. As in the integrated school, parental ability estimates respond only to conduct marks in third grade (in the single well-fitting model).

Children's expectations show a single highly significant effect on third-grade reading marks, but eight of nine coefficients in the well-fitting models are positive. No lagged effects of children's expectations are significant for the well-behaved models, and the poorly fitting models contribute little, since the significant effects are of mixed sign for both the current and lagged effects.

Parents' expectations show fewer effects on marks than in the other schools. Although all nine parental coefficients are positive, only two first-cycle effects are significant. Parental ability estimates provide three substantial inputs into academic marks in models that fit poorly. Since the only well-fitting model with corresponding significant effects provides one positive

Table 6.15

Summary of Coefficients for Structural Models in Figures 5.3 and 6.1B for the Black Lower-Class School:[a] Metric Coefficients in Upper Half of Table, Standardized Coefficients in Lower Half, and Degree of Determinacy

	IQ	SEX	$ABIL_1$	PE_{R1}	PE_{A1}	PE_{C1}	E_{R1}	E_{A1}	E_{C1}	M_{C1}	M_{R1}	M_{A1}	R^2
$ABIL_1$	.0191*	-.1899											
PE_{R1}	-.0043	-.1698	.6170*										
PE_{A1}	-.0051	-.2476	.4308*										
PE_{C1}	-.0198*	-.1704	.4527*										
E_{R1}	.0031	.0211	-.1771	.1742									
E_{A1}	-.0134	-.1098	.2935		-.0144								
E_{C1}	-.0005	-.0023	.1515			-.0275							
M_{C1}	.0055	-.1658	.0905			.2559+			.1005				
M_{R1}	.0227*	-.3254+	-.0020	.0960			.1935			.1226			
M_{A1}	.0327*	-.0148	-.0962		.3340*			.1809		.2874*			
$ABIL_1$	.3545*	-.1405											.1411
PE_{R1}	-.0769	-.1215	.5969*										.3639
PE_{A1}	-.1021	-.1954	.4594*										.2512
PE_{C1}	-.3654*	-.1253	.4499*										.2551
E_{R1}	.0679	.0184	-.2082	.2116									.0348
E_{A1}	-.2853	-.0930	.3359		-.0155								.1415
E_{C1}	-.0172	-.0028	.2544			-.0465							.0559
M_{C1}	.1183	-.1424	.1050			.2990+			.0695				.1805
M_{R1}	.3647*	-.2079+	-.0017	.0857			.1422			.0912			.2429
M_{A1}	.6532*	-.0118	-.1034		.3366*			.1699		.2260*			.6296

[a]Models estimated only for all cases. The degree of determinacy, labeled R^2, equals 1.0 minus the "latent" variable's error variance in the standardized model solution (where the variances of all the latent variables are scaled to be 1.0). Thus R^2 is the proportion of explained variance in the latent variables (concepts). The latent variables are related to the observed variables by the measurement structure detailed in Table B.1.

*Coefficient is more than twice its standard error.

+Coefficient is more than 1.5 times its standard error.

and one negative value, no conclusions about the effectiveness of ability estimates seem justifiable.

As in the other schools, ability estimates of these parents provide a solid base for the formation of particular expectations (five of six coefficients are significant). Parental ability estimates and academic (but not conduct) expectations display significant persistence, but a weak model again invites caution.

The contribution of conduct to academic performance is less consistent in this school than in the other schools. Eight of ten effects are positive, with two significantly so, but a significant negative contribution appears in the well-fitting third-grade model.

REVIEW OF EFFECTS, VARIABLE BY VARIABLE

The preceding sections reviewed the longitudinal picture for development of young children's expectations and achievement within each school. These longitudinal summaries provided one perspective on the general reasonableness of the models and the possible influence of the cultural context provided by each school. In the next section the data are reviewed from another perspective, by examining the efficacy of particular variables. In this review we consider structural coefficients, regardless of size, for every variable as

Table 6.16

Summary of Coefficients for Structural Models in Figures 5.4 and 6.2B for the Black Lower-Class School:[a] Metric Coefficients in Upper Half of Table, Standardized Coefficients in Lower Half, and Degree of Determinacy

	$ABIL_1$	PE_{R1}	PE_{A1}	PE_{C1}	E_{R1}	E_{A1}	E_{C1}	M_{R1}	M_{A1}	M_{C1}	$PEER_2$	ABS_2	E_{R2}	E_{A2}	E_{C2}	M_{C2}	M_{R2}	M_{A2}	R^2
E_{R2}	-.1801	.1625			.2572			-.1634			.7480	-.0027							
E_{A2}	-.2286		.0109			.1878			.1662		.3510	-.0005							
E_{C2}	-.2508^{+}			.1523			.1064			-.0426	.1396	.0022							
M_{C2}	.0927			.0788			.0638			.7822*	.6541^{+}	-.0072			.1015				
M_{R2}	.0797	.1171			-.2156			.2009			.4439	.0009	.3517			.1947			
M_{A2}	.0293		.0135			-.0310			.6578*		.9682^{+}	.0011		.0828		.1700			
E_{R2}	-.2206	.2058			.2670			-.2317			.3295	-.0678							.2698
E_{A2}	-.2651		.0119			.1907			.1790		.1463	-.0111							.1127
E_{C2}	-.4429^{+}			.2705			.1121			-.0647	.0886	.0777							.2296
M_{C2}	.0913			.0781			.0375			.6631*	.2317^{+}	-.1439			.0566				.6394
M_{R2}	.0776	.1177			-.1777			.2261			.1553	.0176	.2793			.1922			.3415
M_{A2}	.0232		.0101			-.0215			.4847*		.2762	.0174		.0567		.1369			.5694

[a]Models estimated only for all cases. The degree of determinacy, labeled R^2, equals 1.0 minus the "latent" variable's error variance in the standardized model solution (where the variances of all the latent variables are scaled to be 1.0). Thus R^2 is the proportion of explained variance in the latent variables (concepts). The latent variables are related to the observed variables by the measurement structure detailed in Table B.1.

*Coefficient is more than twice its standard error.

$^{+}$Coefficient is more than 1.5 times its standard error.

Table 6.18

Summary of Coefficients for Structural Models in Figures 5.6 and 6.4B for the Black Lower-Class School:[a] Metric Coefficients in Upper Half of Table, Standardized Coefficients in Lower Half, and Degree of Determinacy

	$ABIL_3$	PE_{R3}	PE_{A3}	PE_{C3}	E_{R3}	E_{A3}	E_{C3}	M_{R3}	M_{A3}	M_{C3}	$PEER_4$	ABS_4	E_{R4}	E_{A4}	E_{C4}	M_{C4}	M_{R4}	M_{A4}	R^2
E_{R4}	.2380	-.3277+			.1126			.2741+			.0962	-.0100							
E_{A4}	-.1243		.4028+			.0235			-.0987		.4293	.0009							
E_{C4}	-.0559			.0706			.4021*			.2370+	.1537	-.0013							
M_{C4}	.0404			-.0763			-.0641			.7243*	-.1482	.0003			.2554				
M_{R4}	.5483*	-.0748			-.2293+			.5686*			1.6852*	-.0055	-.2769*			.0995			
M_{A4}	.0827		.0752			.3552*			.8691*		-.4299	.0057		.1321		.1556			
E_{R4}	.2322	-.4081+			.1140			.3558+			.0388	-.2249							.1887
E_{A4}	-.1051		.3968+			.0233			-.0805		.1497	.0169							.1247
E_{C4}	-.0754			.1021			.3848*			.2995+	.0856	-.0400							.3130
M_{C4}	.0394			-.0797			-.0443			.6605*	-.0596	.0058			.1844				.5272
M_{R4}	.4172*	-.0727			-.1812+			.5757*			.5291*	-.0954	-.2160*			.0777			.8638
M_{A4}	.0644		.0683			.3236*			.6533*		-.1382	.1027		.1218		.1244			.7427

[a]Models estimated only for all cases. The degree of determinacy, labeled R^2, equals 1.0 minus the "latent" variable's error variance in the standardized model solution (where the variances of all the latent variables are scaled to be 1.0). Thus R^2 is the proportion of explained variance in the latent variables (concepts). The latent variables are related to the observed variables by the measurement structure detailed in Table B.1.

*Coefficient is more than twice its standard error.

+Coefficient is more than 1.5 times its standard error.

Table 6.19

Summary of Coefficients for Structural Models in Figures 5.7 and 6.5B for the Black Lower-Class School:[a] Metric Coefficients in Upper Half of Table, Standardized Coefficients in Lower Half, and Degree of Determinacy

	IQ	SEX	$ABIL_3$	PE_{R3}	PE_{A3}	PE_{C3}	E_{R4}	E_{A4}	E_{C4}	M_{R4}	M_{A4}	M_{C4}	$ABIL_5$	PE_{R5}	PE_{A5}	PE_{C5}	E_{R5}	E_{A5}	E_{C5}	M_{C5}	M_{R5}	M_{A5}	R^2
$ABIL_5$	-.0093	.2203	.8962*							-.0318	-.1376	.4820*											
PE_{R5}	.0060	-.0542		.3292*						.1062			.5297*										
PE_{A5}	-.0084	.3923*			.3910*						.4586*		.3021*										
PE_{C5}	.0133+	-.0564				.0105						.1297	.1874										
E_{R5}	.0045	-.0492					.5093*			.1254			-.0627	.1497									
E_{A5}	.0011	-.0103						.3147			.0408		-.1138		.1182								
E_{C5}	.0004	-.0864							.2847			-.0805	.0020			.1276							
M_{C5}	.0037	-.1934							-.0423			-.0023	.1003			.0174			.1547				
M_{R5}	.0178+	.1936					-.1201			-.0785			.3423*	-.0170			.2965*			.2579*			
M_{A5}	.0169*	.1010						-.0595			.3072+		.3345*		-.1040			.0978		-.0554			
$ABIL_5$	-.1617	.1524	.7229*							-.0343	-.1349	.4004*											.5293
PE_{R5}	.0895	-.0321		.2902*						.0980			.4536*										.5276
PE_{A5}	-.1489	.2779*			.3767*						.4606*		.3094*										.5493
PE_{C5}	.2782+	-.0471				.0109						.1300	.2261										.2197
E_{R5}	.0858	-.0373					.4612*			.1481			-.0687	.1917									.2885
E_{A5}	.0191	-.0070						.2929			.0392		-.1113		.1129								.1210
E_{C5}	.0116	-.0907							.2616			-.1014	.0030			.1604							.1004
M_{C5}	.0721	-.1499							-.0287			-.0021	.1124			.0162			.1143				.0672
M_{R5}	.3999+	.1734					-.1285			-.1095			.4433*	-.0257			.3502*			.2980*			.6282
M_{A5}	.3400*	.0811						-.0656			.3495+		.3881*		-.1178			.1160		-.0573			.5070

[a]Models estimated only for all cases. The degree of determinacy, labeled R^2, equals 1.0 minus the "latent" variable's error variance in the standardized model solution (where the variances of all the latent variables are scaled to be 1.0). Thus R^2 is the proportion of explained variance in the latent variables (concepts). The latent variables are related to the observed variables by the measurement structure detailed in Table B.1.

*Coefficient is more than twice its standard error.

+Coefficient is more than 1.5 times its standard error.

Table 6.20

Summary of Coefficients for Structural Models in Figures 5.8 and 6.6B for the Black Lower-Class School:[a] Metric Coefficients in Upper Half of Table, Standardized Coefficients in Lower Half, and Degree of Determinacy

	$ABIL_5$	PE_{R5}	PE_{A5}	PE_{C5}	E_{R5}	E_{A5}	E_{C5}	M_{R5}	M_{A5}	M_{C5}	$PEER_6$	ABS_6	E_{R6}	E_{A6}	E_{C6}	M_{C6}	M_{R6}	M_{A6}	R^2
E_{R6}	.0757	.1727			.1826			.0735			-.3164	.0052							
E_{A6}	-.2066		.2404			.3080*			.2794		-.1234	.0084							
E_{C6}	.2133*			.0911			.3863*			.0121	-.1194	-.0019							
M_{C6}	-.0228			.1134			.1017			.7964*	.0598	-.0004			-.0078				
M_{R6}	-.2750*	.1550			-.0949			1.1410*			.5020+	.0049	.1122			-.2224*			
M_{A6}	.2461*		.0000			-.0054			.6791*		.5125	-.0012		.2547*		.0088			
E_{R6}	.0845	.2245			.1867			.0624			-.1206	.1001							.1809
E_{A6}	-.1927		.2204			.2929*			.2260		-.0393	.1346							.2528
E_{C6}	.3084*			.1096			.3731*			.0156	-.0590	-.0464							.2948
M_{C6}	-.0242			.1002			.0722			.7554*	.0217	-.0074			.0057				.6262
M_{R6}	-.2870*	.1886			-.0908			.9068*			.1791+	.0876	.1050			-.2186*			.8508
M_{A6}	.2312*		-.0000			-.0051			.5534*		.1645	-.0190		.2566*		.0078			.7380

[a]Models estimated only for all cases. The degree of determinacy, labeled R^2, equals 1.0 minus the "latent" variable's error variance in the standardized model solution (where the variances of all the latent variables are scaled to be 1.0). Thus R^2 is the proportion of explained variance in the latent variables (concepts). The latent variables are related to the observed variables by the measurement structure detailed in Table B.1.

*Coefficient is more than twice its standard error.

+Coefficient is more than 1.5 times its standard error.

estimated from the full data set, in order to highlight substance more than structure and to offer a means for evaluating relative potency of the variables irrespective of sampling variability.

Exogenous Variables

Effects Associated with IQ

IQ appears as an exogenous variable in models at the start of every school year because successive teachers may take IQ into account in different ways. Also, parents may pay varying attention to IQ—for example, they may pay more attention in second grade than in first grade if they have learned their child's IQ score in the meantime.

Apparently IQ influences parents' earliest expectations and ability estimates. Its influence, furthermore, is not confined to the first year. Parents sometimes readjust their expectations in light of their child's IQ. There seem to be no systematic differences in the pattern from school to school.

Concerning the influence of IQ on children's expectations, the coefficients for the middle-class school appear to be somewhat larger than for the other two schools. In fact, when viewed as a set in Table 6.21, the coefficients associated with IQ suggest, contrary to our earlier opinion (Entwisle and Hayduk 1978a), that middle-class children do indeed use IQ information in constructing their expectations. The negative links between IQ and expectations (four with negative signs reach significance) could imply that brighter children feel they are held to tougher standards, or that less-bright children are less realistic in their expectations. The children, of course, do not know their own IQ scores, but it is likely that the exceptionally able children receive clues from their parents and teachers.

Academic marks respond more strongly to IQ over all three grades in the two lower-class schools than in the middle-class school. In the middle-class school, marks seem particularly unresponsive at the start.

According to school policy, teachers in the middle-class school were supposed to reward effort. Teachers in the other two schools were supposed to focus on grade-level performance norms. As noted in Chapter 5, either policy may be harder and harder to implement as children continue in school. That is, after children have attained some proficiency in reading, it may be impossible to give A's for a high level of effort coupled to a poor performance, or to give B's or C's to children who read well but who seem not to exert as much effort. By the same token, if children are not performing at an A or B level, if the teacher ignores effort and gives all poor performers the same mark regardless of effort, learning may be discouraged.

Effects Related to Race

Because race is such a critical variable for theories of schooling, we have summarized the structural coefficients linking race to the full set of endogenous variables for every cycle in the integrated school (Table 6.22), which is the only school where race could be included as an exogenous variable.

Effects on parent variables are fairly large in three instances (two significant), but they are inconsistent overall. Black parents held lower T1 expectations for conduct and lower T3 expectations for arithmetic. It is difficult to interpret the effects of race on parental expectations because the effects appear erratically, and because there are no consistent trends even in the signs of the smaller coefficients. (None of the coefficients for parent variables in any of the marking areas is consistent in sign for the three years.)

Effects of race on children's expectations and marks appear small, with the possible exception of marks in reading. At the beginning of both first and second grades there are fairly large effects on reading marks: for first grade −0.21 and significant, for second grade 0.18 and of borderline significance. Since different sets of teachers are involved in successive years, it is possible that race can affect teachers' evaluations in reading but that bias is inconsistent in direction—sometimes favoring whites, other times favoring blacks. With thirty-six parameters estimated, we would expect at least one coefficient to exceed twice its standard error, so we are inclined to ignore these exceptions, especially since the two exceptions are opposite in sign.

Altogether, effects associated with race appear negligible or potentially offsetting. In the integrated school, family background factors and teacher credentials are fairly constant across race. Between-school race effects (white middle-class vs. black lower-class) cannot be evaluated easily because race is confounded with residential locus, socioeconomic status, and other school differences. However, lower-class whites in the integrated school resemble the lower-class blacks in that school more than they resemble middle-class whites in the suburban school. (Cf. the means presented at the beginning of Chapter 5 and the general lack of race effects within the integrated school just noted.) The differences between lower-class blacks in the integrated school and lower-class blacks in the all-black school are also smaller than differences between whites in the integrated lower-class school and whites in the middle-class school. Over all, this makes us believe that socioeconomic status or social class, more than race per se, is an explanation for differences between schools.

Entering race as an exogenous variable within the

Table 6.21

Summary of Structural Coefficients Associated with Effects of IQ[a]

Endogenous Variables		T1	T3	T5
ABIL	White Middle-Class School	.050*	.021*	-.002
	Integrated Lower-Class School	.022*	-.008	.001
	Black Lower-Class School	.019*	b	-.009
PE_R	White Middle-Class School	.011+	-.001	.006 +
	Integrated Lower-Class School	.011*	-.004	.010
	Black Lower-Class School	-.004	b	.006
PE_A	White Middle-Class School	.022*	-.006	.006
	Integrated Lower-Class School	.011*	.000	.010
	Black Lower-Class School	-.005	b	-.008
PE_C	White Middle-Class School	.007	-.023*	.003
	Integrated Lower-Class School	.001	-.003	.005
	Black Lower-Class School	-.020*	b	.013+
E_R	White Middle-Class School	.010	-.016+	-.011*
	Integrated Lower-Class School	.004	-.010	.018+
	Black Lower-Class School	.003	b	.005
E_A	White Middle-Class School	.022*	.001	.000
	Integrated Lower-Class School	.006	-.004	-.006
	Black Lower-Class School	-.013	b	.001
E_C	White Middle-Class School	-.009	-.019+	-.007
	Integrated Lower-Class School	.001	-.015*	.001
	Black Lower-Class School	-.001	b	.000
M_R	White Middle-Class School	.001	.010	.007+
	Integrated Lower-Class School	.030*	-.011+	.008
	Black Lower-Class School	.023*	b	.018+
M_A	White Middle-Class School	.008	.013+	-.001
	Integrated Lower-Class School	.015*	.013*	.020*
	Black Lower-Class School	.033*	b	.017*
M_C	White Middle-Class School	.016*	.016	.006
	Integrated Lower-Class School	.012*	.014*	.007
	Black Lower-Class School	.006	b	.004

*Coefficient more than twice its standard error.

+Coefficient more than 1.5 times its standard error.

[a]A positive coefficient indicates high ability is associated with high expectations or superior performance.

[b]The variance-covariance matrix for this model was singular.

models for the integrated school, as described above, reveals average differences by race for endogenous variables. Estimating *separate* models for the two races is an alternative strategy that might identify different patterns of underlying causes that could exist whether or not there were mean differences. For example, children of the two races might display similar levels of expectations for reading, but peers might be a strong influence determining that expectation level for one race while parents played a strong role for the other race. In order to distinguish possible racial differences in causal structure, we estimated each of the six models separately for blacks and whites in the integrated lower-class school.

In this separate analysis by race, it turned out that two of the matrices were not positive definite and several other matrices led to unacceptable solutions (poor χ^2 fits, negative error variances, etc.). Apparently the reduced sample size when the children in the integrated school are divided by race made these matrices unstable and led to problems in model estimation. The only models entirely acceptable for both blacks and whites were the T1 start-up models and the T3–T4 transition models through second grade.

Table 6.22

Summary of Structural Coefficients Associated with Race: Lower-Class Integrated School[a]

Endogenous Variables	T1	T2	T3	T4	T5	T6
ABIL	-.01		.06		-.12	
PE_R	-.09		.11		-.18	
PE_A	.00		.20+		-.12	
PE_C	.19*		.05		-.02	
E_R	-.00	-.07	.10	.01	-.10	.16
E_A	-.04	.05	-.11	.02	-.18	.04
E_C	.04	-.03	-.06	.11	-.05	.01
M_R	-.21*	-.02	.18+	-.04	-.02	.15
M_A	-.07	.10	.11	.08	.06	.02
M_C	.00	.11+	.09	.11	.01	.10

*Coefficient more than twice its standard error.

+Coefficient more than 1.5 times its standard error.

[a]White is coded 1, black is coded 2.

In spite of the estimation problems, all possible racial differences arising from black-white comparisons for each of these models were checked against the "full" model (combined over race) and against whatever information could be gleaned from the models that provided an acceptable solution for only one race. Several differences associated with race appeared in both the T1 and T3–T4 models, but the differences were either inconsistent between the two models or not consistent with the partial information that could be culled from estimating other models in this set. In short, although the analysis is not as straightforward or as thorough as we would like, structural differences by race appear minimal.[12]

A great many differences by race have been scrutinized, and general absence of differences in model structure by race suggest that the processes affecting attainment for children from the two races in the integrated school, where racial differences can be compared with other factors held constant, are very much alike.

Effects Associated with Sex

In contrast with race, effects associated with gender can be checked in every school. Sex was introduced repeatedly as an exogenous variable because we expected that the child's sex might affect the marking practices of teachers in the various grades to different degrees. Also, as children progress in school, they may pick up more and more information about sex-role expectations. Similarly, parents may become increasingly influenced by sex-role expectations.

At the start of school, girls are generally favored, with slightly more positive parents' estimates, except for middle-class girls in arithmetic (Table 6.23). In first grade, parents' ability estimates and parents' expectations have negative coefficients (implying a more positive attitude for girls), with the one exception, and they are significant in four instances. In second grade, we could not estimate parameters for the black lower-class school, and the picture is not very clear in the other two schools. By third grade, parents' expectations seem to show a different reaction to their children's sex. While girls and boys are viewed as being about equal in overall ability, parental reading expec-

[12] One finding from earlier analyses for the first cohort in the integrated school (Entwisle and Hayduk 1978a) was modified in the T1 models for whites and blacks that were estimated for data pooled from four cohorts. The influence of IQ on parents' ability (ABIL) estimates is somewhat stronger for whites than for blacks (0.025 vs. 0.015) but both effects are large enough to be significant. Early in first grade, white parents' forecasts of their children's general ability to do schoolwork were more strongly determined by the child's IQ than were black parents', but black parents also based their forecasts to a significant extent on IQ-like information gleaned from their children's behavior. Since most parents did not know the children's IQ scores, we assume they were observing the kinds of behaviors tapped by IQ tests and basing their opinion on these observations.

Table 6.23

Summary of Structural Coefficients Associated with Sex[a]

Endogenous Variables		T1	T2	T3	T4	T5	T6
ABIL	White Middle-Class School	-.10		.27*		-.11	
	Integrated Lower-Class School	-.15+		.14		.08	
	Black Lower-Class School	-.19		b		.22	
PE_R	White Middle-Class School	-.08		-.00		-.11+	
	Integrated Lower-Class School	-.16+		-.11		-.22+	
	Black Lower-Class School	-.17		b		-.05	
PE_A	White Middle-Class School	.10		.03		.22*	
	Integrated Lower-Class School	-.13		.02		-.11	
	Black Lower-Class School	-.25		b		.39*	
PE_C	White Middle-Class School	-.20*		.00		.03	
	Integrated Lower-Class School	-.17+		-.25+		-.07	
	Black Lower-Class School	-.17		b		-.06	
E_R	White Middle-Class School	-.02		-.09		-.05	
	Integrated Lower-Class School	-.24*		.02		-.42*	
	Black Lower-Class School	.02		b		-.05	
E_A	White Middle-Class School	.03		.07		.12	
	Integrated Lower-Class School	-.02		.04		.28+	
	Black Lower-Class School	-.11		b		-.01	
E_C	White Middle-Class School	-.30*		-.08		.01	
	Integrated Lower-Class School	-.05		.00		-.08	
	Black Lower-Class School	-.00		b		-.09	
M_R	White Middle-Class School	.01		-.06		-.02	
	Integrated Lower-Class School	-.02		-.03		.03	
	Black Lower-Class School	-.32+		b		.19	
M_A	White Middle-Class School	.05		.08		-.05	
	Integrated Lower-Class School	.03		-.01		.06	
	Black Lower-Class School	-.02		b		.10	
M_C	White Middle-Class School	-.27*		-.06		-.17+	
	Integrated Lower-Class School	-.40*		.03		-.01	
	Black Lower-Class School	-.17		b		-.19	

*Coefficient more than twice its standard error.

+Coefficient more than 1.5 times its standard error.

[a]Boys are coded 1, girls are coded 2.

[b]The variance-covariance matrix for this model was not positive definite.

tations come to favor girls, while their arithmetic expectations significantly favor boys in the middle-class and black lower-class schools. Somewhat surprisingly, parents' initial expectations for better conduct from girls are largely eroded by third grade. It is curious that the academic areas in which parents come to hold sex-stereotypic views (reading and arithmetic) generally show the least effects of sex stereotyping in the marks teachers actually assign, while the area where parents are least stereotyped (conduct), the corresponding marks show consistent, and sometimes strong, favoritism toward girls, especially in first grade. The coefficients associated with gender in the middle-class school are, if anything, more consistent than those in the other two schools, suggesting that the prevalence of sex-role stereotypes is as strong among middle-class parents as among lower-class parents (see also Entwisle and Baker 1981).

Being female also tends to increase a child's own initial expectations, but those initially weak effects also gradually shift to a weak pattern in which girls favor reading while boys favor arithmetic (with neither dominating conduct). Thus, the effect of gender on children's expectations comes to be much like gender effects on parental expectations.

Being female is conducive to better initial marks in conduct in all three schools (two significant). With the single exception of the black school in first grade, however, sex differences in reading and arithmetic marks appear to be absent. This is a finding worth notice, because it implies that parents' and children's initial expectations do not have a noticeable direct effect on teachers' marks in the two academic areas. It also demonstrates directly that these teachers do not favor one sex over the other in their assignment of marks. On the other hand, in seven of eight instances, boys received lower marks in conduct than girls. Since conduct is conceptualized as a cause of reading and arithmetic achievement, sex differences may be stronger than is implied by the direct effects above. Specifically, reading or arithmetic achievement may be influenced indirectly through conduct marks. The first-grade coefficients of -0.27×0.26 (middle-class, reading), -0.27×0.14 (middle-class, arithmetic), and -0.40×0.27 (integrated, arithmetic) linking sex to conduct marks and then conduct marks to reading and arithmetic marks (with both coefficients in each case exceeding twice their standard errors) indicate gender does have indirect effects on academic performance. However, the magnitude of these chained effects is small, the largest being -0.109.

All in all, effects attributable to gender are numerous, in some cases substantial, and in first grade probably efficacious. Differences among the three schools that might reflect sex-role stereotypes linked to class are not visible. At the beginning of school, girls appear to hold an edge, both in terms of their parents' hopes and also to a lesser degree because of their own expectations. Teachers do not give different academic marks to boys and girls, but the child's gender indirectly affects early marks in both reading and arithmetic through conduct marks, either because the child's conduct (which is sex-related) colors the teacher's evaluation of performances in the two academic areas, or because poor deportment actually interferes with learning in these areas.

All of the gender effects so far discussed are simple effects. It seemed possible that other interactive effects might occur. For example, sex and ability might interact so that high-ability black girls have high expectations, while high-ability black boys do not. To test for such interactive effects, which amount to gender differences in causal structure, each of the six models was estimated separately for males and females in the integrated school, as already mentioned.

Dividing the data by sex led to a case base reduced by half, and this reduction created some serious estimation problems. Detailed analysis was unavoidably confined to within-year models (Figures 6.2I, 6.4I, 6.6I, estimated separately for children of each sex). Insofar as the data could address the issue, there did not appear to be any structural differences associated with gender beyond those already revealed in the earlier analyses, so the strategy of estimating models separately for boys and for girls was not pursued further.

Effects Associated with Peer Ratings

Peer-popularity ratings were obtained each year in the second semester. In every grade there are some substantial, yet scattered, coefficients linking peer ratings to marks in all schools. Apparently, when peers make a high or low appraisal of a classmate, this has some effects on marks, all other things held constant, and/or the special skills that help children become popular also assist them in attaining superior marks. Effects are at least as noticeable in first grade as later.

Altogether, the influence of peer ratings on children's expectations appears negligible (one effect out of twenty-seven is borderline). Signs are mixed and inconsistent, both within school and within subject areas, and there is certainly no evidence that peers are more influential in one school than in another. All in all, these data relating peer-popularity ratings to expectations suggest negligible influence. Some further findings on friends' expectations are reported in Chapter 7.

Effects Associated with Absence

In the middle-class school, there are two out of nine significant effects of absence on children's expectations, and two out of nine on marks. In the integrated school, effects are more frequent, with four significant effects of absence on children's expectations and seven on marks.[13] Not a single significant absence effect appears for the black lower-class school. All but two of the absence coefficients in the integrated school are positive, implying that more absences lead to lower expectations or marks. Patterns of signs are mixed (twenty of thirty-six positive) in the other two schools—another suggestion that absence effects are not important in those schools. Both the number of absences and the associated standard deviation are larger in the integrated school than in the other two schools (see Table 5.2).

The explanation for the special influence of absence in the integrated school is not clear. Above a certain minimum, absences are discretionary, and perhaps the excess number of absences and the association of frequent absences with low marks and expectations in this school comes about because those with low commitment to school stay away more often. However, there is no way to tell whether this conjecture is correct.

ENDOGENOUS VARIABLES: PERSISTENCE

A critical feature of the models is their use of repeated measures on the same variable. This strategy has a

[13] In each tally, one parameter is inconsistent in sign between subsample applications.

number of advantages. It offers evidence of reliability—if a variable measured at one time exerts influence on that same variable at a subsequent time, we have some evidence that we are measuring the same thing on the two occasions—and, of course, reliability is a necessary condition for validity if time spans are sufficiently short to rule out real changes. It would be worrisome, for example, if marks in the first semester did not at all predict marks in the second. Persistence also offers a validity check in that, as children mature, expectations or marks should become more determinate.

In commenting earlier upon heuristic models proposed by Finn (1972) and Braun (1976), we pointed out that their models did not explicitly incorporate measures of persistence, although such an idea is exceedingly important substantively. If marks persist, for example, one conclusion could be that teachers push children into a mold that will set boundaries on their achievement. Similarly, if children form expectations early that are thereafter maintained, this could be interpreted as evidence of crystallization.

Problems arise frequently in interpretation of change, however, even assuming that it has been correctly assessed. If we observe change, it can be attributed to the measuring instrument just as readily as to the individual. That is, when marks change it is equally valid to conclude that teachers are changing (using different standards to evaluate performance) as that children are changing (performing differently now compared to earlier). Consistency over time is equally difficult to interpret. Marks at one time could affect marks at the next time because whatever causes teachers to assign a mark at one time is also there to be observed at the next time. Or, marks at the first time could cause children to perform at the level represented by that mark—having received an A, the child tries to live up to it. In any single year, these two explanations are completely confounded. However, between years, teachers are different and children are not, so stability between years is properly attributed to children rather than to teachers.

Similarly, change in expectations could signify that the task was being interpreted differently by children in second grade as compared to first—they understand what they are doing better as they get older—or it could be that the task for which they hold expectations is itself changing. With expectations, we would argue that change over time probably is not attributable to changes in our recording procedures, because we took great pains to make sure children understood what they were being asked, and we always asked about the same thing in the same way. However, a change in children's expectations might still reflect the closing of a gap between marks and prior expectations, or expectations shadowing a mark that is itself changing.

Marks on Marks

The longitudinal summaries by school reveal strong persistence in marks (top of Table 6.24), especially in the two lower-class schools. The average structural coefficients for reading and arithmetic persistence over time are high in every instance for the two lower-class schools, except at T5 for the black lower-class school. At the end of third grade, the reading and arithmetic coefficients average 0.91 for the black school and 0.67 in the integrated school.

The middle-class school displays a strong pattern that appears to a lesser degree in the lower-class schools. The within-year coefficients in the middle-class school are fairly substantial—0.42, 0.53, 0.32—although usually smaller than the corresponding coefficients in the two lower-class schools. However, between grades (from first to second grade and from second to third grade), the average coefficients in the middle-class school dropped to 0.06 and 0.15. Each new teacher shows a strong tendency to wipe the slate clean and to re-evaluate each child. This tendency, plus the much smaller effects attributable to IQ in that school in the early grades, go a long way toward explaining why there remains much unexplained variance in the system for middle-class third-graders and little unexplained variance in the system for third-graders in the other two schools (where determinacy coefficients were commonly in the 50% to 75% range).

Expectations on Expectations

All the coefficients for persistence in children's expectations (bottom of Table 6.24) are positive, and in a large number of instances the parameters linking expectations at one time with expectations at the next time exceed 1.5 times their standard error (twelve out of fifteen for both the white and integrated schools, and four out of twelve for the black school). Although models for the black school are not as well determined as those for the other schools, the magnitudes of the coefficients in all three schools reveal a tendency for expectations to persist even as early as first grade.

By third grade, differences in persistence of expectations among schools appear negligible. In the first two grades, persistence of expectations in the integrated school looked more pronounced than in the middle-class school (averaging 0.24, 0.55, 0.30 vs. 0.13, 0.31, 0.14).

Contrary to the pattern of stronger within-year persistence for marks, children's expectations tend to show stronger between-year persistence. Within years it is easy for children to change their minds but not their marks, while between years it is easy to change their marks but not their minds. As mentioned above, the change of teachers accounts for the mark half of

Table 6.24

Summary of Structural Coefficients for the Persistence of Marks and Expectations Over Time

Persistence of Marks to Time	T2	T3	T4	T5	T6
White Middle-Class School					
Reading	.39*	.07	.50*	.14	.33*
Arithmetic	.46*	.04	.56*	.16	.30*
Conduct	.60*	.26*	.67*	.04	.54*
Reading and Arithmetic Average	.42	.06	.53	.15	.32
Integrated Lower-Class School					
Reading	.78*	.72*	.70*	.42*	a
Arithmetic	.45*	.33*	.60*	.33*	.67*
Conduct	.66*	.49*	.79*	.32*	.72*
Reading and Arithmetic Average	.62	.52	.65	.38	.67
Black Lower-Class School					
Reading	.23	b	.58*	-.08	1.14*
Arithmetic	.48*	b	.65*	.31+	.68*
Conduct	.66*	b	.66*	.00	.80*
Reading and Arithmetic Average	.36	b	.61	.12	.91

Persistence of Expectations to Time	T2	T3	T4	T5	T6
White Middle-Class School					
Reading	.14+	.23*	.17*	.10	.34*
Arithmetic	.10	.38*	.11	.34*	.30*
Conduct	.14*	.32*	.16*	.30*	.27*
Reading and Arithmetic Average	.13	.31	.14	.22	.32
Integrated Lower-Class School					
Reading	.20	.46*	.33*	.37*	.13
Arithmetic	.28+	.64*	.28*	.27+	.23*
Conduct	.48*	.30	.27*	.39*	.51*
Reading and Arithmetic Average	.24	.55	.30	.32	.18
Black Lower-Class School					
Reading	.26	b	.11	.51*	.18
Arithmetic	.19	b	.02	.31	.31*
Conduct	.11	b	.40*	.28	.39*
Reading and Arithmetic Average	.22	b	.07	.41	.25

*Coefficient more than twice its standard error.

+Coefficient more than 1.5 times its standard error.

[a]M_{R6} was deleted from this model.

[b]The variance-covariance matrix for this model was singular.

this switch, but it is not obvious what accounts for the differential persistence of expectations.

Other Endogenous Variables

In some respects, the relationships among expectations and marks lie at the heart of our models. The effect of expectations on marks and the subsequent feedback from marks to expectations are key elements in a dynamic process shaping achievement. Obviously, by sampling marks and expectations twice a year, we used only a few discrete points in time to sample variables that are continuously interacting, but the careful timing of our observations helped considerably in the specification of causal orders. Furthermore, both the first-order partial derivatives and some explorations of backward paths for the middle-class school (from M_1 to E_1, for example) also suggested that the model is properly specified, with children's expectations acting as a causal force on marks within the first time period, rather than the other way around (Entwisle and Hayduk 1981). After the first cycle, of course, in every cycle there is opportunity for marks to influence expectations at any subsequent time as well as for expectations to influence marks.

In the sections to follow, the effect of current and lagged expectations on marks, as well as the impact of marks on expectations, are discussed. One theme stands out. In the middle-class school, children's expectations come increasingly into line with marks, but this is not the case in the lower-class schools. A lack of paths from marks at one time to expectations at the next time is characteristic of the structural models for the lower-class schools. The implication is that feedback is processed in one place but not in the other.

Effects of Expectations on Marks

Table 6.25 presents a summary of coefficients linking expectations to marks when current expectations are matched to current marks (E_{R2} with M_{R2}, for example) and also expectations lagged one cycle back are linked to current marks (E_{R1} with M_{R2}, for example).

There appear to be some characteristic differences by school in how current expectations influence marks. In the middle-class school, seven of eighteen coefficients attain a respectable size, and, in all cases but one, the sign is in the expected direction. Effects for the integrated lower-class school are less consistent—respectable size is achieved in only four of eighteen possible instances. In four instances, signs for reading are in the wrong direction, and in no instances is the link for reading significant in size. The black lower-class school is even less consistent—out of three significant parameters, one is of reversed sign.

The picture for lagged expectations is virtually turned around for the white and integrated schools. For the white middle-class school, only one lagged coefficient reaches even borderline significance, and signs are mixed. For the integrated lower-class school, four lagged coefficients are significant, all of these are in the proper direction, and they pertain to the substantive areas of reading or arithmetic. The black lower-class school continues to be very inconsistent—the signs of both the significant and insignificant lagged effects are mixed.

We would not care to overinterpret these patterns, but, generally, children's expectations seem to show modest detectable influences on marks, although effects are somewhat erratic. For middle-class children, the impact is generally one of current expectations on marks (seven significant effects), while the effects of children's expectations in the integrated lower-class school are scattered between effects of current and lagged expectations (four current, four lagged), and the black lower-class appear much less effective, with a sprinkling of three positive and two negative effects. Children's initial expectations in the integrated school may then be more effective than might be judged from analysis of the first cycle alone. When teachers give better marks as the year goes along—as they do in this school—the rewards are apparently bestowed upon children whose initial expectations for themselves were higher. Marks also improved within years in the middle-class school, but there is no evidence of lagged expectations effects there.

Effects of Marks on Expectations

A striking difference appears between the models in how marks at one time affect expectations at a subsequent time (Table 6.26). In fact, this pattern is so clear it stands out even in the longitudinal school summaries. In the middle-class school, in ten out of fifteen cases, previous marks shape later expectations, especially within years, and all coefficients are positive. Mark feedback is evidently processed there. In the lower-class schools, on the other hand, there are seven reversals in sign, and only four (borderline) coefficients connect marks with subsequent expectations. Only two of the four are in the academic areas, and both effects appearing in the black lower-class school are for a model that fits poorly.

Further light can be shed on this comparison by referring to Table 6.27, which reveals how well the children expected to do in comparison with their actual performance. In the middle-class school, children get better and better at anticipating their marks in all three areas, with errors about equal in both directions. In other words, from about the end of second grade on, children in the middle-class school forecast their mark correctly, and the proportion of those expecting

Table 6.25

Summary of Structural Coefficients for Effects of Current and Lagged Children's Expectations on Marks

	T1	T2	T3	T4	T5	T6
Impact of Current Expectations on Marks						
White Middle-Class School						
Reading	.00	.12+	-.06	.12*	.12	.02
Arithmetic	.06	.01	.09	.16*	.07	.22*
Conduct	.10	.05	.15+	.11	.16+	.19*
Integrated Lower-Class School						
Reading	-.08	.13	-.05	-.01	.02	-.02
Arithmetic	.10	.13	.15	.06	.17+	.25*
Conduct	.00	.43*	.44*	.16	.09	.04
Black Lower-Class School						
Reading	.19	.35	a	-.28*	.30*	.11
Arithmetic	.18	.08	a	.13	.10	.25*
Conduct	.10	.10	a	.26	.15	-.01
Impact of Lagged Expectations on Marks						
White Middle-Class School						
Reading		-.01	-.09	.05	.07	.01
Arithmetic		.07	-.07	-.01	-.03	-.11+
Conduct		.07	.09	.03	.08	.04
Integrated Lower-Class School						
Reading		.26*	.02	-.04	.30*	.06
Arithmetic		.20+	-.16	.15+	-.16	-.06
Conduct		-.12	-.28	-.03	.07	.03
Black Lower-Class School						
Reading		-.22	a	-.23*	-.12	-.09
Arithmetic		-.03	a	.36*	-.06	-.01
Conduct		.06	a	-.06	-.04	.10

*Coefficient more than twice its standard error.

+Coefficient more than 1.5 times its standard error.

[a]The variance-covariance matrix for this model was singular.

to do better than they actually did is about equal to the proportion of those expecting to do worse than they actually did.

This kind of symmetry around a set of frequently correct estimates is not seen in the data for the lower-class schools. There, few children made correct estimates and a very large proportion of children did worse than they expected, particularly in reading. Furthermore, although the number of children who display maximal discrepancies (three units) decreases over time, at the end of third grade at least 25% of the children are still off by two units or more in their forecasts in both reading and arithmetic in these schools. For example, 28% of the children in the integrated school either expect an A in reading while getting a C or D, or expect a B while getting a D. This information, together with the information derived from the parameter estimates showing whether marks affect subsequent expectations (Table 6.26), suggests that marks are being well processed by children in the middle-class school, but not very well processed in the two lower-class schools.

Determinants of Parental Expectations

We have already discussed several of the determinants of parental expectatons (sex, IQ, race), but not the responsiveness of parental expectations to mark feedback. Parents in the middle-class school consistently modified their estimates of their children's general ability on the basis of prior reading marks, but not on

Table 6.26

Summary of Structural Coefficients for Effect of Marks on Subsequent Expectations

Effect on Expectations at Time	T2	T3	T4	T5	T6
White Middle-Class School					
Reading	.15	.09	.41*	.07	.33*
Arithmetic	.24+	.10	.28*	.24+	.42*
Conduct	.23*	.16	.25+	.26*	.21*
Integrated Lower-Class School					
Reading	-.16	.15	.03	-.19	b
Arithmetic	-.02	.04	.21+	.12	.18
Conduct	.06	.19+	.09	.12	.06
Black Lower-Class School					
Reading	-.16	a	.27+	.13	.07
Arithmetic	.17	a	-.10	.04	.28
Conduct	-.04	a	.24+	-.08	.01

*Coefficient more than twice its standard error.

+Coefficient more than 1.5 times its standard error.

[a]The variance-covariance matrix for this model was singular.

[b] M_{R5} was deleted from this model.

the basis of arithmetic or conduct marks. In sharp contrast, the parents in the lower-class schools modified their overall ability estimates primarily on the basis of conduct marks. Lower-class parents seem to think their children will be able to do well in school if the children can behave themselves, while middle-class parents think their children will do well in school if the children can read.

All the parents tended to form their expectations for reading and arithmetic by consulting their general ability estimates (fifteen of sixteen coefficients are highly significant). The middle-class parents also considered their ability estimates in forming their conduct expectations (all three coefficients are significant), while the parents in the two lower-class schools apparently did not (one of five significant). It is curious that in the lower-class schools, where conduct marks influenced ability estimates, those ability estimates, with one exception, did not in turn influence conduct expectations, while exactly the opposite is true in the middle-class school. Marks in conduct did not influence ability estimates, but ability estimates did influence parents' conduct expectations.

As for parents' utilization of mark feedback to shape expectations in specific areas, the middle-class parents were influenced by prior marks in five of six cases, while the parents in both the lower-class schools were less likely to use mark feedback (four out of nine cases). Parents' use of mark feedback is rather like their children's use of feedback, in that feedback is more consistently used in the middle-class school. Middle-class and lower-class parents also differed in that the general ability estimates of the middle-class parents primarily reflected prior reading marks, while the general ability estimates of lower-class parents responded more to conduct marks. Once formed, these general ability estimates were used by parents in all three schools to generate specific expectations for reading and arithmetic.

Effects of Parents' Expectations on Children

Parents' expectations could affect children's expectations and/or their marks. The evidence summarized in Table 6.28 suggests that middle-class parents' expectations have some influence on their children's expectations in reading and arithmetic—six of twelve coefficients are significant. Significant coefficients linking parents' expectations to children's expectations appear less often in the other two schools, and several negative coefficients appear. To the extent that children's expectations are determined, middle-class parents appear more important than lower-class parents.

Parents are considerably more efficacious when it comes to children's marks. All coefficients are positive, and a number are sizeable for all schools in the first cycle. After the first cycle, only middle-class par-

Table 6.27

The Proportion of Children Displaying Various Discrepancies between Their Marks and Expectations over Time

White Middle-Class School		T1	T2	T3	T4	T5	T6
Reading							
	3 Better	.01	.01	.00	.00	.00	.00
	2 Better	.02	.01	.01	.01	.00	.01
The child did____	1 Better	.17	.17	.15	.25	.19	.21
than he expected	The Same	.36	.52	.49	.58	.59	.62
to do.	1 Worse	.39	.27	.32	.17	.22	.16
	2 Worse	.05	.03	.03	.00	.00	.00
	3 Worse	.00	.00	.01	.00	.00	.00
N on which proportion is based		373	364	317	310	247	238
Arithmetic							
	3 Better	.00	.00	.00	.00	.00	.00
	2 Better	.03	.04	.01	.00	.01	.02
The child did____	1 Better	.22	.24	.11	.17	.19	.26
than he expected	The Same	.43	.45	.50	.54	.55	.56
to do.	1 Worse	.31	.25	.34	.27	.24	.16
	2 Worse	.02	.02	.04	.02	.02	.00
	3 Worse	.00	.00	.00	.00	.00	.00
N on which proportion is based		373	364	323	317	255	245
Conduct							
	3 Better	.01	.00	.00	.00	.00	.00
	2 Better	.06	.02	.02	.01	.00	.00
The child did____	1 Better	.19	.22	.30	.27	.13	.22
than he expected	The Same	.38	.48	.48	.54	.55	.56
to do.	1 Worse	.32	.24	.17	.17	.29	.21
	2 Worse	.05	.04	.03	.01	.03	.01
	3 Worse	.00	.01	.00	.00	.00	.00
N on which proportion is based		373	362	323	317	255	245

Integrated Lower-Class School		T1	T2	T3	T4	T5	T6
Reading							
	3 Better	.00	.00	.00	.00	.00	.00
	2 Better	.00	.02	.01	.02	.00	.00
The child did____	1 Better	.02	.06	.02	.04	.04	.05
than he expected	The Same	.10	.18	.15	.21	.20	.20
to do.	1 Worse	.18	.31	.28	.29	.31	.32
	2 Worse	.40	.29	.31	.29	.30	.28
	3 Worse	.29	.15	.24	.15	.15	.15
N on which proportion is based		288	337	218	232	141	148
Arithmetic							
	3 Better	.00	.00	.00	.00	.00	.00
	2 Better	.00	.02	.00	.00	.01	.01
The child did____	1 Better	.04	.07	.02	.08	.05	.08
than he expected	The Same	.14	.24	.14	.26	.23	.32
to do.	1 Worse	.42	.33	.34	.37	.33	.34
	2 Worse	.31	.27	.38	.23	.30	.18
	3 Worse	.09	.07	.12	.07	.08	.07
N on which proportion is based		339	342	251	238	184	149
Conduct							
	3 Better	.00	.00	.00	.00	.00	.00
	2 Better	.00	.01	.00	.00	.01	.00
The child did____	1 Better	.05	.11	.08	.14	.05	.18
than he expected	The Same	.35	.46	.37	.44	.50	.45
to do.	1 Worse	.47	.37	.42	.27	.40	.31
	2 Worse	.13	.06	.14	.16	.04	.06
	3 Worse	.00	.00	.00	.00	.00	.00
N on which proportion is based		336	342	252	237	184	150

Table 6.27 (Continued)

Black Lower-Class School		T1	T2	T3	T4	T5	T6
Reading							
The child did___ than he expected to do.	3 Better	.00	.00	.00	.00	.00	.00
	2 Better	.01	.00	.00	.02	.00	.00
	1 Better	.05	.03	.03	.03	.09	.03
	The Same	.13	.16	.13	.20	.24	.15
	1 Worse	.31	.31	.42	.28	.44	.49
	2 Worse	.34	.33	.21	.34	.24	.24
	3 Worse	.17	.17	.20	.12	.00	.09
N on which proportion is based		202	165	99	90	34	59
Arithmetic							
The child did___ than he expected to do.	3 Better	.00	.00	.00	.00	.00	.00
	2 Better	.00	.01	.01	.00	.00	.00
	1 Better	.06	.07	.03	.07	.04	.02
	The Same	.18	.30	.15	.17	.15	.31
	1 Worse	.32	.30	.38	.38	.43	.31
	2 Worse	.36	.24	.36	.31	.27	.27
	3 Worse	.08	.08	.07	.07	.12	.10
N on which proportion is based		215	165	162	116	75	62
Conduct							
The child did___ than he expected to do.	3 Better	.00	.00	.00	.00	.00	.00
	2 Better	.00	.01	.00	.00	.01	.03
	1 Better	.04	.10	.07	.10	.09	.11
	The Same	.31	.28	.40	.54	.46	.40
	1 Worse	.46	.42	.49	.33	.30	.37
	2 Worse	.19	.20	.04	.03	.13	.08
	3 Worse	.00	.00	.00	.00	.00	.00
N on which proportion is based		227	172	163	115	76	62

ents continue to be effective, however, with the major exception of third-grade reading in the integrated school.

Over all, children's expectations appear mildly susceptible to parents' expectations. The direct influence of middle-class parents on achievement is much more important. Parents could affect achievement by offering learning opportunities at home, by supervising homework, and the like. In affecting conduct marks, as parents seem to do appreciably in the middle-class school, they may also provide learning opportunities by explaining standards or by insisting upon acceptable behavior at home. The coefficients for the effects of middle-class parents on conduct marks suggest, in fact, that these parents may have further indirect influences on achievement. In many instances, the conduct mark accounted for part of the mark in reading and arithmetic; therefore, by affecting conduct marks, the middle-class parent probably has considerable indirect influence on academic achievement over the early grades.

Since middle-class parents' expectations do predict conduct marks even after previous conduct marks are controlled, change in conduct marks is also to some degree attributable to the parents' standards.

Effects of Parents' Ability Estimates on Children

Parents' ability estimates have significant effects in an inverse direction on middle-class first-graders' expectations in four out of six instances. This counter-intuitive effect was noted and discussed earlier. Aside from this, there is little to say about the effect of parents' ability estimates on children's expectations. In the two lower-class schools, only two of thirty-three coefficients reach significance, and signs are mixed.

Parents' ability estimates seem to have some effect on middle-class children's marks in conduct (three of six parameters are significant, with two in a negative direction) and on black lower-class children's marks in reading and arithmetic in second and third grade (five of six parameters are significant). However, there are puzzling reversals in sign (−0.28, for example, for reading marks at T6 in the black school), so the patterns are not clear-cut. All in all, consequences of parents' general ability estimates are sometimes seen for

Table 6.28

Summary of Structural Coefficients for Effects of Parents' Expectations on Children's Expectations and Marks

Effects at Time	T1	T2	T3	T4	T5	T6
Children's Expectations						
White Middle-Class School						
Reading	.29	.23+	.06	-.12	.23+	.13
Arithmetic	.17	.43*	.24+	.25+	.22	.12
Conduct	.04	.04	.15	-.01	.15	.13+
Integrated Lower-Class School						
Reading	-.06	.10	-.02	-.08	-.08	.20+ b
Arithmetic	.12	-.25+	.15	.16+	-.06	.12
Conduct	-.02	.05	.13	.00	.13	.02
Black Lower-Class School						
Reading	.17	.16	a	-.33+	.15	.17
Arithmetic	-.01	.01	a	.40	.12	.24
Conduct	-.03	.15	a	.07	.13	.09
Marks						
White Middle-Class School						
Reading	.09	.05	.47*	.09	.14	.30*
Arithmetic	.28*	.25*	.16+	.07	.31*	-.03
Conduct	.50*	.29*	.27*	.06	.11	.16*
Integrated Lower-Class School						
Reading	.27*	.20+	.11	.07	.43*	.32*
Arithmetic	.15+	-.05	.08	.12	.20+ b	.07
Conduct	.29*	.08	.15	.06	.05	.06
Black Lower-Class School						
Reading	.10	.12	a	-.07	-.02	.16
Arithmetic	.33*	.01	a	.08	-.10	.00
Conduct	.26+	.08	a	-.08	.02	.11

*Coefficient more than twice its standard error.

+Coefficient more than 1.5 times its standard error.

[a]The variance-covariance matrix for this model was singular.

children's expectations and marks, but the effects are scattered.

Effects of Conduct Marks on Other Marks

Marks in reading and arithmetic frequently responded to conduct marks.[14] Table 6.29 shows that, with one exception, all effects are in the expected direction and many are significant. The cycles from T2 on are particularly interesting because by then marks in reading and arithmetic are "controlled" by the inclusion of previous marks in those subjects, but conduct remains influential.

Two main mechanisms could explain the influence of conduct marks on reading and arithmetic. The first involves teachers' judgments—children who are well-behaved are apt to be judged more leniently, a "halo" effect. Secondly, children who are better behaved may actually learn more, because children who are quiet and orderly may be able to profit more from instruction.

In the present analysis there is no way to separate halo effects from learning effects. One could inquire to what extent conduct marks predict scores on standard-

[14]Analyses in Appendix C demonstrate that these effects are not reciprocal, that is, that conduct marks are not responsive to marks in reading and arithmetic.

Table 6.29

Summary of Structural Coefficients Linking Conduct Marks to Other Marks

Effects at Time	T1	T2	T3	T4	T5	T6
White Middle-Class School						
Reading	.26*	.18*	.25*	.10+	.13+	.08+
Arithmetic	.14*	.18*	.22*	.12*	.13	.14*
Integrated Lower-Class School						
Reading	.03	.34*	.17+	.10	.18	.16
Arithmetic	.27*	.29*	.10	.16*	.15	.08
Black Lower-Class School						
Reading	.12	.19	a	.10	.26*	.22*
Arithmetic	.29*	.17	a	.16	-.06	.01

*Coefficient more than twice its standard error.

+Coefficient more than 1.5 times its standard error.

[a]The variance-covariance matrix for this model was singular.

ized achievement net of other marks, however, and since halo effects are absent from standardized scores, a correlation between conduct marks and standardized scores could represent a pure measure of the impact of conduct on learning opportunities. Analyses along these lines in Chapter 7 indicate conduct marks do predict achievement scores to a small extent, but the main effect of conduct marks is probably to condition reading or arithmetic marks.

Altogether, Table 6.29 suggests that conduct is an appreciable component of academic performance in early schooling. Its effects appear largest in the earlier cycles but are present later as well. Later on, of course, indirect effects could also be appreciable.

Summary of Variable Effects

A bird's eye view of the schooling process as revealed by these models suggests that children's expectations, insofar as we have been able to measure them, are about as well determined in one place as in another, but that in the two lower-class schools they are less likely to affect marks. Parents there are also less likely to affect marks by any route except in the first cycle. IQ rather consistently has effects on marks in the lower-class schools. Most important, perhaps, marks tend to persist strongly between years in the two lower-class schools (with the exception of T5 in the black school), but they persist mainly within years in the middle-class school. Between years in the middle-class school, mark persistence is significant only once. However, children in that school use feedback from marks to calibrate their expectations. In the other two schools, average expectation levels declined, but the decline is not a clear consequence of mark feedback. All in all, the total system in the middle-class school appears looser and the child appears to be better articulated within it. Socioeconomic status appears to be much more likely than race as an explanation of differences between schools, and in the one school that enrolled both black and white students, race effects are few and inconsistent.

The mode of operation of IQ looks different from place to place. It affects parents' initial expectations. It also affects middle-class children's expectations to some extent. Academic marks in the lower-class schools responded strongly to IQ at first, and later marks responded to some extent in all three schools. Effects of gender are in the expected direction, favoring girls, especially in the first cycle. Most of the early gender effects are linked to some aspect of conduct. There appear to be no consistent differences in gender effects across schools. There are some absence effects in the integrated school, and scattered effects of peer-popularity ratings on marks in all schools.

Marks in conduct generally affected marks in the academic areas, especially in the early grades. Expectations persisted to a lesser degree than marks, but they persisted similarly in all schools. Parents have numerous effects upon marks for all children in the first cycle, and middle-class parents' influence continues. There are scattered effects of parents' expectations on children's expectations. Children's expectations have some effects on their current marks in the middle-class school and a few current and lagged effects in the other schools in a complex pattern. The most striking difference across schools is that children's marks in the middle-class school generally affected later expectations, whereas in the lower-class schools only a few borderline influences of this sort appear. Patterns of parental expectations parallel those of their children—middle-class parents seem to take more account of academic mark feedback than lower-class parents do.

RELATIVE SIZES OF EFFECTS

So far we have emphasized comparisons among models over time (within one school) or across schools (at one time). The same variables sampled in different populations naturally have different variances, so in these comparisons metric parameters have served as the primary basis for discussion. In addition to the metric structural coefficients, Tables 6.3 to 6.20 provide standardized coefficients for the full data sets. These standardized coefficients give notions of relative sizes of effects within any one model.

Fortunately, as mentioned earlier, parents' expectations, children's expectations, and marks have a similar metric (1,2,3,4) and sex, race, and peer ratings are also coded in a narrow range, so that most metric coefficients turn out to be much like the standardized coefficients. The main exceptions are IQ (with values ranging from about 70 to 140 points) and absences (ranging from eight to about twenty-two per year).

We do not give a systematic review for standardized scores, and a few comments along the line have been based on standardized coefficients in any case. However, standardized coefficients for IQ suggest that it is relatively important—the significant standardized coefficients usually are in the 0.20 to 0.40 range, and occasionally higher. Standardized coefficients for absences are mostly in the range from 0.10 to 0.20, suggesting less relative importance. Where effects are stable enough to be portrayed as paths in the various diagrams, standardized effects associated with gender are a little smaller than the metric coefficients; standardized IQ effects are much larger (ten to twenty times), peer-rating effects are about half or less, and absence effects are ten or more times the metric coefficients. In other words, when scaled to have equal variances, IQ and absence look as potent as other variables, and peer and sex effects look somewhat less efficacious within any model than the metric coefficients would suggest.

IQ would certainly be expected to play a role, but the *nature* of the role changes in different schools. IQ affects mainly first- and second-grade conduct marks in the middle-class school, but reading and arithmetic marks in the two lower-class schools. This kind of conclusion warrants some attention, because it is based not on subsample replication, but on successive samples over time in the same schools.

Chapter 7

Alternate and Additional Models of the Schooling Process

The models developed so far focus on two cognitive outcomes (teachers' marks in reading and arithmetic) and four affective outcomes (teachers' marks in conduct and children's expectations in reading, arithmetic, and conduct). Considering the complexity of the process we are describing, the models include relatively few variables. In this chapter, the models are elaborated a little further. One elaboration involves estimating a model for "lasting effects." Another elaboration is directed at the critical question of whether the models can account for children's performance as measured by objective tests rather than by teachers' marks. Still further elaborations take notice of teachers' expectations and friends' expectations.

MODELS INVOLVING LASTING EFFECTS

So far all models pertain to relatively short time periods. The models can be considered sequentially, however, to yield a more extended picture of the schooling process. It is possible to estimate a model that spans the first 2 years of school by combining the inputs for the T1–T2 model with outputs of the T3–T4 model. Since this time-spanning model omits the intervening information on T2 and T3 marks and expectations, it corresponds to what might have been found if children had been observed only near the beginning of first grade and then again at the end of second grade. It evaluates the net effects of early expectations and marks after intervening events have had an opportunity to disrupt the patterns created by initial marks and expectations.

Only the models for the white middle-class and integrated lower-class schools could be estimated. (The covariance matrix was singular for the black lower-class school.) Both these models provide acceptable fits ($\chi^2 = 36.9$, d.f. 42, not significant, for the white school; and $\chi^2 = 53.2$, d.f. 42, not significant, for the integrated school). The parameter estimates appear in Tables 7.1 and 7.2.

Even a cursory examination of these tables indicates that the net effects of many of the early variables are either very weak or absent. This is not altogether surprising, since the only way the early variables could remain as efficacious as they are in the short-term models would be for the events intervening at times T2 and T3 to be ineffective. From our previous modeling we know that patterns did not remain unchanged. The key question is thus whether all, or only some, of the initial impacts are obscured by the intervening events.

Parents' initial expectations display no significant net effect on children's expectations or marks 2 years later in either school (one exception: a borderline effect for conduct in the integrated school). Parental ability estimates are more efficacious—they may influence children's subsequent reading expectations, and high initial parental ability estimates consistently boost marks in the integrated school. Parents' ability estimates in the integrated school affect marks about as strongly as previous marks do.

The effects of children's initial expectations are largely obscured by intervening events. Five of the six estimates of the persistence of children's initial expectations display positive values, but none of the coefficients even approaches significance. Children's initial expectations seem only randomly related to second-year marks.

Marks display patterns reminiscent of previous analyses. Initial marks persisted strongly in the integrated school and moderately (yet significantly in

Table 7.1

Summary of Coefficients for the Lasting Effects Model for the White Middle-Class School: Metric Coefficients in Upper Half of Table, Standardized Coefficients in Lower Half, and Degree of Determinacy[a]

	$ABIL_1$	PE_{R1}	PE_{A1}	PE_{C1}	E_{R1}	E_{A1}	E_{C1}	M_{R1}	M_{A1}	M_{C1}	$PEER_2$	ABS_2	SEX	IQ	E_{R4}	E_{A4}	E_{C4}	M_{C4}	M_{R4}	M_{A4}	R^2
E_{R4}	.2262^{+}	-.1377			.1230			.2160^{+}			.2236	-.0038	-.0460	-.0071							
E_{A4}	-.0694		.3194			.1576			.1087		-.1292	.0051	.1093	-.0092							
E_{C4}	.1102			.1098			.0421			.1252	-.5860*	.0097	-.0303	-.0103							
M_{C4}	.1789			.1226			-.0164			.2668*	.0550	.0159^{+}	-.1214	-.0079			.2790*				
M_{R4}	.1247	-.0645			-.0585			.2439*			-.0724	.0093	-.0856	.0090	.2058*			.1503^{+}			
M_{A4}	.0866		-.0604			.0021			.0450		.2291	.0112	.0529	.0156^{+}		.2663*		.1921*			
E_{R4}	.3008^{+}	-.1340			.1473			.1972^{+}			.0986	-.0371	-.0395	-.1175							.1162
E_{A4}	-.0812		.2746			.1682			.0790		-.0501	.0432	.0827	-.1339							.0984
E_{C4}	.1561			.1110			.0600			.1427	-.2752*	.1000	-.0278	-.1823							.1575
M_{C4}	.2231			.1091			-.0206			.2678*	.0227	.1451^{+}	-.0980	-.1222			.2458*				.2916
M_{R4}	.1858	-.0704			-.0785			.2495*			-.0358	.1014	-.0825	.1673	.2306*			.1795^{+}			.3541
M_{A4}	.1264		-.0648			.0028			.0408		.1110	.1197	.0499	.2846^{+}		.3325*		.2249*			.3602

[a] The model χ^2 of 36.9 with 42 d.f. is insignificant.

* Coefficient is more than twice its standard error.

\+ Coefficient is more than 1.5 times its standard error.

Table 7.2

Summary of Coefficients for the Lasting Effects Model for the Integrated Lower-Class School: Metric Coefficients in Upper Half of Table, Standardized Coefficients in Lower Half, and Degree of Determinacy[a]

	$ABIL_1$	PE_{R1}	PE_{A1}	PE_{C1}	E_{R1}	E_{A1}	E_{C1}	M_{R1}	M_{A1}	M_{C1}	$PEER_2$	ABS_2	RACE	SEX	IQ	E_{R4}	E_{A4}	E_{C4}	M_{C4}	M_{R4}	M_{A4}	R^2
E_{R4}	.2059	-.1308			-.0347			-.1355			.3242	$.0115^+$	-.0220	-.0901	-.0045							
E_{A4}	-.2486		.0297			.2226			.1359		.0334	.0021	.1417	-.0059	.0019							
E_{C4}	-.1209			$.1865^+$			.3172			.0246	-.2196	-.0033	.0426	$-.2134^+$	.0014							
M_{C4}	.1675			.0911			-.2093			$.4889^*$	.2970	-.0013	.2117	-.1899	.0023			.2609				
M_{R4}	$.4573^*$	-.1743			$-.3649^+$			$.5538^*$			.7449	-.0039	.1268	$-.3281^+$	-.0125	.0169			.1755			
M_{A4}	$.3157^+$		-.1211			.2119			$.2487^+$		1.1626^*	-.0030	.1794	-.0081	.0054		.1910		$.1721^+$			
E_{R4}	.2221	-.1500			-.0307			-.1575			.1310	$.3270^+$	-.0182	-.0753	-.1042							.1329
E_{A4}	-.2549		.0316			.1785			.1476		.0128	.0575	.1113	-.0047	.0431							.1065
E_{C4}	-.1673			$.2369^+$			.1824			.0342	-.1138	-.1191	.0451	$-.2288^+$	.0417							.2323
M_{C4}	.1407			.0703			-.0730			$.4129^*$	.0934	-.0287	.1361	-.1236	.0420			.1583				.4099
M_{R4}	$.3500^*$	-.1418			$-.2294^+$			$.4571^*$			.2135	-.0788	.0743	$-.1945^+$	-.2065	.0120			.1600			.4587
M_{A4}	$.2607^+$		-.1038			.1368			$.2175^+$		$.3596^*$	-.0655	.1135	-.0052	.0956		.1538		$.1692^+$			.5702

[a] The model χ^2 of 53.2 with 42 d.f. is insignificant.

* Coefficient is more than twice its standard error.

+ Coefficient is more than 1.5 times its standard error.

reading and conduct) in the white school. In view of the importance of conduct for early achievement, it is noteworthy that the first conduct mark is the strongest influence on the conduct mark three semesters later. There is no visible effect of initial marks on children's expectations in the integrated school. In the middle-class school, children's reading marks affected second-grade expectations (borderline significance). Unlike children's earliest expectations, early marks *do* display effects capable of weathering the disturbances provided by the intervening school years.

In the integrated school, being popular with one's first-grade peers boosted children's second-grade marks (significantly so for arithmetic) just as was true for models within each of these grades separately. Peer effects in the white middle-class school also continue a pattern seen previously for both marks and children's expectations. The pattern is one of mixed signs and weak effects. Effects of peer-popularity on children's conduct expectations were consistently small and negative in previous models for the white school, and none of the previous effects even approached the substantial negative effect noted here.

First-grade absences appear to have one borderline effect in each school. As before, race has no discernible effects whatever.

Although gender effects continue to favor girls in both reading and conduct, only two effects in the integrated school attain borderline significance (conduct expectations and reading mark). The absence of IQ effects in the integrated lower-class school represents a noticeable weakening of effects compared to the basic models, while the absence of IQ effects for the white middle-class school is much the same as before. It is noteworthy that IQ has so little impact, especially considering the mandate in the integrated school for teachers to mark in terms of absolute achievement levels.

The effects in the endogenous portions of the models (the effects of conduct marks on reading and arithmetic marks, and the effects of children's current expectations on current marks) are minimally stronger than those for the corresponding basic models. The explained variance declined for both expectations and marks, but the decline for expectations (averaging 4%) is considerably smaller than the decline for marks (averaging 19%). The omission of immediately preceding marks as predictors probably accounts for all these observations.

Over all, the marks and expectations intervening between the beginning of the first semester and the end of the fourth, which are excluded from these models, contain a considerable amount of information that would have been missed had only the corresponding cross-sectional data been collected. From the perspective of enduring effects, these reduced models indicate that the intervening events are sufficient to disrupt the effects of initial expectations, marks, and peer group structure, with the following exceptions: parents' initial ability estimates may have lasting influences on marks; intitial marks, especially the conduct mark, display substantial persistence; and first-grade peer-popularity assists arithmetic performance in the integrated school and hinders conduct performance in the white school. The intervening events are sufficient to disrupt the paths from IQ to performance, even though these paths had consistently significant and relatively strong effects in the integrated school and noticeable effects on conduct in the middle-class school.

Altogether, much of the interplay between marks and expectations would have been missed if a two-year time frame rather than a half-year time frame had been adopted, and the influence of some exogenous variables would have been distored. In fact, with very young children we suspect even shorter time frames (matched exactly to each marking period) would be preferable.

Since this analysis shows that first marks persisted in both schools and the influence of IQ faded, and since other analyses indicate that initial marks affected children's expectations in the middle-class school and parents' second-grade expectations in both schools, our judgment is that the teacher's first formal evaluations of children's reading and arithmetic have great importance. We know that these evaluations are substantially determined by children's conduct, and that conduct evaluations in turn responded to gender and IQ in both the middle-class and the lower-class integrated schools. In fact, IQ affected only the conduct mark, not the other marks, in the middle-class school in the first cycle. *These data argue that children's deportment when they begin first grade may be a prepotent determinant of the level of their academic performance two years later (perhaps longer).* It would be hard to overrate the significance of this general cluster of findings.

ADDITIONAL VARIABLES: STANDARDIZED ACHIEVEMENT

Structural Models

A major purpose of this research is to understand the interplay between expectations (both children's and parents') and each child's unique marking history. This emphasis captures the daily routine of schooling as viewed by the participating individuals, but it has forced aside another basic issue, namely, the implication of various persons' expectations for children's eventual ability to read and to do arithmetic as judged by *objective* standards.

Marks are fallible indicators of actual proficiency. They have different distributions from school to school and they often bear different relations to IQ and to the other predetermined variables. For the schools involved in this research, marks could also have signified different kinds of behavior. In the black and integrated urban schools, for example, marks were supposed to reflect children's actual performance capabilities, while in the white suburban school children were supposed to be marked in terms of effort. Fortunately, as it turned out, these two seemingly polar marking policies led to marking practices that were remarkably similar across schools. The correlations between marks and standardized achievement (Table B.3) indicate that, while there might be some differences among schools in the way marks are assigned in the first grade, there is little difference in the later grades. Also, evidence drawn from questions about marking standards to which teachers replied directly in writing shows that assigned marks reflect both effort *and* caliber of performance in all three schools. Therefore, despite different official policies in the various schools, similar considerations actually governed how teachers assigned marks.

Having said this, we believe it is still desirable to study scores on standardized tests—ratings of performance purged of subjective judgments. Data from two standardized achievement tests for some of the children in the sample allow intensive investigation of the relation between objective performance capabilities and other variables. (The custom of giving IQ tests was abandoned by both school systems while this research was in progress.) The two tests, the *Iowa Test of Basic Skills* (ITBS) and the *California Achievement Test* (CAT), were the only achievement tests administered in more than one school in third grade. These tests were given only in third grade, so any patterns observed reflect the outcome of the schooling process for the entire series of cyclic models.

The Iowa tests were administered to three cohorts of children in the white suburban school, two cohorts in the integrated school, and one cohort in the black school. Each cohort was comprised of three to four classes. The California test was administered to a single cohort in both the integrated and black schools. Both tests were given as a routine part of school-district-wide testing programs. Information is available on fewer cohorts from the lower-class schools because these schools were included in our research later than the middle-class school. (Thus the reduced case base is not a consequence of selective attrition.)

Table 7.3 presents the means and standard deviations for these tests by cohort. This table duplicates findings already seen in Table 5.1. Differences within a school between the average level of children's reading and arithmetic performance are small compared to differences between the white middle-class school and the other two schools. The middle-class children outperformed the children in both lower-class schools, with the lower-class children about 1 year or more below the standards specified by the tests, and the middle-class children generally over half a year above the test norms.

Outcomes for the two different tests agree remarkably well in both lower-class schools, especially considering that the Iowa test was given about 6 months later than the California test. Another fact worth noting is that differences within schools are small. This provides direct support for the fact that the reduced case base caused by absence of some entire cohorts should not be considered a serious threat to the overall analysis.

Correlations presented in Appendix B indicate that third-grade marks in reading and arithmetic in both the white and integrated schools correlate about 0.5 with Iowa scores,[1] and that correlations are slightly higher (averaging about 0.6) for the black school. The California scores for tests taken in third grade correlate about 0.7 with third-grade marks in the integrated school; in the black school these correlations average 0.7 for reading but below 0.5 for arithmetic. Thus, between one-quarter and one-half of the variance in marks is associated with objectively measured performance capabilities. This provides indirect evidence that the models, in predicting school marks, do predict actual performance capabilities.

More direct evidence of the models' validity for predicting standardized achievement can be adduced from the models themselves, however. Standardized achievement scores can replace marks as the ultimate endogeneous variables in the basic models and we can then observe whether model structure changes as a consequence.

We now turn specifically to this question. We inserted the standardized achievement measures as the dependent variables in the model for the transition into third grade (T4–T5), the latest model for which the timing of the standardized achievement testing could be unambiguously specified.[2] Tables 7.4, 7.5, and 7.6 contain the parameter estimates for the model in Figure 5.10, with M_{R5} and M_{A5} replaced by scores from the ITBS in the white and integrated schools, and by scores from the CAT in the integrated school.[3]

[1] The signs on all correlations between marks, expectations, and achievement test scores are changed so that relationships emerge in the intuitively correct direction.

[2] The April-May ITBS testing could have overlapped the securing of children's expectations at the end of third grade (T6).

[3] The comparable models for the black lower-class school could not be estimated because the appropriate covariance matrices were not positive definite. This is not surprising given the few cases in the single cohorts in this school receiving each of the standardized tests. The covariance matrix for the single cohort with CAT scores in the integrated school was also not positive definite.

Table 7.3

Means and Standard Deviations for Third Grade Iowa Test of Basic Skills and California Achievement Test Scores by Cohort[a]

	Reading			Arithmetic		
	Mean	S.D.	N	Mean	S.D.	N
IOWA TEST OF BASIC SKILLS						
White Middle-Class School						
Cohort 1	4.6	1.07	98	4.3	.86	98
Cohort 2	4.9	1.03	106	4.7	.63	103
Cohort 3	4.6	1.08	72	4.6	.77	72
Integrated Lower-Class School						
Cohort 1	2.7	.82	96	3.0	.70	94
Cohort 2	2.8	.73	72	3.0	.76	74
Black Lower-Class School						
Cohort 1	2.8	.81	73	2.8	.60	71
CALIFORNIA ACHIEVEMENT TEST						
Integrated Lower-Class School						
Cohort 1	2.0	.93	98	2.0	.79	94
Black Lower-Class School						
Cohort 1	2.0	1.13	88	2.0	.71	87

[a]Testing was carried out in April-May (ITBS) or October (CAT) of the third-grade year. Scores for both tests are recorded as grade equivalents. A child with a score of 2.5 is performing at a level typical of students half-way through second grade. A superior second-grade student receiving a score of 4.0 is therefore not doing fourth grade work, but rather is doing as well on the test as a typical student beginning fourth grade.

The χ^2 values for the original models in the T4–T5 cycle were rather poor as a set, and the substitution of achievement test scores for marks as ultimate endogenous variables leads to similarly poor fits. The only model with an acceptable fit involves the odd cases in the white school with ITBS. Some χ^2's improved substantially compared to the previous models containing M_{R5} and M_{A5}, but others became worse—notably the even cases with ITBS in the integrated school and the full data set with ITBS for the white school. Overall, however, there seem to be no systematic differences between the present χ^2's and those reported previously.

To anticipate a little, comparison of Tables 7.4, 7.5, and 7.6 with Tables 6.7 and 6.13 leads to a single basic conclusion: the insertion of achievement test scores in place of marks for reading and arithmetic leads to minimal differences in the paths not directly connected to these variables and to only minor changes in the paths directly related to the substituted variables.

The structure of the achievement model in the white middle-class school is very similar to that of the mark model, the largest difference being the increased importance of the direct contribution of IQ to performance. To the extent that teachers were capable of controlling ability in assigning marks on the basis of effort, this would be expected. Perhaps the most encouraging difference between models is the improved determinacy in children's achievement (69% reading, 61% arithmetic) compared to marks (38%, 22%). IQ undoubtedly accounts for much of the improvement. It is, of course, critical to know that the overall model fares well in explaining children's achievement, because the implication is that objectively standardized performance responds to the same forces as the fallible indicators (teachers' marks). There would be much less incentive for explaining marks if one believed that they did not reflect children's capability to read and to do arithmetic.

When marks in reading and arithmetic in the integrated lower-class school are replaced by the corresponding ITBS scores, structural patterns also change very little. The paths indirectly related to the achievement variables show miniscule changes, while the paths directly involved with achievement show some minor changes.

With information available for CAT scores for only a single cohort, it is not surprising that the model is not entirely well behaved. The few differences with respect to paths, the fact that ACH_{R5} is perhaps too well explained, as well as problems with a covariance matrix,

Table 7.4

Structural Coefficients for Figure 5.7 with Standardized Achievement Test Scores (ITBS) as Dependent Variables[a]: White Middle-Class School, Metric Coefficients in Upper Half of Table, Standardized Coefficients in Lower Half, and Determinacy[b]

	IQ	SEX	$ABIL_3$	PE_{R3}	PE_{A3}	PE_{C3}	E_{R4}	E_{A4}	E_{C4}	M_{R4}	M_{A4}	M_{C4}	$ABIL_5$	PE_{R5}	PE_{A5}	PE_{C5}	E_{R5}	E_{A5}	E_{C5}	M_{C5}	ACH_{R6}	ACH_{A6}	R^2
$ABIL_5$	-.0163+ -.0024	.1987 -.1080	.8410* .8176*							.6090* .4295*	.0437 -.0758	.0809 .0524											
PE_{R5}	.0069 .0053	-.0298 -.1112		.4964* .3600*						.3232* .2727*			.0507* .1461*										
PE_{A5}	.0066+ .0061+	.2821* .2148*			.0687+ .1262+						.1486 .1169		.2824* .2099*										
PE_{C5}	.0061 .0035	.1369 .0228				.3517* .3621*						.3037* .2202*	.0409+ .1249+										
E_{R5}	-.0157* -.0099+	-.0313 -.0579					.1315 .1051			.1254 .0602			.0108 .0651	.1579+ .2288+									
E_{A5}	-.0048 .0000	.2488+ .1152						.4380* .3381*			.3028+ .2377+		-.1732 -.0316		.3198 .2207								
E_{C5}	-.0031 -.0070	.0854 .0080							.3236* .2994*			.3386* .2620*	.0457 .0690			.0497 .1463							
M_{C5}	.0034 .0062	-.0335+ -.1734+							.1919 .0809			.1116 .0419	.0585 .0718			.1383 .1054			.0066+ .1645+				
ACH_{R6}[b]	.0467* .0360*	-.2853 -.2109					.0969 .0916			-.0864 -.0532			.2020+ .2256+	.4879+ .6711*			.1369 -.0389			.0174 -.0051			
ACH_{A6}[b]	.0317* .0285*	-.2962+ -.1628						-.1737 -.0732			.1357+ .2230+		.1175+ .1321+		.3359 .1734			.2407+ .1525		.1116 .0389			
$ABIL_5$	-.0341	-.0632	.7670*							.2655*	-.0482	.0381											.7258
PE_{P5}	.1194	-.1028		.3873*						.2664*			.2308*										.6364
PE_{A5}	.1599+	.2295*			.1577+						.1358		.3836*										.4796
PE_{C5}	.0762	.0202				.3806*						.2422*	.1893+										.4053
E_{R5}	-.2445+	-.0583					.1231			.0641			.1121	.2493+									.1849
E_{A5}	.0001	.0955						.3705*			.2140+		-.0447		.1711								.3496
E_{C5}	-.1482	.0069							.2814*			.2793*	.1013			.1417							.2899
M_{C5}	.1415	-.1612+							.0822			.0483	.1142			.1105			.1780+				.2016
ACH_{R6}[b]	.4650*	-.1112					.0562			-.0296			.2034+	.3829*			-.0204			-.0029			.6864
ACH_{A6}[b]	.5031*	-.1173						-.0698			.1746+		.1628+		.1170			.1326		.0301			.6066

[a] Ach_{R6} and Ach_{A6} are Iowa Test of Basic Skills scores. Metric coefficients are for the odd-numbered and full data sets. The data matrix for the even data set was singular. Standardized coefficients are provided for the full data set only. χ^2 with 96 d.f. = 115.1 and 129.9 for the even and full data sets respectively.

[b] The Iowa tests are scored in grade equivalents. The signs on paths leading to the Ach_{R6} and Ach_{A6} variables have been reversed to make them intuitively correct.

*Coefficient is more than twice its standard error.

+Coefficient is more than 1.5 times its standard error.

Table 7.5

Structural Coefficients for Figure 5.7 with Standardized Achievement Test Scores (ITBS) as Dependent Variables[a]: Integrated Lower-Class School, Metric Coefficients in Upper Half of Table, Standardized Coefficients in Lower Half, and Determinacy[b]

	RACE	IQ	SEX	$ABIL_3$	PE_{R3}	PE_{A3}	PE_{C3}	E_{R4}	E_{A4}	E_{C4}	M_{R4}	M_{A4}	M_{C4}	$ABIL_5$	PE_{R5}	PE_{A5}	PE_{C5}	E_{R5}	E_{A5}	E_{C5}	M_{C5}	ACH_{R6}	ACH_{A6}	R^2
$ABIL_5$	-.2422 .0841 -.1121	.0039 -.0075 -.0003	.0306 .1860 .0849	-.0889 c .2312+							.0656 .3296 .1696	.3147 -.0401 .0304	.2214+ .3475* .2802*											
PE_{R5}	.0633* -.4597 -.1815	.0000* .0369 .0118	-.0976 -.3271+ -.2252		.0445 .1874 .1003						.1817 -.2046 .0902			.4819* .2853* .3750*										
PE_{A5}	-.0585+ -.2116 -.1222	.0028* .0197 .0098	-.1920 -.0053 -.1066			.3918* .5333* .3741*						.0386 .0057 .0657		.4656* .0451* .2500										
PE_{C5}	-.0205 -.0767 -.0145	.0030 .0083 .0049	-.1427 -.0049 -.0694				-.0155 .1598 .0796						.5237* .2205+ .3384*	.0378 .0746 .0740										
E_{R5}	-.0902 -.1462 -.0959	.0190 .0053 .0174	-.3731+ -.4533* -.4179*					.2583* .3772* .3609			-.1981 -.0336 -.1816			-.1539* .3483 .1794	.0628 -.1686 -.0821									
E_{A5}	-.3701+ .0171 -.1784	-.0015 -.0104 -.0067	.2128 .2760+ .2814						.2554 .2394+ .2758			-.0299 .1778 .1252		.3323 .1610 .1915		-.1564 .0798 -.0582								
E_{C5}	-.1115 -.0200 -.0573	.0059 .0052 .0031	-.0424 -.1865 -.0867							.3081* .5107* .3968			.2130 -.0669 .1123	-.0524 .0158 -.0193			.0526+ .2180 .1320							
M_{C5}	-.0127 -.0545 .0111	.0074 .0079 .0064	-.0654 .0640 -.0114							.2343 .0478 .0725			.3971* .2750* .3166*	-.0338 .0843 .0155			.0229 .0138 .0561			.1002 .0662 .0851				
ACH_{R6}[b]	-.3584+ .0890 -.0669	.0091 .0277 .0149	.0480 -.0424 .0269					-.0808 .0349 -.0165			.5265* -.0132* .3085			-.1463 .1316 .0295	.1993 -.0278 .1157			-.1023 .2113 .0569			.0357 -.0586 -.0622			
ACH_{A6}[b]	-.2366 .1456 -.0433	.0259* .0350* .0288*	-.1211+ -.2331+ -.1702+						-.1584+ .2265 .0983			.4136* .1635* .2733		-.1354 -.0894 -.0525		.2082+ .0192 .1097			.1091+ .1639+ .1192+		-.0397 -.0669 -.0223			
$ABIL_5$	-.0744	-.0052	.0570	.2294+							.1944	.0327	.2890*											.2709
PE_{R5}	-.1168	.1748	-.1465+		.0920						.1002			.3634*										.3464
PE_{A5}	-.0872	.1613	-.0769			.3504*						.0761		.2687*										.3453
PE_{C5}	-.0120	.0939	-.0582				.0886						.4361*	.0924										.3336
E_{R5}	-.0676	.2824	-.2980*					.3087*			-.2211			.1904	-.0899									.1973
E_{A5}	-.1150	-.0992	.1836+						.2252+			.1310		.1860		-.0526								.1339
E_{C5}	-.0571	.0707	-.0874							.3715*			.1739	-.0289			.1587							.3160
M_{C5}	.0098	.1299	-.0102							.0600			.4334*	.0206			.0596			.0752				.3543
ACH_{R6}[b]	-.0473	.2419	.0192					-.0141			.3767*			.0314	.1272			.0571			-.0499			.3938
ACH_{A6}[b]	-.0330	.5053*	-.1314+						.0950			.3382*		-.0604		.1173			.1410+		-.0193			.7302

[a] Ach_{R6} and Ach_{A6} are Iowa Test of Basic Skills scores. Metric coefficients are for the odd, even and full data sets, while the standardized coefficients in the lower portion of the table are for only the full data set. For the odd data set, χ^2=159 with 96 d.f.: for the even data set χ^2=292.1 with 87 d.f.; and χ^2=126.3 with 96 d.f. for the full data set. The small case base for the odd and even replications make the modest differences between these models of doubtful importance.

[b] The Iowa tests are scored in grade equivalents. The signs on paths leading to the Ach_{R6} and Ach_{A6} variables have been reversed to make them intuitively correct.

[c] $ABIL_3$ was deleted from the even-case model, making this model comparable to the earlier even model with marks as the dependent variables.

*Coefficient is more than twice its standard error.

+Coefficient is more than 1.5 times its standard error.

Table 7.6

Structural Coefficients for Figure 5.7 with California Achievement Test Scores (CAT) as Dependent Variables;[a] Integrated Lower-Class School, Metric Coefficients in Upper Half of Table, Standardized Coefficients in Lower-Half, and Determinacy[b]

	RACE	IQ	SEX	$ABIL_3$	PE_{R3}	PE_{A3}	PE_{C3}	E_{R4}	E_{A4}	E_{C4}	M_{R4}	M_{A4}	M_{C4}	$ABIL_5$	PE_{R5}	PE_{A5}	PE_{C5}	E_{R5}	E_{A5}	E_{C5}	M_{C5}	ACH_{R5}	ACH_{A5}	R^2
$ABIL_5$	-.1123	-.0004	.0797	.2354							.1593	.0389	.2751+											
PE_{R5}	-.1655	.0058	-.2060		.1657						.1289			.3634*										
PE_{A5}	-.1358	.0140	-.1077			.3892*						.0277		.2400+										
PE_{C5}	-.0101	.0043	-.0726				.0764						.3350*	.0769										
E_{R5}	-.1009	.0195	-.4193*					.3983+			-.2064			.1741	-.0715									
E_{A5}	-.1891	-.0021	.2803						.2684			.0893		.1876		-.0618								
E_{C5}	-.0460	.0003	-.0865							.3815*			.1218	-.0085			.1348							
M_{C5}	.0160	.0055	-.0102							.0642			.3181*	.0198			.0495			.1021				
ACH_{R5} [b]	-.0888	.0600*	-.2817+					.7140*			-.0301			-.0228	.3962*			-.1304			.1051			
ACH_{A5} [b]	.0345	.0250*	.1705						.0266			.4296*		.0018		.1210			-.0679		.1937			
$ABIL_5$	-.0746	-.0055	.0535	.2337							.1826	.0419	.2838+											.2678
PE_{R5}	-.1060	.0859	-.1334		.1513						.1425			.3504*										.3422
PE_{A5}	-.0963	.2289	-.0774			.3623*						.0319		.2563+										.3596
PE_{C5}	-.0084	.0830	-.0611				.0853						.4328*	.0963										.3264
E_{R5}	-.0708	.3158	-.2978*					.3393+			-.2501			.1840	-.0784									.2172
E_{A5}	-.1220	-.0319	.1829						.2191			.0934		.1822		-.0562								.1300
E_{C5}	-.0459	.0076	-.0872							.3572*			.1887	-.0128			.1616							.3035
M_{C5}	.0141	.1110	-.0091							.0532			.4365*	.0246			.0526			.0904				.3496
ACH_{R5} [b]	-.0505	.7849*	-.1620+					.4924*			-.0296			-.0195	.3517*			-.1056			.0676			.9942
ACH_{A5} [b]	.0246	.4100*	.1232						.0241			.4975*		.0019		.1219			-.0752		.1567			.8648

[a] Ach_{R5} and Ach_{A5} are California Achievement Test scores. All coefficients are for the full data set. $\chi^2 = 135.9$, d.f.=96.

[b] The California Achievement Test is scored in grade equivalents. The signs on paths leading to the Ach_{R5} and Ach_{A5} variables have been reversed to make them intuitively correct.

*Coefficient is more than twice its standard error.

+Coefficient is more than 1.5 times its standard error.

lead us to discount this model. Clearly, however, this analysis at least shows that a change of standardized tests is not likely to challenge substantially our contention that the models behave similarly to what we would expect had standardized test scores been used in place of teachers' marks throughout the whole model estimation process.

Again, the overall conclusion is that the structure of the model is very similar when standardized achievement test scores replace marks as the ultimate endogenous variables.

Single Equation Regression Models

The previous section concludes that the findings presented in Chapter 6 would probably have not been substantially altered if achievement measures had been substituted for marks in the models for the white and integrated schools. By analogy, the implication for a similar substitution in the models for the black school may be the same.

More direct evidence on this matter is provided by several single equation regression models that could be estimated for the black lower-class school, and for purposes of comparison, the single equation regressions were also estimated for the other two schools. These equations are of two kinds. The first equation focuses on the contribution of teachers' marks and of children's and parents' expectations to standardized achievement. The second equation includes an additional set of predictors and hence controls for these further variables.

The parameters for the single equation regression models are summarized in Table 7.7. Two conclusions are reached. First, for the black school, marks explain a large fraction of the variance in achievement. Second, study of marks and other variables in relation to standardized achievement reveals that, while the results for the black school do not fit very closely with the results presented in Chapter 6, the results here are consistent with respect to our understanding of the behavior of marks, as well as children's and parents' expectations.

Overall, insertion of the achievement information in the models made only minor changes in the paths previously estimated when marks were the ultimate endogenous variables. This invariance provides strong direct evidence that the implications drawn from the mark models in Chapter 6 can be applied equally well to discussions of children's standardized achievement. The close match of the achievement and mark models in the middle-class school is especially gratifying, because it demonstrates that the particular marking policy supposedly in force in this school did not interfere with the modeling of children's achievement measured objectively.

The Relationship between Conduct and Standardized Achievement

Some further regression models were estimated to assess the role of conduct in predicting standardized achievement. Using conduct as a predictor of reading and arithmetic performance is one way to filter nonperformance factors out of the other coefficients affecting marks. As noted, however, conduct could contribute to marks either because of halo factors or because children's conduct affects their ability to learn. Or, of course, both cases could be true. To shed light on the relative weight of these two explanations, conduct marks were inserted as direct predictors of achievement scores. The direct contributions of the conduct mark to standardized achievement are, with one exception out of ten, small in size and mixed in sign (Table 7.8). This finding undercuts the notion that poor conduct directly depresses achievement as a consequence of the misbehaving child's being distracted from learning. It thus seems more likely that poor conduct leads the teacher to assign a lower mark on the basis of (negative) halo effects, and that indirect negative effects follow.

On the whole, the analyses leave little doubt that early social development, insofar as it is measured by the conduct mark, has important effects on marks, and indirectly thereby on achievement. Berkeley (1978) found that kindergarten teachers in the middle-class school are aware of this. They spend much of their time training students in conduct, in the belief that such preparation can enhance performance in the first grade. Berkeley found that kindergarten teachers in the two lower-class schools spent less time this way. Our analysis underscores the wisdom of the middle-class teachers' kindergarten strategy, because marks in reading and arithmetic often responded to conduct marks in all three schools, especially in early cycles. Along similar lines, parents have considerable efficacy on conduct performance and this offers a conduit for positive influences to flow from home to academic achievement.

Differences in conduct associated with gender may be particularly important in the first two grades. Teachers' "biases" in the sample are expressed entirely via conduct marks and not by marks in the other two areas. The schooling process is similar for both sexes—conduct always affects achievement—but the outcome differs because girls are universally rated better in conduct than boys. Also, since expectations *follow* rather than precede achievement, early high marks in conduct could contribute positively to the self-image, which then later could mediate superior achievement.

There is no outside criterion, like standardized test scores, against which to assess the validity of conduct measures. However, since conduct has considerable

Table 7.7

Prediction of Standardized Achievement Scores (ITBS, CAT)[a,b,c,d]

Dependent Variable	Independent Variables									Determinacy
ITBS - READING	M_{R5}	E_{R5}	PE_{R5}	RACE	SEX	IQ-G3	$ABIL_5$	$PEER_6$	ABS_6	
White Middle-Class School										
3 Variables	+.540*	-.161	+1.029*							.553
All Variables	+.267^{+}	+.040	+.577*	----	.186^{+}	.036*	+.176^{+}	-.077	-.003	.725
Integrated Lower-Class School										
3 Variables	+.526*	-.013	-.033							.336
All Variables	+.426*	-.025	-.084	.060	.013	.014^{+}	+.031	-.118	-.002	.389
Black Lower-Class School										
3 Variables	+1.364*	-.217^{+}	-.113							.864
All Variables†	+1.454*	-.247	+.028	----	.301^{+}	.009	-.540*	-.430	-.002	.939
CAT - READING										
White Middle-Class School[e]										
Integrated Lower-Class School										
3 Variables	+.830*	+.031	+.111							.762
All Variables	+.659*	+.001	+.038	.034	.218^{+}	.033*	-.077	e	e	.922
Black Lower-Class School										
3 Variables†	1.672*	-.127	+.264^{+}							.941
All Variables†	1.834*	-.167	+.535*	----	-.249	-.016	-.396^{+}	e	e	.941
ITBS - ARITHMETIC	M_{A5}	E_{A5}	PE_{A5}	RACE	SEX	IQ-G3	$ABIL_5$	$PEER_6$	ABS_6	
White Middle-Class School										
3 Variables	+.500*	+.131	+.485*							.379
All Variables	+.443*	+.087	+.094	----	.159^{+}	.032*	+.119^{+}	-.042	.002	.672
Integrated Lower-Class School										
3 Variables	+.366*	+.069	+.268*							.397
All Variables	+.235*	+.155^{+}	+.162^{+}	.094	.219*	.037*	-.032	.686^{+}	.001	.673
Black Lower-Class School										
3 Variables	+.613*	-.017	+.123							.598
All Variables	+.491^{+}	+.003	+.033	----	-.213	.010	+.123	-.055	.002	.667
CAT - ARITHMETIC										
White Middle-Class School[f]										
Integrated Lower-Class School										
3 Variables	+.694*	-.095	+.241*							.751
All Variables	+.527*	-.084	+.167^{+}	-.065	-.098	.024*	+.030	e	e	.868
Black Lower-Class School										
3 Variables	+.355*	+.052	+.488*							.549
All Variables	+.238	+.073	+.404*	----	-.381*	.012	+.068	e	e	.651

[a]ITBS = Iowa Test of Basic Skills (recorded in units of grade equivalents)
CAT = California Achievement Test (recorded in units of grade equivalents)

[b] * indicates parameter is at least twice its standard error.
+ indicates parameter is 1.5 to 1.99 standard errors.
† indicates the error variance was set as near 5% of the total variance as possible to eliminate small negative variances provided by LISREL without this condition. This additional constraint made no substantial changes to the other parameter estimates.

[c]χ^2 = 0 for all models with free error variances (since d.f.=0). χ^2 indicated acceptable fits for all models noted in † above except for CAT reading in the black school with all variables where χ^2 = 11.0, d.f.=1.

[d]Signs of parameters related to marks, expectations, ability estimates and IQ changed so that they are intuitively correct.

[e]The timing of CAT testing eliminated this as a justifiable control variable.

[f]The CAT was not taken by pupils in this school.

Table 7.8

Prediction of Standardized Achievement in Reading and Arithmetic with Conduct Mark Included[a,b]

Dependent Variables	Independent Variables						Determinacy
White Middle-Class School	M_{C5}	M_{R5}	SEX	IQ	ABS	RACE	
ITBS-Reading	.0638	.6417*	-.2911*	+.0446*	.0031	---	.5921
Integrated Lower-Class School							
ITBS-Reading	-.1216	.4158*	-.0149	+.0156*	.0017	-.0429	.3915
Black Lower-Class School							
ITBS-Reading	.0938	1.1747*	-.0853	-.0014	.0015	---	.8214
White Middle-Class School	M_{C5}	M_{A5}	SEX	IQ	ABS	RACE	
ITBS-Arithmetic	.0588	.5368*	-.1322	+.0360*	-.0010	---	.6372
Integrated Lower-Class School							
ITBS-Arithmetic	-.0809	.2577*	-.1882*	+.0355*	-.0024	-.0670	.5988
Black Lower-Class School							
ITBS-Arithmetic	.0310	.5007*	.1919+	+.0153+	.0005	---	.6447
White Middle-Class School[c]	M_{C5}	M_{R5}	SEX	IQ	ABS[d]	RACE	
Integrated Lower-Class School							
CAT-Reading	-.0251	.6519*	-.2292+	+.0336*	---	-.0366	.9186
Black Lower-Class School							
CAT-Reading†	-.0878	1.9771*	.1613	-.0176	---	---	.9399
White Middle-Class School[c]	M_{C5}	M_{A5}	SEX	IQ	ABS[d]	RACE	
Integrated Lower-Class School							
CAT-Arithmetic	.0879	.5402*	.0665	+.0258*	---	.0588	.8418
Black Lower-Class School							
CAT-Arithmetic	.3431*	.2288	.4465*	+.0289*	---	---	.5803

[a]Signs of coefficients reversed so that high marks, high achievement and high IQ are positively related. Other signs are in direction implied by definitions of variables Chapter 5.

[b]χ^2 = 0 for all models with free error variances (since d.f.=0). χ^2 indicated acceptable fit for model noted in † above.

[c]The CAT was not taken by pupils in this school.

[d]The timing of CAT testing eliminated this as a reasonable predictor.

* indicates the coefficient is at least twice its standard error.
\+ indicates the coefficient is 1.5 to 1.99 standard errors.
† indicates error variance was set as near 5% of the total variance as possible to eliminate small negative variances provided by LISREL without this condition. This additional constraint made no substantial changes to the other parameter estimates.

influence on marks in reading and arithmetic, some of its importance is reflected in the caliber of the child's academic performance. Other important effects could be the labeling of the child as a "troublemaker" or "inattentive." Unfortunately, we have no way to assess these effects.

ADDITIONAL VARIABLES: FRIENDS' EXPECTATIONS

For the young child there are at least four important sets of expectations: their own, parents', teachers', and peers'. All of these are discussed previously except for peers', so far mentioned only in terms of the peer-popularity ratings (PEER). We now turn to more direct evidence about peers' expectations, available only for second- and third-grade children in the last two cohorts. The data are thus somewhat limited.

Which peers are important to children? It seems unlikely that children could respond to the expectations of as many as thirty classmates. Rather, a child's close friends are probably the peers likely to communicate expectations about the child. We therefore obtained children's expectations for "best friend" and "second-best friend." Since it takes time for friendships to develop and for children to come to recognize one another's academic strengths and weaknesses, we ascertained friends' expectations near the end of the school year. This timing also made it less likely that measurement operations would disrupt the natural course of peers' expectation formation.

Gathering expectations for friends involved a minor modification of the usual method for gathering expectations. After the children had given their self-expectations during the year-end interview, they were asked to name their best friend, and then to guess how well this friend would perform in both reading and arithmetic. The interviewer then asked for the name of the second-best friend and about how well the child expected that second-best friend to perform in reading and arithmetic.

By asking for specific names of friends we could determine the set of children who selected any particular child for a friend and hence could ascertain the expectations that this set of self-selected friends held for the child. "Friends' expectations in reading and arithmetic" (FE_R and FE_A) are the average value of the expectations held for a child by the set of children who volunteered themselves to be either the best or second-best friend of the child in question. If no one claimed to be the best or second-best friend of a particular child, that child received no score for friends' expectations. Both this "lack of selection" and occasional selection of friends outside the classroom slightly reduced the sample size for friends' expectation measures compared to the total number of children interviewed.

Patterns in Friends' Expectations

Children's expectations for their best friends uniformly exceeded those for their second-best friends (Table 7.9). So consistent a pattern is unlikely to occur by chance ($P < 0.001$), and several of the specific differences between best and second-best friends' expectations reach significance at the 0.05 level (T4 reading in the white and integrated schools, T4 arithmetic in the black school). This pattern meshes well with the notion that the closer a friend, the more difficult it is to think of that person as being inferior; or, alternatively, the more highly one regards a person, the closer a friend one tries to become.

Expectations for friends are consistently lower in the two lower-class schools than in the middle-class school. Marks *are* generally lower in the lower-class schools (Table 5.2), but the difference in marks across schools is much more pronounced than the modest differences across schools in expectations for friends. In the middle-class school, average expectations for friends and the average marks assigned, with one exception (grade-two arithmetic), differ by less than a quarter of a grade-point. In the lower-class schools, this gap is about a full grade-point. The substantial gap between actual marks and children's expectations for friends in the lower-class schools is reminiscent of the gap noted for the children themselves. The lower-class children hold unrealistic expectations for their friends in the same way they hold unrealistic expectations for themselves. This invites the conclusion that whatever causes lower-class children to hold unrealistic expectations is not likely to hinge entirely on factors that involve only the children themselves. It suggests that a failure to process information, rather than some kind of psychological defense mechanism, is at work in causing expectations to be off-target. Indeed, in the lower-class schools, comparisons of self-expectations (Table 5.2) with those for best friends (Table 7.9) reveals no consistent pattern or significant differences. In contrast, in the middle-class school the children's expectations for themselves are consistently (and significantly in three of four instances) lower than the expectations they hold for their best friends. In fact, in the middle-class school children's self-expectations are even consistently (although not significantly) lower than their expectations for their second-best friends. In the lower-class schools, the reduction in expectations from best to second-best friend is sufficient to make self-expectations consistently higher than expectations for second-best friends (significant in five of eight comparisons) in these schools.

Table 7.9

Means and Standard Deviations for Friends' Expectations[a]

	Child's Expectations for Best Friend			Child's Expectations for Second-Best Friend			Friends' Expectations for Child		
	N	Mean	S.D.	N	Mean	S.D.	N	Mean	S.D.
White Middle-Class School									
Grade 2 Year-end (T4)									
Reading	144	1.47	.57	144	1.63	.59	119	1.59	.57
Arithmetic	144	1.54	.55	144	1.67	.61	119	1.66	.57
Grade 3 Year-end (T6)									
Reading	158	1.52	.54	158	1.61	.58	123	1.62	.57
Arithmetic	158	1.61	.56	158	1.66	.58	123	1.68	.53
Integrated Lower-Class School									
Grade 2 Year-end (T4)									
Reading	127	1.66	.85	125	1.92	.89	102	1.93	.82
Arithmetic	127	1.83	.81	125	1.99	.96	102	1.95	.81
Grade 3 Year-end (T6)									
Reading	152	1.77	.92	152	1.86	.93	122	1.87	.82
Arithmetic	152	1.88	.81	152	1.99	.91	122	2.00	.82
Black Lower-Class School									
Grade 2 Year-end (T4)									
Reading	127	1.79	.87	128	1.95	.98	116	1.97	.85
Arithmetic	127	1.78	.87	128	1.98	.97	116	1.96	.85
Grade 3 Year-end (T6)									
Reading	130	1.75	.85	129	1.95	.92	111	1.91	.82
Arithmetic	130	1.81	.82	130	1.95	.92	111	1.97	.83

[a]Limitations on the comprehension and reporting abilities of the youngest children precluded our gathering friends' expectations in first grade.

Average expectations held for the child by each child's self-professed friends look very much like those the child holds for second-best friends. Children's self-expectations are uniformly lower than those held for them by their friends in the middle-class school, while children's self-expectations are uniformly higher than those held for them by friends in the two lower-class schools.

In sum, while the middle-class children have generally realistic expectations, they hold slightly less optimistic expectations for themselves (1.71 to 1.89) than they do for their friends (1.47 to 1.67). In the lower-class schools, children's expectations for themselves are generally more optimistic than middle-class children's, especially in reading, but they view themselves (1.63 to 1.93) as being about as good as their best friend (1.66 to 1.88) and better than their second-best friend (1.86 to 1.99). The gaps between marks and *all* expectations (for self, best friend, and second-best friend and friends' average expectations) are much smaller in the middle-class school than in the lower-class schools, although marks fall below the expectations for friends at all times in all schools with one trivial exception (grade-two reading, white middle-class: 1.61 vs. 1.63).

In the integrated school there were no consistent differences between the expectations that blacks and whites held for their friends, or in their friends' expectations for them. Friends' expectations did, however, differ by sex in the two lower-class schools. Girls in the lower-class schools held higher expectations for their friends than did boys (0.17 points on average) and girls' friends held higher expectations for the girls than boys' friends held for boys (0.25 grade-points on average). Since children's friends are often other children of the same sex, all these observations may be accounted for by the proposition that lower-class children of both sexes held higher expectations for girls than for boys. This proposition, along with the sex specificity of friendships, would account for the findings that lower-class girls hold higher expectations for their friends, and that friends of the girls hold higher expectations for them. There are no sex differences in peers' average expectations in the middle-class school. It is not clear why sex differences emerged only in the lower-class schools. In only the black school at T1 did we detect any differences by gender in teachers' reading marks. In no school did we detect differences in arithmetic marks, and girls were rated better in conduct in all schools.

Effects of Teachers' Marks

Children's expectations for their friends are based, to a modest extent, on the actual classroom performance of their friends: significant correlations between childrens' marks and their friends' expectations appear in all three schools in both second and third grades (upper half of Table 7.10). Since friends' expectations were measured at year's end, it is not surprising that slightly larger correlations tend to appear for year-end marks compared to mid-year marks.

Children's own expectations show only scattered (eight out of twenty-four) significant, although generally positive, correlations with their friends' expectations for them (lower half of Table 7.10). Children's expectations for themselves are therefore far from a perfect mirror image of their friends' expectations for them, and the correlations are about as large as one would expect if both the children's own expectations and their friends' expectations converged minimally on the child's classroom performance (marks).

Examination of the correlations between children's self-expectations and the expectations they hold for their best and second-best friends reveals that the mid-year correlations for both second and third grades are essentially zero, while the year-end correlations are consistently positive and range from 0 to 0.32 (about half attain significance). These correlations indicate there is a slight, although measurable, tendency for children to come to expect their friends to do about as well as the children themselves expect to do over the school year.

It is possible that something in our procedure for obtaining expectations produced this relation as an artifact—perhaps some children merely repeated for their friends what they had responded for themselves. However, this is made less likely by the consistent mean differences between expectations for the self and others, and by the consistent differences found between best and second-best friends. It seems more plausible that children form friendships within ability levels; that is, children of high ability form friendships with other high-ability children. Some models presented below implicitly control for marks and hence provide a test of this hypothesis. There, the absence of paths between self-expectations and friends' expectations (with marks controlled) indicates no direct effects are necessary to explain the correlations; therefore, formation of friendships within ability levels remains a reasonable explanation.

A parallel question concerns the consistency between children's expectations for their friends and those friends' expectations for them. Is there a reciprocity between friends' expectations—if I expect you to do well, do you also think I will do well? Our data are not perfectly suited to answering this question because the set of children who provided expectations for a child does not necessarily include the children that child would select as best and second-best friends. Nonetheless, there is probably no reciprocity of expectations, because correlating children's expectations for best and second-best friends with friends' expectations for them produces many mixed signs, with only two of twenty-four values being positive and significant. While children's friends may be a social mirror reflecting information back to the child, the expectations children send out are not at all like the expectations reflected back. The friendship mirrors in the white middle-class and integrated lower-class schools are like carnival "distorting mirrors." The friendship mirror in the black lower-class school may be slightly less distorting—and hence provide a more exact reflection—than in the other schools, since both the significant correlations occurred in this school and all values in this school were positive.

The lack of consistency in the social reflection of expectations is matched by dissonance or imbalance in expectations for best and second-best friends. Only three of the twelve correlations between children's expectations for their best and second-best friends attain significance and all three are for arithmetic, one coming from each of the three schools. These correlations are too small (averaging 0.10 over all) and too scattered to indicate any substantial responsiveness to "cognitive dissonance" or "balance" considerations. Children are seemingly oblivious to the dissonance created by holding differential expectations for two highly regarded friends.

In contrast, the children may be responsive to the more obvious dissonance of holding two different expectations for the same highly valued friend. Nine of the twelve correlations between the reading and arithmetic expectations held for a friend (either best or second-best) are significant (six beyond the 0.001 level) and the correlations average 0.22 over all (Table 8.1). There is some pressure for children to think of their friends as likely to do consistently well or poorly across the academic areas, but there is no corresponding pressure to think of their friends as a set as likely to perform similarly well or poorly.

What is the relation between popularity and friends' expectations? For the correlation between peer-popularity and expectations in both second and third grade, the pattern is relatively clear. Children's popularity seems slightly related to the expectations held for them by their friends (r's range from -0.02 to

Table 7.10

Correlations Involving Friends' Expectations[a]

Correlation of Children's Marks with Their Friends' Expectations

	Grade 2		Grade 3	
	T3	T4	T5	T6
White Middle-Class School				
Reading	.21* (109)	.32*** (111)	.34*** (114)	.38*** (119)
Arithmetic	.23** (109)	.34*** (111)	.22** (114)	.47*** (119)
Integrated Lower-Class School				
Reading	.36*** (76)	.40*** (97)	.39*** (93)	.41*** (121)
Arithmetic	.30*** (100)	.35*** (101)	.45*** (122)	.40*** (121)
Black Lower-Class School				
Reading	.32** (67)	.30** (79)	.07 (65)	.31*** (109)
Arithmetic	.21* (109)	.39*** (107)	.18* (105)	.25** (109)

Correlation of Children's Expectations with Their Friends' Expectations

	Grade 2		Grade 3	
	T3	T4	T5	T6
White Middle-Class School				
Reading	.02 (113)	.10 (104)	.11 (112)	.19* (111)
Arithmetic	.08 (113)	.06 (104)	.08 (112)	.17* (111)
Integrated Lower-Class School				
Reading	.13 (88)	.20* (82)	-.06 (114)	.06 (107)
Arithmetic	-.12 (87)	.04 (82)	.19* (114)	.27** (107)
Black Lower-Class School				
Reading	.04 (107)	.02 (83)	.22* (102)	.10 (88)
Arithmetic	.16* (107)	.20* (83)	.16 (102)	.13 (88)

[a] Friends' expectations were obtained only at the ends of grades two (T4) and three (T6). N's appear in parentheses below the correlations.

*P < .05

**P < .01

***P < .001

0.33, with four out of twelve values significant). Popular children tend to receive high expectations from their friends, and unpopular children tend to receive low expectations, but the relationships are very weak.

Children's own popularity seems completely unrelated to the expectations they hold for their best and second-best friends in all the schools (about half the twenty-four correlations are negative). Thus, children's popularity predicts what their friends expect of them but not what they expect of their friends.

Models Involving Friends' Expectations

Friends' expectations were added to the basic models for grades two and three by placing friends' expectations in an endogenous position in the models prior to children's own expectations (Figure 7.1). We think a set of significant others is much more likely to influence one child than that child is to influence the significant others.[4]

The variables potentially causing friends' expectations are all the area-specific variables in the usual T3–T4 and T5–T6 models, with the exception that parental expectations are not thought to influence the expectations of children's friends directly. There is some possibility that friends know parents, but it is unlikely that academic concerns would occupy a sufficiently central focus in their interaction to produce any effects.

[4] If reciprocal effects were present, we would be likely to overestimate these paths, but since in every case the paths turned out to be small and did not attain even a minimal level of significance, there is no support for the reverse causal ordering.

Five of the six models provide acceptable χ^2 fits (Table 7.11) and the one model that originally fit poorly continues to do so (the T5–T6 model in the integrated school). One other model originally fit poorly, but now it provides an acceptable fit.

Most of the coefficients are very similar to those for the models in Chapter 6.[5] Most parameters remained very close to their prior values, although the significance of a few was reduced because of the smaller case base associated with the incomplete friends' data. Even when significance was reduced, however, the magnitude of the coefficients remained stable. On the average, introduction of the new variables increased the explained variance in children's expectations by about 1%, and that in marks by about 3%.

Children's own expectations seem to have negligible impact on expectations of their friends (Table 7.11). A reasonably consistent pattern links friends' expectations with the child's prior marks, but these effects are weak. The child's popularity (PEER) also shows a tendency to influence friends' expectations, but only one coefficient is more than twice its standard error. Only two borderline effects appear for absence. Over all, none of the exogenous variables is a particularly good predictor of friends' expectations and together they manage to explain only between 9% and 38% of the variance in friends' expectations, about what was seen for the child's own expectations.

The effects of friends' expectations are easily summarized. The expectations held by friends have no

[5] Full results for these models are available from the authors upon request.

Figure 7.1

A Model Including Friends' Expectations for T3-T4

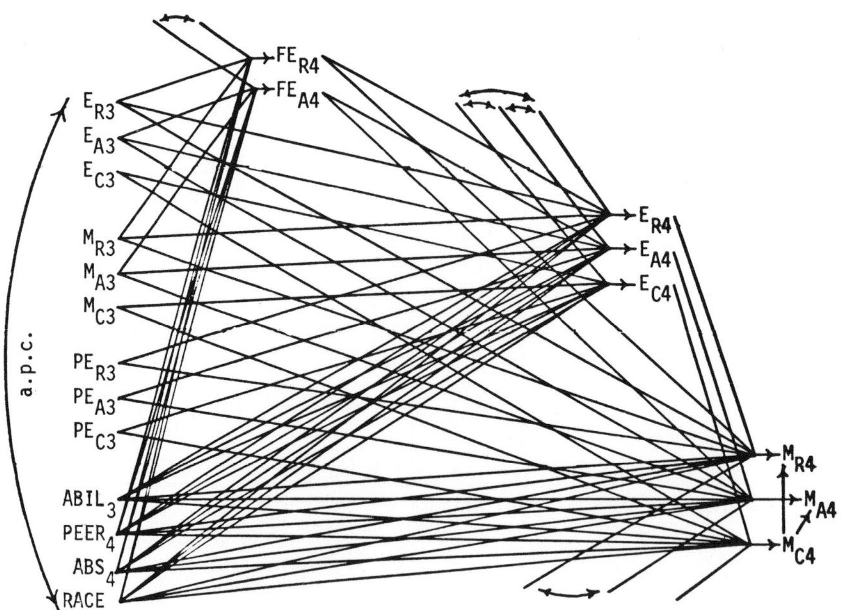

Table 7.11

Selected Coefficients from Friends' Expectations LISREL Models[a]

	Friends' Expectations	Variables Causing Friends' Expectations							Variables Affected by Friends' Expectations						
		E_{R3}	E_{A3}	M_{R3}	M_{A3}	$PEER_4$	ABS_4	RACE	E_{R4}	E_{A4}	M_{R4}	M_{A4}	R^{2b}	χ^2	d.f.
Grade 2 Models (T3-4)															
White Middle-Class School	FE_{R4}	.0348		.2225$^+$		.1302	.0194$^+$	---	.0249		.1458		.1171	55.3	66
	FE_{A4}		.0088		.2623$^+$	.2021	.0095	---		-.0155		.1701$^+$	.0860		
Integrated Lower-Class School	FE_{R4}	.2207		.2598$^+$		.8301$^+$	.0055	-.0290	.2583		.2804		.3770	76.7	66
	FE_{A4}		-.3011$^+$		.5663*	-.1145	-.0072	-.3289$^+$		.0982		.3672*	.3269		
Black Lower-Class School	FE_{R4}	-.0921		.3265$^+$		.0674	.0080	---	-.0499		.0391		.2036	78.1	66
	FE_{A4}		.1947		.3157	-.1720	.0067	---		.3106		.1372	.1388		
		E_{R5}	E_{A5}	M_{R5}	M_{A5}	$PEER_6$	ABS_6	RACE	E_{R6}	E_{A6}	M_{R6}	M_{A6}			
Grade 3 Models (T5-6)															
White Middle-Class School	FE_{R6}	.0373		.3315*		.4230$^+$	.0087	---	-.0124		.1391$^+$		.1785	66.1	66
	FE_{A6}		.0331		.2124$^+$	.3901$^+$	.0026	---		.0539		.3352*	.1007		
Integrated Lower-Class School	FE_{R6}	-.0992		---[d]		.8918$^+$	.0028	-.0491	.0484		.2967*		.1083	133.4[c]	61
	FE_{A6}		.0805		.1687	.5725	.0050	.0723		.2438$^+$		.1142	.1779		
Black Lower-Class School	FE_{R6}	.3092$^+$		-.1340		1.0396*	.0074	---	-.0169		.1323		.2090	64.7	66
	FE_{A6}		.0845		.0103	.4975	.0162$^+$	---		-.0702		.1745$^+$	.1376		

[a]Full models available from authors on request.

[b]This is 1.0 minus the standardized error variances for these variables.

[c]$p < .01$.

[d]M_{R3} was deleted from this model as it was in the corresponding model without friends' expectations.

*Coefficient is more than twice its standard error.

$^+$Coefficient is more than 1.5 times its standard error.

measurable impact on children's own expectations, but friends' expectations do display a consistent, yet weak, tendency to influence children's marks. This effectiveness may come from friends' detecting cues related to performance in the classroom, or it may come from phenomena such as support roles or classroom deference to those thought to be of high standing. Probably both explanations have some validity, since a child who is supported by the high expectations of others may engage in more behaviors that benefit achievement.

Although friends' expectations were omitted from the general models because they were not measured for any first-grade children, it is clear in retrospect that they would have minimal effects on model structure except for the fact that they mediate effects of marks. There are several paths from prior marks to friends' expectations and exactly half of the paths linking friends' expectations to subsequent marks achieve some level of significance. Over all, however, increments of explained variance in children's marks are small (3%) and even smaller for children's own expectations (around 1%). There is little reason to think that including friends' expectations would substantially improve or alter the basic models.

ADDITIONAL VARIABLES: TEACHERS' EXPECTATIONS

Previous research involving teacher expectations (Chapter 2 and 3) generally ignores the link between teachers' expectations and teachers' marks. This omission is all the more curious since there are so many ways for the two variables to be related (see Darley and Fazio 1980). The single previous sociological study (Lockheed and Morgan 1979) that, to our knowledge, includes both teachers' expectations *and* students' self-expectations did not include a variable representing teachers' marks. Since there is a high correlation between teachers' expectations and their marks, effects attributed to expectations could easily flow from marks. We are inclined to believe that, from the child's point of view, a teacher's expectations and the marks she assigns are closely intertwined. This makes it more problematic to include teachers' expectations as separate entities in schooling models than it is to include marks because marks are directly presented to children, whereas expectations are less visible. In this section we address these issues to the extent some limited data permit.

How do teachers' expectations arise and what are they likely to influence? If teachers' expectations respond to classroom behavior, they should arise like marks and act like marks. There are components of marks not included in teachers' expectations, however, and components of expectations not included in marks, although both essentially reflect an evaluation of children's classroom activity.

A teacher's moment-to-moment behavior changes. She may variously reward, punish, press, or ignore a student, and her expectations for that student may bob up and down. However, over a semester a teacher probably shapes her overall expectations to match a child's level of performance. In other words, as a consequence of classroom interaction, teachers' expectations and the marks they bestow should become highly correlated. This is exactly what we have observed. Since we have also seen that teachers' marks in the present study predict the quality of children's performance as judged by standardized tests, we would guess that teachers' expectations would predict standardized test scores as well.

We refrained from asking teachers at the beginning of the school year about the expectations they held for children in their classrooms because we were afraid that the asking of such a question would distort the usual schooling process. Most of the teachers whose pupils we studied were well aware of Pygmalion-in-the-classroom research and its implications. However, at the end of the school year, questions about expectations could be asked in the way of "forecasts" for the coming year, at a time when it was not possible for the asking of such questions to affect the schooling process in the year just terminating. Accordingly, we wrote to the kindergarten, first- and second-grade teachers *after schools closed for the summer* and offered them a modest payment for forecasting the marks they expected children to receive the following year in reading and arithmetic.[6] We thus employed the same "projective" strategy with teachers that we had employed with parents and children; we operationalized the expectation construct by asking for forecasts of specific marks. The simplicity and confidentiality of the task makes these forecasts relatively pure measures of teachers' expectations. The teachers did not have to be concerned with student motivation or parental reprisals. (The values in Table B.1 indicate our belief that, at most, 10% of the variance in these scores is error variance.)

Teachers' expectations shadow marks in that they are lower and slightly more variable in the two lower-class schools than in the middle-class school (Table 7.12). When first- and second-grade teacher expectations are compared to marks (Table 5.2), in eleven of twelve instances the teachers' expectations are slightly lower than the corresponding marks. Teachers tend to be a little less optimistic about children's capabilities

[6] A few kindergarten teachers' forecasts were procured even though marks in kindergarten were not available. No third-grade teachers were included because children were dropped from the research after third grade.

Table 7.12

Means and Standard Deviations of Teachers' Expectations

	White Middle-Class School			Integrated Lower-Class School			Black Lower-Class School		
	N	Mean	S.D.	N	Mean	S.D.	N	Mean	S.D.
Kindergarten Teacher's Forecast									
Reading	190	1.92	.80	158	2.54	.94	128	2.06	.99
Arithmetic	94	1.92	.76	120	2.63	.92	128	2.10	.96
First Grade Teacher's Forecast									
Reading	321	1.89	.76	353	2.90	.84	193	3.10	.81
Arithmetic	258	1.79	.62	350	2.87	.80	194	2.91	.87
Second Grade Teacher's Forecast									
Reading	337	1.95	.63	269	3.23	.83	103	2.96	.89
Arithmetic	335	1.95	.68	266	2.99	.79	103	2.89	.85

than their marks indicate, but teachers' average expectations were usually within a quarter of a grade-point of their marks and were about as variable as marks. Since marking scales and standards do not change much between grades, these similarities to marks are not surprising.

Correlations between these forecasts and marks teachers had actually given in the preceding year and the marks given by the new teacher in the next grade are shown in Table 7.13. In all schools, correlations of forecasts with the teacher's own year-end marks are high for both reading and arithmetic. They average 0.66 in the middle-class school, 0.71 in the lower-class integrated school, and 0.75 in the lower-class black school. As would be expected, correlations between forecasts procured after the end of the school year and marks given by that same teacher in the middle of that year are somewhat lower in all schools, with the smallest values being those in the middle-class school (ranging there from 0.42 to 0.59).

The teacher forecasts turned out to be accurate in the sense that they predicted marks a year later in the next grade almost as well as marks in the prior semester. The predictions were generally better in the two lower-class schools than in the middle-class school, as would be expected on the basis of the high mark stability in the two lower-class schools and because effort was supposedly more influential in determining marks in the middle-class school.

Teachers' expectations for black or white children in the integrated school were nearly identical in the beginning (differences are 0.03 or less in reading and arithmetic in first grade) but moved slightly toward favoring whites by grade two (0.26 grade-points higher in reading and 0.25 higher in arithmetic). The only difference in teacher expectations by gender is that teachers in all grades in the lower-class schools seemed to slightly but consistently favor girls. The middle-class teachers showed no consistent difference in their expectations for boys and girls.

There is considerable agreement between teachers' reading and arithmetic expectations (top panel of Table 7.14). Teachers generally expect some children to do well in both subjects and expect others to do poorly in both. Perhaps a high general ability component contributes to teacher expectations in the same way that a general ability component (ABIL) contributed to parental expectations. While we did not ask teachers for such overall ability ratings, inter-area consistency may reflect the grounding of the two expectations in a single ability judgment. Strong evidence for this is that teachers' reading expectations correlate with current arithmetic marks, and teachers' arithmetic expectations correlate with current reading marks. These correlations (not presented) are surprisingly similar to those presented in Table 7.14. Teachers' reading expectations predict future arithmetic performance almost as well as they predict future reading performance, and teachers' arithmetic expectations predict future reading performance almost as well as they predict future arithmetic performance. Similarly, prior reading performance contributes to teachers' arithmetic forecasts and prior arithmetic performance contributes to reading forecasts about as

Table 7.13

Correlation of Teachers' Expectations with Children's Marks

	First Grade		Second Grade		Third Grade	
	Mid-Year	Year End	Mid-Year	Year End	Mid-Year	Year End
White Middle-Class School						
Kindergarten Teacher's Forecast						
Reading	.17* (174)	.39*** (174)	.14 (105)	.28** (105)	.27* (68)	.37*** (68)
Arithmetic	-.17 (85)	.18 (85)	.33* (28)	.29 (28)	---	---
First Grade Teacher's Forecast						
Reading	.42*** (297)	.61*** (302)	.45*** (208)	.41*** (208)	.27*** (134)	.32*** (134)
Arithmetic	.47*** (241)	.69*** (244)	.34*** (156)	.31*** (156)	.22* (89)	.42*** (89)
Second Grade Teacher's Forecast						
Reading	.41*** (277)	.58*** (286)	.54*** (318)	.60*** (320)	.51*** (206)	.52*** (207)
Arithmetic	.20*** (276)	.37*** (285)	.59*** (322)	.72*** (323)	.41*** (213)	.34*** (213)
Integrated Lower-Class School						
Kindergarten Teacher's Forecast						
Reading	.41*** (144)	.42*** (137)	.28* (51)	.38*** (68)	.39* (19)	.35 (19)
Arithmetic	.38*** (114)	.51*** (111)	.20 (41)	.38** (41)	---	---
First Grade Teacher's Forecast						
Reading	.60*** (304)	.69*** (332)	.61*** (156)	.48*** (188)	.66*** (93)	.60*** (122)
Arithmetic	.66*** (318)	.70*** (330)	.60*** (187)	.62*** (188)	.60*** (118)	.55*** (117)
Second Grade Teacher's Forecast						
Reading	.48*** (160)	.59*** (212)	.74*** (215)	.74*** (247)	.73*** (105)	.71*** (149)
Arithmetic	.48*** (199)	.53*** (215)	.61*** (244)	.71*** (251)	.50*** (145)	.54*** (144)
Black Lower-Class School						
Kindergarten Teacher's Forecast						
Reading	.25** (97)	.55*** (103)	.38 (19)	.38* (36)	.19 (26)	.41** (35)
Arithmetic	.60*** (108)	.68*** (109)	.44*** (44)	.50*** (44)	.29* (36)	.54*** (35)
First Grade Teacher's Forecast						
Reading	.54*** (153)	.63*** (172)	.43*** (48)	.67*** (61)	.29 (28)	.44*** (60)
Arithmetic	.71*** (168)	.74*** (178)	.59*** (84)	.62*** (82)	.41*** (60)	.45*** (61)
Second Grade Teacher's Forecast						
Reading	.39*** (66)	.36** (61)	.62*** (65)	.80*** (72)	.53*** (45)	.68*** (72)
Arithmetic	.47*** (59)	.51*** (61)	.65*** (95)	.84*** (99)	.34*** (73)	.58*** (72)

*P < .05

**P < .01

***P < .001

Table 7.14

Correlation of Teachers' Expectations between Subjects and between Grades[a]

	White Middle-Class School	Integrated Lower-Class School	Black Lower-Class School
Correlation between Teachers' Reading and Arithmetic Expectations			
Kindergarten	.88*** (94)	.84*** (120)	.93*** (128)
Grade 1	.51*** (255)	.76*** (348)	.81*** (191)
Grade 2	.66*** (335)	.68*** (266)	.79*** (103)
Correlation between the Kindergarten and First Grade Teachers' Expectations			
Reading	.36*** (159)	.44*** (133)	.57*** (74)
Arithmetic	.29** (81)	.58*** (103)	.61*** (74)
Correlation between the First and Second Grade Teachers' Expectations			
Reading	.53*** (214)	.59*** (180)	.67*** (41)
Arithmetic	.43*** (158)	.64*** (176)	.66*** (42)
Correlations between the Kindergarten and Second Grade Teachers' Expectations			
Reading	.38*** (107)	.31** (62)	.49** (29)
Arithmetic	.70*** (28)	.60*** (41)	.58*** (29)

[a]N's appear in parentheses beneath the correlations.

**P < .01

***P < .001

much as prior performance in each area contributes to forecasts for that area (not presented but similar to Table 7.14).

The lower portions of Table 7.14 indicate that teachers' expectations are not only consistent between areas, but are consistent across teachers. A teacher's expectations for a child are strongly related to expectations held by the child's teacher in the previous year. In fact, teacher expectations at the end of grade two are even strongly related to kindergarten teacher expectations obtained 2 years earlier (see Table 7.14). This is another way in which teacher expectations resemble marks. As with marks, this stability may be attributed to stability in the children's behavior or to stability in children's reputations as transmitted through informal communications among teachers. (It was possible, although rare, for a child to have the same teacher over 2 or more years.) To the small extent that students do have the same teacher, and to the extent that teachers' expectations crystallize [which is likely to be only slightly (Reschly and Lamprecht 1979)], the stability of teachers' expectations may reflect teacher consistency and not consistency in children's performance. (A similar argument might be made for stability in marks.)

The stability of teacher expectations between years can be seen either as reassuring or as unsettling. If teachers act as unbiased assessors of children's performance, stability across school years simply confirms teachers' abilities to spot superior children. On the other hand, if teachers work largely from unfounded biases and favoritism, such stability could provide a cause for concern, because consistent teacher biases could perhaps become engrained in children's expectations for themselves.

Do teacher expectations actually rub off on children and on parents? Teachers' expectations are more strongly related to parents' expectations than to children's expectations (Table 7.15), but to properly examine the causal impact of teacher expectations requires models that include teacher expectations and that provide the appropriate controls. We now turn to such models.

Models Involving Teachers' Expectations[7]

One way to examine teachers' expectations is to adopt the same strategy as with standardized achievement, that is, to replace marks with the corresponding year-end teacher expectations in the basic models, making teachers' expectations the ultimate endogenous variables. All six models provided acceptable χ^2 fits.[8] In general, the coefficients influencing other endogenous variables (children's expectations and conduct marks) remained nearly identical to those reported when reading and arithmetic marks appeared as the ultimate endogenous variables, so no further comment is required concerning these portions of the models. The coefficients directly influencing the replaced variables show slightly larger perturbations, but about as many get larger as get smaller, with a few minor exceptions.[9]

There is some hint of a difference by race in teachers' expectations. Teachers in the integrated school consistently held expectations that favored white children, but none of the four relevant coefficients reached twice its standard error. (A slight difference in means by grade was mentioned earlier.)

The impact of conduct marks on teacher expectations was slightly less in the schools where the strongest effects had appeared for marks (the white and integrated schools) and was slightly greater in the school where the weakest effects had appeared for marks (the black school). The net result is that conduct marks show a slightly more uniform influence on teacher expectations across schools than was the case when marks were modeled, but in no cases are the effects particularly strong. The coefficients range from 0.10

[7]An exploratory strategy for inclusion of teachers' expectations (forecasts) was to use both the teachers' forecasts and marks as observed indicators of a single underlying concept "teacher's evaluation of the child's performance" (TEP) in the models for the transitions through grade one (T1-T2) and through grade two (T3-T4), with TEP_R and TEP_A replacing marks. We scaled the concept "teacher's evaluation of performance" in units of assigned marks by fixing the corresponding LISREL lambda at unity and provided for the measurement error in both indicators by fixing their measurement error variances at the appropriate proportions of the variable's total variance. (The lambda for the teacher's expectations is determined by the known TEP, total, and error variances.)

The net result of combining strong measurement assumptions with a belief in the common basis of teacher expectations (forecasts) and marks is a multiple indicator model with a completely determined measurement structure. Inclusion of the additional teacher expectations in the covariance matrix provides more degrees of freedom for testing, but there are the same number of parameters to estimate, since the structure of the models is identical to the T1-T2 and T3-T4 models estimated previously.

The resultant parameter estimates are almost identical in both significance and magnitude to those obtained using only marks as the endogenous concepts and indicators. The proportion of explained variance increased only slightly. However the χ^2's for five models turned out to be extremely large, and the sixth model, that for T3-T4 in the black school, could not be estimated because the covariance matrix was singular. The poor χ^2's came about because the observed covariances between marks and teacher expectations were lower than the multiple indicator models implied. As a consequence, the models fit larger covariances between marks and teacher's expectations than are consistent with the data. The current data are thus at odds with the notion that a single, well-measured, evaluative factor underlies both marks and teachers' expectations. Since the indicator covariance is over- rather than underestimated, no more common factors are required. The single existing common factor already provides too much covariance. What is required may be additional "factors" contributing uniquely to either one *or* the other of the indicators, for example, a "current effort" factor influencing marks but not teacher expectations. The single postulated factor "teacher's evaluation of performance" fails by providing too strong a relationship between its specific indicators, yet it functions well with respect to all the other portions of the model by providing parameters comparable to those seen previously.

A second tack was to alter the measurement structure for marks from that of "marks as mark indicators" to "marks as performance indicators." This emphasizes the performance aspect rather than the expressed evaluation aspect of "teachers evaluation of performance." This strategy weakened the measurement assumptions for marks substantially but yielded only four usable models. (For the black school the T1-T2 model encountered estimation problems and the T3-T4 model had a singular covariance matrix.) While the revised measurement structure improved the χ^2's considerably, three of the four estimable models still produced unacceptable χ^2's ($P < 0.01$). Examination of the models indicated the measurement assumption for "marks as performance indicators" was so weak that teachers' expectations were completely controlling the models' behavior while marks were only loosely integrated into the models.

Accordingly, attempts to include expectations in the measurement model, rather than in the structural model, were abandoned.

[8]The χ^2 values and metric and standardized coefficients for such models are available from the authors upon request.

[9]Children's expectations had almost no effect on teacher expectations, although they had a slight impact on the corresponding marks in reading and arithmetic (twelve coefficients average 0.01 for teachers' expectations and 0.08 for marks). Parents' expectations influenced teachers' expectations slightly more than they influenced marks (coefficients average 0.14 and 0.08, respectively). Parents' ability estimates had more impact on teachers' expectations than on marks (coefficients average 0.14 and 0.08, respectively).

Table 7.15

Correlation of Teachers' Expectations with Children's Expectations[a]

	White Middle-Class School		Integrated Lower-Class School		Black Lower-Class School	
	Child's Corresponding First Grade Expectations		Child's Corresponding First Grade Expectations		Child's Corresponding First Grade Expectations	
Kindergarten Teacher's Forecast	Midyear	Year-End	Midyear	Year-End	Midyear	Year-End
Reading	.01 (189)	.13 (170)	.20** (134)	-.01 (121)	-.03 (118)	.01 (84)
Arithmetic	-.13 (94)	-.12 (79)	.01 (105)	.01 (92)	-.13 (118)	.23* (84)
First Grade Teacher's Forecast						
Reading	.13** (308)	.18*** (296)	.05 (284)	.11* (308)	.05 (170)	.15* (139)
Arithmetic	.13* (249)	.13* (235)	.15** (281)	.08 (305)	.05 (171)	.17* (138)
	Child's Corresponding Second Grade Expectations		Child's Corresponding Second Grade Expectations		Child's Corresponding Second Grade Expectations	
Second Grade Teacher's Forecast	Midyear	Year-End	Midyear	Year-End	Midyear	Year-End
Reading	.06 (325)	.28*** (315)	.16** (233)	.09 (235)	.09 (93)	-.06 (60)
Arithmetic	.26*** (323)	.32*** (314)	.15** (229)	.17** (233)	.14 (93)	.19 (60)

Correlation of Teachers' Expectations with Parents' Expectations[a]

	White Middle-Class School	Integrated Lower-Class School	Black Lower-Class School
	Parent's Corresponding First Grade Expectations	Parent's Corresponding First Grade Expectations	Parent's Corresponding First Grade Expectations
Kindergarten Teacher's Forecast			
Reading	.54*** (158)	.25** (136)	.34** (68)
Arithmetic	.22* (80)	.36*** (107)	.22* (67)
First Grade Teacher's Forecast			
Reading	.44*** (268)	.48*** (293)	.37** (52)
Arithmetic	.37*** (213)	.35*** (292)	.33** (52)
	Parent's Corresponding Second Grade Expectations	Parent's Corresponding Second Grade Expectations	Parent's Corresponding Second Grade Expectations
Second Grade Teacher's Forecast			
Reading	.51*** (258)	.51*** (227)	.53*** (32)
Arithmetic	.48*** (257)	.37*** (227)	.52*** (32)

[a] N's appear in parentheses below the correlations.

*P < .05

**P < .01

***P < .001

to 0.34 for marks and from −0.01 to 0.33 for teacher expectations.

On the average, about 4% more variance in teachers' expectations is explained than was explained for the corresponding marks. Since only minor differences appeared in model structure, we conclude that replacing endogenous reading and arithmetic marks with teachers' expectations does not lead to much change in model structure. In fact, teachers' expectations and marks are nearly equivalent in behavior as far as our models are concerned.

A reverse strategy is to examine the impact of teacher expectations on other variables. One serious drawback to this strategy is that the most visible dimension of teacher expectations is assigned marks, and inserting teacher expectations as independent variables in models containing year-end marks as dependent variables amounts to controlling for the dependent variable in some of the equations. Such collinearity is likely to make the effects of the other exogenous variables appear unstable for artifactual reasons.

Nevertheless, we constructed these models, which have TE_R and TE_A added to the list of exogenous variables for first and second grades in each school,[10] and two general features of these models turned out exactly as one might expect. Teachers' expectations strongly and significantly influenced both reading and arithmetic marks in all schools at both times, and the proportion of explained variance in marks increased between 5% and 25%. The larger increase in explained variance when teachers' expectations are used to predict marks as compared to increases when marks are used to predict expectations (averaging 4% in the previous modeling strategy) can be taken as support for Crano and Mellon's (1978) finding that teachers' attitudes affect children's achievement to a greater degree than students' performance impinges on teachers' attitudes.

The other coefficients in these models tended to be weakened slightly, and usually the impact of earlier marks on later marks was substantially reduced—sometimes to insignificance. Only a few other coefficents were markedly reduced, and the general pattern of effects seen earlier was not systematically altered, just weakened. Most of these effects are probably artifactual, the consequence of including proxies for the dependent variables as independent variables, rather than real effects.

One finding that cannot be discounted as an artifact—and the major finding that makes these models worth discussing—is the observation that teachers' expectations, unlike marks, provided no significant impact on children's expectations in either reading or arithmetic in any school at any time. Thus, teachers' expectations had no influence whatever on children's expectations over and above the effects provided by their earlier report card evaluations. Since this finding emerges from equations with no "control" problem, it is strong evidence that *inclusion of prior marks as exogenous variables captures all the effects of teachers on children's expectations.*

Still another way to model teacher expectations as causal factors is to examine the effects of teachers' expectations that carry over into the following grade. To do this, we inserted teacher expectations as exogenous variables in the models for the transition between grades. That is, the first-grade teacher's expectations appear as exogenous variables in the model for the transition from the end of grade one into grade two, and second-grade teacher's expectations appear in the model for the transition into third grade. These models are similar to Figures 5.8 and 5.10, except that both the teacher expectation variables were allowed paths to the subsequent parental ability estimate, while only within-area paths were allowed to marks, children's expectations, and parents' expectations.

Both the models that did fit and those that did not (Table 7.16) have similar implications, with a few exceptions to be noted below.[11] Several sets of coefficients for these models are very similar to the corresponding coefficients in the original models (Tables 6.5, 6.7, 6.11, and 6.13) and hence require no further comment. These similarities include race and gender effects, the stability and impacts of children's expectations, mark influences on parental ability estimates, ability estimates' effects on particular parental expectations, and the influences of conduct on reading and arithmetic marks.

Compared to the original models, the effects of IQ fluctuated somewhat, and slightly weaker effects appeared for mark feedback on parents' expectations, for parents' expectations on children's expectations, and for arithmetic (but not reading and conduct) marks on children's expectations. These changes, however, are much too small to challenge the overall patterns discussed previously for these variables. The most pronounced change in the replication portion of the models is the reduced persistence of reading and arithmetic marks between years. These effects had

[10] Adding the two new teacher variables made the covariance matrix singular for the black lower-class school in second grade. Allowing only within-area effects of teacher expectations (TE_R influences only E_R and M_R while TE_A influences only E_A and M_A) caused no problems for the remaining five models, since all χ^2's were acceptable. The largest was $\chi^2_{50} = 59.2$, n.s.

[11] Both models for the black school had singular covariance matrices and two of the models had unacceptable χ^2 fits. Of the models fitting poorly, one (the T4–T5 integrated model) had fit poorly even without teachers' expectations, and the other (the T2–T3 model) had fit poorly in both the odd and even replications even though the χ^2 using all the cases was acceptable (see Table 6.1). Thus the poor fits may not be entirely attributable to the new teacher variables.

Table 7.16

Summary of Metric Coefficients Obtained by Inclusion of Teachers' Expectations as Independent Variables: Degree of Determinacy in Parentheses

	X^2	d.f.	P	Independent Variables	ABIL	PE R	PE A	E R	E A	M R	M A
The Transition into Grade 2					$ABIL_3$	PE_{R3}	PE_{A3}	E_{R2}	E_{A3}	M_{R3}	M_{A3}
White Middle-Class School	151.2	108	P < .01	TE_{R2}	.2635+	.2126*		-.0769		.0986	
				TE_{A2}	-.5932*		.3171+		.0943		.1911
					(.7240)	(.5311)	(.4729)	(.0900)	(.2924)	(.4485)	(.3832)
Integrated Lower-Class School	95.1	108	n.s.	TE_{R2}	-.0296	.5288*		-.1597		-.1413	
				TE_{A2}	.0885		.1380		.3819+		.2362
					(.4396)	(.4779)	(.2355)	(.2213)	(.4400)	(.8998)	(.5377)
The Transition into Grade 3					$ABIL_5$	PE_{R5}	PE_{A5}	E_{R5}	E_{A5}	M_{R5}	M_{A5}
White Middle-Class School	119.2	108	n.s.	TE_{R4}	.1232	.0423		.0918		.2388*	
				TE_{A4}	.2377		.1442		.2303		.2205
					(.7433)	(.6441)	(.4878)	(.1992)	(.3672)	(.4139)	(.2551)
Integrated Lower-Class School	226.4	108	P < .01	TE_{R4}	-.1989	.4072+		.0500		.6237*	
				TE_{A4}	.2435		.2355+		.2196		.3471*
					(.2916)	(.3737)	(.3651)	(.1881)	(.1479)	(.8775)	(.5149)

*Coefficient is more than twice its standard error.

+Coefficient is more than 1.5 times its standard error.

been small in two cases and modest in two cases, but here they are essentially zero in three of the four models and modest in the last model (T2–T3 in the integrated school). Thus the contrast noted earlier involving the weak between-year stability and the strong within-year stability in academic marks is even sharper than seen previously. Even this most pronounced change, however, merely enhances a pattern noted previously.

The effects for the portions of these models directly involving teacher expectations are summarized in Table 7.16. The well-fitting models (the transition into second grade for the integrated school, and the transition into third grade for the white school) provide only two significant effects. The second-grade teachers' reading expectations influenced the reading marks assigned in third grade in the middle-class school, and the first-grade teachers' expectations influenced later parental reading expectations in the integrated school. The other significant effects appear in models that fit poorly and that are therefore open to question.

If we seek out patterns having both reasonably consistent signs and some hint of significance, only two effects merit attention. Both parents' expectations and marks the following year may respond to teacher's expectations. There is no convincing support for any lasting effect of teachers' expectations on children's expectations (over and above those effects captured by assigned marks). Thus the correlations between teachers' and children's expectations in Table 7.15 are probably spurious, while the slightly stronger correlation for parents' expectations in the same table may be the result of a direct causal impact of teachers' expectations on parents' expectations. There is no consistent support (in Table 7.16) for teacher influences on parental ability estimates. (As in the original models, parental ability estimates continued to respond sporadically to marks assigned by the teacher.)

In sum, inclusion of teachers' reading and arithmetic expectations as exogenous variables left the basic models essentially unchanged and provided tantalizing hints at possible effects of teachers' expectations on both parents' expectations and marks assigned the following year. Although these effects appear in several places, caution is warranted, since much of the evidence appears in poorly fitting models. The minimal increases in explained variance (the average increase is less than 2%) convinces us that teachers' expectations provided little new information.

Summary of Findings on Teachers' Expectation Models

Over all, there is no convincing evidence that exclusion of teachers' expectations from the basic models poses any real challenge to either the substantive findings or to the structure of the basic models as long as marks are included. Including teachers' expectations might have added a little to the explained variance in marks and in parents' expectations, but it would not have altered the structure of the basic models appreciably. This is not to say that teachers' expectations are ineffective, but rather that our inclusion of marks as the most visible component of teachers' expectations captured enough of the effects of teachers' expectations to make their explicit inclusion largely unnecessary.

Teacher evaluations and expectations *may* differ in micro-models, but our data suggest that they probably cannot be distinguished in mid-range models, where assigned marks capture the effects of teachers' expectations (Table 7.13), no doubt because teachers base their expectations upon achievement (Clifton 1980). Teachers' expectations have minimal effects on children's expectations over and above effects coincident with mark effects. This conclusion could imply that considerable previous research effort has been misplaced. To the extent that researchers have ignored marks in favor of teachers' expectations, explanations of schooling linked to teachers' expectations may be spurious. A teacher's expectation is an expected future evaluation often communicated to the child indirectly by behaviors like smiling, ignoring, pressing, and so on.[12] A mark, on the other hand, is a written evaluation communicated directly to the child, peers, parents, and other teachers.

What are the implications of the overlap between teachers' expectations and marks? If the future mark is consistent with the teacher's forecast, the mark itself will pick up the effects of teachers' expectations. If the mark is inconsistent, it will mitigate the effect of prior teachers' expectations. If marks are left out of the model, however, the schooling process will be seriously mis-specified, because we have seen that teachers' expectations do not affect children's expectations but that often marks do. These considerations make a strong argument for using marks, rather than teachers' expectations, in models of early schooling. It is especially noteworthy that children's expectations *never* responded to teachers' expectations, although they did respond in some cases to marks.

There are other drawbacks associated with using teachers' expectations in a model. To find that teachers hold students for whom they have high expectations to higher standards may illuminate a micro-process, but this observation does not readily transfer to schooling issues. Several questions must be answered

[12] One very difficult problem in research on teachers' expectations is the effect of teachers' non-responses. Non-reaction could increase low-achievers' expectations (if they usually are criticized) and decrease high-achievers' expectations (if they are usually praised). How and when to measure non-response is a problem. With marks issued to all students, however, there is no possibility for non-response.

to bridge this gap. To what extent are "standards" operationally distinct from teachers' expectations or evaluation? What are the complications when teachers' standards and students' standards are not the same? How does momentary teacher-pupil interaction translate into pupil achievement? The models involving teachers' expectations put forward by Finn (1972) and Braun (1976) appear to be largely beyond the reach of realistic research until some of these questions are answered. In our view, mid-range models involving evaluation (marks) as a behavioral expression of expectations offer more promise at present than approaches involving only teachers' expectations.

The model proposed by Lockheed and Morgan (1979) includes a number of status variables as determinants of students' and teachers' expectations, and so is more satisfactory than many previous studies of teachers' expectations on this score. It also predicts second- and fifth-grade children's *gains* in reading and arithmetic achievement, and thereby avoids mis-specification of the magnitude of any expectations effect. However, since teachers' marks do not appear explicitly in these models, effects of evaluation are confounded with effects of teachers' expectations, and the observed effects may as well be attributed to evaluations as to expectations. Perhaps students' expectations would not respond to teachers' expectations in the Lockheed and Morgan data if teachers' marks were included.

SUMMARY

The various structural alternatives to the basic models (Appendix C), as well as the more elaborate models incorporating additional variables explored in this chapter, strengthen our confidence in the validity of the basic models. These supplementary investigations lead us to restate and extend some conclusions drawn earlier.

Conduct is an important determinant of the early schooling process. The models with reciprocal paths indicate that conduct affects academic marks rather than the reverse. Its effects on early reading and arithmetic marks are visible in every school, especially in the earliest time period. We suspect that, if we had been able to secure standardized achievement measures for reading and arithmetic in grades one and two, a direct influence of conduct on standardized achievement might even have emerged. Since such a direct effect did not appear in the available third-grade data, however, we lean toward concluding that conduct effects come about more through halo effects than through the active interference of poor conduct with learning. Effects linked to gender arise mainly in respect to conduct, and, except for a few differences in influence of middle-class mothers on boys' expectations in arithmetic (Entwisle and Baker, forthcoming), there appear to be no structural differences by gender, so we see conduct as the chief mechanism leading to gender differences in achievement.

Children's own expectations appear to be consequences of schooling rather than antecedents, a conclusion consistent with Gottfredson's (1980) observation that psychological characteristics of high-school youth respond to achievement rather than the reverse. The small size of parameters from first expectations to first marks plus the low but gradually increasing determinacy of children's expectations is evidence in support of this. Further evidence of the causal priority of achievement is that expectations of middle-class children responded to marks, and, even though the same cannot be said of lower-class children (they failed to process mark information for themselves), they did use mark information in forming expectations for their friends. The implication is that achievement determines expectation levels except when knowledge about achievement is too painful or too confusing to be assimilated.

The disparity between children's expectations and their marks in the two lower-class schools seems to be a consequence partly of some defense mechanism—children cannot bring themselves to process negative information about themselves. However, the data for friends' expectations suggests that part of the disparity is a simple failure to understand information about marks, perhaps because it is presented in a confusing form. In the middle-class school, gaps between expectations and marks and between expectations for friends and expectations for the self are much smaller than those in the other two schools. Mark information is being processed by middle-class children for their friends as well as for themselves. In the lower-class schools, gaps between expectations for friends and friends' marks are noticeably smaller than gaps between expectations for the self and own marks, but gaps are still significant in size. Since expectations for friends are unrealistically high and since there is no need to construct psychological defenses for friends in the same way that there is need to construct psychological defenses for the self, we conclude that simple failure to process information about marks is one reason that expectations and marks of lower-class children are not in agreement.

The psychological literature does not speak definitively to the issue of a "self-enhancing" feedback bias, although there are explanations for adults parallel to those we here propose for children. Miller and Ross (1975), for example, emphasize motivation (parallel to a defense mechanism) and Zuckerman (1979) directly discusses information processing. Piagetian accounts of development point to children's exaggerated feelings of self-efficacy, but since Piaget is not concerned with individual differences there is little insight into why some children (lower-class) might have more exaggerated ideas than others (middle-class).

Introducing teachers' expectations into the models suggests teachers' expectations and the marks they assign do not have identical effects, but that the unique components of teachers expectations would add little explanatory power and alter the model structure only minimally. Since the implications of these findings are summarized in the preceding section, we do not repeat them here.

Chapter 8

The Early Schooling Process

There may be much to be gained from expanding sociological research on schooling to younger children, and Chapter 1 reviews the strategic advantages that may come from studying children in the early grades. First, the early grades may be precisely the time that schools have their strongest effects. Except when mandatory busing or other kinds of changes are specifically introduced, elementary schools tend to mirror the neighborhoods they serve. For this reason, school and home influences are probably most congruent at this life stage. Second, many people believe children's eventual attainment level and their track in school are fixed after the first few years (Husen 1969; Kraus 1973), because it is then that basic skills in reading and arithmetic are learned. Third, despite the general lack of differential school effects for secondary students, several investigators recently have found sizeable differences among teachers and/or across schools in the achievement of elementary-school children (Brookover et al. 1978; Murnane 1975; Summers and Wolfe 1977). Our research now adds to the work on differential school effects by showing that the *process* of schooling can differ from one school to another. Thus, even when outputs are equivalent, the processes by which output is reached may not be the same.

Early affective growth may be particularly sensitive to school climate. To our knowledge, however, no one has tried to see how children form ideas about their own capabililties or how they go about creating an academic self-image. By studying how young children developed expectations for their own performance and how these expectations changed, our research tried to avoid the monolithic focus of educational research on standardized tests (Spady 1976). Moreover, there seems to be much to learn about the interplay between affective and cognitive development, a topic that is broader than schooling per se. In the long run, the importance of affective outcomes of schooling could outweigh that of cognitive outcomes, because children who learn early to dislike schoolwork or who are unsure about their academic worth may be at a disadvantage in all future learning. Children who like learning, on the other hand, may continue their own education outside school hours, or even long after they leave school.

Employing self-concept measures with older children can be criticized on grounds that measuring children's self-perceptions of academic ability is tantamount to collecting self-reported data on academic achievement (see Gottfredson 1980). That same criticism cannot be leveled at research on the academic self-image of children starting school, however, because first-graders have not yet established a level of academic achievement. In fact, first grade may be the only point in life where the two variables are actually distinct.

The quality of children's lives, an important consideration in its own right, provides another reason for studying children's expectations. Schools should not be the "factories for failure" that some researchers picture (Rist 1973). No matter what their eventual effect on attainment, school climates that make children overanxious or undermine their self-esteem are objectionable.

In this chapter we review and discuss what we have found out about children's early schooling, and we try to draw some policy implications. While reading this chapter the reader should be mindful of the methodological limitations of our research, particularly its purposive sampling base. Rather than repeat caveats in every section of the chapter, however, we have summarized the limitations of the research in Appendix A.

THE MODELS

Durkheim's (1961) demonstration of the importance of social structure for interpreting individual behavior has sometimes had the unfortunate effect of leading investigators to ignore individual-level variables entirely, and psychologists often lean in the opposite direction, failing to take social structure into account. The mid-range models we offer point to the fruitfulness of blending these two traditions in modeling early schooling.[1] Fortunately, the final models are relatively simple and the variables appearing in them turned out to be the same from year to year and from school to school. Also, by estimating the models separately for children of the two sexes and the two races, and finding solutions to be roughly equivalent, we have provided some evidence that the schooling process is the same by gender or ethnic groupings. Stated another way, the models remain linear, since they do not require interaction terms.

Most research on schooling examines only standardized achievement. Our research suggests that the process of schooling is not correctly specified with this single dimension of output, because there is an interplay between cognitive and affective outcomes. The interplay among the cognitive and affective outputs varied from school to school. To be specific, the relation between expectations and marks was not the same across schools, which is evidence that the process of schooling differs. Furthermore, looking only at standardized achievement, we would not have been able to see that teachers' marks are much more fully determined in one school than in another, or that early IQ scores act to condition marks more strongly in one school than in another. As suspected, the schooling process includes variables that act reciprocally upon one another, so the strategy of studying the cognitive and affective outcomes separately with the idea of combining them later may be futile.

Models employing a series of repeated measures may be especially useful when dealing with data for children beginning elementary school. We suspect that these years are a time of rapid change. In the middle-class school, for example, some children greatly underestimated their own performance early in first grade. However, by the end of first grade they became attuned to the (high) range of marks teachers in that school awarded. Also, before their first marks were issued, children's expectations in all three schools were largely unpredictable, but they became better determined as the year progressed. If we had obtained measures to assess expectations only late in the year, we might have concluded that expectations determine performance to a greater extent than now seems likely. Findings related to parents also appear to be sensitive to timing. Parents everywhere appeared to influence first marks, but only the middle-class parents retained their influence over the latter part of first grade. If we had waited until the end of first grade to measure parents' expectations, it might have appeared that their influence was felt only in the middle-class school or that the influence of lower-class parents continued to the end of first grade. In addition, some "lasting-effects" models (T1 to T4 with intervening cycles ignored) led to the same conclusions as models repeated cycle after cycle, but others did not. Much of the interplay between marks and expectations is lost if a longer time frame, like that in the lasting-effects models, is adopted. Intervening events disrupted some of the effects of initial expectations, initial marks, and epecially IQ. Understanding the intervening events could be particularly important for understanding differences in the schooling process and could shed light on theories of continuity and change (Kagan 1980). There is more continuity, for example, in children's expectations than the lasting-effects models suggest.

Another feature of this style of modeling is worth noting. It is linear in form, but, because of its cyclic nature, may approximate more complicated functional forms. Our choice of cycle length was dictated by convenience. In future work we would recommend choosing cycles exactly one marking period in length.

A particularly appealing feature of cyclic models and a multi-wave sample is that the time dependencies among some variables are established by the sampling design. In this research, data pertaining to each child were collected from several different respondents at the times most appropriate for establishing causal dependencies. In macro-models of secondary-school attainment, on the other hand, students report data at one point in time even though the life events they are describing have occurred at various times in the past. This retrospective reporting requires inferring the time-ordering among variables operating in the past, with the obvious risk of misspecification. The only ambiguities in specifying causal dependencies in our first cycle models centered on whether children's expectations should precede their first marks, and whether the conduct mark should precede the other two marks. Substantive information and the outcomes of alternative modeling strategies answered these questions satisfactorily, and at the same time provided insights into the early schooling process.

[1] See also similar models recently discussed by Lockheed and Morgan (1979), Schneider (1980), and others.

Our style of modeling offers some potential for exploring the limits of expectations-states theory (see Berger, Rosenholtz, and Zelditch 1980). Although the principles of this theory *could* apply in real-life situations, to our knowledge there are almost no naturalistic studies of children's expectations besides our own. [The study by Lockheed and Morgan (1979) is an exception.] Most research previously used to challenge the theory consists of either laboratory or field experiments, so we know little about expectations held over relatively long periods. In addition, since children cannot be subjected to artificial procedures that would cause them to lower their expectations, it is hard to judge whether experimental findings would apply to daily classroom work, where children's expectations are sometimes pushed downward.

There are other problems with experimental work on expectation-states theory. For example, contingencies between evaluations and expectations are usually arranged so that it is very difficult for subjects to ignore or misinterpret evaluations. Experiments are contrived to force subjects to attend to relevant variables. In real-life settings, however, children may misinterpret evaluations or miss them altogether. An outstanding instance of this was uncovered in our sample when children from less-favored backgrounds failed to process feedback from marks. Relationships discovered between expectations and evaluations in the laboratory may therefore not hold up when systems are "noisy" or when subjects can erect psychological defenses. In fact, our work suggests that the theory may need to be modified to take account of self-evaluations that disagree with others' evaluations. In the laboratory, expectations for the self are artificially pegged by information from a single source. In real life, expectations are in flux and respond to self-evaluations as well as to evaluations provided by others.

Mid-range models could enrich expectation-states theory by demonstrating the action of expectations in environments that are more complex than experiments can tolerate. In a laboratory it is virtually impossible to create multiple expectations (in reading, arithmetic, and conduct) from multiple sources (parents, peers, etc.) and then to join them to multiple simultaneous outcomes (performance in reading, arithmetic, etc.), but life itself is complex and variables do not act one at a time. If expectations of significant others interact or offset each other, or if specific expectations are nested under a hierarchy of more general expectations, or if various performances are simultaneously visible in real life, a robust theory must acknowledge these facts. It may be essential to model expectations in natural situations if the scope of expectations-states theory is to be realistically mapped.

Our work relates also to another body of theory. It now seems possible to elaborate our mid-range models to incorporate and test Bandura's (1977) theory of efficacy and outcome expectancies. To explain learning, Bandura invokes self-reinforcement, a cognitive process that regulates behavior through self-evaluation.[2] The cognitive process is divided into an outcome expectancy ("a person's estimate of the likelihood that a given behavior will lead to certain outcomes") and an efficacy expectancy ("the conviction that one can successfully execute the behavior required to produce the outcome").

One way to test Bandura's expectancy theory would be to invent vignettes combining particular behaviors with particular outcomes, and then to ask children to comment on the vignettes in ways that would reveal their own outcome expectancies and efficacy expectancies in parallel situations. These two kinds of expectancies could then be included as variables in mid-range models along with children's specific expectations for school marks. Our measure of children's expectations may actually be a combination of Bandura's two expectancies, because if children believe they are going to receive an A in reading, they may also believe that they know *what* behaviors to execute and how to execute them to obtain an A. If so, Bandura's expectancies could be tied to actual academic performance and Bandura's two expectancies could be included at either the structural or measurement levels.

SIGNIFICANT OTHERS

From the time of Cooley and Mead, the view has been widely held that opinions of the self are derived from reactions of others. The empirical implications of this idea in terms of human development have not been followed up, however (Brim 1976). No one has yet explicitly traced the history of self-concept development. If our data can be trusted, when children begin school they apparently have little in the way of a self concept for themselves as academic performers. However, presumably as a consequence of being evaluated by others *and* of being evaluated by themselves, they slowly manufacture images of themselves as academic performers.

The looking-glass theory assumes that, through a self-monitoring process, the "generalized other" becomes internalized. The self comes to observe the self and to produce its own evaluations, but the self also continues to process evaluations reflected from the social environment, *and the self can filter or distort in various ways the evaluations provided by others.* The

[2] As noted above, it is this kind of concept that may need to be added to expectation-states theory.

generalized other may or may not match objective reality. Thus the same level and quality of social feedback could have quite different consequences depending upon how that reflected feedback compares to self-produced feedback, and also upon how the reflected feedback is processed internally. In our data it appears that teacher evaluations that are very discordant with self-evaluations are filtered. It also appears that, to the extent that evaluations of some significant others (parents) are out of tune with *other* significant others' evaluations (teachers'), power is dissipated. *All* parents' expectations predicted marks in the first cycle, but thereafter it was mainly middle-class parents, whose predictions were close to teachers' marks, who continued to have influence on marks. In other words, the children acted as if they were processing and integrating various self-images generated by significant others and by the self. However, the data that children process have first to be perceived, and perceptions appear to be heavily edited if they are in mutual disagreement.

Teachers' expectations (as distinct from evaluations) apparently have little independent influence on children's expectations. A major finding is that children's expectations are well shielded from teacher expectations, either directly (as seemed to be true for all the children irrespective of school) or indirectly because mark feedback is largely ignored (the two working-class schools). To the extent that teachers' expectations determine marks, however, they could be important. Our analysis suggests that the "evaluation" component of teachers' expectations is very important, and, because of this, using teachers' marks to capture teachers' expectations may be more appealing than the prevailing strategy of gathering only teacher expectations and ignoring marks. From a research perspective this is most fortunate. Teachers are required to give marks, so they can be gathered unobtrusively. Collecting teachers' expectations, on the other hand, requires teachers to do something they do not ordinarily do, and the very collecting of expectations could alter the schooling process.

We have tried to emphasize that evaluation is not a unitary concept. The teacher's expectations as well as her objective assessment of any given student performance contribute to the evaluation she makes. A teacher who expects a low-quality performance, for example, would likely evaluate a mediocre performance more highly than would be the case if she were expecting a high-quality performance. On the other hand, after some interaction has occurred between teacher and student, we find that the publicly recorded evaluations—the marks—incorporate teachers' expectations fairly completely.

There is another strand of evaluation that is related to the student: Students evaluate their own work and have expectations for the quality of that work. For this reason, the same teacher evaluation might produce different effects in students whose self-expectations are different. Children *do* respond to significant others, but they also respond to themselves, and we believe that their responses to themselves are not only direct inputs to the development of the self but also a critical factor in how input from others is interpreted.

Peers

Generally speaking, our analysis shows little influence of peer-popularity ratings on the schooling process of these young children. Although all but one of the effects on reading and arithmetic marks are positive, the patterns formed by the half-dozen effects that are significant are not consistent enough to be convincing. Peer-popularity is essentially randomly related to children's expectations in all schools in all grades. This agrees with the findings of Ruble et al. (1980) who report that achievement-related self-evaluations are little affected by relative comparisons until fourth grade. In two studies of first- and second-graders, they found that only the second-graders made any use at all of social comparison information. Elementary-school children do not seem to be as dependent upon a wide set of peers as secondary-school students, and children of the two sexes, when left to themselves, usually play separately and avoid interacting.

There may also be methodologic reasons peculiar to this research that account for inconsistent early peer-popularity effects on marks. For one thing, peer ratings were recorded only in the latter half of each school year and so had less opportunity to display effects. For another thing, because captains chose teams, the peer ranking is no doubt a combination of popularity *and* the captain's estimate of the child's ability. There was also no definitive way to check overall validity of the several versions of the peer-popularity measure, and the strength of effects may vary with the nature of the measure used.

More convincing evidence that peers lacked influence was found when friends' expectations were added as specific variables to the models. These variables were measured only for the older children and used a single procedure that was a minor variant on the usual strategy for eliciting expectations. The friends' expectations seemed to have considerable internal consistency—best friend's expectations exceeded second-best friend's, and the like.[3] However,

[3] Before obtaining expectations from the "best" and "second-best" friends, we thought many children might have friends outside the classroom and thus that the child's peers who could affect classroom achievement might not actually have been interviewed. It turned out, however, that most children's friends were in the same class as the child, so even this threat to the validity of the friends' expectations measures failed to materialize.

inclusion of even these stronger variables failed to find any substantial peer effects and led to only minimal increase in explained variance, strengthening our conclusion that peer effects are very small for children at this stage.

Best- and second-best friends' responses turned out to be exceedingly informative in a way we did not anticipate. As discussed in Chapter 7, the middle-class children held higher expectations for their friends than for themselves, while the lower-class children held lower expectations for their friends than for themselves, but lower-class children's expectations for their friends exceeded the level of their friends' marks in much the same way that their own expectations exceeded their own marks. This observation provokes the conclusion that not all of the discrepancy between lower-class children's expectations and performance is likely to be a consequence of intrapsychic stress. Although in constructing a self-theory children may reduce anxiety to bearable levels by a "clouding of consciousness" (Epstein 1967) and thus be able to maintain too-high expectations, they do not need to do this for their friends. Expectations for friends are closer to friends' attainment levels than are expectations for the self, but they are still far too high.

The significant, although smaller, discrepancy between lower-class children's expectations for friends and friends' performance seems best explained by the children's ignorance of school marking norms. While the children may know the meaning of particular marks, they may be ill-formed about the kinds of marks that are usually assigned.[4] This ignorance would affect their expectations for themselves as well as those for their friends. If expectations for friends early in first grade, which we did not collect, were as much too high or higher than they are later, it would be especially appealing to see unawareness of norms as an explanation for too-high expectations. Lower-class parents' expectations suggest this, because their expectations are too high in the first semester of school, before any marks have been awarded. (Lower-class parents' expectations, like their children's, also remained too high.) Children are unlikely to be as well informed about friends' marks as they are about their own, but the discrepancies are biased in the same way for friends as for self. It therefore seems likely that misperception of group norms contributes to the discrepancies. An easy way to check this in future work would be to ask parents and children how well they think the "average" child will do in reading and arithmetic. Note, however, that by third grade the children know what marks mean and precisely how well or poorly they personally have done. If self-expectations continue to be unrealistically high, it is in spite of this obvious personal history, which includes considerable feedback in terms of marks.

[4]Direct evidence that some lower-class children had trouble understanding marks per se was procured by re-interviewing some first-graders.

It has often been speculated that blacks are more responsive to peer influences than whites, and therefore that blacks' school achievement suffers either because individual blacks eschew achievement (it erodes group solidarity) or because the peers of blacks are more likely to be from lower socioeconomic levels than the peers of whites (and hence less able to provide the resources linked to high achievement). Although in our data it is not possible to test for such racial differences in the influence of peers as carefully as we would like, we can see no evidence of structural differences in peer effects across the two racial groups when separate models involving friends' expectations are estimated for blacks and whites in the integrated school. Conclusions were not clear-cut, because samples were small and the data generally were not of sufficient quality to support a full analysis, but neither the regular models within schools nor the separate models for blacks and whites in the integrated school support the hypothesis of differential sensitivity to peers according to race.

Parents

Most of the variables initially included to measure parent influence did not turn out to be useful. For example, parents' general interest in the child (whether measured by parents' knowledge of children's friends, involvement in conversation with the child at mealtimes, or long-term expectations for schooling) did not influence either expectations or marks. A homework-help question was not useful either, perhaps because the socially desirable response was not obvious. (Most parents say they will help with homework.)

Previous research shows that parents help establish feelings about the self early in life (Ausubel et al. 1954; Jourard and Remy 1955) and that parental evaluations are associated with elementary children's self-concepts of academic ability (Bilby, Brookover, and Erickson 1972). In our research, to the extent that children's expectations are explained at all, specific parental expectations offered some limited predictive power, especially for arithmetic, and relatively more for middle-class children. Four out of six paths from parent ability judgments (ABIL) to middle-class children's expectations in first grade are significant, and *all negative* (Table 6.35). Parental ability estimates that were higher than the already high averages for this school thus appeared to dampen these first-graders' expectations. As noted earlier, children may be made anxious by sensing very optimistic, yet unfocused, expectations on the part of their parents.

Even with IQ controlled, parents' specific expectations are important determinants of children's *first* marks in all three schools.[5] A striking pattern, especially in view of the key role that conduct plays in early attainment, is that in the middle-class school conduct marks responded significantly to parent expectations in four out of the six cycles (Table 6.29), while conduct marks responded only once in each of the other schools. After the middle of first grade, the influence of the lower-class parents appears to be considerably less than that of their middle-class counterparts—with the exception that parents of third-graders in the integrated school seem as effective in influencing academic marks as middle-class parents.

Children's marks continued to respond to parental expectations at the beginning of second grade in the middle-class school, although second-grade marks did not respond to first-grade marks. In contrast, parents' expectations were not effective at the beginning of second grade in the integrated school, where marks were strongly conditioned by prior marks. To the extent that marks persisted, parent influence was mitigated. Parent influences also seem generally stronger in the first cycle of each year, when previous marks are less efficacious, but this could also happen because parental variables were measured only once a year, during the first term.

What could explain the generally greater efficacy of parents in the middle-class setting? One possibility is that lower-class parents interact less with their children. We did find that lower-class parents ate dinner less often with their children and knew fewer of their children's friends. If lower-class parents spend less time with their children, they may not be readily available to talk about school or to provide help with schoolwork. In other words, a child who does not spend enough time with a parent to learn of parental expectations could hardly be affected by them. Another possibility is that after parents' expectations are proved to be off target by the first marks the lower-class children receive, the parents may become less credible sources of information about school. This kind of reaction by children could explain why parents' expectations impinged strongly on marks of lower-class children during the first cycle and then not ever again in the black lower-class school, and not until several cycles later in the integrated school.

Another potential explanation for the greater efficacy of parents' expectations in the middle-class school is that teachers are relatively less influential there. This explanation, however, is not very consistent with various structural coefficients, such as the third-grade resurgence of parental effects in the integrated school.

Still another line of reasoning to explain differential parent influence is that the absolute amount of variance in marks could limit the number of explanatory sources. That is, if there is more variation to be explained, it might be possible for more factors to come into play. In absolute terms, however, there is *more*, rather than less, mark variance to be explained in the integrated as compared to the middle-class school. Table 5.2 shows that the standard deviations for all marks over the 3-year period of the study ranged from 0.51 to 0.69 in the middle-class school and from 0.65 to 1.02 in the integrated school. A larger number of significant others being influential in the middle-class school runs directly counter to this explanation.

It is important to note that, although parents' expectations in all three places affected first marks to about the same extent in the first marking period, parents were not equally accurate in each place. Parents' expectations in the middle-class school were very close to their children's first marks (1.78, 1.80, and 1.78 vs. 1.82, 1.85, and 1.80 in reading, arithmetic, and conduct, respectively), whereas in the other two schools parents' expectations were close to children's marks only in conduct (2.44, 2.36, and 1.70 vs. 3.31, 3.00, and 1.87 in the integrated shcool; 2.39, 2.39, and 1.78 vs. 2.96, 3.01, and 2.12 in the all-black school). When parents' expectations are off target, their efficacy apparently declines.

Perhaps children do not process input from their parents for the same reasons they do not process information from their marks—it is painful—but this explanation cannot account for the resurgence in effectiveness of third-graders' parents in the integrated school, since these parents' expectations remained as overly optimistic in third grade as they were in first grade. Lower-class parents' expectations tended to be lower than their children's expectations, although they were higher than the corresponding marks, and lower-class parents' expectations remained overly optimisitic despite their consistent (and borderline significant) responsiveness to marks at the end of first grade.

The composite picture suggests that all parents were influential at the start of school but that middle-class parents were more influential in matters of conduct, a key area in predicting early academic performance, and that, perhaps because their forecasts were correct, or pleasing, or possibly because of more parent/child contact, middle-class parents' influences continued after the beginning of first grade, to the end of first grade and beyond.

The fact that acceptance by peers (Reese 1961) and parents (Bilby et al. 1972) has been shown to be

[5] Parents' general ability estimates had some effects on middle-class children's conduct marks (three out of six significant) but they are hard to interpret because signs are mixed. Parental ability estimates also had effects on black children late in second grade and in third grade, but mixed signs and the weakness of the models for this group make these effects questionable.

associated with more-positive attitudes toward the self could merely imply that favorable feedback is more likely to be processed. Very little is known about negative feedback.

The relative influence of significant others has been of much greater interest to sociologists of education than to developmental psychologists. It seems likely that peers would become relatively more influential with age, but more data are needed to trace this out. Our data suggest that the relative influence of significant others could also depend on social context, since middle-class parents retained influence while lower-class parents did not.

Teachers

The influence of teachers as significant others is discussed mainly in a later section devoted to marks and evaluations, since teachers' expectations had no effect on children's expectations above that captured by teachers' marks. This finding has a number of important implications, the first being that, as significant others, the teachers, through their behavioral expression of expectations—giving marks—may exert their influence mainly via this one channel. Another implication is that previous research, almost all of which emphasizes teachers' expectations to the exclusion of teachers' marks, may have left us with a distorted image of teacher-student influence patterns.

Teachers responded strongly to children's conduct and apparently only by this means did gender affect teachers' evaluations. Conduct is a strong determinant of teachers' marks in reading and arithmetic in the first year of school, and testing models with reciprocal paths suggests this influence is mainly unidirectional—*from* conduct *to* performance in reading and arithmetic. The regression models with conduct as a predictor of standardized test scores suggested that conduct had little direct effect on standardized performance measures, but the coefficients were uniformly positive. The timing of these standardized measures (third grade) may lead this effect to be underestimated.

There were hints that, as children advanced in age, race began to affect teachers' expectations slightly, although in first grade no differences associated with teacher and/or pupil race matching or mismatching could be uncovered (Entwisle and Hayduk 1978b).

A fruitful area for future investigation is the relation of teacher characteristics other than race to student evaluations; for example, the relations between teachers' gender or years of experience and marks. In this study it appeared that evaluations were stricter when children were of lower socioeconomic status than the teacher. Except for race, however, teachers' demographic characteristics in this research are unknown, so it was not possible to check findings like Schneider's (1980), which indicate that the more extensive a teacher's background is and the greater her experience, the lower children's achievement.

EFFECTS OF ASCRIPTIVE VARIABLES

Concern with equality of opportunity for minority groups prompted much educational research during the sixties and seventies. Concern for equity along gender lines came later and has mounted as more and more women have entered the labor force. Controversies concerning the extent to which gender differences are innate or environmentally produced (Benbow and Stanley 1980; Maccoby and Jacklin 1980) are not likely to be settled any sooner than the similar disputes about IQ, and our research does not speak directly to these concerns. However, we did observe some structural differences across schools that were associated with the ascriptive exogenous variables, especially IQ. On the one hand, race, gender, and IQ, in and of themsleves, did not turn out to be nearly as influential on early schooling as many people would have guessed. On the other hand, the response of attainment to IQ varied somewhat across schools, suggesting rather different effects of IQ upon the schooling process. Most important, in the lasting-effects model, IQ effects washed out, even in the integrated school, where cycle-by-cycle effects of IQ were substantial.

Race

Black children and white children attending the integrated school were exposed to similar learning environments. Many factors commonly confounded with racial differences, especially the socioeconomic composition of the school, were fairly well controlled for children of the two races attending this particular integrated school. We found no evidence for *structural* differences by race in the process of schooling for children in this school, and, in particular, the role of significant others (e. g., parents, peers) did not appear to differ by race in this sample.

Children of the two races in the integrated school had the same expectations, and, as far as we could tell, they responded to peers in an equivalent fashion. Their achievement in reading and arithmetic was about equal. Black teachers and white teachers evaluated children of the two races in similar terms (see Entwisle and Hayduk 1978b), with the possible exception that teachers held slightly higher expectations for white children by the end of second grade. The structural patterns explaining expectations and marks in the various cycles were the same for children of the two races, with one exception, a possible difference in the effect of IQ on parents' estimates of their child's ability to do schoolwork in first grade. Our findings therefore agree with those of Heyns (1978, p. 64), who found only slight structural differences by race in the influences of particular variables for sixth- and seventh-graders in Atlanta, and with those of Beady and Hansell (1981), who report no difference in teachers' expectations by race for student achievement and effort. In other studies where model structure has been found to differ for students of the two races (Winkler 1972), blacks and whites are exposed to different kinds of peer groups, with blacks having a much higher proportion of low-socioeconomic-level peers than whites.

Effects of race could be evaluated from another standpoint, by comparing whites in the integrated school with whites in the all-white school and blacks in the integrated school with blacks in the all-black school. In these comparisons there were marked differences in socioeconomic level between the white children in the integrated lower-class school and whites in the middle-class school. The structural parameters explaining performance differed between these groups of whites. There was little difference in socioeconomic status of children in the integrated and black schools, and blacks *and* whites in the integrated lower-class school resembled blacks in the all-black lower-class school. These comparisons suggest that socioeconomic status, rather than race, is the dominant factor associated with attainment differences across these schools. When socioeconomic status was comparable, race mattered little. When it was not, children differed in numerous respects.[6]

These findings must be interpreted cautiously, however. Race may be much more salient when children attend schools outside their immediate neighborhoods, because then the racial composition of the school is likely to differ from the racial composition of the neighborhood. Moreover, we suspect the salience of race for children increases as they become older and become aware of the significance of race in the larger society. Children are thought to gain this awareness around the end of elementary school. We learned accidentally that fifth-grade children in the integrated school did not know that blacks are a minority group in the United States, so the salience of race may be especially low in this school.

As mentioned, much of the research on educational attainment has been motivated by concern for equity. However, St. John (1975, p. 36) concludes that "adequate data have not yet been gathered to determine a causal relation between school racial composition and academic achievement. There are no definitive positive findings." To the best of our knowledge, St. John's conclusion still holds. However, apparently no one has looked for *structural* differences in the early attainment process associated with racial composition of schools along the lines suggested by our models. Structural modeling could shed light on the mechanisms that mediate desegregation effects. For example, black students in integrated schools with a high percentage of whites may do well because their parents, who see to it that their children get into such schools and who are therefore perhaps different from other black parents, hold expectations that provoke relatively higher levels of attainment. Or they may do well because they respond to the peer influences of their white classmates. (The latter explanation is often mentioned, but, insofar as our data can test it, the explanation is not supported.) It is quite possible that offsetting effects occur, with affective development impeded and cognitive development improved as the percentage of blacks declines (McPartland 1968). There is little prior work on how desegregation ratios may affect development of the academic self-image. In the integrated school studied in this research, there were more blacks than whites, but the racial division was not extreme, and a balance had prevailed for many years. If one race predominates or if there is racial tension in a school, the picture may be different.

Sex

Our finding that marks in conduct reveal gender differences is in accord with previous research (Alberti 1971; Brophy and Good 1970). On the other hand, in contrast to previous investigators (Averch et al. 1972; Doma 1972; Dwyer 1973), we did not observe sex bias in marks for reading and arithmetic. Marks in conduct responded strongly to gender (favoring girls over boys) at the beginning of first grade in the middle-class and integrated schools and to a smaller extent in the black school. It is during the first cycle that marks in conduct have their most noticeable influence upon marks in reading and arithmetic. The standardized coefficients for middle-class children show that gender is the strongest influence on children's conduct expectations at that time, and it is about as strong an influence on conduct marks as IQ is. For children in the integrated school, gender affects three of the four parent variables in the first cycle (always to the benefit of girls) and has more impact on marks in conduct than either IQ or parents' expectations. After the first cycle, however, gender effects appear less important, although occasionally they do crop up. The weak pat-

[6] As emphasized in Appendix A, comparisons between the lower-class schools and the middle-class school are confounded in a number of ways: by differences in average IQ, by the emphasis on absolute levels of achievement as compared to effort, and by the degree of parent participation. Except for marking policy, however, these differences are the usual correlates of differences in socioeconomic status.

terns that do appear in all schools are generally consistent with traditional sex stereotypes of girls excelling in reading and conduct while boys dominate arithmetic.

This overview suggests that gender has fairly strong effects on the early schooling process by way of conduct. The early impact of gender could have long-lasting consequences because first marks tend to persist, especially in the lower-class schools. Also, parent variables displayed several responses to gender, and several gender effects on parent variables appeared as late as third grade in all the schools.

To our knowledge no one has previously examined structural models to see whether the schooling process is different for males and females in elementary school. Murnane (1975) reports interactions by gender among teachers, students, and subject matter—male teachers being more effective teaching black children, especially arithmetic. In our data there were no male teachers, so the opportunity for gender differences to arise was limited. However, to the extent that we could look for structural differences by gender, they were absent.

IQ[7]

IQ is a particularly difficult variable to intepret in this research, both because of its inherent nature and because, for several cohorts, there were no IQ scores available. Also, as noted in Appendix A, the IQ distribution is not the same from school to school, and the average IQ level fluctuates considerably from year to year within schools. How seriously the latter two problems may afflict this data set is impossible to say. In addition, IQ is taken only as an exogenous variable. To place it in a dependent position with our data would be awkward for practical reasons, but we would avoid doing it in any case because there is so much ambiguity involved in IQ measures. IQ scores reflect arithmetic, reading, and other skills and in different proportions depending upon the age of the child. For this reason it may be a mistake to implicitly assume, as most macro-studies do, that IQ is a continuously distributed unitary variable across schools. In one school a "high IQ" may be 110, and in another school a "low IQ" may be 110. The score is the same, but the social meaning of the score, which is what the parent or teacher attends to, varies.

In this research, IQ scores seem best interpreted as a kind of ascriptive variable that can affect teacher evaluations. Since we never pooled data across schools, the IQ effects are just as school-specific as marks. We mainly inquired how influential IQ may be within a given social setting and whether its effects are direct or indirect.

We pay most attention to IQ effects over first grade in the black school and over the first two grades in the middle-class and integrated schools because of problems of fit, and because the model for entry into second grade could not be estimated at all for the black school. IQ had more effects in the lower-class schools than in the middle-class school. In the integrated school, *all* marks responded to IQ in the first and second grades (once negatively), and reading and arithmetic marks responded strongly in the black school. Marks in the middle-class school responded to IQ only sporadically—a different area reaches significance in each grade.

Parents in all three schools apparently incorporated IQ into their initial ability estimates, and the middle-class parents even adjusted their second-grade ability estimates in terms of IQ. The initial academic expectations of parents in the white and integrated schools also mirrored IQ, but later responses in these schools were less consistent. The IQ variable appeared to influence parents in the middle-class school more strongly than it affected children's performance there! Initially at least, parents *and* performance in the integrated school responded to IQ comparably.

Teachers' ratings of conduct in both the middle-class and integrated schools for the first marking period, when conduct had strong effects on reading and arithmetic marks, responded directly to IQ. Children with higher IQ's received better marks in conduct in *both* places. However, the IQ picture may be more complex than is commonly assumed. At times, parents expected exactly the opposite would happen—brighter children were expected to be less docile in the classroom (T1 black school, T3 white school). Even the brighter children themselves at times thought they would be judged to be poorly behaved (second grade, white and integrated schools) or that they would be judged to be poor readers (second and third grade, middle-class school) although some positive effects appear as well. With this mixture of effects it is not surprising that IQ did not prove particularly efficacious in the lasting-effects models, where potentially contrasting effects are accumulated.

The findings here need to be explored much further. It would be particularly desirable to know how much IQ contributes to in-school and out-of-school achievement. Heyns (1978) finds that "home factors" improve more affluent children's achievement over the summer, but that during the school year, children of all socioeconomic levels are learning at a fairly comparable rate. To the extent that her findings could apply to our data, IQ may be a fairly weak or negligible influence on early learning *in school*, but it may serve

[7] Because the metric for IQ is so different from other metrics, structural coefficients for IQ in standardized form are much different than they are in metric form.

as a proxy for the relative levels of academic resources available to children outside of school. (We have no measure of the academic climate of the home.) A child who enters first grade knowing how to read would probably get a high IQ score, but that competence may be as stongly correlated with home resources (parents who teach children) as with the child's IQ level.

Knowledge of IQ scores consistently improved prediction of standardized test scores (Chapter 7), but the mechanisms by which IQ affected children's competence, particularly its effects on parents, children, and teachers, are complex. In our data its effects varied drastically, not only in size from one school to another, but in nature.

Summary

This overview of the influence of ascriptive variables on the schooling process suggests that race per se, divorced from socioeconomic status, had little impact. Gender had some influence, but surprisingly little direct influence on academic marks. (It mainly affected early conduct marks, which in turn affected early marks in reading and arithmetic.)

IQ had considerably less influence on marks than we would have guessed. The differences in structural patterns of IQ across schools merit attention. The higher average level of IQ in the middle-class school may diminish the influence of IQ there, because children are well above any critical level for being able to learn basic skills, and the range of variation for IQ is restricted enough to attenuate relationships.

IQ also has less of a unique influence upon standardized achievement than we would have guessed. For example, in Table 7.7, when three variables that include marks but not IQ are used to predict standardized achievement of third-graders in the two lower-class schools, the coefficients of determination are generally large (eight coefficients average 0.658) and the addition of six other variables, including IQ, to the equation improves the average prediction only to 0.757.[8]

It is noteworthy that, even this early in the schooling process, the effects of IQ on achievement are mediated by other variables linked to the *behavior* of significant others, especially teachers' marks and parents' expectations, through their conceptions of children's ability.

[8] It could be objected that the joint contribution of marks and IQ is, by this analysis, allocated entirely to marks. True, but there is some logic in the ordering. Since we are interested in portraying the internal functioning of a system, we should attribute as much as possible to the most concrete elements of that system, namely marks. If IQ provided no additional variance contribution, we would not claim that ability was unimportant, but rather that the other model elements carried all the essential ability information.

Gender influenced teachers' evaluations mainly via conduct. This kind of effect may explain Murnane's (1975) and Summers and Wolfe's (1977) observations concerning teacher effectiveness. Teachers whose sex and race match those of their pupils probably have standards for conduct that are better tuned to the children's own standards. Perhaps for this reason, both boys and girls are reported to have a strong tendency to prefer adults of their own sex (Stevenson et al. 1967). This explanation could also account for Murnane's observation that increasing experience on the job contributed to teacher effectiveness for about 3 years, but that effectiveness declined with additional years of experience. [Schneider (1980) confirms the negative relation between years of experience and effectiveness.] Years of experience, of course, are also strongly related to the teacher's chronological age. With advancing age, teachers may become less and less tolerant of boisterousness and confusion. The noisy roughhouse of small boys, for example, may be much better tolerated by a teacher in her twenties than by a teacher in her fifties. Since direct effects of conduct are most noticeable in first grade, this would provide one reason for assigning the youngest teachers to first grade.

THE DETERMINANTS OF CHILDREN'S EXPECTATIONS AND THEIR IMPACT UPON PERFORMANCE

Because reading and arithmetic lie at the heart of the elementary school curriculum, we traced the developmental history of children's expectations for performance in those two specific areas. Conduct is academically vacuous but may capture halo effects and other facets of teacher evaluation that are not tied to a child's actual competence. Teachers form "affective" as well as "cognitive" evaluations (Williams 1976), and part of the distinction between the two kinds of evaluations is manifest in how teachers rate reading and arithmetic in comparison with conduct. Non-cognitive factors cannot be ignored by a teacher confined all day in a single room with twenty or thirty children.

To see whether expectations were formed in the same way in each school and to plot the timetable for expectation development, we tracked expectations through the first three grades in the three distinct social environments. What little we knew about young children's expectations at the time this research began did not indicate whether self-expectations were fixed by the time children entered first grade or whether they developed over the early school years. The causes of high or low expectations, particularly in terms of how responsive children's expectations are to ascriptive variables like gender or race, were not clear.

The major clue provided by previous work was Rosenberg and Simmons' (1971) survey pointing to the specific kinds of life experiences that affected the self-esteem of black children. The child's status relative to friends and classmates, not the absolute level of a child's socioeconomic status, determined children's ideas about themselves. Rosenberg and Simmons reported that poor black children in Baltimore did not lower their self-image as long as they were surrounded by children like themselves. Therefore, we looked to the immediate social context of the children in our sample for the determinants of self-expectations.

It makes sense that the *local* social context, rather than children's position in the larger society, dominates their self-image. Elementary schools, because they draw their clients from neighborhoods close around them, may effectively shelter children from social interactions that would erode their self-regard. Although adults may suffer a diminished self-image if the group to which they belong is looked down upon by the rest of society, children's vision is limited. They do not have clear notions of how the larger society is structured, and their social world is circumscribed.

Expectation Levels

In line with other investigators (Nicholls 1979; Parsons and Ruble 1977), we observed that children's expectations declined somewhat and became more predictable with increasing age. Variance in expectations of third-graders was better explained than variance in expectations of first-graders in every school. Children in every school held initial expectations that were higher on average than their marks, but the expectations of the lower-class children were inordinately high. Eighty-seven percent of the children in the integrated school received poorer reading marks than they anticipated on their first report card, and the comparable figure for the all-black school was 81%. In contrast, only 44% of the middle-class children did worse than they expected on the first report card, and a majority did the same or slightly better than they expected.

All first-grade children failed to predict their first report card marks with accuracy above chance, but 36% of the middle-class children *happened* to be correct in their reading forecasts. Many fewer children in the other two schools happened to be correct—only 10% in the integrated school and 18% in the all-black school, because on average the marks in these schools were low. At the beginning of school the average discrepancy between expectations and marks for the integrated school was −1.85, −1.30, and −0.71 (expectations higher than marks) compared to −0.22, −0.06, −0.09 for the middle-class school. All children overestimated, but the estimates of the middle-class children were much more accurate. As time went on, all children's accuracy improved, but only the middle-class children were actually on target. For example, at the end of grade three the discrepancies were still large in the integrated school— −1.34, −0.83, and −0.25, respectively. In contrast, middle-class children's estimates were on the conservative side by the end of grade three. By then, middle-class children were *under*estimating their marks in reading and arithmetic, while the lower-class children were still overestimating them by a sizeable margin. Not only were the initial expectations of lower-class children higher than those of middle-class children, but, even after the lower-class children had repeatedly received marks much lower than they hoped for, their expectations were generally as high as middle-class children's. For example, children's expectations in reading, arithmetic, and conduct at end of grade three were 1.74, 1.89, and 1.79 in the middle-class school, compared to 1.74, 1.85, and 1.66, and 1.67, 1.93, and 1.57 in the integrated and black schools, respectively. Lower-class children's expectations did drop relatively more over the 3-year period (declines of −0.28, −0.15, −0.50 in the integrated school and −0.14, −0.15, −0.24 in the black school, compared to −0.14, −0.10, −.08 in the middle-class school), but they did not drop enough to come into line with the marks the children received.

Initially, lower-class parents' expectations were about 0.60 grade-points lower for reading and arithmetic than middle-class parents', but all parents expected about the same performance in conduct (slightly above a B). Parents' and children's expectations did not closely coincide in any school. In the lower-class schools, however, where parental expectations were relatively lower and children's expectations were relatively higher, lack of agreement was striking. For example, in the integrated school in the first cycle, parents' expectations were 2.44, 2.36, and 1.70, compared to children's expectations of 1.46, 1.70, and 1.16. Both the difference between children's expectations and their marks and the difference between children's expectations and parents' expectations were much smaller in the middle-class school than in the lower-class schools. Middle-class parents were the only persons "well-tuned" in terms of marks.

Average expectation levels by school are the opposite of what might have been predicted. Lower-class children's expectations might be relatively modest, for example, because their older siblings and friends probably did less well in school than the older siblings and friends of the middle-class children did. Also, as noted, lower-class parents held lower expectations, on the average, than middle-class parents did. However, a pattern of too-high expectations for these lower-class youngsters is not out of line with other empirical findings. St. John (1975, p. 56), for example, reports college aspirations of black adolescents as being higher than those of whites.

The patterns involving expectations for reading and arithmetic are not the same. In every school differences between expectations and marks are smaller for arithmetic than for reading, and children's expectations for arithmetic are lower than their expectations for reading at every time. In addition, at the end of third grade in all the schools, there are paths from children's expectations in arithmetic to their marks in arithmetic, while there are no corresponding connections between children's expectations for reading and their reading marks. In other words, children's expectations in arithmetic are everywhere predictive of performance by the end of third grade, while their reading expectations are not.[9]

One tentative conclusion is that, when expectation levels are more realistic, they play a stronger role in determining performance. This conclusion is supported by several findings: in the middle-class school, where expectations and marks are generally closer than they are in the other two schools, seven out of eighteen paths between children's current expectations and marks are significant, compared to seven out of thirty-three in the other two schools; final expectations for third-grade arithmetic are predictive in all three schools, as cited above; and parents' expectations display less power after the first cycle in the lower-class schools.

Although the causal power of expectations appears stronger when expectations are realistic (by matching the distribution of assigned marks), such realism is neither a necessary nor a sufficient condition for effectiveness. At times expectations are effective in the integrated school, despite the fact that expectations there exceeded marks on the average, and at times expectations are ineffective when discrepancies are small. For example, after the first cycle, parents' conduct expectations in the lower-class schools are ineffective, despite discrepancies averaging only about one-tenth of a grade-point. Thus, while expectations display their greatest effectiveness when the means of marks and expectations correspond, ineffectiveness sometimes appears, in spite of such correspondence, and effectiveness sometimes appears, in spite of lack of correspondence.[10]

The inaccuracies of children in the various schools are very different qualitatively. We have already noted that, in the first cycle, 56% of the children in the middle-class school did as well or better than they expected in reading, whereas in the integrated and black schools the comparable figures are 12% and 19%. Furthermore, with the passage of time, the percentage of middle-class children who did worse than they expected in reading declined over the six cycles—44%, 30%, 34%, 16%, 22%, and 16%—whereas in the other two schools most children continued to do worse than they expected. In the integrated school, 87%, 75%, 83%, 73%, 76%, and 75% did worse, and, in the black school, 82%, 81%, 83%, 74%, 68%, and 82% did worse over the six cycles. Middle-class children frequently underestimated their performance and so could be happily surprised when their pessimistic forecasts proved wrong. Almost all lower-class children, on the other hand, were in for unpleasant surprises, because their estimates were consistently over-optimistic and the degree of their over-optimism diminished little. One consequence of the very high level of lower-class children's expectations is that the variability of their expectations is small—smaller than the variability of their marks. The variability of children's initial expectations in the middle-class school, on the other hand, is not only larger than that of lower-class children's, but larger than the variability either of their parents' expectations or of the marks they received. Their estimates encompassed a wide range.

Distinctiveness of Expectations

There are consistent biases in children's expectations favoring reading over arithmetic, and only 25% of the children in the middle-class school and 28% in the integrated school had the same initial expectations in reading and arithmetic. This represents a deficit in matching over what would be expected by chance. By the end of the year, a matching deficit is still present, but it is not large enough to be significant in either school. Children in both places thus behaved similarly, in that they strongly differentiated the two subject areas when they started school. The relatively homogeneous levels of arithmetic expectations over the three schools, together with the lack of homogeneity between schools in reading expectations, also suggests that children differentiated among their expectations in these two areas.

Even stronger evidence that the two expectations are distinct is contained in the patterns of correlations between children's expectations for reading and arithmetic (Table 8.1). Only one correlation is significantly positive, and in ten out of eighteen instances the correlations are actually negative. [One that is negative (−0.14) is relatively large, just short of the 5% level.]

[9] At earlier times no clear superiority of either area is evident.

[10] The lagged effects of children's expectations appear predominantly where there are substantial discrepancies, but this is simply because the lagged effects occur primarily in the integrated school.

Table 8.1. Correlations Related to Children's Expectations in Reading and Arithmetic

	T1	T2	T3	T4	T5	T6
Children's expectations for reading and arithmetic						
White middle-class school	.03	-.02	.03	-.04	-.01	.14*
Integrated lower-class school	.00	.13	-.05	-.06	-.06	-.01
Black lower-class school	.01	.03	-.14	-.08	-.04	.00
Marks for reading and arithmetic						
White middle-class school	.34**	.47**	.51**	.47**	.36**	.45**
Integrated lower-class school	.60**	.64**	.60**	.58**	.55**	.55**
Black lower-class school	.51**	.69**	.44**	.78**	.48**	.64**
	For best friend		For second best friend		Friends' expectations	
	T4	T6	T4	T6	T4	T6
Expectations for reading and arithmetic						
White middle-class school	.05	.28***	.17*	.28***	.16*	.30***
Integrated lower-class school	.11	.34***	.32***	.33***	.26**	.50***
Black lower-class school	.17*	.06	.29***	.18*	.33***	.31***
	T1	T2	T3	T4	T5	T6
Expectations for conduct with reading						
White middle-class school	.13**	.01	.13*	.09	.11*	.16*
Integrated lower-class school	.19**	.14*	.20**	.09	.20**	.15
Black lower-class school	.19**	.13	.07	n.a.	.25**	.26**
	T1	T2	T3	T4	T5	T6
Expectations for conduct with arithmetic						
White middle-class school	-.02	.06	-.01	.06	-.04	.08
Integrated lower-class school	.10	.20**	.01	-.05	-.05	.11
Black lower-class school	.10	.19**	.30**	.23*	.13	.01

* P < .05

** P < .01

*** P < .001

Over all, there is no visible relation between expectations in the two areas.[11]

In contrast, the correlations between children's marks in reading and their marks in arithmetic are substantially positive and significant beyond the 1% level in every case. Teachers assign very similar marks in the two areas. Parents have consistent expectations for the two areas (correlations averaged 0.44 in the white middle-class school, 0.59 in the integrated school, and 0.64 in the black school). Children appear to be oblivious to these facts with respect to their own expectations, even though they seem to perceive them with respect to other children. Children's expectations for their friends and their friends' expectations for them in reading and arithmetic are generally correlated (Table 8.1).

Could the independence of children's self-expectations for reading from their self-expectations for arithmetic come about because one or both sets of expectations consist entirely of error? Several kinds of evidence deny this: 1) the generally significant test-retest correlations for children's expectations shown in Table B.2; 2) the relatively large correlations (0.40 to 0.55) between children's expectations in arithmetic obtained by interview and their expectations obtained independently from answers to an item on the self-esteem test (Table B.2); 3) the consistently positive correlations between children's expectations for conduct and their expectations for reading (eleven of seventeen are significant in Table 8.1)

In addition, children's expectations are better predicted as children mature, even though the correlations between children's expectations for reading and arithmetic show no pattern with increasing age. The children are also able to hold independent expectations for their best and second-best friends, although they expect similar performances in reading and arithmetic for *each* friend. Thus, another kind of cognitive inconsistency appears that could no more be predicted than the inconsistency in reading and arithmetic ex-

[11] Earlier (Entwisle and Hayduk 1978a, p. 131), from observation of only three cohorts, we believed the association between children's expectations for reading and arithmetic was actually inverse. On the basis of the more extensive data now in hand, it seems likely that the association between children's expectations for reading and arithmetic is negligible or zero.

pectations for the self. All in all, children apparently perceive their own performances in reading and arithmetic as being unrelated, and it seems unlikely that one or both sets of expectations are random.

The independence of young children's reading and arithmetic expectations has some practical implications. First, of course, it vindicates our separate-area assumption in modeling. Second, if children's expectations are distinct, low expectations in one subject would not be expected to affect learning in the other. Third, if changing children's expectations proves in the future to be either feasible or desirable, the likelihood of being able to design some "treatment" appears to us to be greater if children perceive the two areas as distinct. That is, one can more easily imagine a set of exercises to improve a child's ideas about his or her ability in arithmetic than one can imagine a set of exercises to improve a child's entire academic self-image.

The divorce between children's expectations in reading and arithmetic and the greater predictive capacity of arithmetic expectations may reflect norms present in both social classes. Most Americans make light of poor performance in arithmetic—the "I-can't-balance-a-checkbook" phenomenon—but we have yet to see a parent who takes poor performance in reading as lightly. As a consequence, children may experience less pressure for high aspirations in arithmetic and so find it possible to be more realistic. Besides having lower expectations for arithmetic than for reading, individual children may be able to face their own limitations in arithmetic more easily.

Determinants of Expectations

There are many studies of the effects of children's self-image on achievement, but only a few examine effects of teacher's expectations on students' expectations. To our knowledge there is only one study of how children's expectations develop starting from the time of school entry: it is Rist's (1970) report based on data from a single class of black kindergarteners. By measuring children's expectations very early in their school career and *before* marks were received, we hoped to measure the "initial" levels of children's expectations, to see if children did enter school with clear ideas about their own capabilities. Rist's research, which was entirely observational, concluded that the teacher's expectations formed in the first few days of school, apparently in response to ascriptive factors, and were resistant to change thereafter. Then children's achievement came to be matched to the teacher's expectations, perhaps in part because the children developed low expectations for themselves. Our data disagree. In our study, teachers' expectations did not respond to ascriptive factors [nor did they in the Haller and Davis (1981) study], and children's expectations did not respond to teachers' expectations.

The first time their expectations were measured, children in our study had been in school for about 2 months. At that time the children's expectations were amorphous—from 4% to 5% of reading, 5% to 14% of arithmetic, and 2% to 6% of conduct expectation variance could be accounted for by parental and background factors (Table 6.2).

IQ might be thought to be an especially potent determinant of early expectations because either high-ability or low-ability children might get more distinctive feedback. That is, children who stand out may get more explicit reactions than those who are in the middle of the distribution. (Low-ability children might receive more clear statements from classmates or teachers that their performance is not up to standard and revise their expectations downward, and, similarly, a high-ability child might get clearer positive daily reinforcements than a child of mediocre ability.) This conjecture does not hold up, however, because only one coefficient out of nine linking IQ to children's expectations in the first cycle was significant. Later, a scattered mixture of positive and negative effects appears.

In all three schools, children's expectations at the time they began first grade were poorly determined and equally unresponsive to parent influences. After one semester in school, children's expectations began to be more predictable. Some expectations early in the school year determined expectations later in the year (reading and conduct in the middle-class school, arithmetic and conduct in the integrated school), and parents did seem to have a little more influence on expectations later in first grade than earlier. However, children's expectations in all three schools were not very well determined, even at the end of third grade. By then the explained variance in children's expectations is highest in the middle-class school (36%, 29%, and 22% for reading, arithmetic, and conduct, respectively), but less in the integrated school (8%, 13%, and 28%). The black school falls in between (18%, 25%, and 29%). Our conclusion is that in the black school children's expectations were largely indeterminate at the start of school and developed somewhat over the early school years, but remained rather poorly determined even at the end of grade three. Expectations were considerably less well determined than marks or standardized achievement scores, a finding that is consistent with Epstein's (1980) conclusions about seventh-graders.

The indeterminacy of children's expectations forces an important conclusion, namely that children's early expectations do not crystallize. In all three schools, all the paths linking children's prior expectations with their current expectations are positive, and most of the twenty-eight (of forty-two) that are significant are even highly significant. The magnitudes of the effects, however, are not large (the standardized coefficients average 0.23, 0.31, and 0.25 in the white, integrated, and black schools, respectively) and imply modest contributions to the variance explained in later expectations by earlier expectations. Children's expectations do consistently display persistence between time periods, but the persistence is not strong enough to be dubbed crystallization.

The considerable reshuffling of expectations that appears between adjacent time periods implies that year-to-year expectations persist even less. If expectations do become predictable, not much of the stabilization is attributable to psychological commitment or rigidity. An alternate explanation would be that expectations mirror other stable factors, such as marks, and we discuss children's responses to mark feedback below.

The indeterminacy of children's expectations, if corroborated in future work, is a key finding. It suggests that early expectations are far from indelible. Children in this study who had low initial expectations often had high expectations later, and vice versa. Expectation indeterminacy is in agreement with Gottfredson's (1980) conclusion that achievement shapes expectations rather than the other way around. Cognitive theorists who accord expectations a central role in their explanation of behavior but who do not emphasize evaluation by the self as a separate concept may be at a handicap in explaining children's behavior if young children's expectations are not stable. Mead and Cooley, on the other hand, emphasized that evaluations by others lead to the mergence of a "generalized other," which can be regarded as a mechanism for generating self-evaluations. To the extent that self-expectations can be differentiated from self-evaluations, the latter may prove the more useful concept, just as we suggest for teachers' expectations and evaluations.

Generally, parents of middle-class children seemed to affect their children's expectations more than lower-class parents did. Significant effects of parents' expectations upon children's expectations in the academic subjects were noted in five out of twelve possible instances in the middle-class school, but fewer effects of this kind appeared in the other two schools (four positive, one negative, out of twenty-two). At times, the strength of parents' expectations relative to other predictors is impressive in the middle-class school. Parents' expectations are the largest single source of children's expectations in reading and arithmetic at the end of first grade (standardized coefficients of 0.23 and 0.36, respectively). With one exception, parents' expectations for conduct were not related to children's expectations for conduct in any school at any time. This is surprising, since conduct would seem to be the area where parents could communicate expectations most effectively.

Parents' general ability estimates had fewer effects on children's expectations than on parents' specific expectations, and early effects on children's expectations appeared to be negative. This is further evidence of the importance of distinguishing among expectations for reading, arithmetic, and conduct, and differentiating them from general ability estimates.

Besides revealing expectations of lower-status children to be higher than those of middle-class children, our data suggest differences by social class in the determinants of children's expectations. As far as we can tell, the ascriptive variable one would suspect of being the most potent—race—had negligible effects. As time passed, children's expectations became better determined in all three schools but only in the middle-class school did performance itself play a clear role in shaping expectations. Perhaps most important, in the middle-class school marks appeared to influence later expectations (ten of fifteen significant). In contrast, significant parameters linking marks to later expectations in the other two schools are very few (four of twenty-six) and a number of insignificant signs are reversed. In the middle-class school, feedback from marks strongly modulated children's academic expectations, and in the other two schools it apparently did not. Without taking notice of evaluations in relation to ideas of their own competence, children in the lower-class schools could maintain unrealistic ideas about their own capabilities—children's expectations for reading and arithmetic remained higher than their marks over the first three grades. In the middle-class school, however, children's expectations declined somewhat and came into line with their marks.

The feedback patterns suggest that mark feedback is not processed by children in the two lower-class schools because marks in reading and arithmetic are painfully distant from expectations. We think it is no accident that two of the four exceptions involving feedback from marks to expectations in the lower-class schools involve conduct, because average conduct marks given by teachers in the two lower-class schools were higher than marks in the other areas, making them less distant from the children's expectations.

The patterns generally suggest an achievement basis for children's expectations in the middle-class school and some other basis for children's expectations in the other two schools. The sequential structural models reveal that the drop in lower-class children's expectations over the 3-year period is apparently not a consequence of mark feedback, and the discrepancies between marks of lower-class children and their expectations still present at the end of grade three testify to the functional divorce between them. In addition, expectations of children in the two lower-class schools affected marks less often (four out of eighteen possibilities in the integrated school and three positive out of fifteen possibilities in the black school) than was true for middle-class children (seven out of eighteen possibilities). These findings imply that lower-class children's ideas about their own capabilities are not strong determinants of their performance levels at this age. The difference across schools in feedback patterns could help explicate socioeconomic differences in school achievement.

Evidence from two studies of secondary-school students (Gottfredson 1980; Marjoribanks 1979) and a panel study of second- and fifth-graders (Lockheed and Morgan 1979) suggests that teachers' expectations respond to prior achievement. Gottfredson's work shows that students' motivational outlooks respond to prior achievement and that commitment to academic goals comes *after* students attain a satisfactory level of achievement, rather than the other way around. When children achieve at a level unsatisfactory to them, as children did in the two lower-class schools, expectations for future performance seem not to respond to achievement. Thus it appears that one consequence of the failure to achieve is that young students come to base their expectations on non-achievement information. This may be the first step in developing an external control function, a feeling that external events and circumstances, rather than oneself, are responsible for life events. After more time passes and students get older, they could then gradually bear to lower their expectations, because they are convinced that school achievement is not under their personal control (i.e., they have an external control function).

Summary

These data shed light on the developmental history of children's expectations. Some authors (e.g., Rist 1970) have speculated that children's academic expectations crystallize very early and match their socioeconomic status. Our data do not agree. At least for the children in the present study, expectations show limited persistence and appear to be almost random until well into the first-grade year, expectations are fairly amorphous even at the end of grade three, and children's expectation levels are inversely related to status.

The relationships among expectations and marks lie at the heart of the models. The impact of expectations on marks and the subsequent feedback from marks to expectations constitute a dynamic process shaping achievement. By sampling marks and expectations twice a year, we used only a few discrete time points to monitor variables that are continuously interacting, but the careful timing of our observations helped considerably in the specification of causal orders (see Appendix C). There are almost no paths from marks in reading or arithmetic at one time to expectations at the next time for children in the two lower-class schools, even though such paths are substantial and rather consistently present in the middle-class school.

Another theme also stands out. In the middle-class school, children became better and better at anticipating their marks, with errors of underestimation and overestimation being about equally frequent. From the end of second grade on, most children in the middle-class school forecast their mark correctly and the proportion of those expecting to do better than they actually did is about equal to the proportion of those expecting to do worse. This kind of symmetry around a set of frequently correct estimates is not seen in the data for the lower-class schools. There, even in third grade, fewer children made correct estimates and a very large proportion of children did worse than they expected, particularly in reading. The number of lower-class children whose expectations were far off the target decreased a little over time, but at the end of third grade a majority were still incorrect. *More than 25%* of the children were still off by two or more units in their forecasts for both reading and arithmetic in the lower-class schools. The failure to forecast marks, together with the negligible effect of marks on subsequent expectations, suggests that marks are poorly processed in the two lower-class schools.

Contrary to much speculation in the literature, lower-class children did not have low expectations that damped achievement. Lower-class children's expectations were so high that they consistently exceeded those of the middle-class children, but this proves to be of no benefit since their marks are unresponsive to their expectations. Although high, their expectations are ineffective at boosting achievement. Paradoxically, their too-high expectations even seemed to be a drawback. Children's expectations affected marks modestly in the middle-class school—between one-third and one-half the time. In the two lower-class schools, children's expectations affected marks considerably less often—about one-fifth of the time. We suspect that mark feedback was so negative in comparison with their expectations that they failed to process it.

These findings are quite different from the usual explanation invoking the "self-fulfilling prophecy," namely that children of low socioeconomic status have low expectations that cause them to make low forecasts for themselves, and the low forecasts limit achievement. It seems instead that the excessively high expectations of lower-class children forced them to shield themsleves from unpleasant feedback.

The unrealistic expectations of the lower-class children may interfere with the causal efficacy of expectations via at least two mechanisms. First, shielding oneself by ignoring feedback may be self-protective, but it also eliminates the information necessary for learning. One cannot improve without paying attention to the initial failure. Recognizing one is doing poorly is a necessary first step to improving, and later steps require continual monitoring of evaluations after each attempted improvement. Without constant evaluative checking, there is no way to be assured that one's new activities are improvements. Doing things differently does not guarantee they are being done better. It is this monitoring, or attention to evaluative feedback, that sorts out productive from unproductive strategies.

Another way high expectations may undercut the effectiveness of expectations is that, if one truly believes one is already doing well, there is no reason to try to improve. If "I am the greatest," the goal has been attained, and there is no need for further improvement and no reason to keep trying.

The first explanation for why high expectations may undercut the potency of expectations implies a shielding of oneself from negative evaluations, while the second explanation implies an indifference to evaluation that may look like "not paying attention" or "not caring" about academic pursuits.

The development of notions about the self is a critical issue in child development (see Brim 1976). Notions about the "academic self" could be particularly important for school achievement. Our research suggests that middle-class children have more accurate conceptions of their academic selves. Not all of the inaccuracy of lower-class children can be attributed to the need to shield themselves from negative feedback, however, because they also have less accurate perceptions of their friends' levels of performance than the middle-class children do. Presumably, confusion in marking schemes or conflict between evaluations given verbally in the classroom and report-card evaluations cause some of the misperception.

All signs point to development of notions about the self as being consequences of schooling rather than determinants of it, and to teachers' evaluations rather than their expectations as the agents of change. If true, the literature on children's self-esteem and expectations will require some re-interpretations, because it is usually assumed that self-esteem is a cause, rather than a consequence, of achievement, and that teachers' expectations are critical determinants of children's attainment by way of children's expectations. The present research suggests that teachers' expectations appear effective precisely because they are highly correlated with evaluations.

MARKS, EVALUATIONS, AND ATTAINMENT

The information we gathered concerning children's marks was plagued by several kinds of inconsistency. First, the system of reporting marks varied from school to school, from time to time in the same school, and even from teacher to teacher in the same grade for the same marking period. Some first-grade teachers in the integrated school, for example, used the child's reader level as the basis for assigning the reading mark, while others used a composite criterion. Also, different series of readers used the same letter to designate different levels of performance (P standing for Primer, and P standing for Preprimer), so in the same marking period a P from one teacher could indicate a satisfactory level of performance and a P from another teacher could indicate a deficient level. In coding marks for use in our analysis, such inconsistencies were eliminated, but the effect of the inconsistencies upon parents and children may have been considerable, especially in first grade.[12]

When marks are taken strictly as indicators of teachers' evaluations, the differences in how they were defined are less troublesome than when they are taken as barometers of actual proficiency. A mark of B, for example, may have the same impact upon children whether it is based on grade equivalent performance or on effort, but marks assigned strictly on the basis of effort could attenuate correlations between marks and scores on standardized tests.

The basis for assigning marks, as judged from the teachers' written statements that we solicited, often seemed to differ less among schools than schools' announced policies did. Also, the options open to the teacher to implement differential marking standards become less viable as children progress from grade one to grade three. At the start of first grade, for example, it is possible for a teacher to adhere rather rigidly to a policy of assigning marks in terms of effort. As time passes, however, the child's objective performance level inevitably intrudes. It is virtually impossible for a third-grade teacher to give a high mark to a poor performer who is trying hard or to give a low mark to an outstanding performer who appears to exert little effort.

Like expectations, effects of marks can be considered from two main points of view, in terms of level and in terms of structural models. These are discussed in turn below, but first we comment on the several functions of marks.

The Nature of Marks

One purpose of the elementary school is to teach children to read and to do arithmetic, and one func-

[12] This could perhaps account for the lack of feedback effects in first grade. However, as children grew older, their understanding of marks increased and ambiguities in marks were lessened, so the lack of feedback effects later on is not likely to be explained in these terms.

tion of marks is to tell children and parents about progress in these subjects. However, for obvious reasons, teachers' marks are not perfect indicators of children's accomplishments—different teachers have different standards, and so on. A student may receive an A if he or she is the best in a class, but if other students in the class are not high achievers, the absolute performance level signified by that A may be far below the level signified by an A in another class. Standardized test scores circumvent such problems.

For our research it would have been ideal to elaborate every model to include standardized test scores as well as teachers' marks. Unfortunately, information on standardized achievement scores was limited to a relatively small part of the sample, so we could not expand the basic models in this fashion. However, information was available for some cohorts in third grade, and we used this information to estimate models that had test scores replacing marks in order to assess effects of background variables and school factors on objectively measured performance. The same structural patterns of causation prevailed whether the models were used to predict marks *or* standardized test scores. As shown in Chapter 7, the structural patterns of models were practically invariant when standardized test scores were substituted for marks as the ultimate endogenous variables. Thus marks can serve as proxies for absolute measures of achievement as far as the schooling process is concerned. The uniformly significant correlations between teachers' marks and children's scores on standardized tests also document the validity of teachers' marks as indicators of competence. The correspondence between marks and standardized test scores is critical, of course, if the models are to serve as descriptors of the process of educational attainment.

There is no "standardized conduct test" and so there is no easy way to calibrate conduct marks. The lack of an objective anchor for conduct may be somewhat irrelevant in terms of predicting standardized scores, however, because, as we have seen, effects of conduct are mediated to a large extent through other marks.

A second function of teachers' marks is that they serve as written evaluations seen by the child. They are statements of the teacher's opinion of the child. The child who receives an A is receiving a positive evaluation, and this in itself has implications apart from any significance the mark may possess in terms of the child's actual proficiency. Evaluations have emotional impact on the child *and* the child's classmates and parents. Evaluations probably affect the actual learning process, and for this reason the models in Chapter 7 also suggest how teachers' evaluations (marks) may affect standardized test performance, a topic that previously has received scant attention.

Marks turned out to have a third meaning that became clear only in retrospect: marks and teachers' expectations turned out to overlap to a very considerable degree. In this study, a teacher's mark was also a very good measure of that teacher's expectations for the student. This redundancy has important theoretical implications, because it means that in many research studies "teachers' expectations" could probably be replaced by "teachers' evaluations." The two concepts imply different things conceptually, however, if only because one refers to the past and the other refers to the future. Nevertheless, in practice, and especially from the child's point of view, evaluations may be the best indicator of teachers' expectations.

Research summarized in Chapter 2 suggests that, in natural settings, teachers' expectations respond to children's achievement. Teachers forecast for the future what they have observed in the past. In studies where teachers are asked to name children for whom they hold high or low expectations, the expectations could relate to past experience with the child, specifically the evaluations the teachers have made of prior performances. This line of reasoning is suggested by the fact that, in such studies, teachers are observed to press the children for whom they hold high expectations to give answers and to ask them more questions, for example. Teachers avoid pressing students for whom they hold low expectations, students who are unlikely to provide answers. Therefore, pupils could readily interpret the pressing behavior as a positive evaluation, because only a sadistic teacher would keep after a child who was not able to make an adequate response. In short, teacher expectations could well be derived from prior evaluations and in turn prompt evaluations. Since children have no way of knowing teacher expectations except through the teacher's behavior that encodes evaluations, from the child's point of view, "teacher expectations" *are* evaluations.

In experiments where teachers have been given misleading information about children's IQ scores, in some cases no measurable changes occur in children. These failures are commonly ascribed to failure of the experimental maneuver—presumably the teachers failed to process the communications given to them by the experimenters about IQ. An equally plausible idea is that teachers will act on the basis of the behavior they observe in children. They have processed the false IQ information but do not act upon it when it is not relevant to observed behavior.

In many psychological models, teacher expectations are seen as determinants of children's performance. Like West and Anderson (1976), we are arguing the reverse here: children's performance determines teacher evaluations, and teachers' evaluations are indistinguishable from teacher expectations. Once feedback cycles start, the order of the variables makes little difference—there is a continuous loop linking evaluations and both teachers' and children's expectations. The only point at which the order could make much difference is at the start, perhaps at the beginning of first grade. To the extent that our models can be believed, teachers' *first* evaluations in reading and arithmetic in all schools responded consistently to the child's deportment and to parents' forecasts, and, in addition, to IQ in the lower-class schools. This overall pattern can be interpreted as supporting the idea that children's achievement determines teacher evaluations.

The facts that blacks received higher marks in reading in the integrated school in the first cycle (the one isolated effect associated with race) and that only marks in conduct responded to gender (higher for girls in the white and integrated schools) are also in line with the idea that children's achievement, rather than other factors, affects teachers' judgment. If blacks had received lower marks at first, or if gender had acted on marks in reading and arithmetic independent of conduct, one could more easily believe that teachers' evaluations were biased by expectations.

Explicitly in some models (Braun 1976; Finn 1972), and implicitly in experiments and observational studies, teachers' expectations are taken as causes of students' expectations—Pygmalion studies claim improved performance after teachers' expectations for particular students are raised, implying that expectations cause achievement. The alternative, that student achievement causes teachers' expectations, was mentioned above, and we find it more appealing. In fact, teacher expectations and marks are so intertwined that, operationally, students would have a difficult time distinguishing a teachers' expectations from her evaluations, because the evaluations are explicit—marks, words, or even facial expressions—whereas expectations are implied future standards for behavior that can be expressed forthrightly, but need not be.

In the Pygmalion studies, there is actually no way to distinguish between effects of teachers' expectations and teachers' evaluations. Even if teachers' expectations are raised artificially, teachers may respond by altering their standards of evaluation in ways that improve the quality of actual performance. The same interpretation applies to naturalistic studies. In research where teachers identify students for whom they hold high expectations (those previously evaluated positively) and where teacher behavior is then observed, as already mentioned, teachers are seen to press students more for answers, to give them more action opportunities, and the like. From the student's point of view, the key aspect of the teacher's behavior may be that she presses the student until she gets a performance for which she is willing to award the same high level of evaluation. She could give hints about the answer, alter her standards if necessary, and by her behavior instigate a student performance that deserved a high evaluation. A teacher could hardly press a student on repeated occasions without providing some means for the student to be rewarded, or without having some justification for expecting to be able to provide a reward.

The three views of marks—as proxies for standardized test scores, as evaluation, and as operational definitions of teachers' expectations—have separate implications.

Marks form a critical link between naturalistic studies and expectations-states theory because evaluation is a central concept in that theory. Children and parents are presumed to revise their expectations on the basis of marks (evaluation). Marks allow students to monitor performance. Evaluations are linked to children's relative status in the classroom. Peers probably derive their expectations from evaluations as well. Evaluations are the vehicles of social approval or disapproval—the motivational component that drives the schooling process.

Marks as proxies or replacements for teachers' expectations could also have important implications for theory and practice, as discussed above and in Chapter 7. At the very least, marks should be included in future models of teacher-expectation effects.

Levels of Marks

It is curious that the educational literature on children's attainment emphasizes teachers' marks so little and teachers' expectations so much. We have already noted that "teachers' expectations" may be surrogates for marks, and in this research they actually appear to be efficacious because they are confounded with marks. Marks certainly affected parents' ability judgments and parents' expectations in the middle-class school, and to some extent in the two lower-class schools. The mutual effects, or their lack, between marks and children's expectations have already been commented upon at length, but the absolute level of marks awarded in a school may be of considerable importance as well, particularly in the first cycle.

There were large differences across schools in the average levels of the marks awarded students. In the middle-class school, average marks were always above a B and within each year marks went up in every area. In the integrated school, average marks in reading and arithmetic started at or below a C and generally improved within the year. In the black school at the beginning of the year, average marks were about equal to those in the integrated school, but did not improve over the year.

These differences in average marks are well reflected in the average differences in third-grade standardized test scores. For example, the average reading mark in the middle-class school (1.66) was 1.42 units above the reading mark in the integrated school (3.08), and the standardized scores were about 1.95 units apart in these two schools (Table 5.1). Similarly, in the middle-class school, the mathematics mark was 1.07 units higher and the mathematics test score was about 1.46 units higher. However, across schools, the gap between marks and standardized scores in mathematics is less than the corresponding gap in reading, i.e., the difference in objectively measured proficiency in mathematics is smaller. Average marks in reading exceeded marks in arithmetic in five of the six cycles in the middle-class school. In the integrated school the opposite was true—average marks in arithmetic exceeded those in reading in five of the six cycles. We saw earlier that children consistently held lower expectations for arithmetic than for reading in all schools, which means that arithmetic expectations and arithmetic marks are closer together in the lower-class schools (the average discrepancy is about 1.13 grade-points) than are reading expectations and marks (averaging 1.39 grade-points). Perhaps this is the reason children's standardized scores in arithmetic were relatively higher in the integrated school.

We found no evidence of teacher marking bias in connection with race. In the integrated school, white teachers gave pupils similar marks irrespective of race, and black teachers did the same.

Determinants of Marks

In the two schools with lower attainment levels there was a high degree of determinacy in even the earliest marks (58% and 35% in reading and arithmetic in the integrated school, and 24% and 63%, respectively, in the all-black school). IQ was a strong determinant of first marks in both places. In addition, in these two schools marks persisted between years as well as within years. In contrast, in the middle-class school, which had the highest attainment level, marks were much less well determined at the start (18% and 20%) and the transitions from grade one to grade two and from grade two to grade three show only one persistence effect (conduct from first to second grade), although within each grade there is mark persistence. In all schools, as children passed to a new grade a new teacher assigned marks, but only in the middle-class school did this change of teacher lead to a complete reshuffling of marks. From the children's viewpoint this means that in the middle-class school the slate is wiped clean—each year there is a new opportunity to achieve. In the other two schools past performance cannot be forgotten. Aside from IQ, persistence is the major force that leads to the high degree of mark predictability in these schools, and marks there seldom responded to child or parent variables (with the exception of the response to parents in the very first cycle). We also saw in the lasting-effects model that at the end of second grade in the integrated school marks in all subjects responded strongly to marks in the first cycle, whereas lasting effects of marks in the middle-class school were much smaller. Whatever the causes of these first marks in the integrated school, their consequences are far-reaching.

Parents' influence is much greater on marks than on children's expectations, especially in the first cycle. In seven of the nine possible instances in the first cycle, parents' expectations affected children's first marks, and effects were sizeable. Since first marks tended to persist and parent influence at this point is noted in all three schools, the early influence of parents is clearly important. However, the influence of parents on marks after the first marking period is less regular and looks different across schools, with the greatest influence occurring in the middle-class school (eight out of fifteen possible paths), the next greatest in the integrated school (four out of fifteen possible paths), and no instances visible in the all-black school. Another indicator of the power of middle-class parents is that their notions about general ability directly influenced conduct marks in the first two grades (negatively at first, positively later). This kind of influence is lacking for parents in the other two schools.

One interpretation of these findings is that parents affect schooling through *direct* avenues: with IQ controlled, children of parents with high expectations do better than children of parents with low expectations, and this is not a consequence of parents' expectations acting upon children's expectations. In the middle-class and integrated schools, there are some large effects of this sort on reading, even in third grade. The standardized coefficient linking middle-class parents' third-grade reading expectations to the year-end reading mark is 0.33, almost identical to the standardized persistence effect in that year (0.34). In the integrated school, an equally large standardized effect of parents' expectations is noted. (The lack of effects in the all-black school in third grade may be on account of the much smaller case base.) Parents who think their children will do well must provide the means for their children to achieve, especially before the beginning of first grade.

This rationale also gains credibility from the fact that parents' specific expectations are more potent than their ideas about the child's general ability. It seems likely that parents promote specific achievement-related activities rather than just provide an "overall" positive atmosphere. Another reason to think that parents exert influence by way of direct coaching or by provision of specific resources for the child is that a number of other parent variables that were investigated in formulating the models had to be discarded when they proved ineffectual. Most of these variables pertained to parental influences on the child's self-esteem as uncovered by Rosenberg (1965)—the number of the child's friends the parent knew, whether verbal interaction at home involved the child, how often the family ate dinner with the child, whether the parent was emotionally involved with the child's school achievements, and so on. All of these variables were related to children's global self-esteem, but we found that neither they nor global self-esteem had reliable effects on children's achievement.

Teachers influenced students through evaluations (marks), but first marks and some third-grade marks responded noticeably to parent influences. Children themselves seemed to have little independent influence (their expectations had many fewer and smaller effects on marks than their parents' expectations did), and the impact of peers was less than that of parents. This pattern is somewhat different from what is noted for secondary-school students, for whom peer influence on ultimate educational attainment is substantial and is judged equal to parent influence (Hauser, Sewell, and Alwin 1976, p. 328).

In terms of policy, actions taken with regard to parents offer promise—the present research points toward area-specific practices or coaching at home. By engaging in reading or arithmetic-oriented activities, a parent may signal high expectations to the child. If our speculations are correct, however, it is the net increment that such activities contribute to academic performance, rather than the holding of realistic expectations per se, that proves efficacious. Since ability is controlled, the improved performance implies that some parents are directly preparing their children for work in first grade better than others.

Conduct

The forward effect of the conduct mark on the reading and arithmetic marks in all three schools was confirmed by testing models with reciprocal paths. In the first two grades, conduct was an *important* determinant of performance (fourteen out of twenty-two possibilities were significant).

To the extent that various explanations for the efficacy of conduct can be examined in our data, we judge that it is more teacher bias, as manifest in conduct marks, than children's poor behavior actually interfering in learning, that accounts for conduct effects. That is, positive evaluations of conduct are a cause of positive evaluations in reading or arithmetic via halo effects. Conduct marks did not add much to the prediction of standardized achievement in grade three, although coefficients were positive (with one exception). This judgment could be contradicted by more data, however. Conduct might be a stronger direct predictor of standardized achievement if we could test a model with first-grade standardized achievement data. The strongest effects of conduct on marks occurred in first grade, and thereafter marks persisted strongly. Because we had to use third-grade achievement tests, which were the only ones available, the earlier effects of conduct may be somewhat obscured.

The major effects of gender are that, when the sexes differ, boys tend to get poorer marks in conduct in all schools, and parents initially expect boys to receive poorer marks in conduct than girls.

The conduct mark also mediates some parent effects in the middle-class school because the parents' general-ability estimate had direct effects on conduct marks in three of the four semesters in the first two grades, and indirect effects were exerted through parents' expectations for conduct. In addition, effects of peers and absences are manifest almost exclusively on the conduct mark for middle-class children. Children who are absent more often may be less well behaved because they are less familiar with classroom routines or with work done on the previous day. Also, teachers may unconsciously rate absences as a form of misbehaving. The fact that conduct marks responded to peer-popularity ratings could suggest either that children who receive low peer ratings misbehave because they feel rejected, or, conversely, that children who misbehave are downgraded by other children. Since peer ratings were never entered as dependent variables, we cannot choose between these explanations.

A survey of the relative size of IQ effects (comparing sizes of standardized coefficients within any one model) shows that IQ has as much effect on conduct as on the other two marks in the white and integrated schools. Children who test higher are judged to be better behaved. IQ has strong direct effects on marks in reading and arithmetic in the lower-class schools, but marks in conduct are also effective influences on the academic marks (all of the fourteen coefficients in the first two grades are positive and six are significant). Even in the lower-class schools, where absolute performance level was supposed to determine marks, the child's deportment shaped early attainment. It is noticeable that the rather consistent links between conduct marks and marks in the other two areas fade by third grade. This chronological pattern suggests that children's conduct in the first two grades is a causal factor in achievement, but after that, no doubt partly because there is strong persistence in marks, the effects of deportment weaken.

The importance of conduct for early school attainment, if it holds up on further investigation, has several implications. One is that conduct effects may explain gender differences in reading attainment.[13] Another is that conduct deserves study by itself. Fostering good conduct in children may outweigh the relative benefits of emphasizing some particular method of instruction (see Eder 1981).

One way to alter conduct performance, of course, is to alter the standards of the judges. Some teachers are much more lenient in their judgments of conduct than others. One reason that male teachers stimulate higher achievement in boys than female teachers do (Murnane 1975) may be that male teachers' standards for the conduct of young males are different from the standards of female teachers. Perhaps male teachers have greater tolerance for restless or aggressive behaviors by young boys. [Other studies show young males to be more frequent targets of blame than young females (Felsenthal 1971).]

Another way to improve conduct is by manipulation of the environment. A schedule that allows for frequent and satisfying physical activity may lead to better classroom conduct than a schedule that requires young children to remain seated for long periods. Regrouping within the classroom or changing classrooms for different subjects may be efficacious in part just because physical movement has salutary effects on conduct.

Marking Policy

It seems to us that confusion about marks would be reduced if fewer marks were awarded. Some report cards in use over the period of this research required teachers to award over thirty marks per child. In addition, confusion would be decreased if the basis for assigning marks were as simple as possible and consistent from teacher to teacher and subject to subject. Parents would be more helpful to their children if they knew the distributions of marks that teachers awarded. At the very least, they should be informed of the actual criteria that teachers use in assigning marks.

Of all the variables considered, marks are the easiest to use as instruments of policy. Children's expectations can sometimes be changed (see Entwisle and Webster 1974a), but manipulation of children's expectations has ethical as well as practical drawbacks. On the other hand, marking policies are often intentionally and rather capriciously changed by schools, teachers, or whole school districts. Usually, the basis for such changes is educational fashion or administrators' intuition, rather than careful scientific evaluation. We believe changes in marking policy could be meaningfully assessed net of effects of other variables by employing mid-range models like those we propose.

A mark is a critical variable from several vantage points. Dornbusch and Scott (1975) see evaluation as a critical control mechanism. In expectation-state theory (Berger et al. 1980) evaluation is a key concept in expectation formation and maintenance. Furthermore, in earlier days educational psychologists were more mindful of the importance of written evaluations than they appear to be now. For example, in a study by Page (1958), comments of a positive, neutral, and negative sort were placed on the papers of random groups of students. Students who were evaluated (*either* positively or negatively) consistently outperformed those who received non-evaluative (neutral) comments. [In a similar but smaller study in an elementary school, Entwisle, Cornell, and Epstein (1972) replicated Page's findings.] However, surprisingly, evaluation does not appear as a variable in models of schooling formulated recently by educational psychologists (e.g., Braun 1976; Finn 1972). One easy way to incorporate evaluation in such models would be to reconceptualize "teachers' expectations" as "evaluations," as we have already stated.

Dornbusch and Scott emphasize that evaluation criteria must be clear. We observed that standards were unclear in the lower-class schools because many parents asked interviewers questions about report cards and marking schemes. Even teachers were unclear in their own minds about some subjects they were marking in first grade. We found teachers' written descriptions of their criteria for marking spelling and language so ambiguous that we eliminated marks in these subjects from the research. We strongly suspect that part of the discrepancy between children's expectations and marks in the lower-class schools is because marking practices were not clear.

There is often confusion in the public mind about subverting "academic excellence" and the use of ranked grading systems. Children, the reasoning goes, should not be given high marks unless they are really performing well; otherwise, the standards of the school will be corrupted, to the eventual confusion of all. But surely the curriculum of the early elementary school is within the grasp of all normal children. For this reason it does not necessarily make sense to enforce arbitrary standards if the aim is, for example, to enable six-year-olds to start reading and to derive enough pleasure from reading so that they will try to do it outside school. Learning might be more efficient if children were given evaluations in relation to their own progress, but this may require a reorganization of school timetables (see Scarr 1980, p. 82). In colleges

[13] The fact that in some cultures young males learn to read more easily than females could imply that the sex difference in reading attainment in the United States may be attributable more to social factors like conduct than to biological factors (Dwyer 1973).

and universities, adherence to marking practices based on objective standards of quality makes sense, say, for classifying applicants to professional or graduate school, and college students have the option of changing courses, schools, or even dropping out. Elementary students have few such options.

It is not possible to conclude much about particular marking policies from the present research. Although marking policies supposedly differed across schools, policies were not implemented consistently even within a school. On the other hand, when children's expectations were closer to the marks awarded, expectations seemed both to have more impact and to be more responsive. For expectations to be close, children must have some idea of the average and range of the mark distribution.

OTHER IMPLICATIONS OF MARKS, EXPECTATIONS, AND CONTROL

There are no benchmarks against which to judge children's ideal expectations. It is impossible to say what the level of children's expectations "should" be. Earlier (Entwisle and Hayduk 1978a, pp. 170 ff.) we drew attention to the close conceptual relation between early self-expectations and a child's sense of control. Just as self-esteem or expectations have been studied only in older children, so also a person's sense of control has not yet been traced to its sociopsychological roots.

In the present research, expectations and performance levels converged for middle-class children but did not for lower-class children. Expectations in the lower-class schools did not respond to prior marks. Children there may have misread their actual performance, not recognized its significance, or even been rewarded for not discovering the nature of the correspondence between level of effort and level of achievement. If children form consistently high expectations that are unrealized, they would be expected to develop some intrapsychic stress. They would also be expected to score low on efficacy, because they predict outcomes that do not occur and fail to predict the outcomes that do occur. In short, they would be expected to develop an external control function that produces high performance expectations irrespective of effort.

Children in the middle-class school, in contrast, must feel themselves to be more in control because their predictions come true. They may have started school with an internal control function already under construction, but marked improvement in their predictions occurs over the first three grades, and sharply at first. These improvements apparently come about because they take account of their previous performance levels.

The foregoing resolves some paradoxes, because it suggests how high expectations can be dysfunctional and how lower-class children could simultaneously have high expectations and low sense of control. In fact, the specific findings that have emerged in this book allow a sensible integration of previously inconsistent sets of findings concerning aspirations and control. Unrealistically high aspirations may be the seeds that produce control failure later on.

Plainly, high aspirations and competence are not necessarily connected. Rather, it appears that, when achievement is somewhere close to expectations, expectations respond. Children's response to achievement appears to be contingent upon the distance between the level of their expectations and the level of their achievement.

The matter of evaluation is also spotlighted in Darley and Fazio's (1980) analysis of expectancy confirmation processes. They address in a more general way issues we raised earlier about teachers' evaluations. Students may interpret the teacher's action according to whether that action agrees with one the student would take. Example: if a black student evaluates his or her performance lower than the teacher does, the student could interpret the teacher's action as "institutional racism"—the assigned marks are seen as determined by the student's race rather than by the student's performance. Teachers' evaluations are no doubt interpreted in many different ways according to the student's perceptions, and hence effects of evaluations cannot be completely assessed without taking into account the student's own expectations, evaluations, and attributional styles. Furthermore, it can be misleading to isolate teachers' evaluations from their other behaviors. For example, Becher (1978) found that teachers who tended to provide more evaluations asked more "drill" questions than reflective questions and also asked students to clarify ideas less often. Thus the amount of evaluative feedback children receive may be embedded in structurally different daily routines. Even with a data set as rich as the one we were able to assemble, many such concerns remain beyond our analytical grasp.

A better understanding of the early schooling process may be critical for shaping children's long-term achievement. Our research indicates that background variables are extremely important—gender, for example, showed effects in early first grade. Finally, the present research also testifies to the key role played by evaluation very early in children's educational careers. Early evaluations had persistent effects, net of other variables, and effects were stronger in the lower-class schools.

A SOCIOLOGY OF CHILDHOOD

Even a casual glance at the sociological literature reveals that sociologists pay little attention to children. For example, in diagrams of society (see Riley, Johnson, and Foner 1972, p. 400) "young" refers to high-school or college-age persons. Children are left out. In a similar vein, Kohn's (1969) work on child socialization is based on interviews with adults. Actions *parents* take toward their children, whether *parents'* disciplinary actions reflect their work values, and so on, are the center of interest. No attention is given to the influence of children upon parents, or to the balance of reciprocal influences between parents and children.

The narrowness of this view excludes two truths: first, human influences are always reciprocal—even newborn infants shape their parents behavior (Entwisle and Doering 1981); second, the causes of adult behavior may be difficult to understand outside of a life-cycle perspective—the child is indeed father, or mother, to the adult.

Childhood experiences often predict where children finish in the stratification race and how they go about founding families of their own (Kagan and Moss 1962), and children's social experience is expanding as more and more women enter the labor force. When mothers go to work, they leave their children in day care, nursery schools, or kindergartens. Social experiences in these places could have many long-lasting consequences for children. Attending an integrated nursery school, for example, could shape a child's lifelong attitudes toward members of minority (or majority) groups. Outside the home, children learn how the social system is organized. Even in nursery school, children head down a path that leads to their ultimate place in the world of work. A nursery school in the suburbs cares for children of professionally employed women. A day care center in the city watches over the children of clerks and factory workers. Every high school has feeder junior highs, every junior high has feeder elementary schools, and elementary schools have feeder nursery schools. It is likely that children are really "tracked" long before they reach secondary school, and chains of schools are probably much stronger than curricular tracks within high schools.

Children are of interest in themselves, apart from the need to understand how children turn into adults. Children's social groups, their role in the family, and the role that social institutions play in their lives are all of intrinsic interest. Children too have friendship groups, reactions to illness, religious views, buying habits, tastes in entertainment, political preferences, and sex-role attitudes. Early schooling represents the main source of children's experience outside the family, and for this reason it is of sociological interest in itself.

Elementary Schools

The main institution that affects children in the United States—the elementary school—has no real counterpart for adults.[14] Attendance is compulsory, children can seldom initiate moves from one school to another, and, as noted earlier, elementary schools tend to be highly parochial. They enroll children who live close to the school, even in large cities. Since they are usually small and limited to three or four classrooms per grade, they bring together children who are highly similar in socioeconomic status, intellectual endowment, and general world view. These like-minded children stay together for many hours a day, for 10 months a year, usually for 7 to 9 years.

Being neighborhood schools, elementary schools reflect the stratification patterns of the larger society. In cities, there are elementary schools that enroll only poor children, who attend classes in buildings close to federal housing provided for the inner-city poor, or in buildings set in the midst of old city rowhouses and tenements surviving from the nineteenth century. Other schools, on the fringes of these cities, are set on large expanses of ground, off tree-lined streets, among single-family houses with tennis courts and swimming pools. They tend to enroll more affluent white students. These elementary schools, which draw from small geographic areas, vary sharply in terms of social climate. An elementary school in an urban ghetto is just a different social institution from a school in a well-to-do suburb. Even when a school building in the inner city is as modern as one in suburbia and when teachers' salaries are equivalent, there is little overlap in world outlook in the two places. Standards of dress and behavior, habits of speech, attitudes of parents, and teachers' relative power differ as markedly between such schools as drinking beer at a corner bar in the city differs from sipping cocktails on a patio in the suburbs. Parents in the poorer urban areas are as non-involved with schools as they are with other social institutions, and as much intimidated by teachers and principals as they are by their work

[14] For adults the nearest counterpart is the armed forces. There, enlisted men are grouped homogeneously (by educational level) and remain together for extended periods. They are taught values and norms as well as skills, they too learn what to feel and what to think, and, like children in elementary school, personnel in the armed forces have little control over their work assignments and are almost totally under the control of their supervisors. They must serve a specific number of years whether they like it or not. Curiously, while lack of control is universally recognized as a condition of military service, it is not recognized as a condition of elementary education.

supervisors. Parents of children in suburban schools, on the other hand, often express their competitiveness through their children's school accomplishments, and they do not hesitate to intimidate teachers. People's beliefs about the purpose of school, the value of education, the relative power of teachers and parents, and children's role in society differ from one elementary school to another, and we believe the quality of children's school experience responds strongly to these beliefs. The elementary school masquerades as a single social institution, but in fact is a wide variety of institutions, depending on its locus within the social system.

It is not just that young children may react to schooling differently from older children, then, that persuaded us to direct our research toward children in the first three grades. The schools that young children attend are more socially diverse and more intense in focus than secondary schools generally are. The characteristics of the elementary school match those of the family more closely than schools do later, so if social structure does affect schooling, the effects of school and home would potentiate each other. Three schools do not provide a sufficient basis for generalization, but to the extent that the sharp inter-school differences that appeared in this research are duplicated elsewhere, more intensive study of the elementary school by sociologists may prove worthwhile. In fact, schooling in the early grades may be the opposite of the leveling influence many so devoutly hope for.

Research with high-school students may be incapable of revealing attainment-related differences among schooling environments because, by high school, students' academic habits and attainment levels are set. Cook and Alexander (1980) point to the necessity of tracing attainment over time—the best predictor of students' attainment at any level of school is attainment at the previous level. If attainment at prior levels is ignored, then the pattern of influence of other variables, such as home background, is distorted. In our research, when intervening levels of attainment were ignored, effects of first marks were visible at the end of second grade, but effects of IQ and initial expectations were not. Yet IQ and expectations did have effects along the way. In fact, students' background may condition secondary attainment mainly because it shapes attainment in elementary school, when schools match home background. Children have the same kinds of peers in grade school as in high school; therefore, to the extent that peers do affect achievement, their effects early in a child's schooling career may only become manifest later. We suspect that effects of schooling may be most variable *before* children reach the secondary level. The cumulative nature of schooling argues that the crucible years of school are likely to be the early ones.

Differential School Effects

Differential high-school effects have so far been judged to be absent or small (Chapter 1). For example, after examining students' aspiration levels in relation to the socioeconomic characteristics of the neighborhoods in which they resided, Sewell and Armer (1966) conclude that, with ability and family background controlled, any influence attributable to neighborhood context itself is exceedingly small. The conclusion that achievement is unresponsive to school differences has held up under repeated re-analysis since the Coleman (1966) report.

With minor exceptions, however, students' earlier educational experience has not been taken into account, and therefore is confounded with "background factors" in these studies (Alexander et al. 1981). If differences among elementary schools *do* lead to differences in achievement among students, and if these differences among students continue in high school, such elementary-school effects would be attributed to background in most models of educational attainment by way of specification error. The failure to find differential school effects for high-school students and the complementary finding that individual and background factors account for most of the variance in achievement of secondary-school students can thus be interpreted as an argument in favor of a critical role for elementary school.

Smith (1972) makes this point:

> I have argued that the relationship between background variables and achievement is initially strong at the first grade . . . Three causal mechanisms might combine . . . first, there is strong evidence that the first few years of life are important in preparing the child for school and the level of early preparation is correlated with readiness and achievement; second, the family has a continuing influence on a child's achievement; and third, the selection and assignment practices carried out by the schools might well serve to exacerbate the relationship between class and achievement in the early grades while stabilizing it in the higher grades . . . (p. 265).

Smith emphasized grouping practices within elementary schools as one reason for the strong relations observed between background and early achievement. He could also have emphasized that home and school are usually more consonant at the elementary level and that the range of variation in social climate across elementary schools is much more pronounced than for secondary schools.

Lack of school differences for high-school students is curiously at odds with the findings lately emerging for younger children. For example, Summers and Wolfe (1977), Murnane (1975), and others find differences by teacher and/or school. Brookover et al. (1978) report that, among elementary schools in

Michigan, some schools with students of low socioeconomic level but with especially favorable social climates enrolled students who outperformed similar students in less favorable climates.

For this research we intentionally chose schools that seemed to typify the frustrations confronting educational planners: schools that had equal resources but that quickly prompted very different levels of children's achievement. In the two lower-class schools, children's achievement by the end of third grade was more than a grade equivalent below achievement in the middle-class school, no matter what measure is used (Table 5.1). There are suggestive differences among schools in model structure and also in the magnitude of parameters that could explain this widening gap in achievement. Average marks were considerably higher and less persistent in the middle-class school than in the two lower-class schools. For example, most of the structural coefficients representing the persistence of marks between grades are three times as large in the integrated school as they are in the middle-class school. Another difference across schools is linked to parental variables. Parents in all three schools had significant impact on children's very first marks, but only middle-class parents appeared to retain their influence after the first semester. One reason for this may be that lower-class parents' expectations were off target, but a further reason that deserves emphasis here is parents' differential involvement with school. Although we have little systematic data on involvement, we nevertheless observed that the middle-class fathers as well as mothers made more frequent school visits and we often received letters and calls from the middle-class parents but not from the lower-class parents. The principal and teachers in the middle-class school anticipated high levels of parental involvement. In future research it would be desirable to devise measures to rate parental interest or participation.

Children's expectations for themselves also shaped up differently across schools. By the end of third grade, the middle-class children's expectations were as likely to be too low as too high, whereas the lower-class children's expectations were almost never too low. Students in every school were more optimistic about their reading performance than about their arithmetic performance, but only in the middle-class school was that optimism warranted in terms of teachers' evaluations.

Children from less advantaged backgounds *are* capable of learning the basics of reading and arithmetic, because almost all eventually do. What are the requisites for them to learn sooner? One may be adequate feedback. If the difference in assimilation of feedback according to socioeconomic status observed in this research holds more generally, and if some parents provide better feedback than others, these facts could provide a powerful explanation for the perplexing and widespread differences in educational attainment associated with social class. For learning to occur, students must actively try out behaviors and then pay attention to how their performances are evaluated (Estes 1970). Feedback sometimes comes from the teacher, sometimes from others, but most reliably from students themselves. Without feedback the learning cycle breaks down, because students can modify behavior (i.e., learn) only when they know whether their new behavior is "correct" or not. Feedback must be informative. If, as Dornbusch and Scott (1975) point out, evaluations are contradictory or pertain to behaviors over which students have little control, feedback becomes either confusing or irrelevant. Also, when students are unable to predict the relation between work performed and its evaluation, or when students are held to unattainable standards, they are unable to provide feedback for themselves. When 40% of first-graders receive D's in reading on their first report cards, as did the students in the integrated school, they may view the task before them as being insurmountable.

We observed ineffective feedback where attainment is low—reading and arithmetic marks had little effect on subsequent expectations in the lower-class schools. We believe that some part of this failure is attributable to unintelligible or confusing marking schemes. We also believe part of the failure to process feedback is attributable to psychological defense mechanisms; however, these defense mechanisms are not likely to be uniquely personal mechanisms, since the expectations the lower-class children held for their friends were as high and unrealistic as those they held for themselves. These children shield both themselves and their friends from evaluations that are so low as to be threatening.

All the problems associated with evaluation cited by Dornbusch and Scott (1975) seem more likely to occur in the two lower-class schools. Contradictory evaluations seem especially likely for several reasons. 1) Standards of lower-class parents may overlap relatively less with those of teachers, who are mostly lower middle-class. Thus, behaviors rewarded in school may not be rewarded at home, and vice versa, especially in the key area of conduct. 2) Students may perceive the behavior of teachers in the lower-class schools as contradictory. Teachers must give positive evaluations—smiles and praise—to keep a classroom functioning, yet they issue report cards with a very high proportion of C's and D's. 3) Teachers of one social background and children of another may have conflicting ideas about the importance of various activities, as when children think sports are more important than academic work, for example.

The clearest instance of a control failure occurs when

children are unable to predict the relation between work performed and its evaluation. Children in the two lower-class schools were much less accurate in predicting how they would be evaluated than children in the middle-class schools, and the errors were always in a direction that led to punishment or unpleasant surprises. Since children expected higher marks than they received, they could not avoid being disappointed, and since their parents also tended to overestimate future marks, the children were probably further punished when they took home report cards that disappointed their parents.

Other differences among schools, like absence and peer effects, are consistent but less coherent. There is some evidence that absences have an effect on both children's expectations and their marks in the integrated school but not elsewhere. The reasons for this are not clear. The effect cannot be written off as a consequence of a wider sampling range, because absences in the black lower-class school are almost as numerous and have almost as large a standard deviation as in the integrated school.

All in all, despite Hauser et al.'s (1976) assessment that "the observed differentiation of educational outcomes among American students has not been traced directly or in large measure to systematic variations in the social environment from school to school" (p. 310), there are enough differences among our elementary schools in *patterns* of effects to suggest that the issue is not dead. Many fruitful paths for future investigation are opened by investigating the schooling process as well as educational outcomes.

OTHER IMPLICATIONS

The process of schooling, even for children as young as those surveyed in this research, seems far more complex than casual inspection is likely to reveal, and, as stated in Chapter 2, most psychological theorists who do research that is related to schooling work at the micro level. They deal mostly with single variables like individual teacher expectations or similar molecular-type variables. Stephens (1967), to our knowledge, is the single major exception. His psychological theory of schooling is at a different level entirely. In fact, he is concerned with even more basic schooling issues than we are. He is interested, for instance, in how the psychological makeup of human beings and survival value have led to the establishment of institutions such as schools in the first place. He wants to understand how inborn psychological mechanisms knit together "significant others" who care about children or who influence children. In other words, he is not content, as we have been in this book, to take it as a given that schools exist, that a teacher or a parent dispenses social approval or disapproval to children, and that actions of parents and teachers lead children to change their behavior. He asks *why* parents and teachers are disposed to pay attention to children at all and *why* societies invest resources in schools.

He believes that schooling depends to a considerable degree on strong human predilections that adults have to teach children in the absence of any deliberate intention. He points to automatic or non-deliberative behavior of adults that reinforces learning in children (facial expression, tone of voice), or that produces closure (commenting on why a particular event came out as expected or "as it should"). He believes that schooling of children is such a strong urge in many adults that they are literally helpless to stop themselves and would continue to act in ways to teach children if there were no formal schools at all. Stephens calls attention to commonly ignored daily activities that give clues about powerful psychological forces so taken for granted they are below the level of explicit awareness.

Stephens feels that one reason researchers have had so little success in finding differences among effects of secondary schools is that *all* schools exert powerful effects and, compared to huge overall effects, differences among schools are so small as to be undetectable. If we compared students who attended school and others who did not, he believes we would lay bare large school effects. The problem is, of course, that in modern society we cannot find comparable schooled and unschooled children, and in addition we have powerful schooling effects from influences outside the classroom, including the media. Happily, as noted in Chapter 2, some evidence of just the kind Stephens' theory predicts has been provided recently by Heyns (1978), who isolates large school effects by contrasting learning during the school year with amounts of learning over the summer vacation. The fact that we find that the same basic models account well for children's attainment across three schools and over a 3-year time span can be interpreted as further evidence consistent with Stephens' theory.

In addition to more research along the lines of Heyns', research is needed on pupils' perceptions of the schooling process as affected by social structural variables (e.g., race, gender, socioeconomic context). The possibility of structural differences in the process of early schooling seems clear. Evaluation, and whether parents and children are in tune with evaluation, appears to hold one key to explaining the schooling differences we have observed. In addition, evaluation seems to be a much more feasible way to take account of teachers' expectations in schooling research than measuring teachers' expectations directly. The neglect of teacher evaluations in prior studies is as unfortunate as it is curious.

Teachers' evaluations of children's conduct directly affects their academic performance, but it is hard to know the standards for evaluating conduct. We do know from other work (e.g., Kohn 1969) that conduct is assessed differently by middle-class and working-class parents. Middle-class parents are not very disturbed by a child's boisterousness because they pay attention to the child's intent. Working-class parents are disturbed by wild play even if it is just high spirits boiling over—they take children's destructive behavior at face value and downplay intent. There is no obvious reason why Kohn's analysis of parents could not apply to teachers. When some of the teachers in this research were asked to describe the criteria they used to rate children's conduct, teachers in all three schools emphasized consideration for others and following adult requests (directions). Teachers in the lower-class schools added that they assigned high conduct marks to children who "work but don't talk out" and low marks to children who are "talkative." The teachers of middle-class children did not mention "talking out." These comments are free-response and were provided by only a few of the teachers, so they are not necessarily either valid or representative, but they do make us suspect there may be class differences in how teachers evaluate children's conduct.

A little evidence indicates that teachers of middle-class children are especially aware of the key role played by conduct early in school. A careful minute-by-minute observational study of kindergarten teachers in the same three schools as those attended by the first-, second-, and third-graders in our sample revealed that kindergarten teachers in the middle-class school spent significantly more time than teachers in the other two schools on "procedural activities"—instructing children in classroom and school routines, teaching children to raise hands rather than call out, and so on (Berkeley 1978). When interviewed, the middle-class teachers expressed their belief that learning to behave well in kindergarten would be especially helpful to children later on. The teachers in the two lower-class schools did not express this point of view.

A number of studies also reveal class-related differences in teaching style. Lower-class black parents use more negatives in instructing their children (Hess and Shipman 1965). Lower-class kindergarten children respond best to positive intonations, while middle-class children respond similarly to positive, neutral, or negative tones (Kashinsky and Wiener 1969). These examples and many more suggest that the nature of face-to-face evaluation and children's interpretation of it are strongly linked to social class. The evaluative process and its interpretation, furthermore, may be one area in which similarity between home and school environments is particularly critical for young children.

It would be useful, since conduct is such an important element of early school performance, if conduct could be explicitly studied. Hundreds of studies have been directed at methods for teaching reading, but none to our knowledge investigates the relation between conduct and reading. What *are* teachers' and parents' actual standards for conduct? Are the standards of middle-class parents more congruent with those of most teachers than are those of lower-class parents, as seems likely?

The educational literature contains its share of loose thinking about expectations of lower-class and minority-group children, much of it based on fantasy rather than hard evidence. In the schools we studied, blacks did not look for failure, nor did they hold low expectations for themselves, and the blacks in the integrated school thought of themselves in the same terms as the blacks in the all-black school. Other careful research also concludes that blacks do not typically hold low opinions of themselves—Rosenberg and Simmons (1971) reported (also for a Baltimore sample) that black children did not have low self-esteem if they were in consonant or protective settings. Young children starting school may almost always be in protective settings because of the parochial nature of elementary schools. Young minority-group children may seldom be aware of society's evaluation of the group to which they belong.

Contrary to recommendations favored in the past, the way to improve performance of groups with educational deficits (like blacks or other minorities) does not seem to be to raise expectations levels. Unrealistically high expectations may prove to be a handicap for these children. For example, children in the present research did not appear to do poorly because they thought they would do poorly—the self-fulfilling prophecy remains unfulfilled. Rather, a set of circumstances combined to rate their performance at a low level and then they were unable to readjust their thinking. The lasting-effects model suggests that IQ did not have lasting effects. If this is true, and if emphasis on absolute standards led IQ to play a strong part in early low evaluations of these children, one may question the utility of the evaluation strategy. The emphasis on absolute levels of achievement forced the students to turn away and to look for other cues in the environment.

Havighurst (1970) believes that an important avenue for improving schools is to arrange schooling so that children can learn how to control their own environment on the basis of the reality principle, the idea that they are in control of their own actions and that these actions have foreseeable consequences. Havighurst's belief, which we share, is consonant with the major findings of our research. The failure of expectations to respond to previous evaluations seems to be as clear-cut a case as can be imagined of the failure of the reality principle. In schools where mark determinacy is high to start with, and where marks strongly persist, and where for these reasons children have little power to effect change without encountering other potent forces, average achievement is lower. In such schools, children appear unable to monitor their actions according to external reality because their expectations remained out of line with performance. "Reality" awareness means processing feedback.

Along other lines, theories of stress (Lazarus 1966; Janis 1958) also relate to the gap between expectations and performance, because such a gap must be stressful. Stress can be mitigated by increased feelings of control or exacerbated by feelings of powerlessness. Although some anxiety may stimulate learning because it increases the person's level of arousal, too much anxiety is clearly a handicap for learning. We have no direct measures of children's feelings of efficacy or of stress, but we suspect that having unrealistic expectations is stressful because there is a continuing need either to discount or to deny reality.

If our hunches are correct, what could be done?

Parents could easily be informed about the range of marks awarded in any school. Parents could also be informed about the importance of conduct and the standards for judging conduct in the school their children attend. We suspect that, if parents' expectations for first marks in the lower-class schools had been more accurate, their expectations would have retained some effectiveness after the first cycle. Parents could also be given information about how the "average" child in the school is performing whenever they receive their own child's report cards.

Teachers could also be informed about the distribution of grades being awarded in their school. We suspect that, if they are told that they are awarding 40% D's, teachers would probably mark less stringently. Without knowing what other teachers are doing, one teacher can believe that her class is not performing at the same level as other classes in the school, and therefore it is possible for her to be less disturbed by a negative skew in the mark distribution than she would otherwise be. It is doubtful that teachers in the lower-class schools were clearly and unequivocally aware of the extremely low marks given by all the teachers to first-grade children and of how confusing their marking schemes were.

There must be ways to put children and their parents in better tune with their elementary schools. To us it seems that parents' learning informal norms and customs could go far in this direction.

Appendix A

Limitations of Sample Design and Data

The findings and implications of our research must be weighed in view of its limitations. Several methodological drawbacks are described in this appendix. The prime drawback is that, in interpreting findings based on naturally occurring groups, differences between schools are confounded with socioeconomic differences, racial differences, and IQ differences.

LIMITATIONS OF THE SAMPLE

The sample of children participating in this research is purposive and suffers from all the drawbacks that a non-random sample implies. We made three extensive case studies, each based on a single school. Results of the research therefore cannot be safely generalized to any larger population, because there is no way to tell how representative the schools may be. To aid the reader in judging the character of the three schools, data are provided from the 1970 census, and from two Maryland school accountability surveys (Table 5.5).

Fortunately, the size and quality of staff in the three schools were similar, except that teachers in the lower-class schools were assisted by classroom aides and could call upon resource teachers (Title I). The large differences in achievement favoring the middle-class school cannot therefore reasonably be taken as consequence of differences in school resources; if anything, the lower-class schools commanded greater resources. Besides having fewer teachers, the middle-class school had larger class sizes.

Social Climate

The atmosphere in the three schools was very different, especially in respect to parents. When parents in the all-white school were invited to school, a very high percentage of them came. Fathers as well as mothers came, and sometimes both parents appeared together. In the other two schools, we never observed a father responding to an invitation to visit school, and a low percentage (generally 10% or less) of mothers responded.

In the middle-class school the teachers and principal were very sensitive to parents' views and were diligent in responding to parents' inquiries. Parents from this school at times wrote letters to the researchers. The PTA officers there frequently expressed interest in having the researchers address parent meetings. In the other two schools, the teachers and principal seemed to be in a different power relation with parents. Parents who visited the schools did so mainly to resolve discipline problems. It was difficult to get these parents to respond to consent forms. Communications to us from parents in these two schools were very rare.

Children were seldom late in the middle-class school. They arrived by school bus, on foot, and often by private automobile. In the other two schools, the use of automobiles or buses was rare. Children were often late, especially in the integrated school. Children were frequently walked to school by relatives, and first- and second-graders usually went to and from school with an older sibling or neighbor's child.

Personnel in all three schools tended to remain in place over the period of our research. The schools appeared somewhat more stable in terms of personnel than other schools in the city at that time (1971 to 1976).

Geographical Location

Wider generalizability could be affected by the noticeable cultural differences between Baltimore and other urban areas in the U.S. Baltimore has proportionately fewer middle-class blacks than Washington, D.C., for example, and such demographic characteristics may have pronounced effects on people's views of themselves and of others. In Baltimore there is yet to be a black mayor, whereas Washington has had several black mayors. In Baltimore blacks could perceive themselves to be less powerful relative to whites than blacks in cities like Washington. Such perceptions could have important implications for black parents' expectations for their children. The extent to which such differences affected the results of this study is an open question.

TECHNICAL PROBLEMS RELATED TO THE SAMPLING STRATEGY

All the sampling weaknesses enumerated in what follows bear on the interpretation of the findings. Every research undertaking involves trade-offs, however, and in order to be able to devote the time and resources needed to study young children as carefully as we believed was required, we sacrificed breadth of coverage for depth. A longitudinal design with multiwave sampling carried out in three different physical locations offers a number of potential advantages. These include measuring variables at times consistent with causal hypotheses so that specific causal orderings may be more clearly tested, as well as possible reduction in specification error because of repeated measurements of the same variables. The most important gain was a hoped-for increase in validity of the measures used with the young children. By working in only a few schools, we could devote as much time as was needed to interviewing children.

Pairwise Data

By taking overlapping two-wave panels, and thus combining several short-term longitudinal studies to form a longer one, we avoided the severe attrition that affects many longitudinal studies. Even with this strategy, however, there turned out to be enough missing data to require the use of pairwise, rather than listwise, covariance (correlation) matrices. In any particular cycle it was difficult to secure data for every child on each of the many required variables. However, more severe causes of attrition were some changes in school archives and in our own research procedures. In some years, IQ measures and standardized test scores were completely lacking because the schools did not give the tests in those years. Also, in earlier years we did not gather all the information from parents that we gathered later (notably their ability estimates).

The only feasible way to deal with these missing data was to use pairwise measures and to estimate standard errors on the basis of conservative pairwise sample sizes. There may be consequences in terms of model structure from using pairwise-present data. The inability to invert some variance-covariance matrices may be attributable to this problem. On the other hand, the close correspondence in fit revealed by stacking data for the odd and even sample replications suggests that problems stemming from the pairwise nature of the data are not serious.

Dependence among Sampling Units

Since many of the students had the same teachers, there is some dependence among the sampling units. For this reason and because the sample is not random, it is not strictly legitimate to use standard errors to estimate the statistical significance of parameters, although for convenience we have tagged parameters that are relatively large compared to their standard errors. Also, children in one classroom would be expected to resemble one another more than children from different classrooms, and sampling of entire classrooms could lead to specification error in the models. Some teachers taught children in successive cohorts, so "teacher effects" are not independent and could bias the findings in unknown ways.

Pooling of Cohorts

By pooling all the first-graders who began first grade in a particular school over the several years of the study, we have ignored any systematic differences among cohorts. There may be real differences among them. The report-card format, for instance, was changed from from time to time. If this had effects on students, we cannot detect it. The pooling of cohorts could lead to mis-specification and/or bias. Furthermore, the effects of pooling may differ from school to school because of the varying nature of year-to-year differences in each school.

Confounding of Inter-School Differences with Other Differences

Most comparisons involving socioeconomic status are confounded by school differences. When white children from the lower-class school are compared with white children from the middle-class school, for example, any differences between them could as well be attributed to differences between schools as to differences in socioeconomic status.

One difference, pointed out in Chapter 5, is that teachers in the two lower-class schools were supposed to base marks on absolute levels of performance and teachers in the middle-class school were supposed to base marks on effort. We believe, however, from written statements solicited from the teachers describing their marking standards, that teachers' criteria in all schools were similar, especially after first grade.

Another difference among schools is the average IQ level. First-grade children in the middle-class school tested about 15 points higher than first-graders in the integrated school, and the differences between these two schools in average IQ for second- and third-graders were close to 25 points. There were also large fluctuations in average IQ over the three grades in the middle-class and integrated schools. For example, the averages over the three grades in the middle-class school were 113, 104, and 112; in the integrated school, 97, 83, and 90; and in the black school 90, 91, and 90. There is no obvious reason for the large grade-to-grade fluctuations within schools, but since differences close to 10 points occur often from year to year, differences of the same size between two schools in any one year may be of less import. The averages in both lower-class schools appear to be fluctuating around a grand mean in the neighborhood of 90.

The effects of the average IQ differences between schools cannot be analytically distinguished from other "school" effects. The IQ range in each school is different, so IQ could interact with other variables in one way in the middle-class school and in another way in the lower-class schools. We tried to address this problem by obtaining subsamples of children with IQ's in a comparable range from the all-white and the integrated schools. Our hope was to estimate models using equivalent IQ subsamples and thus to investigate whether, with similar inputs, IQ and other effects were similar in the two places. Unfortunately, the subsamples proved too small to provide useful analyses.

Our interpretation of the consistent and comparatively large IQ effects in the two lower-class schools, and the relatively smaller IQ effects in the middle-class school, is that the teachers in the lower-class schools were at least partially successful in adhering to marking policies that emphasize the absolute level of achievement. However, the fact that marks in reading and arithmetic were more responsive to IQ in the two lower-class schools than in the middle-class school could also be a consequence of differences among schools in the range of IQ. IQ differences between 75 and 100 may be more important for predicting reading success in the first three grades than differences between 100 and 120. In any case, the fact that the lasting-effects models do not reveal significant long-term effects associated with IQ in either the middle-class or integrated school suggests that IQ differences may create fewer problems for the interpretation of the findings than we anticipated.

Occasionally, the particular nature of the results does allow an "unpackaging" of confounded variables that makes the interpretation of inter-school differences clearer. One important instance of this occurs when the middle-class and lower-class schools as a whole differ in some way, yet where the results for the white subsample of the lower-class school resemble results for the all-white middle-class school, or when the two lower-class schools as a whole differ in some way yet where the black subsample in the integrated school resembles the all-black group in the other school. In such instances inter-school differences cannot be simple social-class effects or global school effects. Such effects must be attributed to race or some variable associated with race. For a reverse example, differences in average expectations are small between the black and the white children in the integrated school, small between black children in the integrated school and black children in the all-black school (where socioeconomic status is held fairly constant), but large between white children in the integrated school and white children in the all-white school (where socioeconomic status also differs). In this case it seems likely that average expectation level is associated with socioeconomic level rather than race.

DIFFERENCES BETWEEN MODEL CYCLES AND SCHOOL MARKING PERIODS

There is a lack of strict correspondence between school marking periods and the cycles mentioned. Only two cycles per year are included in the models, even though in the middle-class school there were three marking periods in first grade and four marking periods in the second and third grades. There were always three marking periods in the two lower-class schools, with the first matched to the first-cycle model of each academic year, and the latter two matched to the second-cycle model of each school year. Thus feedback from marks is measured in terms of the impact of the first mark in any school year on variables measured at or near the end of that year.

The consequences of the mismatch between model cycles and school marking periods are not known, but they generally should bias parameter estimates downward. For example, if an expectation obtained at T1 is taken as a direct determinant of a mark at T2, but an intervening mark has occurred at T1.5, correlations between expectations at T1.5 and marks at T2 would presumably exceed correlations between expectations at T1 and marks at T2.

Since the timing of variable measurement is better matched to first-cycle models generally, we examined the fits of the first-cycle models in each year compared to those for the second cycle. The χ^2 fit in the first cycle for each year does not appear superior to the fit for the second cycle (Table 6.1). There is some tendency, however, for the explained variance in children's expectations to increase and then to fall back cycle by cycle, as might be predicted if the first cycle model each year provided a more veridical model than the second. For example, in the integrated school the predicted variance in children's reading expectations over the six cycles (6.0, 12.5, 20.7, 18.3, 20.2, 7.6) and arithmetic expectations (6.3, 15.1, 37.0, 24.1, 13.4, 12.7) follows a sawtooth pattern in the second and third grades. In that school the first cycle was matched to the first marking period (which extended to the end of November) and the second cycle covered the remainder of the year (two marking periods). In the middle-class school, arithmetic expectations follow this pattern (8.9, 15.8, 28.7, 14.1, 35.0, 29.4) but reading expectations do not (5.1, 12.7, 11.3, 16.9, 19.3, 35.5). There the first cycle matched the first semester (two marking periods) and the second cycle matched the second semester (also two marking periods).

QUESTIONS ABOUT EXPECTATION MEASURES

Questions about the validity and reliability of children's expectations for themselves or others are the most pressing questions in terms of the overall significance of this research. Indeed, we were so acutely aware of possible threats to validity that we restricted our sample to three schools to guarantee sufficient attention to these problems. But should young children's expectation statements be taken at face value, particularly in the lower-class schools? Perhaps the children did not understand what they were doing when they were asked about expectations, or perhaps first-grade children in the lower-class schools overestimated their forthcoming marks because they were ashamed to acknowledge to the interviewers anything less than high expectations. There is no completely adequate response to such speculations. On the other hand, since our research personnel entered each school several times a year, and since children came to accept the presence of these personnel as routine, we believe that effects of interviewers were small.

Self-Expectations

We took several steps to improve validity and to check it (see Chapter 5 and Appendix B). First, every interviewing session in which expectations were obtained was conducted in private and in the spirit of a guessing game. Interviewers tried hard to get children to guess without pressing them, and it is doubtful that the children were even aware their guesses were being recorded. Second, real efforts were made to ensure that every child knew what was being asked. At the time of the inital interviews, when children guessed the marks they would get on their first report card, they were gently asked at the beginning of the interview if they knew the meaning of "report card," "arithmetic," and so on. A large plastic replica of a report card helped define the task. This brightly colored plastic sheet was spread out on a table or on the floor. Interviewers took as much time with each child as was needed, and only after the interviewer was satisfied that the child understood what was being asked did the interview proceed.

As mentioned in Appendix B, the validity of the children's expectation measure was checked by some extensive re-interviewing. Every first-grader in cohort S-2 of the middle-class school and every first-grader in cohort L-1 of the integrated lower-class school was re-interviewed completely. The purpose was to see whether children's understanding of report cards and of the marking system was clear enough for them to have made a meaningful response in the "expectation interview" held earlier that year. All children at the time of the re-interview (late in first grade) seemed to know the major fact about report cards—report cards evaluate how well children do in school—and in the middle-class school about 90% of children, and in the working-class school about 70%, had a good grasp of the meaning of all facts about report cards, according to the second interviewer's ratings.

Some of the strongest evidence for the validity of the expectation measure is that children clearly differentiated between their expectations for reading and arithmetic. Children expected to do better, on the average, in reading than in arithmetic, and there was no correlation between children's initial expectations for these two subjects (Table 8.1). Furthermore, reading expectations tended to be higher than arithmetic expectations irrespective of whether children were first asked about their reading expectations and then asked about their arithmetic expectations, or were asked about their expectations in the reverse order. In the first 3 years of the study, children were asked reading expectations first, arithmetic expectations second. However, the order of eliciting expectations was reversed in later years and the differences remained. Average arithmetic expectations never exceeded average reading expectations, independent of the order in which they were procured. Therefore, relatively higher reading and lower arithmetic expectations were not an artifact of the order in which the questions were asked. Children's differentiation of expectations by area, in addition to being a strong point of consistency across schools, also agrees with what has been found for older children (see Crandall 1969; Morse 1967). If children were merely giving high guesses because they thought this was what the interviewer wanted to hear or because they did not understand what they were doing, overmatching (rather than undermatching) of expectations in the two areas would be expected.

Other evidence of validity is provided by correlations between expectations for arithmetic obtained by two different procedures: from interviewers asking children to guess their forthcoming marks in arithmetic vs. answers to an item on a self-esteem test that happened to cover the same point. The self-esteem item was procured at a different time and under completely different testing conditions (see Appendix B).

Additional evidence of validity in the expectation measures is found in the developmental trends. In all three schools, even though the total amount of explained variance was not large, increasing amounts of variance in children's expectations are accounted for at each cycle. For example, at the end of second grade, more variance is accounted for in every area and in every school than was true at the end of first grade.

Estimates of reliability for the expectation measure are hampered because a single question was used to determine expectations in each area (reading, arithmetic, and conduct), and test-retest procedures pose obvious threats to a longitudinal research plan. However, data summarized in Table B.2 vouch for short-term stability. Persistence of expectations over longer time periods can be regarded as a test-retest measure, but, because of the long intervening time interval, we prefer to regard agreement between expectations at the middle and end of first grade as evidence of validity.

Peer-Popularity Ratings

The measurement of peer-popularity ratings was the least consistent of any of the variables in terms of operational procedures, and it may be weak. Early in the study, peer-popularity ratings in the middle-class school were obtained from a complicated "game" in which children repeatedly chose others in their class. Each child was ranked by his/her classmates several times, so the validity of the ultimate ranking may be secure. On the other hand, the procedure was so difficult to carry out that we never ventured to try it twice with the same class in order to check its consistency, and it proved impossible to use in the integrated school.

Consequently, most measurements of peer-popularity were secured by observing the order in which two competing team "captains," one boy and one girl, chose other children to join them in playing a reading game. The actual basis for choosing children was probably dual, because the order of choices to some extent reflected proficiency, although it was clear that a child's popularity or close friendship with the team captain was also influential. Gender frequently governed the choices, and occasionally a girl captain chose an entire team of girls while a boy captain chose a team composed entirely of boys. Some children who were chosen late were newcomers to the class or were frequently absent. When this procedure was repeated with one first-grade class in the integrated school after 1 week had elapsed, the correlations between ranks was 0.73.

A final strategy for obtaining peer-popularity ratings was an offshoot of the procedure for obtaining second- and third-grade childrens' expectations for their friends. The number of times a child was selected as a "best or second-best" friend by all the other children in the class was scaled as an indicator of peer-popularity.

Low validity or the presumed multifactor structure of the peer-popularity variable could account for its failure to predict children's expectations both generally and within cohorts, where only single-measurement strategies were used. The signs of structural parameters linking peer ratings with children's expectations are mixed and inconsistent. On the other hand, in the first two grades, half of the coefficients linking peer ratings to children's marks are large enough to attain borderline significance, and the lasting-effect model reveals significant effects of peer ratings on marks.

The problems associated with obtaining a reliable and valid measure of young children's liking for their peers and measures of peer-popularity are not easy to solve. There are ethical questions involved—it does not seem right to ask children whom they like least, and most schools frown on it. Children in the first three grades cannot write the names of other children, so choices of peers must be ascertained either from interviews or from some behavioral indicator. Indicators that can be observed in a short time have all the drawbacks that plagued the several measures that we tried.

A more workable method for obtaining peer-popularity ratings might be to ask a teacher to estimate popularity by ranking the boys and girls (separately) in her classroom. Rankings of more than one teacher could be obtained (physical education instructors, vocal music instructors, etc.) to make the measurement of popularity more reliable.

We should emphasize that our final measurement strategy attempted to separate the academic and social components of peers' evaluations by specifically requesting children's expectations for their friends and then operationalizing peer-popularity as the number of choices received. Unfortunately, we did not try this procedure for the first-grade children, and since it is obtrusive, it may tend to create, rather than measure, friends' expectations. The methodology for measuring peer-popularity and expectations for peers requires more investigation.

Parents' Expectations

Parents' expectations were obtained in settings that were as reassuring as possible. For example, the race of the interviewer was the same as that of the parent in the all-white and all-black schools, and interviewers were mixed by race in the integrated school. Nevertheless, the validity of the parent expectation measure probably differs across schools. Lower-class parents may be more threatened by interviewers (who were mostly middle-class) than middle-class parents are. Lower-class parents also may have had less information upon which to base an expectation estimate, since they conferred with teachers less frequently and were much less likely to visit school than were middle-class parents. Such differences in parents' responses or in the objective information available to parents may contribute to the generally lower year-to-year correlations for parents' expectation estimates observed in the two lower-class schools as compared to the middle-class school. (The year-to-year correlations between parents' expectations for reading were 0.28 and 0.23 in the integrated school, 0.32 and 0.50 in the black school, and 0.36 and 0.64 in the middle-class school; the correlations of year-to-year arithmetic estimates in these schools were 0.33 and 0.40, 0.07 and 0.48, 0.43 and 0.47, respectively.) It is also possible that, when asked about their expectations for the conduct mark, lower-class parents used different standards for judgment than middle-class parents, for example, taking it for granted that children's inattentiveness is "misbehavior" rather than a consequence of curricular inadequacies. Their perceptions of children's capabilities may be less consonant with the teacher's perceptions than middle-class parents' because teachers are generally recruited from the lower middle-class.

SUMMARY

While the list reviewed above is long, there is no particular finding we currently view as being challenged or jeopardized by the preceding discussion. Within the constraints posed by the data, we challenge the basic models in every way we can think of in Chapter 7 and in Appendix C. Also, we have focused attention mainly on findings that were sensible across cycles or across schools. For example, the failure of mark feedback to affect children's expectations was noted repeatedly across all cycles in both lower-class schools. The work is highly exploratory and we have tried to adapt the methodology to that fact. Fortunately, the subsample replications and across-cycle or across-school patterns provide some assistance in judging the overall reasonableness of many findings.

Appendix B

Issues of Measurement

As part of our modeling strategy, we hypothesized both structural models and measurement models. We therefore assembled as much information as possible on likely errors of measurement. That information is summarized in this appendix.

A basic modeling decision concerned whether we should analyze covariance or correlation matrices. Analyzing correlation matrices leads to standardized parameters, of course, and raises the well-known concern that differences among the variances of the variables in different populations are confounded with the magnitudes of the effect parameters. For comparisons among populations, unstandardized coefficients are preferable. Since we wish to compare parameters for three different schools, or to compare parameters across three grades within any single school, structural coefficients obtained from covariance analyses are preferred over those from correlation analyses. Actually, since LISREL provides standardized coefficients as well as metric coefficients, we obtained both kinds.

THE MEASUREMENT STRUCTURE

Table B.1 provides coefficients that are our estimates of the proportion of true variance in each of the variables. These may be thought of as either the test-retest reliability coefficients of each measure or as the square of the correlation between the true values of each concept and its indicator values. The complement of the tabled values is the proportion of error variance in the measures.

Each unobserved variable is assumed to be linked to a single observed variable, and the same measurement is used for a variable no matter where in a model, or in how many models, that variable appears.

When running covariance analyses, we fixed the lambda coefficients in LISREL as equal to 1.0 in order to facilitate interpretation. This forces our concepts to have the same units of measurement as our indicators. Fixing the error variances at "1 minus the tabled value, times the variance of the indicator" provides the correct proportion of true and error variance in our indicators. Therefore, the concept and indicator have the same scale of measurement, and the variance of the indicator is appropriately partitioned between the true (conceptual) variance and the error variance.

In practice, we fixed both the true concept variance and error variance at the appropriate values if the variable was exogenous (by fixing the corresponding LISREL ϕ and θ_δ values). For endogenous variables the error variances (θ_ϵ values) could be fixed directly, but the conceptual (true) variance had to be fixed indirectly by also fixing the measurement scales to be equal (lambda = 1.0). While this implies the true (conceptual) variance is the total indicator variance minus the error variance, the LISREL program was free to modify the variances of the endogenous concepts. Since any such change in variance made a direct increase in the χ^2 fit for the model (by violating the measurement variance equation) such "program" emendations to our measurement structure were minimized. While this was somewhat less than desirable, there was no alternative available within LISREL to directly fix the variance of the endogenous concepts.[1]

A part of all our models is a matrix of the covariances among the exogenous concepts. Fixed values were entered in this (phi) matrix, thereby making it

[1]A check on this aspect of the measurement structure showed that the variances of endogenous concepts were usually within 1% of the proper value, although occasionally discrepancies ran to 3% or 4% of the true-concept variances. The three largest differences ever found were 9.1%, 7.3%, and 4.5%.

Table B.1

Proportion of True Variance in the Indicators

	Children's Marks			Children's Expectations				Parent Variables										Peers' Expectations				Achievement Measures		
	Reading	Arithmetic	Conduct	Reading	Arithmetic	Conduct	Replicate Arithmetic	Reading Expectation	Arithmetic Expectation	Conduct Expectation	Ability Estimate	Peer Popularity Rating	Absences	Lateness	IQ	Sex	Race	Best Friend	Second Best Friend	Friends' Expectations	Teacher's Forecasts-Expectations (Kindergarten, Gr 1, Gr 2)	Likes School	Iowa Test of Basic Skills	California Achievement Test
White Middle-Class School																								
Grade 1	.90	.90	.90	.81	.81	.81	.56	.81	.81	.81	.90	.72	.90	.81	.76	1.0	X	X	X	X	.90	.72	X	X
Grade 2	.90	.90	.90	.90	.90	.90	.72	.90	.90	.90	.90	.72	.90	.81	.76	1.0	X	.90	.90	.90	.90	.72	X	X
Grade 3	.90	.90	.90	.90	.90	.90	.72	.90	.90	.90	.90	.72	.90	.81	.76	1.0	X	.90	.90	.90	X	X	.81	X
Integrated Lower-Class School																								
Grade 1	.81	.90	.90	.49	.49	.49	.30	.81	.81	.81	.81	.64	.81	.81	.76	1.0	1.0	X	X	X	.90	.72	X	X
Grade 2	.81	.90	.90	.64	.64	.64	.42	.90	.90	.90	.81	.64	.81	.81	.76	1.0	1.0	.64	.64	.64	.90	.72	X	.81
Grade 3	.81	.90	.90	.81	.81	.81	.64	.90	.90	.90	.81	.64	.81	.81	.76	1.0	1.0	.81	.81	.81	X	X	.81	.81
Black Lower-Class School																								
Grade 1	.81	.90	.90	.49	.49	.49	.30	.81	.81	.81	.81	.64	.81	.81	.76	1.0	X	X	X	X	.90	.72	X	X
Grade 2	.81	.90	.90	.64	.64	.64	.42	.90	.90	.90	.81	.64	.81	.81	.76	1.0	X	.64	.64	.64	.90	.72	X	.81
Grade 3	.81	.90	.90	.81	.81	.81	.56	.90	.90	.90	.81	.64	.81	.81	.76	1.0	X	.81	.81	.81	X	X	.81	.81
Relevant Notes:	1	1	1	2	2	2	2	2	2	2	3	4	5	6	7	8	8	9	9	9	10	11	12	12

[1]The only errors influencing these variables are recording or keypunching errors which are small in magnitude and uniform across schools. First-grade reading marks receive a lower coefficient because some of the cohorts received marks based on reading book level (which we converted into a 1 to 4 scale) which may have been confusing to both students and parents.

[2]These coefficients are discussed in the body of the text.

[3]The clarity of the questions and answer categories provide the high values while the school differences arise from the greater contact the middle-class parents have with the school. The wording of the answer categories minimized social desirability concerns.

[4]A test-retest measurement of the most frequently used procedure for measuring peer popularity provided a correlation of .72. In two classes the game for obtaining popularity ratings was played twice, one week apart. In one class the rank-order correlation was .68, and in the other it was .76. While this is reliability information, this also closely reflects our estimate of the validity of this item. The smaller coefficients in the lower-class schools reflect the slightly increased difficulty of gathering this information in these schools.

[5]Only recording and keypunching errors influence the middle-class school estimates while the frequent possibility of confusing substantial lateness with absence reduces the coefficients in the other schools.

[6]The infrequency of lateness in the middle-class school encouraged some laxity in keeping these records. In the lower-class schools there was more lateness but the care and consistency with which these records were kept is still questionable.

[7]The tabled coefficient of .76 is our estimate of the reliability of our IQ measures. The IQ tests used were:

Test	Grade Level	Cohorts Receiving Test	No. of Cases Receiving This Test	Published Reliabilities
Primary Mental Abilities (PMA)	Kingergarten	3	297	--
	First Grade	4	367	.83
Primary Cognitive Abilities Test (PCAT)	Kindergarten	4	275	.774
	First Grade	4	338	.788
	Second Grade	3	241	.814
Cognitive Abilities Test (CAT)	Third Grade	5	410	.93+
Short Form Test of Academic Aptitude (SFTAA)	Second Grade	1	102	

The reliabilities for the Primary Cognitive Abilities Test are test-retest correlations with a 13-month interval as reported by Thorndike, Hagen, and Lorge (1974). The Cognitive Abilities Test value indicates all three sections of this test had Kuder-Richardson 20 reliabilities in excess of .93 as reported by Thorndike and Hagen (1971). In first grade the PMA test had a test-retest reliability of .83 with both a 1 and a 4 week interval (Thurstone and Thurstone, 1965). While no kindergarten values are available we assume they would be slightly lower than this.

The SFTAA test in grade two has published reliabilities of .93 for a two-week interval and .75 for a 14-month interval (Sullivan, Clark, and Tiegs, 1974).

Three types of information condition our acceptance of these published values. First, individually administered tests typically provide slightly better reliabilities. For example, Honzik, MacFarlane, and Allen (1948) provide values of .82 and .83 for children tested and retested at the ages of 6 and 7, 7 and 8, respectively. Second, scores on different IQ tests are less consistent than test-retest reliabilities. Harcourt, Brace, and World Test Department (1961, 1968) reports correlations ranging from .53 to .80 for the application of several different tests to children in the first three grades, while Hieronymus and Stroud (1969) report fourth-grade inter-test correlations ranging from .50 to .83. And third, actual developmental changes in IQ which produce differing rankings of individuals are occurring at this stage of the life cycle. Bloom (1964), for example, reports that even perfectly measured IQ's measured at the ages of 5 and 17 correlate about .8 while those measured at 8 and 17 correlate about .9--with these values not reaching 1.0 due to real developmental changes. The tabled value of .76 is the same for

(Notes continue on next page.

unnecessary to estimate numerous coefficients in this matrix. Since the phi matrices for the second-semester models contained far too many parameters for the existing version of LISREL to estimate, we had no alternative but to find a way to obtain the exact values for the elements in this matrix. Fortunately this was easy to do, given that we had a single indicator of each concept and that the measurement scales of the concepts and indicators were the same.

The measurement procedure discussed above establishes that the variance of any true concept (ξ) is the proportion of true variance in the indicator (X). That is: $\text{Var}(\xi) = P\,\text{Var}(X)$ where P is the appropriate coefficient (proportion of true variance) from Table B.1. The remaining proportion of the variance in the indicator, $(1 - P)\text{Var}(X)$, is error variance. Thus, as already discussed, to calculate the diagonal elements of the phi matrix, use $P\,\text{Var}(X)$ to obtain the variance of the concepts.

The covariances among the unobserved exogenous concepts remain to be discussed. If we had needed the correlation between a pair of unobserved concepts, we could have obtained this by using the usual formula for correcting a correlation between observed variables for attenuation:

$$r_{12}^{*} = \frac{r_{12}}{(r_{11}r_{22})^{1/2}}$$

or, thinking of our tabled P's as test-retest reliabilities,

$$r_{12}^{*} = \frac{r_{12}}{(P_1P_2)^{1/2}}$$

Thus the correlation between two concepts is larger than the correlation between the corresponding indicators, and how much larger it is depends on how far P_1 and P_2 fall short of the perfect measurement value of 1.0.

To obtain the covariance between two concepts, we use the definitional relation between correlation and covariance:

$$r_{12}^{*} = \frac{\text{Cov}(12)^{*}}{[\text{Var}(1)^{*}\,\text{Var}(2)^{*}]^{1/2}}$$

[where the asterisks (*) indicate that all the terms in this equation refer to true rather than measured variables]. We arrange this as:

$$\text{Cov}(12)^{*} = r_{12}^{*}\,[\text{Var}(1)^{*}\,\text{Var}(2)^{*}]^{1/2}$$

Since the variance of any concept is P times the variance of the corresponding indicator, the following equation holds:

$$\text{Cov}(12)^{*} = r_{12}^{*}\,[P_1\text{Var}(1)\,P_2\text{Var}(2)]^{1/2}$$

Using the usual correction for attenuation to obtain the concepts' correlation, we can write this as:

$$\text{Cov}(12)^{*} = \frac{r_{12}}{(P_1P_2)^{1/2}}\,[P_1\text{Var}(1)\,P_2\text{Var}(2)]^{1/2}$$

which reduces to:

$$\text{Cov}(12)^{*} = \frac{r_{12}}{(P_1P_2)^{1/2}}\,(P_1P_2)^{1/2}\,[\text{Var}(1)\,\text{Var}(2)]^{1/2}$$

$$\text{Cov}(12)^{*} = r_{12}\,[\text{Var}(1)\,\text{Var}(2)]^{1/2}$$

$$\text{Cov}(12)^{*} = \text{Cov}(12)$$

This demonstrates that decrementing the concept variances to make them equal to the true portion of the indicator variances implies that the observed covariances are precisely those covariances that would appear if we were to correct the concepts' "correlations" for attenuation and then multiply this by the concepts' variances to obtain the concepts' covariance. Traditional procedures for dealing with measurement error require that the variance of both the indicator and the concept variables are held constant at 1.0 (in doing a correlation) while the covariance is adjusted upward. The equations above demonstrate that we can accomplish precisely the same thing by holding the covariances constant and reducing the variances (by making the variances of the concepts equal to the true portion of the variance of the indicator).

Hence, since we have a single indicator of each concept, and since the measurement scales of our concepts and indicators are the same, the required covariance matrix for the exogenous concepts (phi) is the covari-

---

Table B.1 (Continued)

all schools. Any poorer testing in the lower-class schools would be offset by the fact that low IQ's are more reliably measured than high IQ's (Robert Gordon, personal communication).

[8] The obvious nature of these items, combined with repeated checks due to the longitudinal nature of this study eliminate even keypunching errors in these variables.

[9] Children are about as able to report reading and arithmetic expectations for their friends as they are able to report expectations for themselves. The potency, veracity, or reasonableness of these expectations is to be accounted for by the model structure, not measurement error.

[10] There was no reason for teachers to conceal their forecasts so these values reflect their excelling reporting abilities.

[11] Though daily contacts make teachers aware of childrens' liking for school, their status as participants and the day-to-day variation in events influencing whether or not children like school render the measurements less than perfect.

[12] These values correspond to (are slightly less than, greater than) those reported in the test manuals for the Iowa Test of Basic Skills and the California Achievement Test. For the ITBS the <u>Fifth Mental Measurements Yearbook</u> (1959) reports (p. 17) values of .84 to .96 for the major tests. For the CAT the <u>Eighth Mental Measurements Yearbook</u> (1978) reports (p. 36) values of .87 for reading and .85 for mathematics.

ance matrix for the corresponding indicators with the diagonal variances reduced from those of the indicators to those of the corresponding concepts. This is precisely how we calculated the elements of the phi matrix for entry as fixed values in each of our models.

Measurement Assumptions

The remaining portion of this appendix presents the details of the measurement considerations that resulted in the measurement parameters presented in Table B.1. As mentioned, these values are interpretable as either the square of the correlation between the values of the true concepts and the corresponding indicators, or as the test-retest reliabilities of the indicators. As indicated above, our primary use of these parameters is to determine 1 minus the table value, the proportion of error variance to be fixed for each of our indicators, and the true variances of the exogenous variables for deriving the fixed phi matrix.

The measurement coefficients are allowed to vary by school and by grade (see Table B.1). In general, measurement was best in the white middle-class school and less precise in the integrated and black lower-class schools. This finding reflects many things, including the greater hesitancy of lower-class children to talk to adults, the greater difficulty of locating both lower-class parents and children (more absences and lateness), and the greater difficulty in gathering data as scheduled and the more confusing set of marking schemes in the lower-class schools.

The coefficients generally increase as grade level increases, indicating that data for third-graders are rated as generally of better quality than data for first-graders. By third grade, the students were more familiar with the different academic areas (they could easily separate reading from spelling, for example); they were more familiar with the use of report cards and the associated marking schemes; they were less hesitant about talking with the researchers, who were initially strangers but who by third grade had been seen several times; and both children and parents were more familiar with the interview procedures, having participated on several previous occasions.

The tabled reliability values were selected prior to our having "tried them out" with any model. Therefore, there is no possibility of their being selectively chosen to support our models and conclusions. In fact, we tried to estimate the coefficient as accurately as possible, because making these coefficients either consistently too large or too small incurs costs.

The series of notes appended to Table B.1 lists some of the considerations weighed in assigning coefficients for particular variables. Our original decisions were made in terms of having the square roots of the tabled values correspond to the early use of LISREL lambdas, in order to capture measurement precision rather than scale metrics. Since our use of these values is always in terms of the proportion of true variance in the variables, it is these proportions that we present in Table B.1, even though the implicit squaring makes them appear to be a somewhat unusual set of "considered estimates." Many of the minor decisions, for example, making a choice to table 0.64 or 0.72 (0.8 or 0.85 in our original unsquared version) rested on our familiarity with the overall data set and the behavior of these variables during preliminary analyses. Some initial attempts to use extremely conservative measurement coefficients introduced estimation problems, because the small coefficients made several sets of parameters equally admissible and so ruled out any single maximum likelihood solution. Accordingly, artificially small measurement coefficients were avoided.

The following sections discuss the measurement coefficients for children's and parents' expectations and for children's marks in detail.

Children's Expectations

Several types of information bear on the measurement of children's expectations. The first is how well children understand what they are being asked to rate when they give their expectations—if children do not understand what a report card is or what it signifies, the remainder of the task is meaningless.

To check on children's understanding, in June 1973, first-grade children from both the integrated lower-class and white middle-class schools who had reported on their expectations earlier in the year were individually re-interviewed by a different interviewer and were asked to explain what a report card was and what each of the marks issued by their school meant. (This questioning did not inquire about expectations.) All children in both schools were able to explain that a report card was the teacher's written evaluation of that child's performance. Thirty-five percent of the seventy-seven children in the integrated school verbalized the basics of the letter marks issued there in reading and arithmetic, and 42% of these children could verbalize the ranking implied by the numerical grades issued in conduct. Eighty-one percent of the ninety-five children interviewed in the all-white school correctly verbalized the numerical marking system used in all marking areas in this school. Thus, with a stringent criterion—whether the children on a separate occasion could correctly state aloud to a different interviewer both what report cards signified and what all the valuations on report cards signified—a high percentage of the children understood the basic concepts they would have to employ in voicing their expectations correctly.

The sharp difference between the number of students in the integrated and all-white schools (35% vs. 81%)

who correctly verbalized the essence of the marking scheme implies that measurement coefficients should differ between the two schools in the first grade. On the other hand, we are convinced that the actual magnitude of the difference should not be nearly as large as the differences in percentages between the two schools, because requiring lower-class children to verbalize information to our interviewer greatly underrates their competence. It is well-known that lower-class children will not converse readily with strangers (particularly if the strangers are middle-class), and that dialect-speaking children often react with silence or "non-work" responses when addressed by a non-dialect speaker.

A second kind of information bearing on how well children's expectations were measured came from a test-retest reliability study of all three grades in all schools in June 1976 (at the end of the data-collection period). Children's expectations were first obtained by employing the usual procedures at the end of the year. Then the children were re-interviewed after a period of 1 to 2 weeks, yet before the issuance of report cards. Besides reassessing the children's prevailing expectations, the second interview probed to see if the children recalled the expectations they had given earlier. Table B.2 presents the correlations between the children's initial, retested, and recalled expectations.

If considered alone, the first three columns of Table B.2 suggest that second- and third-grade expectations are moderately stable over the test-retest period, but that, in first grade, the arithmetic expectations of children in the integrated school and the reading expectations of children in both lower-class schools are measured very poorly. Considering recalled expectations (the second set of three columns), we find increases in a majority of the coefficients; this suggests that although the children could recall what they had said previously, they sometimes chose to provide other responses. Evidently some real changes in expectations occurred, as might be expected given the intervening time interval (about 5% of the year). Two first-grade measures remain troublesome according to these data—reading expectations of children in the black school and arithmetic expectations of children in the integrated school. We present more information regarding arithmetic below. Reading was assigned the same coefficient as the other areas since the measurement procedure was identical across areas.

Of the 276 children providing expectations at both times, 16% volunteered their recollection of the earlier proceedings, and 84% recalled the earlier interview when asked directly about it. Only one child failed to recall the earlier interview even with substantial prompt-

Table B.2 Correlations for Children's Retested Expectations[1]

	Initial with Retested Expectations			Initial with Recalled Expectations			Recalled with Retested Expectations			Year-end Arithmetic Expectations with Arithmetic Expectations Derived from the second term Self-esteem Tests		
	Gr.1	Gr.2	Gr.3	Gr.1	Gr.2	Gr.3	Gr.1	Gr.2	Gr.3	Gr.1	Gr.2	Gr.3
White Middle-Class School												
Reading	.35 (22)	.36* (26)	.46*** (30)	.90*** (19)	.43* (23)	.93*** (29)	.47* (19)	.54** (23)	.59*** (29)			
Arithmetic	.52** (22)	.82*** (26)	.79*** (30)	.55* (17)	.86*** (23)	.91*** (30)	.89*** (17)	.87*** (23)	.73*** (30)	.25*** (362)	.42*** (317)	.55*** (241)
Conduct	.64*** (22)	.52** (26)	.06 (30)	.89*** (17)	.68*** (24)	.55*** (28)	.55* (17)	.73*** (24)	.44** (28)			
Integrated Lower-Class School												
Reading	-.13 (27)	.38* (32)	.76*** (26)	.24 (27)	.46** (31)	.58*** (26)	.22 (27)	.43** (31)	.73*** (26)			
Arithmetic	-.31 (27)	.41** (32)	.82** (26)	.00 (26)	.54*** (32)	.53** (26)	.36* (26)	.58*** (32)	.67*** (26)	.12* (296)	.15* (205)	.40*** (143)
Conduct	.56*** (27)	.61*** (32)	.50** (26)	.38* (25)	.60*** (32)	.77*** (25)	.40* (25)	.68*** (32)	.53** (25)			
Black Lower-Class School												
Reading	.01 (22)	.58*** (25)	.58*** (60)	-.04 (21)	.63*** (24)	.65*** (59)	.58** (21)	.38* (24)	.64*** (59)			
Arithmetic	.41* (22)	.06 (25)	.57*** (60)	.46* (20)	.75*** (23)	.69*** (57)	.84*** (20)	.05 (23)	.56*** (57)	.03 (172)	.31*** (122)	.51*** (128)
Conduct	.73*** (22)	.82*** (25)	.47*** (60)	.58** (21)	.62*** (25)	.41*** (58)	.79*** (21)	.34* (25)	.50*** (58)			

[1]N's appear in parentheses, and grade level is indicated as Gr.1, Gr.2, Gr.3.

*one-tailed p < .05

**one-tailed p < .01

***one-tailed p < .001

ing. A number of children, however, failed to recall the specific expectations they had voiced on the prior occasion. The percentages of children who recalled both the prior interview and the particular expectations they voiced are 94%, 92%, and 93% in reading, arithmetic, and conduct, respectively. Table B.2 indicates that the accuracy of recall was higher for the higher grades.

A fortunate coincidence provided additional information concerning the measurement of arithmetic expectations in all three schools. A self-esteem questionnaire was completed by all children during the latter part of the second term of each grade.[2] In this test, the children indicated how good they thought they were at various activities, such as running, playing ball, being polite, etc. One of the items on both the boys' and girls' forms of this questionnaire was about arithmetic. Children were asked how good they thought they were at doing arithmetic, using as response categories "very good," "good," "not good or bad," "bad," and "very bad."

This information (with the last two categories, which were used the least frequently, combined) gives a measure of arithmetic expectations independent of the measure obtained from the standard interview procedure used for all children. Self-esteem measurements, and hence these additional arithmetic expectations, were obtained from interviews 2 to 5 weeks prior to report-card issuance and always before specific expectations (collected about 1 to 3 weeks prior to report cards). The timing of the collection of these additional data thus did not correspond precisely with the actual collection of expectations. This hiatus provides time for real changes in expectations to occur between the self-esteem interviews and year-end expectation interviews. Also, the context of inquiring about expectations differed in that the usual procedure couched the expectation questions in the academic context of report cards and marking schemes, while the question on the self-esteem questionnaire was not focused on a particular upcoming report card and was surrounded by a range of questions reflecting many other activities, such as skating, helping others, and so on. Thus the time span, the frame of reference, and the administration procedures may all have contributed to variation between findings from the standard procedure and those inferred from the self-esteem test. For these reasons the modest correlations (the last three columns of Table B.2) between these arithmetic "expectations" and those gathered by the standard procedure are about as expected.

The products of the square roots of the measurement coefficients in Table B.1 for the true expectations and the slightly smaller corresponding values for the esteem-replicate arithmetic expectations provide predicted correlations about 0.3 units larger than the values in Table B.2 (a difference reasonably attributable to real changes in expectations). The products of the roots of the tabled values much more closely approximate the correlations for the test-retest procedure reported above.

Fortunately, there are several places where the extra set of arithmetic data nicely complement the short-term replication data on expectations. Such comparison suggests that both the largest negative value (integrated school, first grade) and a nearly zero value (black school, second grade) are unquestionably too low. Also, the smallest value from the self-esteem procedure (black school, first grade) corresponds to a substantial value in the short-term replication. Together they suggest that, while the measures are far from perfect, they do tap the dimensions they were designed to tap.

All in all, we conclude that first-grade children's expectations are measured with considerable reliability in the middle-class school and with somewhat less reliability in the other two schools. The precision of expectation measurement definitely improves for children in higher grades in all three schools.

Parents' Expectations

No test-retest data for parental expectations are available, but several points are pertinent.

The strongest argument that there was precision in measurement of parents' expectations centers on how the expectations were obtained. Parents filled out a replica of their school's report card that contained brief descriptions of how performance is rated in reading, arithmetic, and conduct. Interviewers explained whatever was unclear, and offered to record the parents' verbal guesses if the parents wished. The parents' task was thus extremely well defined and precisely focused.

Conduct expectations may be slightly less stable than reading or arithmetic expectations because of the inherent lability of conduct. A month of good behavior can be overshadowed by one bad incident. Also, children's conduct is influenced by that of other students: If surrounded by well-behaved youngsters, a child is more likely to display acceptable conduct. The inherent uncertainty associated with conduct, however, may be offset by the fact that conduct is an aspect of behavior for which parents themselves can marshal the most direct evidence.

Table 5.2 indicates that, although one might think that parents would voice only the highest expectations for their children, a majority of parents expressed only

[2]Because preliminary analyses cast doubt on the construct validity of this measure, self-esteem scores were not included as variables in the final version of our models.

moderately optimistic expectations. This conservatism suggests that parents were being realistic.

We believe parental expectations were equally well formed in all schools, but that in first grade expectations are slightly harder to measure. Accordingly, the coefficients in Table B.1 indicate that about 81% of the variance in parents' initial reading and arithmetic expectations is considered true variance, while about 90% of the variance in their expectations in the later grades is considered true.

Children's Marks

Our transcription of report-card marks from school records provides almost error-free measurement. The only error component would arise from coding or keypunching errors, strictly minimized to less than 1%. Even teacher errors, such as recording a mark in the wrong column, do not necessarily contribute error variance, because the consequences of such a mark are real, even if unintended.[3]

Although our modeling strategy conceptualizes marks as the evaluation of children's behavior that influenced children, parents, teachers, and peers, it is essential to consider the extent to which actual performance capabilities contribute to marks. To this end, we gathered all the data available in the school files on standardized tests. Standardized testing was not under our control, so the information is less complete than we might wish. There is, however, sufficient information to support some basic conclusions. Teachers' marks are substantial indicators of standardized achievement in all three schools, particularly in later grades. Table B.3 presents the correlations between report-card marks and the available standardized measures. The upper portion of the first two columns refers to the Iowa Test of Basic Skills (ITBS) taken in grade three in the middle-class school. Second- and third-grade marks in this school correlate about 0.5 with both the reading and arithmetic sections of the test, while first-grade marks correlate about 0.35 with this third-grade testing.

The lower portion of the first two columns concerns the Gates-MacGinitie reading test (vocabulary and comprehension sections), administered in all three grades. The first-grade administration of this test provides values of above 0.4, while the second-grade administration consistently provides correlations of 0.5 or above. The second- and third-grade correlations for the Gates-MacGinitie reading test do not substantially alter the 0.5 correlation suggested by the ITBS for these grades. This is especially true if one discounts the weaker correlations on the basis that there are many ways to fail standardized tests (distractions, failure to follow instructions, the need for a washroom, time wasted due to broken pencils, etc.) while there are many fewer ways to do well.

Table B.4 provides test-retest correlations that fortunately arose when a change in testing schedules in the two lower-class schools provided the California Achievement Test (CAT) and the Test of Basic Experience (TOBE) in both October and May of the same year. These data suggest that the tabled value of 0.81 for the CAT seems a little conservative in the integrated school and a little optimistic in the black school. The values for the TOBE are considerably lower, even though all the relevant coefficients exceed those reported by the test authors for a comparable time span (see the note to Table B.4). Considerably higher coefficients for a shorter time span were reported in the test manual.[4]

Table B.3 points to the best estimates of the correlations between marks and standardized achievement as 0.65, 0.65, and 0.70 for first to third grades, respectively, in the integrated lower-class school. The California Achievement Test correlations again suggest a slight boosting of the correlations above those suggested by the third-grade administration for the Iowa Test of Basic Skills.

The data in Table B.3 pertaining to the black lower-class school suggest that first-grade marks there do not reflect standardized achievement particularly well, but that the second- and third-grade marks there are almost as good as those in the integrated school. For reading, summary values of 0.40, 0.60, and 0.65 may be used for the first to third grades, respectively. For arithmetic, summary values may be taken as 0.60, 0.50, and 0.50.

Those values in general, and the 0.60 value for first-grade arithmetic in particular, are also supported by the mark-achievement correlations obtained from the repeated use of the TOBE taken in first grade and the CAT taken in second grade. The mark correlations of an early TOBE testing and a later CAT testing are only slightly smaller than those presented in Table B.3. Since both these tests were administered in the integrated school with the same replication timings and since they lead to similar correlations, we place a little extra confidence in these coefficients.

One factor that could complicate the interpretations above is that the correlations between marks and the

[3]In the two lower-class schools, reading marks were frequently reported as the level of the reader the child was working in. Since this necessitated recoding to our 1 to 4 marking schema, additional errors may have been introduced here, so slightly lower coefficients appear in Table B.1. Again, however, the error component is assumed to be small.

[4]With a 6-week interval, TOBE reliabilities are 0.72 (math) and 0.57 (reading). "Alternate form" reliabilities for the Gates test for all grades cluster around 0.85, while grade three validity correlations with other tests are 0.84 (vocabulary) and 0.79 (comprehension). The Iowa information is not available.

Table B.3
Correlations between Standard Achievement Measures and Marks for All Schools[a]

IOWA TEST OF BASIC SKILLS Reading and Arithmetic sections Test taken in third grade		Middle-Class White School Reading Mark	Middle-Class White School Arithmetic Mark	Lower-Class Integrated School Reading Mark	Lower-Class Integrated School Arithmetic Mark	Lower-Class Black School Reading Mark	Lower-Class Black School Arithmetic Mark
First Grade	mid year	.36 (182)	.30 (180)	.42 (86)	.54 (113)	-.02° (41)	.27° (35)
	year-end	.39 (188)	.38 (186)	.38 (117)	.63 (117)	.14° (42)	.15° (40)
Second Grade	mid year	.55 (214)	.48 (216)	.42 (104)	.52 (129)	.42** (33)	.33** (51)
	year-end	.44 (215)	.46 (217)	.47 (137)	.61 (136)	.55 (39)	.34** (50)
Third Grade	mid year	.48 (242)	.43 (248)	.47 (120)	.49 (163)	.73 (33)	.65 (61)
	year-end	.46 (252)	.48 (256)	.53 (164)	.55 (162)	.44 (66)	.57 (66)

GATES-MacGINITIE READING TEST		Reading Mark With Vocabulary	Reading Mark With Comprehension
Test taken in first grade			
First Grade	mid year	.36 (144)	.39 (144)
	year-end	.45 (146)	.49 (146)
Test taken in second grade			
First Grade	mid year	.50 (199)	.51 (199)
	year-end	.55 (121)	.55 (121)
Second Grade	mid year	.39 (144)	.35 (141)
	year-end	.59 (143)	.53 (143)
Third Grade	mid year		
	year-end		
Test taken in third grade			
First Grade	mid year	.31** (84)	.47 (82)
	year-end	.47 (87)	.58 (85)
Second Grade	mid year	.33 (100)	.40 (98)
	year-end	.43 (100)	.48 (98)
Third Grade	mid year	.46 (129)	.42 (125)
	year-end	.53 (135)	.49 (131)

TEST OF BASIC EXPERIENCE[b] Reading and Arithmetic sections Test taken in first grade		Lower-Class Integrated School Reading Mark	Lower-Class Integrated School Arithmetic Mark	Lower-Class Black School Reading Mark	Lower-Class Black School Arithmetic Mark
First Grade	mid year	.37 (88)	.48 (86)	.18° (62)	.61 (84)
	year-end	.39 (90)	.52 (87)	.35 (83)	.67 (92)

CALIFORNIA ACHIEVEMENT TEST[c] Reading and Arithmetic sections		Lower-Class Integrated School Reading Mark	Lower-Class Integrated School Arithmetic Mark	Lower-Class Black School Reading Mark	Lower-Class Black School Arithmetic Mark
Test taken in second grade					
First Grade	mid year	.59 (54)	.65 (53)	.43 (61)	.59 (69)
	year-end	.65 (58)	.57 (59)	.71 (64)	.61 (72)
Second Grade	mid year	.66 (66)	.59 (66)	.82 (25)	.36** (62)
	year-end	.54 (66)	.61 (66)	.81 (44)	.37 (62)
Third Grade	mid year			.36* (33)	.40** (51)
	year-end			.63 (46)	.45 (50)
Test taken in third grade					
First Grade	mid year	.47 (58)	.45 (56)	.21° (50)	.44 (47)
	year-end	.64 (58)	.54 (60)	.29** (49)	.29** (51)
Second Grade	mid year	.62 (34)	.62 (69)	.53 (49)	.31** (71)
	year-end	.54 (75)	.73 (77)	.56 (50)	.43 (69)
Third Grade	mid year	.70 (84)	.71 (80)	.84 (36)	.45 (78)
	year-end	.69 (83)	.65 (79)	.58 (74)	.43 (78)

[a]The signs of these correlations have been reversed so that they will be intuitively correct. N's appear in parentheses. All coefficients are significant at the $p < .001$ level with one-tailed test unless denoted as:

° not significant
* $p < .05$
** $p < .01$

[b]These correlations are for a test taken in May. The same test taken the preceding October provided almost identical correlations, based on slightly smaller N's.

[c]The second-grade CAT correlations are based on a test taken in October. The same test taken the following May provided comparable, though minimally smaller correlations, based on similar N's.

Table B.4

Standardized Achievement Test Replication Correlations

		California Achievement Test Administered in Grade Two			
		Integrated School		Black School	
		Replicate Score		Replicate Score	
		Reading	Arithmetic	Reading	Arithmetic
Initial Score	Reading	.89*** (65)	.69*** (65)	.72*** (65)	.54*** (62)
	Arithmetic	.57*** (66)	.80*** (66)	.21* (66)	.58*** (64)

		Test of Basic Experience Administered in Grade One[a]			
		Integrated School		Black School	
		Replicate Score		Replicate Score	
		Reading	Arithmetic	Reading	Arithmetic
Initial Score	Reading	.67*** (78)	.61*** (80)	.50*** (76)	.59*** (76)
	Arithmetic	.40*** (78)	.39*** (81)	.48*** (77)	.69*** (77)

[a]The TOBE Level L Examiner's Manual provides a comparable correlation matrix of

$$\begin{pmatrix} .36 & .36 \\ .38 & .37 \end{pmatrix}$$

for a Richmond, Va. Catholic sample of size about 200 using Form K and L but with a comparable time span.

*one-tailed p < .05.

**one-tailed p < .01.

***one-tailed p < .001.

various standardized tests in Table B.3 may reflect yearly differences in teachers' marking policies. Thus, using higher correlations from one year and test to rule out lower correlations for another test given to the same grade level in another year may not be entirely justified.

This potential criticism is strongest under two conditions: first, if the different tests are extremely highly correlated with one another, and second, if restricting the correlation case base to include only those cases receiving both standardized tests eliminates the differences in the correlations. That is, if eliminating case base differences also eliminates the systematic differences in the correlations, we would be suspicious that the systematic differences in Table B.3 are cohort (marking) differences rather than testing differences.

Examining both these concerns in the relatively few instances where children received more than one form of standard test indicates that the tests do not correlate with one another excessively, and that this does not abolish the differential relationships. Therefore, we feel some confidence in relying on the higher correlations. The details of the test interrelations are as follows: ITBS reading total with Gates, comprehension $r = 0.71$ in second grade and $r = 0.78$ in third grade in the middle-class school; ITBS with third-grade CAT, $r_R = 0.62$, $r_A = 0.71$ in the integrated school and $r_R = 0.64$ and $r_A = 0.57$ in the black school; while second-grade CAT and the TOBE for the black school was $r_R = 0.28$, $r_A = 0.61$ and $r_R = 0.32$ and $r_A = 0.66$ for the *first* and *second* testing of TOBE, respectively. (The TOBE Manual Level L provides first-grade correlations between TOBE and CAT as $r_R = 0.42$, $r_A = 0.46$ for a Richmond, Virginia, Catholic sample of about 184 cases.)

We address the relationships between these standardized tests and other variables in Chapter 7.

Appendix C

Structural Variants of the Basic Models

Some structural variants of the basic models are discussed in this section. Other structural variants, such as separate estimation of the basic models by race and gender, are presented in Chapter 6. These separate estimates allowed us to see whether model structure is similar within each race or gender subgroup.

Parameter estimates for the separate models by race and sex closely resembled estimates for models based on combined gender or racial groups. Insofar as we could tell, the attainment process in the present sample is the same for boys and girls, and for blacks and whites. Also, in Chapter 6 we report that the forward specification of paths from children's first expectations to their first marks, rather than reciprocal paths, seemed preferable on substantive grounds, and exploration of models with reciprocal paths supported use of only the forward paths in the initial cycle.

Other structural variants, such as including reciprocal paths between conduct marks and marks in reading and arithmetic, and the re-introduction of the ascriptive exogenous variables in every cycle rather than in alternate cycles, are now discussed. These variants are, in many ways, as reasonable a priori as the structures we initially chose.

RECIPROCAL PATHS BETWEEN MARKS IN CONDUCT AND MARKS IN READING AND ARITHMETIC

The basic models are almost fully recursive. In particular, there are no backward paths in any of the models. Conduct marks are taken as determinants of marks in reading and arithmetic in spite of the fact that all three marks were measured simultaneously. Poor conduct is assumed to cause poor reading or arithmetic for two reasons: 1) Unruly children are likely to be inattentive to instruction; hence they are likely to spend less time learning how to read and do arithmetic. 2) It is reasonable to assume that teachers will give better marks to well-behaved children.

While placing conduct marks in a prior position seems well founded (and we ultimately came to prefer it), we also considered the reverse causal ordering—that marks in the two substantive areas could be causes of the mark in conduct. Perhaps children who are not learning well become disruptive because of their poor academic performance, through frustration or boredom, or both. It is also possible that all three causes could operate simultaneously and produce effects operating in two directions. If so, reciprocal causal paths would be the proper specification. To resolve the issue, we tested models with reciprocal paths inserted between marks in conduct and the other two marks, and observed the outcome.

Models with reciprocal paths between conduct marks and marks in reading and arithmetic but with all other structures unchanged were estimated for each of the three schools for each of the six time periods (Table C.1). Four of the eighteen models provided unacceptable solutions.[1] For none of the fourteen models with acceptable solutions was there an improvement in fit, as measured by a significant decrement in χ^2 in the revised as compared with the original models. Of the twenty-eight backward paths (fourteen from reading to conduct, fourteen from arithmetic to conduct) eighteen were positive, as predicted, and ten were negative.

[1]Three had standardized error variances exceeding 1.0 (T1 and T4–T5 in the black school, T4–T5 in the integrated school), and, as noted elsewhere, one had a non-positive definite covariance matrix (T2–T3 in the black school).

APPENDIX C

Table C.1

Comparison of Results Obtained With and Without Reciprocal Paths from Marks in Reading and Arithmetic to Marks in Conduct[a]

	Model for:	Backward Paths $M_R \rightarrow M_C$	Backward Paths $M_A \rightarrow M_C$	Forward Paths $M_C \rightarrow M_R$: In Original Model	Forward Paths $M_C \rightarrow M_R$: In Model with Reciprocal Paths	Forward Paths $M_C \rightarrow M_A$: In Original Model	Forward Paths $M_C \rightarrow M_A$: In Model with Reciprocal Paths	Reduction in Model χ^2, d.f. = 2
T1	White Middle-Class School	.4017[+]	-.0330	.2577[*]	-.0435	.1379[*]	.0760	3.20
	Integrated Lower-Class School	.6609[+]	-.2564	.0265	-.2528	.2705[*]	.2195	3.03
	Black Lower-Class School[b]	---	---	.1226	---	.2874[*]	---	---
T1-2	White Middle-Class School	-.0334	.0691	.1761[*]	.1837[*]	.1772[*]	.1530[*]	0.38
	Integrated Lower-Class School	.0783	.1000	.3431[*]	.2719[*]	.2854[*]	.2037[*]	3.74
	Black Lower-Class School	.2228	.0617	.1947	.0367	.1700	.0917	0.80
T2-3	White Middle-Class School	.3038[+]	.2368	.2506[*]	.0457	.2174[*]	.0617	5.79
	Integrated Lower-Class School	.0746	-.3058[+]	.1674[+]	.1827[+]	.1040	.2552[+]	2.18
	Black Lower-Class School[c]	---	---	---	---	---	---	---
T3-4	White Middle-Class School	-.0622	-.1103	.0981[+]	.1291[+]	.1172[*]	.1592[*]	2.05
	Integrated Lower-Class School	.0573	.0063	.0967	.0581	.1572[*]	.1454[+]	0.48
	Black Lower-Class School	.3924[+]	-.1139	.0995	.0289	.1556	-.0038	3.78
T4-5	White Middle-Class School	.3809	.2648	.1283	-.1786	.1319	-.1517	3.99
	Integrated Lower-Class School[b]	---	---	.1807	---	.1548	---	---
	Black Lower-Class School[b]	---	---	.2579[*]	---	-.0554	---	---
T5-6	White Middle-Class School	.1190	-.1284	.0838	.0520	.1416[*]	.1908[*]	1.46
	Integrated Lower-Class School	-.1672	.2054[*]	.1641	.2938[*]	.0759	-.0962	5.28
	Black Lower-Class School	-.2907[*]	.1697	-.2224[*]	-.1937[+]	.0088	.0060	4.05

[a]All coefficients are unstandardized.

[b]This model provided standardized structional disturbance variances (PSI) greater than unity.

[c]The data matrix for this model was not positive definite.

[*]Coefficient is more than twice its standard error.

[+]Coefficient is more than 1.5 times its standard error.

Only one positive path and one negative path of the twenty-eight exceeded twice their standard error. Insertion of the backward paths also tended to reduce the magnitude of the forward paths from conduct to reading and arithmetic marks, but seven of the twenty-eight forward paths continued to exceed twice their standard errors (compared to fifteen originally) and twelve exceeded 1.5 times their standard error (compared to seventeen originally). The insertion of reciprocal paths also made the models slightly less appealing, in that a few negative paths from conduct to reading and arithmetic appeared. Only two of the twenty-eight original forward paths was negative while seven (usually small) negative paths appeared with the insertion of reciprocal paths.

These various facts build a rather strong case against including reciprocal paths between conduct and the two academic subjects: the fit of the models was not improved; most of the backward paths were not significant (twenty-six of the twenty-eight) and the two that were large enough to attain significance had mixed signs; the models became more unreasonable in other ways (more negative forward paths), while the general role played by the forward paths from conduct to reading and arithmetic was little changed. Thus the substantive arguments that persuaded us to place conduct ahead of marks in reading and arithmetic are consistent with conclusions derived from estimating a set of models with non-recursive properties. Although a reciprocal causal structure between conduct and marks in the academic areas may be plausible at higher grade levels, we are inclined to believe that, especially in the first two grades, conduct determines academic performance rather than the other way round. The schooling process may be qualitatively different for younger, as compared to older, children.

Other hints here and there are also consistent with assuming only forward paths from conduct. For one thing, many of the children could not anticipate their marks in reading and arithmetic and tended to estimate marks that were too high. Since they did not forecast their forthcoming marks accurately and believed that their marks would be higher than the marks turned out to be, it is hard to argue that they were at that point discouraged by poor achievement. They believed their achievement levels were high, and on that account poor conduct as a consequence of discouragement is inconsistent with the facts. For another thing, teachers in the middle-class school were specifically instructed to mark on effort, and teachers in the other two schools also took effort into account. Therefore, effort, which would be visible in good conduct, was acknowledged by teachers to be one of the *determinants* they used in assigning marks in reading and arithmetic.

ADDING SEX AND IQ AS EXOGENOUS VARIABLES IN THE SECOND HALF OF THE SCHOOL YEAR

The basic models are of two types: a model for the transition between grades, and a model for the movement through each grade. The between-year models (including the transition into first grade) include sex, IQ, and (where appropriate) race as exogenous variables, while the models for the movement through each of the years exclude direct effects of these variables. The rationale for not including these three variables as exogenous in every cycle is that, if these variables have effects, they probably correspond with the child's entry into a new classroom in the fall of the year. By mid-year, teacher preferences, peer networks, and daily routines are presumed to have become relatively stable in each classroom; therefore, any effects of gender, race, and IQ operating through teachers' preferential treatment or peer friendship patterns would merely continue patterns established during the first part of the year. In short, we postulated only indirect effects of sex, race, and IQ in the second half of each school year.

One way to justify our modeling strategy, as before, is to let the data judge whether inclusion of sex and IQ in the within-year models is advantageous. Accordingly, the within-year models were estimated with sex and IQ inserted as exogenous variables. Of the three possible models in each of the three schools, eight proved acceptable.[2] Both sex and IQ were allowed to influence directly each of the six endogenous year-end variables in these models. With three expectation variables and three mark variables, there are thus a total of twelve "new" coefficients estimated in each of the eight models. Sampling fluctuations would predict that about five of these ninety-six coefficients would appear to be significant by chance, and we found that eleven of the coefficients exceeded twice their standard errors—four for sex, and seven for IQ.

[2]The T3–T4 model in the black school provided an unacceptable negative error variance.

There were no consistent patterns in these effects, and the effects of both variables usually added less than 4% to the explained variances. In particular, for the model contributing four of the seven significant IQ effects (the white school in third grade) predictions did not improve very much (the explained variance increased by an average of 2.5%). For the most part, the other portions of the models remained similar to those presented in Chapter 6.

On balance, the elaboration of the models to include sex and IQ as exogenous variables in every cycle suggests that there might be marginal benefit from including these variables directly in the within-year models. However, for the present data real costs would be involved. The reduction in sample size for some of the models (necessitated by the inclusion of IQ and its relatively weak case base) decreases the power of tests involving parameter significance, and the unreasonable behavior of the T3–T4 model in the black school completely eliminates this portion of the data. As already mentioned, only three of the seven IQ effects occurred in the first two grades.

Although we would be inclined in future work to enter sex and IQ as exogenous variables in every cycle, we believe that their omission here leads to small changes, especially in the first and second grades, where the models are generally most satisfactory. Parameter estimates and other information about these models are available from the authors on request.

SUMMARY OF STRUCTURAL ALTERNATIVES IN THE BASIC MODELS

The supplementary analyses presented in this appendix and some presented in Chapter 6 examine the most controversial parts of our structural models. Our assessments of the various structural alternatives are recapitulated below.

1. The specification of children's expectations as determinants of marks in the initial cycle, rather than the opposite, is supported by examination of the corresponding partial derivatives of the likelihood function for all schools. In the middle-class school, estimating backward paths from marks to expectations as well as forward paths from expectations to marks also upheld the forward specification. Further checks were judged unnecessary because of the small size of the parameters on the forward paths, which amounts to little indication of upward bias. In cycles after the first, feedback allows children's expectations to affect their marks, so the problem is minimized.

2. Although similar outcomes, in terms of average expectation levels and average marks, for the two races do not necessarily rule out structural differences in the attainment process, no structural differences across

races were found when separate models were estimated for children of the two races.

3. Although structural differences in the attainment process could obtain for members of the two sexes, separate model estimates by gender for the integrated school suggest this possibility is not likely. Subsequent work reveals some differences in mother's influence and average expectation levels associated with gender in the middle-class school (Entwisle and Baker forthcoming).

4. Estimation of reciprocal effects between conduct marks and marks in reading and arithmetic suggests that the forward specification from conduct to marks in the other two areas is preferable to a non-recursive formulation. However, this specification may be appropriate only for very young children.

5. Although gender and IQ served as exogenous variables only in cycles matched to the beginnings of school years, and so direct effects of these two variables in the latter half of each school year were disallowed, it is possible that models could be improved if direct effects of these variables in the second half of each year were specified. This is the only alternative structure that challenges the basic models, and the challenge seems most serious for the third-grade models. In future work we would include these variables as separate exogenous variables in every cycle. For the present data the costs far exceeded any benefits, because IQ scores were available for only a fraction of the sample.

Appendix D

Data Matrices Used in Model Estimation

Tables D.1 to D.18 provide matrices of correlations and covariances (below the diagonal) and number of pairwise present observations (above the diagonal) used to estimate the parameters reported in Tables 6.3 to 6.20.

Table D.1

Correlations, Covariances[a], Variances[b], and Number of Pairwise Present Observations for Cycle 1, Middle-Class School (Corresponding to Model in Figures 5.3 and 6.1W)

	$ABIL_1$	PE_{R1}	PE_{A1}	PE_{C1}	E_{R1}	E_{A1}	E_{C1}	M_{R1}	M_{A1}	M_{C1}	SEX	IQ
$ABIL_1$	193 (.6631)	187	187	188	190	190	190	173	173	173	193	50
PE_{R1}	.63327 (.3245)	348 (.3960)	348	342	338	338	338	323	323	323	348	203
PE_{A1}	.58154 (.2992)	.53998 (.2147)	348 (.3992)	342	338	338	338	323	323	323	348	203
PE_{C1}	.34826 (.1739)	.33900 (.1308)	.33814 (.1310)	343 (.3760)	334	334	334	319	319	319	343	197
E_{R1}	-.06095 (-.0384)	.03928 (.0191)	.03006 (.0147)	.14913 (.0708)	408 (.5992)	408	408	373	373	373	408	228
E_{A1}	-.00121 (-.0008)	-.01606 (-.0079)	.12554 (.0622)	.02434 (.0117)	.03335 (.0203)	408 (.6153)	408	373	373	373	408	228
E_{C1}	.10071 (.0709)	-.01278 (-.0070)	.05307 (.0290)	.09720 (.0515)	.13383 (.0896)	-.01585 (-.0107)	408 (.7477)	373	373	373	408	228
M_{R1}	.26266 (.1196)	.27044 (.0952)	.18205 (.0643)	.15570 (.0534)	.03761 (.0163)	.06175 (.0271)	-.02190 (-.0106)	380 (.3126)	380	380	380	226
M_{A1}	.12955 (.0534)	.20022 (.0638)	.30171 (.0965)	.13179 (.0409)	.05342 (.0209)	.16261 (.0646)	.09816 (.0430)	.33993 (.0962)	380 (.2563)	380	380	226
M_{C1}	-.01271 (-.0068)	.12928 (.0533)	.16240 (.0672)	.36398 (.1463)	.11790 (.0598)	-.02342 (-.0120)	.15295 (.0867)	.28946 (.1061)	.21788 (.0723)	380 (.4295)	380	226
SEX	-.04831 (-.0197)	-.08924 (-.0281)	.06263 (.0198)	-.17078 (-.0524)	-.01330 (-.0052)	.04785 (.0188)	-.19113 (-.0827)	-.09298 (-.0260)	.03846 (.0097)	-.28467 (-.0934)	(.2504)	237
IQ	.51372 (4.6328)	.43873 (3.0577)	.50663 (3.5449)	.24517 (1.6649)	.05256 (.4506)	.17944 (1.5588)	-.01996 (- .1912)	.19872 (1.2304)	.26650 (1.4934)	.12151 (.8820)	.01950 (.1081)	237 (122.6490)

[a]Covariances in parentheses.

[b]Variances on diagonal.

Table D.2

Correlations, Covariances[a], Variances[b], and Number of Pairwise Present Observations for Cycle 2, Middle-Class School (Corresponding to Model in Figures 5.4 and 6.2W)

	E_{R2}	E_{A2}	E_{C2}	M_{R2}	M_{A2}	M_{C2}	E_{R1}	E_{A1}	E_{C1}	M_{R1}	M_{A1}	M_{C1}	PE_{R1}	PE_{A1}	PE_{C1}	$ABIL_1$	$PEER_2$	ABS_2
E_{R2}	385 (.3944)	385	385	364	364	361	369	369	369	358	358	358	332	332	327	183	348	281
E_{A2}	-.02230 (.0107)	385 (.5787)	385	364	364	361	369	369	369	358	358	358	332	332	327	183	348	281
E_{C2}	.01226 (.0050)	.06162 (.0302)	386 (.4160)	365	365	362	370	370	370	359	359	359	333	333	328	184	348	282
M_{R2}	.19516 (.0754)	.01727 (.0081)	.12933 (.0513)	387 (.3782)	387	384	372	372	372	373	373	373	317	317	312	173	342	301
M_{A2}	.10893 (.0400)	.16927 (.0753)	.00719 (.0027)	.46839 (.1684)	387 (.3418)	384	372	372	372	373	373	373	317	317	312	173	342	301
M_{C2}	.02047 (.0088)	-.00069 (-.0004)	.20162 (.0894)	.30012 (.1269)	.33478 (.1345)	384 (.4724)	369	369	369	370	370	370	315	315	310	171	339	298
E_{R1}	.15332 (.0745)	.05083 (.0299)	.01683 (.0084)	.03759 (.0179)	.06721 (.0304)	.08262 (.0440)	408 (.5992)	408	408	373	373	373	338	338	334	190	346	291
E_{A1}	.08905 (.0439)	.15506 (.0925)	.08368 (.0423)	.07191 (.0347)	.19319 (.0886)	.04999 (.0269)	.03335 (.0203)	408 (.6153)	408	373	373	373	338	338	334	190	346	291
E_{C1}	.07710 (.0419)	-.04277 (-.0281)	.17105 (.0954)	.09635 (.0512)	.06097 (.0308)	.19482 (.1158)	.13383 (.0896)	-.01585 (-.0107)	408 (.7477)	373	373	373	338	338	334	190	346	291
M_{R1}	.15720 (.0552)	.09965 (.0424)	.06299 (.0227)	.48605 (.1671)	.33772 (.1104)	.21942 (.0843)	.03761 (.0163)	.06175 (.0271)	-.02190 (-.0106)	380 (.3126)	380	380	323	323	319	173	335	295
M_{A1}	.03025 (.0096)	.23799 (.0917)	.06452 (.0211)	.26956 (.0839)	.52234 (.1546)	.23214 (.0808)	.05342 (.0209)	.16261 (.0646)	.09816 (.0430)	.33993 (.0962)	380 (.2563)	380	323	323	319	173	335	295
M_{C1}	.09457 (.0389)	.01625 (.0081)	.24264 (.1026)	.22694 (.0915)	.28217 (.1081)	.63740 (.2871)	.11790 (.0598)	-.02342 (-.0120)	.15295 (.0867)	.28946 (.1061)	.21788 (.0723)	380 (.4295)	323	323	319	173	335	295
PE_{R1}	.16844 (.0666)	.15711 (.0752)	-.03141 (-.0127)	.30475 (.1179)	.27973 (.1029)	.20120 (.0870)	.03928 (.0191)	-.01606 (-.0079)	-.01278 (-.0070)	.27044 (.0952)	.20022 (.0638)	.12928 (.0533)	348 (.3960)	348	342	187	303	242
PE_{A1}	.07274 (.0289)	.22165 (.1065)	-.05797 (-.0236)	.26641 (.1035)	.37883 (.1399)	.20075 (.0872)	.03006 (.0147)	.12544 (.0622)	.05307 (.0290)	.18205 (.0643)	.30171 (.0965)	.16240 (.0672)	.53998 (.2147)	348 (.3992)	342	187	303	242
PE_{C1}	.04949 (.0191)	-.02582 (-.0120)	.07400 (.0293)	.24923 (.0940)	.22990 (.0824)	.44641 (.1881)	.14913 (.0708)	.02434 (.0117)	.09720 (.0515)	.15570 (.0534)	.13179 (.0409)	.36398 (.1463)	.33900 (.1308)	.33814 (.1310)	343 (.3760)	188	299	242
$ABIL_1$	.05836 (.0298)	.03934 (.0244)	-.09298 (-.0488)	.25914 (.1298)	.16909 (.0805)	.11844 (.0663)	-.06095 (-.0384)	-.00121 (-.0008)	.10071 (.0709)	.26266 (.1196)	.12955 (.0534)	-.01271 (-.0068)	.63327 (.3245)	.58154 (.2992)	.34826 (.1739)	193 (.6631)	172	173
$PEER_2$	.09324 (.0177)	.03838 (.0088)	-.02220 (-.0043)	.22579 (.0419)	.19356 (.0342)	.07124 (.0148)	-.01667 (-.0039)	.00772 (.0018)	-.00719 (-.0019)	.17017 (.0287)	.20831 (.0318)	.04361 (.0086)	.21569 (.0410)	.21221 (.0405)	.19687 (.0364)	.16837 (.0414)	364 (.0911)	274
ABS_2	-.15065 (-.5621)	-.06088 (-.2752)	-.09401 (-.3603)	.03710 (.1356)	.02846 (.0989)	.05856 (.2392)	.02715 (.1249)	.01105 (.0515)	-.00705 (-.0362)	-.02285 (-.0759)	-.01445 (-.0435)	.02120 (.0826)	-.14291 (-.5343)	-.03446 (-.1294)	-.00934 (-.0340)	-.13642 (-.6600)	-.01162 (-.0208)	302 (35.3026)

[a]Covariances in parentheses.

[b]Variances on diagonal.

Table D.3

Correlations, Covariances[a], Variances[b], and Number of Pairwise Present Observations for Cycle 3, Middle-Class School (Corresponding to Model in Figures 5.5 and 6.3W)

	$ABIL_3$	PE_{R3}	PE_{A3}	PE_{C3}	E_{R3}	E_{A3}	E_{C3}	M_{R3}	M_{A3}	M_{C3}	E_{R2}	E_{A2}	E_{C2}	M_{R2}	M_{A2}	M_{C2}	SEX	IQ	$ABIL_1$	PE_{R1}	PE_{A1}	PE_{C1}
$ABIL_3$	198 (.7137)	194	194	194	195	195	195	181	186	186	176	176	177	178	178	176	198	112	100	153	153	153
PE_{R3}	.57217 (.2965)	271 (.3761)	270	271	265	265	265	249	255	255	233	233	234	235	235	233	269	172	96	208	208	204
PE_{A3}	.51753 (.2691)	.52421 (.1979)	270 (.3790)	270	264	264	264	248	254	254	233	233	234	235	235	233	268	172	96	208	208	204
PE_{C3}	.38254 (.2018)	.23641 (.0905)	.30553 (.1174)	271 (.3899)	265	265	265	249	255	255	233	233	234	235	235	233	269	172	96	208	208	204
E_{R3}	.06927 (.0343)	.12546 (.0452)	.06010 (.0217)	.12554 (.0460)	344 (.3445)	344	344	317	323	323	283	283	284	287	287	284	339	202	115	245	245	240
E_{A3}	.20908 (.1287)	.27309 (.1220)	.32791 (.1471)	.11560 (.0526)	.02949 (.0126)	344 (.5309)	344	317	323	323	283	283	284	287	287	284	339	202	115	245	245	240
E_{C3}	-.02375 (-.0144)	.02366 (.0104)	-.01302 (-.0058)	.24071 (.1081)	.13060 (.0551)	-.01048 (-.0055)	344 (.5172)	317	323	323	283	283	284	287	287	284	339	202	115	245	245	240
M_{R3}	.25153 (.1212)	.51440 (.1799)	.31104 (.1092)	.12949 (.0461)	.05217 (.0175)	.18080 (.0751)	.07959 (.0326)	332 (.3252)	332	331	277	277	278	282	282	279	330	200	110	242	242	237
M_{A3}	.35369 (.1480)	.36360 (.1104)	.39716 (.1211)	.10773 (.0333)	.12299 (.0357)	.27451 (.0990)	.02853 (.0102)	.50600 (.1429)	338 (.2452)	337	280	280	281	285	285	282	336	202	110	244	244	239
M_{C3}	-.03802 (-.0214)	.17402 (.0710)	.12790 (.0524)	.30537 (.1269)	.12684 (.0496)	.13617 (.0660)	.27091 (.1297)	.38161 (.1449)	.31451 (.1037)	337 (.4432)	280	280	281	285	285	282	335	202	110	244	244	239
E_{R2}	.08510 (.0451)	.18138 (.0699)	.07551 (.0292)	-.06044 (-.0237)	.19523 (.0720)	.10004 (.0458)	.01772 (.0080)	.04480 (.0160)	.08517 (.0265)	.03474 (.0145)	385 (.3944)	385	385	364	364	361	385	227	183	332	332	327
E_{A2}	.03336 (.0214)	.10295 (.0480)	.20864 (.0977)	-.03903 (-.0185)	.01835 (.0082)	.38595 (.2139)	-.06736 (-.0369)	.01470 (.0064)	.03770 (.0142)	.06602 (.0334)	-.02230 (-.0107)	385 (.5787)	385	364	364	361	385	227	183	332	332	327
E_{C2}	-.11227 (-.0612)	-.00580 (-.0023)	-.01547 (-.0061)	.13809 (.0556)	.08004 (.0303)	.03422 (.0161)	.30479 (.1414)	.15902 (.0585)	.01852 (.0059)	.22732 (.0976)	.01226 (.0050)	.06162 (.0302)	386 (.4160)	365	365	362	386	228	184	333	333	328
M_{R2}	.39447 (.2049)	.50637 (.1910)	.35234 (.1334)	.28339 (.1088)	.14066 (.0508)	.10284 (.0461)	.01437 (.0064)	.40077 (.1406)	.33017 (.1006)	.27016 (.1106)	.19516 (.0751)	.01727 (.0081)	.12933 (.0513)	387 (.378[illegible])	387	384	387	227	173	317	317	312
M_{A2}	.23548 (.1163)	.33222 (.1191)	.37779 (.1360)	.15396 (.0562)	.02887 (.0099)	.24310 (.1035)	.01713 (.0072)	.21056 (.0702)	.26620 (.0771)	.18786 (.0731)	.10893 (.0400)	.16927 (.0753)	.00719 (.0027)	.46839 (.1684)	387 (.3418)	384	387	227	173	317	317	312
M_{C2}	.09879 (.0574)	.19526 (.0823)	.12103 (.0512)	.39729 (.1705)	.10300 (.0415)	.04767 (.0239)	.24144 (.1193)	.21925 (.0859)	.14802 (.0504)	.40943 (.1873)	.02047 (.0088)	-.00069 (-.0004)	.20162 (.0894)	.30012 (.1269)	.33478 (.1345)	384 (.4724)	384	227	171	315	315	310
SEX	.08923 (.0377)	-.04247 (-.0130)	.07535 (.0232)	-.10356 (-.0324)	-.11055 (-.0325)	.12585 (.0459)	-.17888 (-.0644)	-.14536 (-.0415	.04162 (.0103)	-.22019 (-.0734)	-.07531 (-.0237)	.14648 (.0558)	-.24288 (-.0784)	-.20758 (-.0639)	-.01524 (-.0045)	-.30004 (-.1032)	(.2504)	237	193	348	348	343
IQ	.56116 (5.2501)	.35316 (2.3987)	.37503 (2.5568)	.12689 (.8774)	-.05966 (-.3878)	.18470 (1.4904)	-.14597 (-1.1626)	.26044 (1.6449)	.36893 (2.0233)	.05784 (.4264)	.17857 (1.2419)	.10532 (.8872)	-.01428 (- .1020)	.29451 (2.0059)	.36818 (2.3837)	.13540 (1.0306)	.01950 (.1081)	237 (122.6490)	50	203	203	197
$ABIL_1$	.70298 (.4838)	.45113 (.2253)	.43227 (.2167)	.31846 (.1619)	.00112 (.0005)	.19509 (.1157)	.05256 (.0308	.28632 (.1330)	.21177 (.0854)	.05364 (.0291)	.05836 (.0298)	.03934 (.0244)	-.09298 (-.0488)	.25914 (.1298)	.16909 (.0805)	.11844 (.0663)	-.04831 (-.0197)	.51372 (4.6328)	193 (.6631)	187	187	188
PE_{R1}	.43708 (.2324)	.36461 (.1407)	.33206 (.1286)	.23237 (.0913)	.07759 (.0287)	.21000 (.0963)	.01874 (.0085)	.20707 (.0743)	.34612 (.1079)	.14659 (.0614)	.16844 (.0666)	.15711 (.0752)	-.03141 (-.0127)	.30475 (.1179)	.27973 (.1029)	.20120 (.0870)	-.08924 (-.0281)	.43873 (3.0577)	.63327 (.3245)	348 (.3960)	348	342
PE_{A1}	.38619 (.2061)	.30606 (.1186)	.42700 (.1661)	.18151 (.0716)	-.00623 (-.0023)	.27336 (.1258)	-.00882 (-.0040)	.24440 (.0881)	.36953 (.1156)	.18155 (.0764)	.07274 (.0289)	.22165 (.1065)	-.05797 (-.0236)	.26641 (.1035)	.37883 (.1399)	.20075 (.0872)	.06263 (.0198)	.50663 (3.5449)	.58154 (.2992)	.53998 (.2147)	348 (.3992)	342
PE_{C1}	.30846 (.1598)	.16623 (.0625)	.14473 (.0546)	.46975 (.1799)	.10484 (.0377)	.06377 (.0285)	.13581 (.0599)	.14701 (.0514)	.19831 (.0602)	.32150 (.1312)	.04949 (.0191)	-.02582 (-.0120)	.07400 (.0293)	.24923 (.0940)	.22990 (.0824)	.44641 (.1881)	-.17078 (-.0524)	.24517 (1.6649)	.34826 (.1739)	.33900 (.1308)	.33814 (.1310)	343 (.3760)

[a]Covariances in parentheses.

[b]Variances on diagonal.

Table D.4

Correlations, Covariances[a], Variances[b], and Number of Pairwise Present Observations for Cycle 4, Middle-Class School (Corresponding to Model in Figures 5.6 and 6.4W)

	E_{R4}	E_{A4}	E_{C4}	M_{R4}	M_{A4}	M_{C4}	E_{R3}	E_{A3}	E_{C3}	M_{R3}	M_{A3}	M_{C3}	PE_{R3}	PE_{A3}	PE_{C3}	$ABIL_3$	$PEER_4$	ABS_4
E_{R4}	330 (.3759)	330	330	311	317	317	312	312	312	309	315	314	252	251	252	184	310	313
E_{A4}	-.04099 (-.0175)	330 (.4851)	330	311	317	317	312	312	312	309	315	314	252	251	252	184	310	313
E_{C4}	.09126 (.0322)	.05885 (.0236)	330 (.3320)	311	317	317	312	312	312	309	315	314	252	251	252	184	310	313
M_{R4}	.35849 (.1224)	.17271 (.0670)	.18201 (.0584)	335 (.3100)	335	335	319	319	319	330	331	330	248	247	248	179	313	331
M_{A4}	.21134 (.0742)	.38902 (.1551)	.08643 (.0285)	.47403 (.1511)	341 (.3275)	341	324	324	324	331	337	336	254	253	254	185	319	335
M_{C4}	.17329 (.0694)	.17543 (.0799)	.30578 (.1151)	.29029 (.1056)	.27888 (.1043)	341 (.4271)	324	324	324	331	337	336	254	253	254	185	319	335
E_{R3}	.15428 (.0555)	.16065 (.0657)	.14893 (.0504)	.11915 (.0389)	.12942 (.0435)	.11147 (.0428)	344 (.3445)	344	344	317	323	323	265	264	265	195	313	319
E_{A3}	.03152 (.0141)	.21540 (.1093)	.08357 (.0351)	.15226 (.0618)	.23406 (.0976)	.08006 (.0381)	.02949 (.0126)	344 (.5309)	344	317	323	323	265	264	265	195	313	319
E_{C3}	.14918 (.0658)	.08780 (.0440)	.25567 (.1060)	.10946 (.0438)	.11133 (.0458)	.24545 (.1154)	.13060 (.0551)	-.01048 (-.0055)	344 (.5172)	317	323	323	265	264	265	195	313	319
M_{R3}	.32215 (.1126)	.12383 (.0492)	.15417 (.0507)	.61984 (.1968)	.43187 (.1410)	.24997 (.0932)	.05217 (.0175)	.18080 (.0751)	.07959 (.0326)	332 (.3252)	332	331	249	248	249	181	311	327
M_{A3}	.14988 (.0455)	.27173 (.0937)	.12254 (.0350)	.38991 (.1075)	.60289 (.1709)	.22070 (.0714)	.12299 (.0357)	.27451 (.0990)	.02853 (.0102)	.50600 (.1429)	338 (.2452)	337	255	254	255	186	317	331
M_{C3}	.18324 (.0748)	.17863 (.0828)	.30249 (.1160)	.33413 (.1238)	.30362 (.1157)	.65147 (.2834)	.12684 (.0496)	.13617 (.0660)	.27091 (.1297)	.38161 (.1449)	.31451 (.1037)	337 (.4432)	255	254	255	186	316	330
PE_{R3}	.20545 (.0773)	.11635 (.0497)	.04047 (.0143)	.43630 (.1490)	.35976 (.1263)	.19573 (.0784)	.12546 (.0452)	.27309 (.1220)	.02366 (.0104)	.51440 (.1799)	.36360 (.1104)	.17402 (.0710)	271 (.3761)	270	271	194	249	250
PE_{A3}	.03782 (.0143)	.28760 (.1233)	-.05449 (-.0193)	.31822 (.1091)	.41713 (.1470)	.10257 (.0413)	.06010 (.0217)	.32791 (.1471)	-.01302 (-.0058)	.31104 (.1092)	.39716 (.1211)	.12790 (.0524)	.52421 (.1979)	270 (.3790)	270	194	248	249
PE_{C3}	.06105 (.0234)	.02044 (.0089)	.08539 (.0307)	.11532 (.0401)	.19280 (.0689)	.31764 (.1296)	.12554 (.0460)	.11560 (.0526)	.24071 (.1081)	.12949 (.0461)	.10773 (.0333)	.30537 (.1269)	.23641 (.0905)	.30553 (.1174)	271 (.3899)	194	249	250
$ABIL_3$	.19814 (.1026)	.15365 (.0904)	-.11393 (-.0555)	.25825 (.1215)	.37994 (.1837)	.10539 (.0582)	.06927 (.0343)	.20908 (.1287)	-.02375 (-.0144)	.25153 (.1212)	.35369 (.1480)	-.03802 (-.0214)	.57217 (.2965)	.51753 (.2691)	.38254 (.2018)	198 (.7137)	184	181
$PEER_4$	.05041 (.0095)	.05394 (.0115)	.02307 (.0041)	.18751 (.0320)	.18260 (.0321)	.01667 (.0033)	-.03772 (-.0068)	.05740 (.0128)	-.00177 (-.0004)	.22474 (.0393)	.12666 (.0192)	.10209 (.0208)	.15516 (.0292)	.18815 (.0355)	.12680 (.0243)	.26331 (.0682)	332 (.0941)	314
ABS_4	-.02144 (-.0812)	.04591 (.1974)	.11530 (.4102)	.10212 (.3511)	.05341 (.1887)	.12484 (.5038)	-.04054 (-.1469)	.11037 (.4965)	.01076 (.0478)	.06722 (.2367)	.03882 (.1187)	.00429 (.0176)	.04229 (.1602)	.17442 (.6603)	-.05238 (-.2019)	-.07816 (-.4077)	.15574 (.2949)	336 (38.1245)

[a]Covariances in parentheses.

[b]Variances on diagonal.

Table D.5

Correlations, Covariances[a], Variances[b], and Number of Pairwise Present Observations for Cycle 5, Middle-Class School (Corresponding to Model in Figures 5.7 and 6.5W)

	$ABIL_5$	PE_{R5}	PE_{A5}	PE_{C5}	E_{R5}	E_{A5}	E_{C5}	M_{R5}	M_{A5}	M_{C5}	E_{R4}	E_{A4}	E_{C4}	M_{R4}	M_{A4}	M_{C4}	SEX	IQ	$ABIL_3$	PE_{R3}	PE_{A3}	PE_{C3}
$ABIL_5$	223 (.8118)	222	223	223	217	217	217	203	211	211	179	179	179	186	190	190	223	136	100	161	160	161
PE_{R5}	.57594 (.2975)	222 (.3287)	222	222	216	216	216	203	211	211	178	178	178	185	189	189	222	136	100	161	160	161
PE_{A5}	.50288 (.2249)	.33407 (.0951)	223 (.2464)	223	217	217	217	203	211	211	179	179	179	186	190	190	223	136	100	161	160	161
PE_{C5}	.33324 (.1762)	.33867 (.1139)	.32142 (.0936)	223 (.3442)	217	217	217	203	211	211	179	179	179	186	190	190	223	136	100	161	160	161
E_{R5}	.23758 (.1124)	.28363 (.0834)	.08378 (.0218)	.12541 (.0386)	270 (.2755)	270	270	247	255	255	212	212	212	221	225	225	270	161	115	179	178	179
E_{A5}	.17785 (.1022)	.07642 (.0279)	.35351 (.1119)	.10822 (.0405)	-.01271 (-.0043)	270 (.4065)	270	247	255	255	212	212	212	221	225	225	270	161	115	179	178	179
E_{C5}	.14708 (.0814)	.08404 (.0296)	-.03710 (-.0113)	.25279 (.0911)	.11448 (.0369)	-.03831 (-.0150)	270 (.3769)	247	255	255	212	212	212	221	225	225	270	161	115	179	178	179
M_{R5}	.42518 (.1998)	.46502 (.1390)	.28389 (.0735)	.19171 (.0587)	.23476 (.0643)	.12593 (.0419)	.08071 (.0258)	259 (.2720)	259	259	205	205	205	214	218	218	259	160	111	173	172	173
M_{A5}	.26930 (.1233)	.19194 (.0559)	.35569 (.0897)	.23069 (.0688)	.03394 (.0091)	.23034 (.0746)	-.03604 (-.0112)	.36381 (.0964)	268 (.2582)	268	212	212	212	221	225	225	268	160	111	178	177	178
M_{C5}	.21118 (.1077)	.26905 (.0873)	.14833 (.0417)	.25488 (.0846)	.08346 (.0248)	.08168 (.0295)	.26987 (.0937)	.30209 (.0891)	.22829 (.0656)	268 (.3201)	212	212	212	221	225	225	268	160	111	178	177	178
E_{R4}	.26610 (.1470)	.31867 (.1120)	.16116 (.0490)	.19982 (.0719)	.23928 (.0770)	.01993 (.0078)	.25522 (.0961)	.25854 (.0827)	.02714 (.0085)	.13604 (.0472)	330 (.3759)	330	330	311	317	317	328	123	184	252	251	252
E_{A4}	.08901 (.0559)	.01131 (.0045)	.31120 (.1076)	-.00465 (-.0019)	.13164 (.0481)	.45783 (.2033)	.07184 (.0307)	.16023 (.0582)	.16724 (.0592)	.07358 (.0290)	-.04099 (-.0175)	330 (.4851)	330	311	317	317	328	123	184	252	251	252
E_{C4}	-.00592 (-.0031)	.08126 (.0268)	-.00132 (-.0004)	.06806 (.0230)	.11888 (.0360)	-.06101 (-.0224)	.35503 (.1256)	.08752 (.0263)	-.00664 (-.0019)	.17538 (.0572)	.09126 (.0322)	.05885 (.0236)	330 (.3320)	311	317	317	328	123	184	252	251	252
M_{R4}	.41055 (.2060)	.56558 (.1805)	.33948 (.0938)	.33971 (.1110)	.21197 (.0620)	.10349 (.0367)	.19765 (.0676)	.43757 (.1271)	.21293 (.0602)	.31872 (.1004)	.35849 (.1224)	.17271 (.0670)	.18201 (.0584)	335 (.3100)	335	335	333	131	179	248	247	248
M_{A4}	.36934 (.1904)	.30780 (.1010)	.39827 (.1131)	.30034 (.1008)	.07412 (.0223)	.39912 (.1456)	.16005 (.0562)	.36796 (.1098)	.34228 (.0995)	.22586 (.0731)	.21134 (.0742)	.38902 (.1551)	.08643 (.0285)	.47403 (.1511)	341 (.3275)	341	339	135	185	254	253	254
M_{C4}	.20262 (.1193)	.12041 (.0451)	.07551 (.0245)	.37270 (.1429)	.02976 (.0102)	.06378 (.0266)	.38314 (.1537)	.11075 (.0377)	.04629 (.0154)	.25923 (.0958)	.17329 (.0694)	.17543 (.0799)	.30578 (.1151)	.29029 (.1056)	.27888 (.1043)	341 (.4271)	339	135	185	254	253	254
SEX	-.04863 (-.0219)	-.14685 (-.0421)	.23923 (.0594)	-.07442 (-.0218)	-.15301 (-.0402)	.17903 (.0571)	-.13352 (-.0410)	-.09533 (-.0249)	.00759 (.0019)	-.19009 (-.0538)	-.05548 (-.0170)	.10519 (.0367)	-.12926 (-.0373)	-.15563 (-.0434)	.03027 (.0087)	-.23219 (-.0759)	(.2504)	176	198	269	268	269
IQ	.26715 (3.3915)	.32099 (2.5929)	.35286 (2.4680)	.20091 (1.6608)	-.07992 (-.5911)	.21251 (1.9091)	-.02850 (-.2465)	.29114 (2.1393)	.15876 (1.1366)	.12274 (.9785)	.04118 (.3558)	.19746 (1.9378)	-.01444 (-.1172)	.32065 (2.5156)	.32544 (2.6242)	.16063 (1.4790)	.14633 (1.0317)	176 (198.5281)	113	114	114	114
$ABIL_3$	.72901 (.5549)	.46958 (.2274)	.50134 (.2102)	.30296 (.1502)	.13526 (.0600)	.12705 (.0684)	.08568 (.0444)	.32471 (.1431)	.18225 (.0782)	.16590 (.0793)	.19814 (.1026)	.15365 (.0904)	-.11393 (-.0555)	.25825 (.1215)	.37994 (.1837)	.10539 (.0582)	.08923 (.0377)	.28974 (3.4489)	198 (.7137)	194	194	194
PE_{R3}	.55651 (.3075)	.63637 (.2237)	.38659 (.1177)	.36601 (.1317)	.31446 (.1012)	.07615 (.0298)	.05270 (.0198)	.41301 (.1321)	.24935 (.0777)	.25069 (.0870)	.20545 (.0773)	.11635 (.0497)	.04047 (.0143)	.43630 (.1490)	.35976 (.1263)	.19573 (.0784)	-.04247 (-.0130)	.17778 (1.5362)	.57217 (.2965)	271 (.3761)	270	271
PE_{A3}	.53383 (.2961)	.37653 (.1329)	.47327 (.1446)	.31266 (.1129)	.12355 (.0399)	.26509 (.1040)	.08033 (.0304)	.29726 (.0954)	.30038 (.0940)	.27567 (.0960)	.03782 (.0143)	.28760 (.1233)	-.05449 (-.0193)	.31822 (.1091)	.41713 (.1470)	.10257 (.0413)	.07535 (.0232)	.35235 (3.0562)	.51753 (.2691)	.52421 (.1979)	270 (.3790)	270
PE_{C3}	.23425 (.1318)	.21880 (.0783)	.13912 (.0431)	.47898 (.1755)	.03701 (.0121)	-.10009 (-.0398)	.23753 (.0910)	.05001 (.0163)	.01257 (.0040)	.08483 (.0300)	.06105 (.0234)	.02044 (.0089)	.08539 (.0307)	.11532 (.0401)	.19280 (.0689)	.31764 (.1296)	-.10356 (-.0324)	.16090 (1.4156)	.38254 (.2018)	.23641 (.0905)	.30553 (.1174)	271 (.3899)

[a]Covariances in parentheses.

[b]Variances on diagonal.

Table D.6

Correlations, Covariances[a], Variances[b], and Number of Pairwise Present Observations for Cycle 6, Middle-Class School (Corresponding to Model in Figures 5.8 and 6.6W)

	E_{R6}	E_{A6}	E_{C6}	M_{R6}	M_{A6}	M_{C6}	E_{R5}	E_{A5}	E_{C5}	M_{R5}	M_{A5}	M_{C5}	PE_{R5}	PE_{A5}	PE_{C5}	$ABIL_5$	$PEER_6$	ABS_6
E_{R6}	256 (.3568)	256	256	238	245	245	242	242	242	230	239	239	210	210	210	210	249	240
E_{A6}	.14138 (.0619)	256 (.5370)	256	238	245	245	242	242	242	230	239	239	210	210	210	210	249	240
E_{C6}	.15711 (.0503)	.07976 (.0313)	256 (.2870)	238	245	245	242	242	242	230	239	239	210	210	210	210	249	240
M_{R6}	.31926 (.0990)	.29912 (.1138)	.05282 (.0147)	269 (.2695)	269	269	248	248	248	259	261	261	204	204	204	204	251	263
M_{A6}	.13082 (.0432)	.43563 (.1767)	.15546 (.0461)	.44635 (.1282)	276 (.3064)	276	255	255	255	259	268	268	211	211	211	211	258	270
M_{C6}	.11589 (.0451)	.18057 (.0862)	.34218 (.1194)	.27818 (.0940)	.28042 (.1011)	276 (.4242)	255	255	255	259	268	268	211	211	211	211	258	270
E_{R5}	.39366 (.1234)	.05975 (.0230)	.12112 (.0341)	.19199 (.0523)	.08418 (.0245)	.01380 (.0047)	270 (.2755)	270	270	247	255	255	216	217	217	217	253	249
E_{A5}	-.00542 (-.0021)	.35317 (.1650)	-.00570 (-.0019)	.14130 (.0468)	.12199 (.0431)	.08921 (.0370)	-.01271 (-.0043)	270 (.4065)	270	247	255	255	216	217	217	217	253	249
E_{C5}	.17557 (.0644)	.05636 (.0254)	.36085 (.1187)	.08182 (.0261)	.07503 (.0255)	.29087 (.1163)	.11448 (.0369)	-.03831 (-.0150)	270 (.3769)	247	255	255	216	217	217	217	253	249
M_{R5}	.42882 (.1336)	.22089 (.0844)	.14217 (.0397)	.52276 (.1415)	.34099 (.0984)	.14964 (.0508)	.23476 (.0643)	.12593 (.0419)	.08071 (.0258)	259 (.2720)	259	259	203	203	203	203	242	253
M_{A5}	.12949 (.0393)	.37242 (.1387)	-.05707 (-.0155)	.27836 (.0734)	.39991 (.1125)	.05035 (.0167)	.03394 (.0091)	.23034 (.0746)	-.03604 (-.0112)	.36381 (.0964)	268 (.2582)	268	211	211	211	211	251	262
M_{C5}	.14752 (.0499)	.17066 (.0708)	.30516 (.0925)	.22041 (.0647)	.24668 (.0773)	.55218 (.2035)	.08346 (.0248)	.08168 (.0295)	.26987 (.0937)	.30209 (.0891)	.22829 (.0656)	268 (.3201)	211	211	211	211	251	262
PE_{R5}	.38116 (.1305)	.17012 (.0715)	.03180 (.0098)	.52577 (.1565)	.24662 (.0783)	.24658 (.0921)	.28363 (.0854)	.07642 (.0279)	.08404 (.0296)	.46502 (.1390)	.19194 (.0559)	.26905 (.0873)	222 (.3287)	222	222	222	212	206
PE_{A5}	.12297 (.0365)	.32602 (.1186)	.04577 (.0122)	.31940 (.0823)	.27636 (.0759)	.13177 (.0426)	.08378 (.0218)	.35351 (.1119)	-.03710 (-.0113)	.28389 (.0735)	.35569 (.0897)	.14833 (.0417)	.33407 (.0951)	223 (.2464)	223	223	213	206
PE_{C5}	.21448 (.0752)	.09672 (.0416)	.23144 (.0727)	.26667 (.0812)	.25412 (.0825)	.34013 (.1300)	.12541 (.0386)	.10822 (.0405)	.25279 (.0911)	.19171 (.0587)	.23069 (.0688)	.25488 (.0846)	.33867 (.1139)	.32142 (.0936)	223 (.3442)	223	213	206
$ABIL_5$	.34858 (.1876)	.24471 (.1616)	.09076 (.0438)	.39531 (.1849)	.32673 (.1629)	.21662 (.1271)	.23758 (.1124)	.17785 (.1022)	.14708 (.0814)	.42518 (.1998)	.26930 (.1233)	.21118 (.1077)	.57594 (.2975)	.50288 (.2249)	.33324 (.1762)	223 (.8118)	213	206
$PEER_6$	.12372 (.0218)	.17867 (.0386)	.04191 (.0066)	.26678 (.0409)	.25430 (.0415)	.21161 (.0407)	-.03051 (-.0047)	.13623 (.0256)	.14691 (.0266)	.15762 (.0242)	.12181 (.0183)	.13725 (.0229)	.23472 (.0397)	.23729 (.0347)	.22793 (.0394)	.24370 (.0648)	271 (.0870)	254
ABS_6	.03330 (.1516)	-.01275 (-0712)	.04075 (.1664)	.04195 (.1660)	.07356 (.3104)	.19033 (.9451)	.02055 (.0823)	.06183 (.3006)	.10633 (.4976)	-.05913 (-.2351)	-.06855 (-.2656)	.04478 (.1932)	-.02519 (-.1101)	.00091 (.0034)	.05072 (.2269)	.00589 (.0405)	.06202 (.1395)	271 (58.1223)

[a]Covariances in parentheses.

[b]Variances on diagonal.

Table D.7

Correlations, Covariances[a], Variances[b], and Number of Pairwise Present Observations for Cycle 1, Integrated Lower-Class School (Corresponding to Model in Figures 5.3 and 6.1I)

	$ABIL_1$	PE_{R1}	PE_{A1}	PE_{C1}	E_{R1}	E_{A1}	E_{C1}	M_{R1}	M_{A1}	M_{C1}	RACE	SEX	IQ
$ABIL_1$	241 (.5145)	241	241	240	213	213	213	217	219	217	236	241	114
PE_{R1}	.44953 (.2459)	348 (.5814)	348	347	303	304	304	281	323	320	342	348	219
PE_{A1}	.45519 (.2430)	.56895 (.3229)	349 (.5540)	348	304	305	305	282	324	321	343	349	220
PE_{C1}	.04867 (.0230)	.16319 (.0820)	.12678 (.0621)	348 (.4338)	303	304	304	281	323	320	342	348	219
E_{R1}	.06171 (.0335)	.00993 (.0057)	.07383 (.0416)	.04656 (.0232)	364 (.5738)	364	364	288	338	336	357	364	226
E_{A1}	.07805 (.0404)	.10260 (.0564)	.12906 (.0693)	-.02073 (-.0098)	.00313 (.0017)	365 (.5198)	365	288	339	336	357	365	226
E_{C1}	.03101 (.0085)	.00852 (.0025)	.00307 (.0009)	-.00117 (-.0003)	.19045 (.0553)	.09885 (.0273)	365 (.1468)	288	339	336	357	365	226
M_{R1}	.34885 (.1936)	.44710 (.2637)	.33066 (.1904)	-.05030 (-.0256)	.01223 (.0072)	.05075 (.0283)	-.12932 (-.0383)	341 (.5983)	337	334	339	341	199
M_{A1}	.32622 (.1684)	.33816 (.1855)	.32444 (.1737)	.10250 (.0486)	.03607 (.0197)	.10455 (.0542)	-.08441 (-.0233)	.60471 (.3365)	397 (.5177)	393	393	397	248
M_{C1}	.11573 (.0567)	.18105 (.0944)	.18106 (.0921)	.26800 (.1206)	.09359 (.0485)	.03224 (.0159)	.02138 (.0056)	.17643 (.0933)	.32907 (.1618)	393 (.4672)	390	393	248
RACE	.08047 (.0285)	.01705 (.0064)	.07816 (.0288)	.14431 (.0470)	.01497 (.0056)	.00259 (.0009)	.05287 (.0100)	-.01561 (-.0060)	.05485 (.0195)	.08767 (.0296)	582 (.2444)	582	280
SEX	-.06363 (-.0228)	-.11768 (-.0449)	-.09438 (-.0351)	-.12619 (-.0416)	-.14736 (-.0558)	-.01623 (-.0059)	-.06054 (-.0116)	.00872 (.0034)	-.05969 (-.0215)	-.30877 (-.1056)	.00509 (.0013)	(.2502)	281
IQ	.35733 (4.1025)	.30389 (3.7088)	.33935 (4.0428)	.06452 (.6801)	.04295 (.5208)	.14094 (1.6264)	.06225 (.3818)	.53648 (6.6419)	.39991 (4.6054)	.18215 (1.9927)	.17512 (1.3858)	.07933 (.6351)	281 (-256.1856)

[a]Covariances in parentheses.

[b]Variances on diagonal.

Table D.8

Correlations, Covariances[a], Variances[b], and Number of Pairwise Present Observations for Cycle 2, Integrated Lower-Class School (Corresponding to Model in Figures 5.4 and 6.2I)

	E_{R2}	E_{A2}	E_{C2}	M_{R2}	M_{A2}	M_{C2}	E_{R1}	E_{A1}	E_{C1}	M_{R1}	M_{A1}	M_{C1}	PE_{R1}	PE_{A1}	PE_{C1}	$ABIL_1$	$PEER_1$	ABS_1	RACE
E_{R2}	350 (.5654)	350	350	337	341	340	287	287	287	275	322	319	294	295	294	195	297	342	348
E_{A2}	.13487 (.0835)	351 (.6777)	351	338	342	341	288	288	288	275	323	320	295	296	295	195	277	343	349
E_{C2}	.13701 (.0577)	.20010 (.0922)	352 (.3134)	339	343	342	289	289	289	276	324	321	296	297	296	196	277	344	350
M_{R2}	.12005 (.0920)	.11280 (.0946)	.10803 (.0616)	404 (1.0388)	400	399	320	320	320	323	372	369	313	314	313	209	308	401	402
M_{A2}	.08576 (.0576)	.17647 (.1298)	.08145 (.0407)	.64269 (.5851)	408 (.7978)	406	327	327	327	326	378	375	317	318	317	213	314	404	406
M_{C2}	.05489 (.0286)	.00144 (.0008)	.24589 (.0954)	.39602 (.2799)	.43205 (.2676)	411 (.4808)	330	330	330	329	381	379	319	320	319	215	315	407	409
E_{R1}	.10199 (.0581)	.09788 (.0610)	.08097 (.0343)	.09627 (.0743)	-.06053 (-.0410)	.07431 (.0390)	364 (.5738)	364	364	288	338	336	303	304	303	213	277	336	357
E_{A1}	.07286 (.0395)	.13064 (.0775)	.05249 (.0212)	.14439 (.1061)	.19723 (1270)	.14863 (.0743)	.00313 (.0017)	365 (.5198)	365	288	339	336	304	305	304	213	277	336	357
E_{C1}	.09657 (.0278)	.00195 (.0006)	.15474 (.0332)	-.02939 (-.0115)	-.08296 (-.0284)	.02817 (.0075)	.19045 (.0553)	.09885 (.0273)	365 (.1468)	288	339	336	304	305	304	213	277	336	357
M_{R1}	.02243 (.0130)	.12294 (.0783)	.01454 (.0063)	.65381 (.5154)	.57016 (.3939)	.20638 (.1107)	.01223 (.0072)	.05075 (.0283)	-.12932 (-.0383)	341 (.5983)	337	334	281	282	281	217	261	337	339
M_{A1}	.06745 (.0365)	.08920 (.0528)	.04445 (.0179)	.52858 (.3876)	.61769 (.3970)	.33596 (.1676)	.03607 (.0197)	.10455 (.0543)	-.08441 (-.0233)	.60471 (.3365)	397 (.5177)	393	323	324	323	219	301	386	393
M_{C1}	.06337 (.0326)	-.01239 (-.0070)	.09971 (.0382)	.30139 (.2100)	.32900 (.2009)	.66847 (.3168)	.09627 (.0485)	.03224 (.0159)	.02138 (.0056)	.17643 (.0933)	.32907 (.1618)	393 (.4672)	320	321	320	217	299	383	390
PE_{R1}	.08561 (.0491)	-.02029 (-.0127)	.07905 (.0337)	.47051 (.3656)	.38037 (.2591)	.27964 (.1478)	.00993 (.0057)	.10260 (.0564)	.00852 (.0025)	.44710 (.2637)	.33816 (.1855)	.18105 (.0944)	348 (.5814)	348	347	241	260	324	342
PE_{A1}	.09494 (.0531)	-.01417 (-.0087)	.06189 (.0258)	.38468 (.2918)	.30643 (.2037)	.23167 (.1196)	.07383 (.0416)	.12906 (.0693)	.00307 (.0009)	.33066 (.1904)	.32444 (.1737)	.18106 (.0921)	.56895 (.3229)	349 (.5540)	348	241	261	325	343
PE_{C1}	.00893 (.0044)	.02569 (.0139)	.05998 (.0221)	.05895 (.0396)	.11448 (.0673)	.28463 (.1300)	.04656 (.0232)	-.02073 (-.0098)	-.00117 (-.0003)	-.05030 (-.0256)	.10250 (.0486)	.26800 (.1206)	.16319 (.0820)	.12678 (.0621)	348 (.4338)	240	261	324	342
$ABIL_1$	.05480 (.0296)	.06712 (.0396)	.08521 (.0342)	.28291 (.2068)	.29415 (.1885)	.15354 (.0764)	.06171 (.0335)	.07805 (.0404)	.03101 (.0085)	.34885 (.1936)	.32622 (.1684)	.11573 (.0567)	.44953 (.2459)	.45519 (.2430)	.04867 (.0230)	241 (.5145)	173	219	236
$PEER_1$	.06862 (.0156)	.07670 (.0191)	.02286 (.0039)	.33356 (.1027)	.37395 (.1009)	.15857 (.0332)	.01887 (.0043)	-.00373 (-.0008)	-.05393 (-.0062)	.37528 (.0877)	.35112 (.0763)	.13541 (.0280)	.21051 (.0485)	.14036 (.0316)	.07185 (.0143)	.03017 (.0065)	327 (.0913)	318	326
ABS_1	.13094 (1.8536)	.11997 (1.8595)	.12450 (1.3122)	.33858 (6.4972)	.29614 (4.9802)	.04928 (.6433)	.06308 (.8997)	.01994 (.2707)	-.04954 (-.3575)	.27397 (3.9899)	.28806 (3.9022)	.08563 (1.1020)	.22684 (3.2567)	.22527 (3.1569)	-.02682 (-.3325)	.16332 (2.2058)	.08434 (.4799)	422 (354.4936)	420
RACE	-.04750 (-.0177)	.01061 (.0043)	.00504 (.0014)	.00349 (.0018)	.09319 (.0412)	.14718 (.0505)	.01497 (.0056)	.00259 (.0009)	.05287 (.0100)	-.01561 (-.0060)	.05485 (.0195)	.08767 (.0296)	.01705 (.0064)	.07816 (.0288)	.14431 (.0470)	.08047 (.0285)	-.06459 (-.0096)	-.02999 (-.2792)	582 (.2444)

[a]Covariances in parentheses.

[b]Variances on diagonal.

Table D.9

Correlations, Covariances[a], Variances[b], and Number of Pairwise Present Observations for Cycle 3, Integrated Lower-Class School (Corresponding to Model in Figures 5.5 and 6.3I)

	$ABIL_3$	PE_{R3}	PE_{A3}	PE_{C3}	E_{R3}	E_{A3}	E_{C3}	M_{R3}	M_{A3}	M_{C3}	E_{R2}	E_{A2}	E_{C2}	M_{R2}	M_{A2}	M_{C2}	RACE	SEX	IQ	$ABIL_1$	PE_{R1}	PE_{A1}	PE_{C1}
$ABIL_3$	258 (.6744)	255	257	258	224	222	223	197	228	228	188	189	189	203	208	208	255	258	187	100	179	180	179
PE_{R3}	.46345 (.2825)	257 (.5512)	257	257	224	222	223	195	226	226	187	188	188	202	207	207	253	257	186	101	179	180	179
PE_{A3}	.27575 (.1547)	.58070 (.2945)	259 (.4668)	259	224	222	223	196	228	228	188	189	189	203	208	208	255	259	187	101	180	181	180
PE_{C3}	.09274 (.0532)	.22029 (.1143)	.19163 (.0915)	260 (.4885)	225	223	224	197	229	229	189	190	190	204	209	209	256	260	188	101	180	181	180
E_{R3}	.00111 (.0007)	.05337 (.0296)	.04785 (.0244)	.01097 (.0057)	286 (.5579)	284	285	218	253	253	220	221	221	236	242	242	284	286	220	112	195	196	195
E_{A3}	-.00254 (-.0016)	.08199 (.0477)	.08757 (.0468)	-.04391 (-.0240)	-.05259 (-.0308)	284 (.6129)	284	216	251	251	218	219	219	234	240	240	282	284	218	111	193	194	193
E_{C3}	-.03429 (-.0177)	.09509 (.0444)	.05011 (.0215)	.21396 (.0941)	.20388 (.0958)	.01272 (.0063)	285 (.3961)	217	252	252	219	220	220	235	241	241	283	285	219	111	194	195	194
M_{R3}	.38262 (.2679)	.49616 (.3141)	.38611 (.2249)	.25324 (.1509)	.10522 (.0670)	.16135 (.1077)	.09364 (.0502)	242 (.7269)	241	242	169	170	170	190	192	192	240	242	183	77	152	153	152
M_{A3}	.25151 (.1430)	.38384 (.1973)	.33378 (.1379)	.16994 (.0822)	.13333 (.0690)	.15354 (.0832)	.01646 (.0072)	.59909 (.3537)	287 (.4796)	287	204	205	205	221	227	227	284	287	216	109	184	185	184
M_{C3}	.13169 (.0780)	.16508 (.0896)	.11613 (.0580)	.40028 (.2045)	.10531 (.0578)	-.12017 (-.0688)	.25641 (.1180)	.36170 (.2254	.30344 (.1536)	288 (.5342)	204	205	205	221	227	227	285	288	216	109	184	185	184
E_{R2}	.12416 (.0767)	.16819 (.0939)	-.02085 (-.0107)	-.03227 (-.0170)	.20777 (.1167)	.11860 (.0698)	.09162 (.0434)	.12234 (.0784)	.15059 (.0784)	.03960 (.0218)	350 (.5651)	350	350	337	341	340	348	350	234	195	294	295	294
E_{A2}	.04267 (.0288)	.08842 (.0540)	.01908 (.0107)	-.06832 (-.0393)	.11412 (.0702)	.33718 (.2173)	.04977 (.0258)	.12874 (.0904)	.06011 (.0343)	-.05603 (-.0337)	.13487 (.0835)	351 (.6777)	351	338	342	341	349	351	235	195	295	296	295
E_{C2}	-.00888 (-.0040)	.12921 (.0537)	-.02515 (-.0096)	.08348 (.0327)	.15167 (.0634)	.10401 (.0456)	.14725 (.0579	.16454 (.0785)	.15157 (.0588)	.11796 (.0483)	.13701 (.0577)	.20010 (.0922)	352 (.3134)	339	343	342	350	352	235	196	296	297	296
M_{R2}	.33151 (.2775)	.40789 (.3086)	.37895 (.2639)	.12147 (.0865)	.07910 (.0602)	.04310 (.0344)	-.02959 (-.0190)	.74266 (.6454)	.56726 (.4004)	.27183 (.2025)	.12005 (.0920)	.11280 (.0946)	.10803 (.0616)	404 (1.0388)	400	399	402	404	256	209	313	314	313
M_{A2}	.36683 (.2691)	.47114 (.3124)	.34892 (.2129)	.19609 (.1224)	.06753 (.0451)	.13226 (.0925)	.03526 (.0198)	.62117 (.4730)	.56051 (.3467)	.26088 (.1703)	.08576 (.0576)	.17647 (.1298)	.08145 (.0407)	.64269 (.5851)	408 (.7978)	406	406	408	262	213	317	318	317
M_{C2}	.19072 (.1086)	.28615 (.1473)	.25612 (.1213)	.43218 (.2094)	-.02112 (-.0109)	-.03146 (-.0171)	.19953 (.0871)	.42381 (.2506)	.38226 (.1836)	.57411 (.2910)	.05489 (.0286)	.00144 (.0008)	.24589 (.0954)	.39602 (.2799)	.43205 (.2676)	411 (.4808)	409	411	264	215	319	320	319
RACE	.08752 (.0355)	.09994 (.0367)	.19678 (.0665)	.10582 (.0366)	.00411 (.0015)	-.05561 (-.0215)	-.06410 (-.0199)	.11298 (.0476)	.19588 (.0671)	.16370 (.0592)	-.04750 (-.0177)	.01061 (.0043)	.00504 (.0014)	.00349 (.0018)	.09319 (.0412)	.14718 (.0505)	582 (.2444)	582	280	236	342	343	342
SEX	-.00947 (-.0039)	-.11902 (-.0442)	-.02882 (-.0098)	-.31989 (-.1118)	-.07091 (-.0265)	.01897 (.0074)	-.13121 (-.0413)	-.16187 (-.0690)	-.05624 (-.0195)	-.20389 (-.0745)	-.11303 (-.0425)	.01542 (.0063)	.03099 (.0087)	-.10260 (-.0523)	-.10895 (-.0487)	-.31547 (-.1094)	.00509 (.0013	(.2502)	281	241	348	349	348
IQ	.24121 (3.1705)	.18070 (2.1472)	.23025 (2.5178)	.05029 (.5626)	-.05388 (-.6441)	.06390 (.8007)	-.18829 (-1.8968)	.35356 (4.8249)	.44273 (4.9073)	.25731 (3.0102)	.06067 (.7302)	.14088 (1.8562)	.13535 (1.2128)	.47964 (7.8245)	.42571 (6.0861)	.25730 (2.8556)	.17512 (1.3858)	.07933 (.6351)	281 (256.1856)	114	219	220	219
$ABIL_1$	.47585 (.2803)	.37286 (.1986)	.14073 (.0690)	.17540 (.0879)	-.07398 (-.0396)	.00769 (.0043)	-.18482 (-.0834)	.36963 (.2261)	.26606 (.1322)	.14702 (.0771)	.05480 (.0296)	.06712 (.0396)	.08521 (.0342)	.28291 (.2068)	.29415 (.1885)	.15354 (.0754)	.08047 (.0285)	-.06363 (-.0228)	.35733 (4.1025)	241 (.5145)	241	241	240
PE_{R1}	.32859 (.2058)	.27803 (.1574)	.20733 (.1080)	.19770 (.1054)	.05447 (.0310)	.05969 (.0356)	-.06810 (-.0327)	.43052 (.2799)	.33162 (.1751)	.23876 (.1331)	.08561 (.0491)	-.02029 (-.0127)	.07905 (.0337)	.47051 (.3656)	.38037 (.2591)	.27964 (.1478)	.01705 (.0064)	-.11768 (-.0049)	.30389 (3.7088)	.44953 (.2459)	348 (.5814)	348	347
PE_{A1}	.23558 (.1440)	.27443 (.1516)	.33073 (.1682)	.14510 (.0755)	.02581 (.0143)	.06484 (.0378)	-.11107 (-.0520)	.32364 (.2054)	.29288 (.1510)	.23931 (.1302)	.09494 (.0531)	-.01417 (-.0087	.06189 (.0258)	.38468 (.2918)	.30643 (.2037)	.23167 (.1196)	.07816 (.0288)	-.09438 (-.0351)	.33935 (4.0428)	.45519 (.2430)	.56895 (.3229)	349 (.5540)	348
PE_{C1}	.13611 (.0736)	.10883 (.0532)	.05335 (.0240)	.28854 (.1328)	-.11915 (-.0586)	-.02630 (-.0136)	.08420 (.0349)	.12841 (.0721)	.03885 (.0177)	.31185 (.1501)	.00893 (.0044)	.02569 (.0139)	.05998 (.0221)	.05895 (.0396)	.11448 (.0673)	.28463 (.1300)	.14431 (.0470)	-.12619 (-.0416)	.06452 (.6801)	.04867 (.0230)	.16319 (.0820)	.12678 (.0621)	348 (.4338)

[a]Covariances in parentheses.

[b]Variances on diagonal.

Table D.10

Correlations, Covariances[a], Variances[b], and Number of Pairwise Present Observations for Cycle 4, Integrated Lower-Class School (Corresponding to Model in Figures 5.6 and 6.4I)

	E_{R4}	E_{A4}	E_{C4}	M_{R4}	M_{A4}	M_{C4}	E_{R3}	E_{A3}	E_{C3}	M_{R3}	M_{A3}	M_{C3}	PE_{R3}	PE_{A3}	PE_{C3}	$ABIL_3$	$PEER_4$	ABS_4	RACE
E_{R4}	245 (.5624)	245	245	232	238	237	210	208	209	200	228	229	208	210	210	209	190	235	244
E_{A4}	-.06127 (-.0360)	245 (.6121)	245	232	238	237	210	208	209	200	228	229	208	210	210	209	190	235	244
E_{C4}	.08801 (.0383)	-.04603 (-.0209)	245 (.3366)	232	238	237	210	208	209	200	228	229	208	210	210	209	190	235	244
M_{R4}	.05535 (.0394)	.10998 (.0816)	-.08939 (-.0492)	297 (.9000)	295	294	248	246	247	241	278	279	222	223	224	223	197	292	295
M_{A4}	.07200 (.0456)	.20040 (.1323)	-.01457 (-.0071)	.58018 (.4645)	302 (.7123)	301	251	249	250	241	283	284	226	228	229	228	203	297	300
M_{C4}	-.01783 (-.0108)	-.01153 (-.0073	.17928 (.0841)	.29849 (.2290)	.34705 (.2368)	301 (.6538)	251	249	250	241	283	284	226	228	229	228	202	296	299
E_{R3}	.19706 (.1104)	.08289 (.0484)	.02490 (.0108)	.07986 (.0566)	.15400 (.0971)	.03591 (.0217)	286 (.5579)	284	285	218	253	253	224	224	225	224	176	252	284
E_{A3}	.10789 (.0633)	.20290 (.1243)	.04924 (.0224)	.15119 (.1123)	.20502 (.1355)	-.01942 (-.0123)	-.05259 (-.0308)	284 (.6129)	284	216	251	251	222	222	223	222	174	250	282
E_{C3}	-.01699 (-.0080)	.07798 (.0384)	.22840 (.0834)	.08851 (.0528)	.05093 (.0271)	.17229 (.0877)	.20388 (.0958)	.01272 (.0063)	285 (.3961)	217	252	252	223	223	224	223	175	251	283
M_{R3}	.07573 (.0484)	.16495 (.1100)	-.06782 (-.0335)	.61932 (.5009)	.59314 (.4268)	.31034 (.2140)	.10522 (.0670)	.16135 (.1077)	.09364 (.0502)	242 (.7269)	241	242	195	196	197	197	160	238	240
M_{A3}	.04671 (.0243)	.21446 (.1162)	-.11003 (-.0442)	.42994 (.2825)	.68952 (.4030)	.33884 (.1897)	.13333 (.0690)	.15354 (.0832)	.01646 (.0072)	.59909 (.3537)	287 (.4796)	287	226	228	229	228	193	283	284
M_{C3}	-.01117 (-.0061)	.07223 (.0413)	.18969 (.0804)	.24812 (.1721)	.26970 (.1664)	.69933 (.4133)	.10581 (.0578)	-.12017 (-.0688)	.25641 (.1180)	.36170 (.2254)	.30344 (.1536)	288 (.5342)	226	228	229	228	194	284	285
PE_{R3}	-.00934 (-.0052)	.20980 (.1219)	-.06247 (-.0269)	.40207 (.2832)	.41133 (.2577)	.16839 (.1011)	.05337 (.0296)	.08199 (.0477)	.09509 (.0444)	.49616 (.3141)	.38384 (.1973)	.16508 (.0896)	257 (.5512)	257	257	255	164	226	253
PE_{A3}	-.05266 (-.0270)	.23411 (.1251)	-.00163 (-.0006)	.21866 (.1417)	.33184 (.1913)	.07565 (.0418)	.04785 (.0244)	.08757 (.0468)	.05011 (.0215)	.38611 (.2249)	.33378 (.1579)	.11613 (.0580)	.58070 (.2945)	259 (.4668)	259	257	165	228	255
PE_{C3}	-.07182 (-.0376)	.05301 (.0290)	.11020 (.0447)	.16158 (.1071)	.15571 (.0918)	.34858 (.1970)	.01097 (.0057)	-.04391 (-.0240)	.21396 (.0941)	.25324 (.1509)	.16994 (.0822)	.40028 (.2045)	.22029 (.1143)	.19163 (.0915)	260 (.4885)	258	166	229	256
$ABIL_3$	-.03804 (-.0234)	.12691 (.0815)	-.05303 (-.0253)	.29725 (.2316)	.32357 (.2243)	.17429 (.1157)	.00111 (.0007)	-.00254 (-.0016)	-.03429 (-.0177)	.38262 (.2679)	.25151 (.1430)	.13169 (.0790)	.46345 (.2825)	.27575 (.1547)	.09274 (.0532)	258 (.6744)	165	228	255
$PEER_4$	.12849 (.0302)	-.02975 (-.0073)	-.03805 (-.0069)	.27958 (.0832)	.41349 (.1095)	.10488 (.0266)	.00853 (.0020)	.03214 (.0079)	-.14722 (-.0291)	.30323 (.0811)	.36379 (.0790)	.00230 (.0005)	.24767 (.0577)	.06640 (.0142)	-.01110 (-.0024)	.21722 (.0560)	211 (.0984)	204	211
ABS_4	.14204 (1.8698)	.01292 (.1774)	.01351 (.1376)	.15799 (2.6312)	.18208 (2.6976)	-.06428 (-.9124)	-.09695 (-1.2712)	.05531 (.7601)	.01852 (.2046)	.16920 (2.5324)	.08556 (1.0401)	-.00793 (-.1018)	.13498 (1.7591)	.07925 (.9505)	-.00579 (-.0710)	.07246 (1.0445)	.15051 (.8289)	307 (308.1570)	304
RACE	-.03347 (-.0124)	.08537 (.0330)	.08481 (.0243)	.05876 (.0276)	.17144 (.0715)	.20014 (.0800)	.00411 (.0015)	-.05561 (-.0215)	-.06410 (-.0199)	.11298 (.0476)	.19588 (.0671)	.16370 (.0592)	.09994 (.0367)	.19678 (.0665)	.10582 (.0366)	.08752 (.0355)	-.07107 (-.0110)	-.08214 (-.7129)	582 (.2444)

[a] Covariances in parentheses.

[b] Variances on diagonal.

Table D.11

Correlations, Covariances[a], Variances[b], and Number of Pairwise Present Observations for Cycle 5, Integrated Lower-Class School (Corresponding to Model in Figures 5.7 and 6.51)

	$ABIL_5$	PE_{R5}	PE_{A5}	PE_{C5}	E_{R5}	E_{A5}	E_{C5}	M_{R5}	M_{A5}	M_{C5}	E_{R4}	E_{A4}	E_{C4}	M_{R4}	M_{A4}	M_{C4}	RACE	SEX	IQ	$ABIL_3$	PE_{R3}	PE_{A3}	PE_{C3}
$ABIL_5$	171 (.6861)	168	168	169	162	163	163	121	152	151	121	121	121	143	148	148	168	171	120	114	113	114	114
PE_{R5}	.40140 (.2677)	170 (.6482)	170	170	161	162	162	119	151	150	120	120	120	142	147	147	168	170	121	115	114	115	115
PE_{A5}	.34180 (.2073)	.63167 (.3724)	170 (.5361)	170	161	162	162	119	151	150	120	120	120	142	147	147	168	170	121	115	114	115	115
PE_{C5}	.25927 (.1345)	.23264 (.1173)	.19319 (.0886)	171 (.3920)	162	163	163	120	152	151	120	120	120	142	147	147	169	171	122	115	114	115	115
E_{R5}	.14008 (.0908)	.05783 (.0364)	.08891 (.0509)	.21788 (.1067)	211 (.6123)	211	211	141	183	183	143	143	143	171	176	176	209	211	144	139	138	140	140
E_{A5}	.15410 (.1087)	.03638 (.0249)	.09364 (.0584)	-.10823 (-.0577)	-.06271 (-.0418)	212 (.7252)	212	142	184	184	144	144	144	172	177	177	210	212	145	140	139	141	141
E_{C5}	.08501 (.0390)	.08445 (.0377)	-.04067 (-.0165)	.31569 (.1096)	.20438 (.0887)	-.05202 (-.0246)	212 (.3075)	142	184	184	144	144	144	172	177	177	210	212	145	140	139	141	141
M_{R5}	.38697 (.2878)	.55658 (.4023)	.41093 (.2701)	.17662 (.0993)	.15492 (.1088)	.07612 (.0582)	.02924 (.0146)	156 (.8060)	153	153	101	101	101	123	127	127	154	156	117	97	95	97	97
M_{A5}	.24123 (.1631)	.24472 (.1608)	.36610 .2188)	.05123 (.0262)	.05849 (.0374)	.18975 (.1319)	-.01950 (-.0088)	.55175 (.4044)	204 (.6665)	203	137	137	137	164	168	168	202	204	157	132	130	132	132
M_{C5}	.19236 (.0941)	.31434 (.1495)	.22400 (.0969)	.34532 (.1278)	.17268 (.0798)	.04301 (.0216)	.26733 (.0876)	.33959 (.1802)	.31739 (.1531)	205 (.3492)	136	136	136	164	168	168	203	205	157	131	129	131	131
E_{R4}	.06369 (.0396)	.01436 (.0087)	-.11085 (-.0609)	-.00552 (-.0026)	.19809 (.1162)	.05835 (.0373)	.15749 (.0655)	.13971 (.0941)	-.02962 (-.0181)	-.07259 (-.0322)	245 (.5624)	245	245	232	238	237	244	245	111	209	208	210	210
E_{A4}	.05302 (.0344)	.12835 (.0809)	.32715 (.1874)	.04004 (.0196)	-.00026 (-.0002)	.16484 (.1098)	.00340 (.0015)	.02328 (.0164)	.09305 (.0594)	-.15570 (-.0720)	-.06127 (-.0360)	245 (.6121)	245	232	238	237	244	245	111	209	208	210	210
E_{C4}	-.04199 (-.0202)	.02731 (.0128)	-.10545 (-.0448)	.20114 (.0731)	.11737 (.0533)	-.02514 (-.0124)	.34323 (.1104)	-.03825 (-.0199)	-.03236 (-.0153)	.16119 (.0553)	.08801 (.0383)	-.04603 (-.0209)	245 (.3366)	232	238	237	244	245	111	209	208	210	210
M_{R4}	.31190 (.2451)	.29864 (.2281)	.22206 (.1543)	.17726 (.1053)	.08837 (.0656)	.05614 (.0454)	.10475 (.0551)	.60287 (.5135)	.58698 (.4546)	.21316 (.1195)	.05535 (.0394)	.10998 (.0816)	-.08939 (-.0492)	297 (.9000)	295	294	295	297	128	223	222	223	224
M_{A4}	.28459 (.1990)	.39490 (.2623)	.39269 (.2427)	.14919 (.0788)	-.01913 (-.0126)	.12779 (.0918)	.07598 (.0356)	.59041 (.4474)	.54494 (.3755)	.24432 (.1218)	.07200 (.0456)	.20040 (.1323)	-.01457 (-.0071)	.58018 (.4645)	302 (.7123)	301	300	302	132	228	226	228	229
M_{C4}	.31897 (.2136)	.32186 (.2095)	.18300 (.1083)	.49243 (.2493)	.11309 (.0716)	-.01488 (-.0102)	.32115 (.1440)	.39303 (.2853)	.20443 (.1349)	.50811 (.2428)	-.01783 (-.0108)	-.01153 (-.0073)	.17928 (.0841)	.29849 (.2290)	.34705 (.2368)	301 (.6538)	299	301	131	228	226	228	229
RACE	.02385 (.0098)	-.05134 (-.0204)	.03860 (.0140)	.10685 (.0331)	-.02278 (-.0088)	-.07665 (-.0323)	.04543 (.0125)	.02689 (.0119)	.15156 (.0612)	.13925 (.0407)	-.03347 (-.0124)	.08537 (.0330)	.08481 (.0243)	.05876 (.0276)	.17144 (.0715)	.20014 (.0800)	582 (.2444)	582	164	255	253	255	256
SEX	-.07133 (-.0296)	-.20581 (-.0829)	-.11421 (-.0418)	-.22332 (-.0699)	-.24877 (-.0974)	.15302 (.0652)	-.25309 (-.0702)	-.19475 (-.0875)	-.00569 (-.0023)	-.19313 (-.0571)	-.05212 (-.0196)	.00231 (.0009)	-.22324 (-.0648)	-.19296 (-.0916)	-.06536 (-.0276)	-.29526 (-.1194)	.00509 (.0013)	(.2502)	164	258	257	259	260
IQ	.21518 (2.3324)	.32638 (3.4387)	.30281 (2.9015)	.25833 (2.1166)	.06288 (.6439)	.04661 (.5195)	.09002 (.6533)	.37780 (4.4387)	.42045 (4.4920)	.26521 (2.0508)	-.14854 (-1.4577)	.23841 (2.4410)	.00571 (.0434)	.48753 (6.0527)	.47761 (5.2752)	.28729 (3.0400)	.18855 (1.2199)	-.03303 (-.2162)	164 (171.2539)	107	105	107	107
$ABIL_3$	.26998 (.1836)	.44275 (.2927)	.36201 (.2177)	.06048 (.0311)	-.04878 (-.0313)	.02898 (.0203)	-.01747 (-.0080)	.18579 (.1370)	.06841 (.0459)	-.00560 (-.0027)	-.03804 (-.0234)	.12691 (.0815)	-.05303 (-.0253)	.29725 (.2316)	.32357 (.2243)	.17429 (.1157)	.08752 (.0355)	-.00947 (-.0039)	.16615 (1.7856)	258 (.6744)	255	257	258
PE_{R3}	.29421 (.1809)	.23112 (.1381)	.24831 (.1350)	.07872 (.0366)	.08841 (.0514)	.00271 (.0017)	-.00923 (-.0038)	.37921 (.2528)	.23290 (.1412)	.02107 (.0092)	-.00934 (-.0052)	.20980 (.1219)	-.06247 (-.0269)	.40207 (.2832)	.41133 (.2577)	.16839 (.1011)	.09994 (.0367)	-.11902 (-.0442)	.38537 (3.7440)	.46345 (.2825)	257 (.5512)	257	257
PE_{A3}	.18362 (.1039)	.15890 (.0874)	.39620 (.1982)	-.03121 (-.0133)	.01105 (.0059)	-.03533 (-.0206)	-.19390 (-.0735)	.13767 (.0844)	.24101 (.1344)	-.01392 (-.0056)	-.05266 (-.0270)	.23411 (.1251)	-.00163 (-.0006)	.21866 (.1417)	.33184 (.1913)	.07565 (.0418)	.19678 (.0665)	-.02882 (-.0098)	.16931 (1.5137)	.27575 (.1547)	.58070 (.2945)	259 (.4668)	259
PE_{C3}	.09644 (.0558)	.23237 (.1308)	.28373 (.1452)	.27864 (.1219)	-.04793 (-.0262)	-.02229 (-.0133)	.07593 (.0294)	.12243 (.0768)	.10657 (.0608)	.16023 (.0662)	-.07182 (-.0376)	.05301 (.0290)	-.11020 (-.0447)	.16158 (.1071)	.15571 (.0918)	.34858 (.1970)	.10582 (.0366)	-.31989 (-.1118)	.05403 (.4942)	.09274 (.0532)	.22029 (.1143)	.19163 (.0915)	260 (.4885)

[a] Covariances in parentheses.

[b] Variances on diagonal.

Table D.12

Correlations, Covariances[a], Variances[b], and Number of Pairwise Present Observations for Cycle 6, Integrated Lower-Class School (Corresponding to Model in Figures 5.8 and 6.6I)

	E_{R6}	E_{A6}	E_{C6}	M_{R6}	M_{A6}	M_{C6}	E_{R5}	E_{A5}	E_{C5}	M_{R5}	M_{A5}	M_{C5}	PE_{R5}	PE_{A5}	PE_{C5}	$ABIL_5$	$PEER_6$	ABS_6	RACE
E_{R6}	151 (.6195)	151	151	148	149	150	135	136	136	115	147	147	134	134	135	135	141	144	150
E_{A6}	-.00691 (-.0045)	151 (.6986)	151	148	149	150	135	136	136	115	147	147	134	134	135	135	141	144	150
E_{C6}	.15317 (.0722)	.11416 (.0571)	151 (.3584)	148	149	150	135	136	136	115	147	147	134	134	135	135	141	144	150
M_{R6}	.07599 (.0496)	.07775 (.0539)	.03712 (.0184)	214 (.6877)	206	208	184	185	185	152	200	200	153	153	154	154	160	204	213
M_{A6}	.02285 (.0179)	.31452 (.2611)	-.10198 (-.0606)	.54848 (.4517)	209 (.9862)	207	180	181	181	151	198	199	149	149	150	150	158	200	208
M_{C6}	.13366 (.0683)	.07223 (.0392)	.15683 (.0609)	.31420 (.1691)	.29525 (.1903)	211 (.4212)	182	183	183	150	200	200	150	150	151	151	159	202	210
E_{R5}	.13311 (.0820)	.08123 (.0531)	.31675 (.1484)	.09986 (.0648)	-.04008 (-.0311)	.08856 (.0450)	211 (.6123)	211	211	141	183	183	161	161	162	162	146	186	209
E_{A5}	.00918 (.0062)	.21331 (.1518)	-.00527 (-.0027)	.05661 (.0400)	.14059 (.1189)	.06485 (.0358)	-.06271 (-.0418)	212 (.7252)	212	142	184	184	162	162	163	163	147	187	210
E_{C5}	.05779 (.0252)	-.02459 (-.0114)	.39981 (.1327)	-.00568 (-.0026)	-.12327 (-.0679)	.22906 (.0824)	.20438 (.0887)	-.05202 (-.0246)	212 (.3075)	142	184	184	162	162	163	163	147	187	210
M_{R5}	.13594 (.0961)	.12636 (.0948)	.14163 (.0761)	.89477 (.6662)	.50141 (.4471)	.40148 (.2339)	.15492 (.1088)	.07612 (.0582)	.02924 (.0146)	156 (.8060)	153	153	119	119	120	121	130	151	154
M_{A5}	.01690 (.0109)	.20608 (.1406)	.02657 (.0130)	.57479 (.3892)	.69688 (.5650)	.34095 (.1807)	.05849 (.0374)	.18975 (.1319)	-.01950 (-.0088)	.55175 (.4044)	204 (.6665)	203	151	151	152	152	157	197	202
M_{C5}	.11058 (.0514)	.02038 (.0101)	.16213 (.0574)	.25908 (.1270)	.16513 (.0969)	.64460 (.2472)	.17268 (.0798)	.04301 (.0216)	.26733 (.0876)	.33959 (.1802)	.31739 (.1531)	205 (.3492)	150	150	151	151	156	196	203
PE_{R5}	.12939 (.0820)	-.07950 (-.0535)	.02399 (.0116)	.45609 (.3045)	.23255 (.1859)	.34249 (.1790)	.05783 (.0364)	.03638 (.0249)	.08445 (.0377)	.55658 (.4023)	.24472 (.1608)	.31434 (.1495)	170 (.6482)	170	170	168	135	153	168
PE_{A5}	.07314 (.0422)	.12773 (.0782)	-.05258 (-.0231)	.37216 (.2260)	.32029 (.2329)	.23276 (.1106)	.08891 (.0509)	.09364 (.0584)	-.04067 (-.0165)	.41093 (.2701)	.36610 (.2188)	.22400 (.0969)	.63167 (.3724)	170 (.5361)	170	168	135	153	168
PE_{C5}	.02904 (.0143)	.06952 (.0364)	.20322 (.0762)	.12957 (.0673)	.06920 (.0430)	.30381 (.1235)	.21788 (.1067)	-.10823 (-.0577)	.31569 (.1096)	.17662 (.0993)	.05123 (.0262)	.34532 (.1278)	.23264 (.1173)	.19319 (.0886)	171 (.3920)	169	136	154	169
$ABIL_5$	.01499 (.0098)	-.01880 (-.0130)	.07073 (.0351)	.35002 (.2404)	.20907 (.1720)	.18272 (.0982)	.14008 (.0908)	.15410 (.1087)	.08501 (.0390)	.38697 (.2878)	.24123 (.1631)	.19236 (.0941)	.40140 (.2677)	.34180 (.2073)	.25927 (.1345)	171 (.6861)	137	154	169
$PEER_6$	-.03545 (-.0082)	.09816 (.0241)	-.09878 (-.0174)	.18329 (.0447)	.27610 (.0807)	.15359 (.0293)	.03445 (.0079)	.17149 (.0430)	-.03165 (-.0052)	.18475 (.0488)	.36315 (.0873)	.16260 (.0283)	.24342 (.0577)	.21213 (.0457)	.01494 (.0028)	.16989 (.0414)	162 (.0866)	157	161
ABS_6	.07688 (1.2353)	.08732 (1.4899)	-.03176 (-.3882)	.32261 (5.4619)	.29330 (5.9465)	.11751 (1.5569)	.14347 (2.2919)	.15142 (2.6324)	-.06171 (-.6986)	.28940 (5.3042)	.26134 (4.3558)	.00381 (.0460)	.15792 (2.5956)	.08665 (1.2953)	-.01092 (-.1396)	.18685 (3.1595)	.27806 (1.6706)	214 (416.7722)	212
RACE	.07480 (.0291)	.02646 (.0109)	.04617 (.0137)	.03770 (.0155)	.08452 (.0415)	.14677 (.0471)	-.02278 (-.0088)	-.07665 (-.0323)	.04543 (.0125)	.02689 (.0119)	.15156 (.0612)	.13925 (.0407)	-.05134 (-.0204)	.03860 (.0140)	.10685 (.0331)	.02385 (.0098)	-.09667 (-.0141)	-.17522 (-1.7685)	582 (.2444)

[a] Covariances in parentheses.

[b] Variances on diagonal.

Table D.13

Correlations, Covariances[a], Variances[b], and Number of Pairwise Present Observations for Cycle 1, Black Lower-Class School (Corresponding to Model in Figures 5.3 and 6.1B)

	$ABIL_1$	PE_{R1}	PE_{A1}	PE_{C1}	E_{R1}	E_{A1}	E_{C1}	M_{R1}	M_{A1}	M_{C1}	SEX	IQ
$ABIL_1$	96 (.5615)	89	87	91	91	91	91	70	74	78	96	30
PE_{R1}	.47157 (.2737)	90 (.5999)	88	90	85	85	85	65	70	74	90	26
PE_{A1}	.36718 (.1931)	.70009 (.3806)	88 (.4927)	88	83	83	83	63	69	72	88	26
PE_{C1}	.26633 (.1503)	.39078 (.2280)	.32844 (.1737)	92 (.5676)	87	87	87	66	71	75	92	27
E_{R1}	-.03525 (-.0216)	.06144 (.0389)	.05778 (.0331)	-.08617 (-.0530)	260 (.6667)	260	260	202	215	227	260	119
E_{A1}	.13918 (.0880)	.16653 (.1089)	.06239 (.0370)	.17380 (.1105)	.00825 (.0057)	260 (.7123)	260	202	215	227	260	119
E_{C1}	.15420 (.0664)	.04780 (.0213)	.03415 (.0138)	.02157 (.0093)	.18941 (.0889)	.10231 (.0496)	260 (.3303)	202	215	227	260	119
M_{R1}	.17263 (.1121)	.13861 (.0931)	.16662 (.1014)	.12588 (.0822)	.10845 (.0768)	.02520 (.0184)	.06020 (.0300)	220 (.7517)	196	205	220	114
M_{A1}	.33587 (.1659)	.34771 (.1776)	.33738 (.1561)	.05908 (.0293)	.04703 (.0253)	.08568 (.0477)	.11979 (.0454)	.51354 (.2935)	231 (.4347)	229	231	107
M_{C1}	.24244 (.1110)	.21785 (.1031)	.10927 (.0468)	.29242 (.1346)	.05631 (.0281)	.11891 (.0613)	.05526 (.0194)	.16319 (.0864)	.33899 (.1365)	243 (.3731)	243	111
SEX	-.11269 (-.0421)	-.17953 (-.0693)	-.23167 (-.0811)	-.17765 (-.0667)	.00361 (.0015)	-.10000 (-.0421)	-.01832 (-.0053)	-.20492 (-.0886)	-.13119 (-.0431)	-.20081 (-.0612)	(.2486)	187
IQ	.27055 (2.9204)	.10618 (1.1847)	.03681 (.3722)	-.15774 (-1.7120)	.00193 (.0227)	-.10189 (-1.2389)	.03237 (.2680)	.30968 (3.8679)	.51776 (4.9177)	.07564 (.6656)	.03740 (.2687)	187 (-207.5357)

[a]Covariances in parentheses.

[b]Variances on diagonal.

Table D.14

Correlations, Covariances[a], Variances[b], and Number of Pairwise Present Observations for Cycle 2, Black Lower-Class School (Corresponding to Model in Figures 5.4 and 6.2B)

	E_{R2}	E_{A2}	E_{C2}	M_{R2}	M_{A2}	M_{C2}	E_{R1}	E_{A1}	E_{C1}	M_{R1}	M_{A1}	M_{C1}	PE_{R1}	PE_{A1}	PE_{C1}	$ABIL_1$	$PEER_1$	ABS_1
E_{R2}	191 (.6296)	191	191	165	165	172	170	170	170	157	158	166	72	71	73	77	167	174
E_{A2}	.03190 (.0212)	191 (.7046)	191	165	165	172	170	170	170	157	158	166	72	71	73	77	167	174
E_{C2}	.12946 (.0560)	.18832 (.0861)	191 (.2968)	165	165	172	170	170	170	157	158	166	72	71	73	77	167	174
M_{R2}	.12326 (.0763)	.19030 (.1246)	.19142 (.0813)	239 (.6084)	234	238	209	209	209	195	213	220	66	65	67	70	206	236
M_{A2}	.04234 (.0312)	.19540 (.1525)	.12190 (.0617)	.69147 (.5013)	250 (.8640)	249	217	217	217	201	224	230	68	67	69	72	211	246
M_{C2}	.12191 (.0697)	.08990 (.0544)	-.03253 (-.0128)	.31881 (.1792)	.37729 (.2528)	262 (.5196)	226	226	226	207	229	240	74	72	75	78	219	258
E_{R1}	.12272 (.0795)	.09761 (.0669)	.02264 (.0101)	.00190 (.0012)	.07038 (.0534)	.14698 (.0865)	260 (.6667)	260	260	202	215	227	85	83	87	91	209	229
E_{A1}	.08216 (.0550)	.08607 (.0610)	.16771 (.0771)	-.03521 (-.0232)	-.01135 (-.0089)	.05329 (.0324)	.00825 (.0057)	260 (.7123)	260	202	215	227	85	83	87	91	209	229
E_{C1}	.08632 (.0394)	.07834 (.0378)	-.00815 (-.0026)	.06666 (.0299)	.08451 (.0451)	.14262 (.0591)	.18941 (.0889)	.10231 (.0496)	260 (.3303)	202	215	227	85	83	87	91	209	229
M_{R1}	-.02192 (-.0151)	.05157 (.0375)	.07264 (.0343)	.28419 (.1922)	.42821 (.3451)	.20640 (.1290)	.10845 (.0768)	.02520 (.0184)	.06020 (.0300)	220 (.7517)	196	205	65	63	66	70	185	208
M_{A1}	.01844 (.0096)	.13747 (.0761)	.07263 (.0261)	.47158 (.2425)	.67156 (.4115)	.37277 (.1771)	.04703 (.0253)	.08568 (.0477)	.11979 (.0454)	.51354 (.2935)	231 (.4347)	229	70	69	71	74	197	228
M_{C1}	.03716 (.0180)	.04847 (.0249)	-.05522 (-.0184)	.15113 (.0720)	.23726 (.1347)	.65778 (.2896)	.05631 (.0281)	.11891 (.0613)	.05526 (.0194)	.16319 (.0864)	.33899 (.1365)	243 (.3731)	74	72	75	78	204	240
PE_{R1}	.04979 (.0306)	.01100 (.0072)	-.15006 (-.0633)	.35857 (.2166)	.35887 (.2584)	.29627 (.1654)	.06144 (.0389)	.16653 (.1089)	.04780 (.0213)	.13861 (.0931)	.34771 (.1776)	.21785 (.1031)	90 (.5999)	88	90	89	71	76
PE_{A1}	.20023 (.1115)	.00710 (.0042)	-.17277 (-.0661)	.16975 (.0929)	.24859 (.1622)	.26789 (.1355)	.05778 (.0331)	.06239 (.0370)	.03415 (.0138)	.16662 (.1014)	.33738 (.1561)	.10927 (.0468)	.70009 (.3806)	88 (.4927)	88	87	70	74
PE_{C1}	-.02308 (-.0138)	-.00369 (-.0023)	.09795 (.0402)	.06450 (.0379)	.10972 (.0768)	.31549 (.1713)	-.08617 (-.0530)	.17380 (.1105)	.02157 (.0093)	.12588 (.0822)	.05908 (.0293)	.29242 (.1346)	.39078 (.2280)	.32844 (.1737)	92 (.5676)	91	73	77
$ABIL_1$	-.05387 (-.0320)	-.07703 (-.0484)	-.21057 (-.0860)	.22774 (.1331)	.25706 (.1790)	.30613 (.1653)	-.03525 (-.0216)	.13918 (.0880)	.15420 (.0664)	.17263 (.1121)	.33587 (.1659)	.24244 (.1110)	.47157 (.2737)	.36718 (.1931)	.26633 (.1503)	96 (.5615)	75	80
$PEER_1$	.18357 (.0441)	.06663 (.0170)	.05362 (.0089)	.26553 (.0628)	.40558 (.1143)	.18797 (.0411)	.12620 (.0312)	-.04425 (-.0113)	.22844 (.0398)	.27207 (.0715)	.35692 (.0713)	.02449 (.0045)	.24334 (.0571)	.32735 (.0696)	.17424 (.0398)	.15554 (.0353)	238 (.0919)	222
ABS_1	-.01904 (-.2308)	.02693 (.3454)	.15414 (1.2831)	.03698 (.4407)	.02432 (.3454)	-.11854 (-1.3056)	.02397 (.2991)	-.00465 (-.0599)	.09353 (.8213)	.16814 (2.2274)	.01202 (.1211)	-.04736 (-.4420)	.05876 (.6954)	.12269 (1.3158)	.23079 (2.6567)	-.10639 (-1.2180)	.05686 (.2633)	265 (233.4601)

[a]Covariances in parentheses.

[b]Variances on diagonal.

Table D.15

Correlations, Covariances[a], Variances[b], and Number of Pairwise Present Observations for Cycle 3, Black Lower-Class School (Corresponding to Model in Figure 5.5; Figure 6.3B Omitted Because Matrix Was Singular)

	$ABIL_3$	PE_{R3}	PE_{A3}	PE_{C3}	E_{R3}	E_{A3}	E_{C3}	M_{R3}	M_{A3}	M_{C3}	E_{R2}	E_{A2}	E_{C2}	M_{R2}	M_{A2}	M_{C2}	SEX	IQ	$ABIL_1$	PE_{R1}	PE_{A1}	PE_{C1}
$ABIL_3$	82 (.4173)	77	77	25	77	77	77	44	74	75	45	45	45	44	47	49	82	68	25	22	22	23
PE_{R3}	.55389 (.2795)	79 (.6101)	79	78	74	74	74	40	71	72	44	44	44	43	46	48	79	65	24	21	21	22
PE_{A3}	.48463 (.2234)	.69724 (.3886)	79 (.5092)	78	74	74	74	40	71	72	44	44	44	43	46	48	79	65	24	21	21	22
PE_{C3}	.17426 (.0738)	.30308 (.1553)	.31914 (.1494)	79 (.4301)	74	74	74	40	71	72	44	44	44	43	46	48	79	65	24	21	21	22
E_{R3}	-.01069 (-.0052)	-.03008 (-.0177)	.18202 (.0980)	.02139 (.0106)	106 (.5694)	183	183	99	162	163	106	106	106	116	118	123	183	147	31	26	26	27
E_{A3}	.07438 (.0408)	.09049 (.0601)	.03323 (.0202)	-.11049 (-.0616)	-.14056 (-.0902)	183 (.7227)	183	99	162	163	106	106	106	116	118	123	183	147	31	26	26	27
E_{C3}	.03600 (.0120)	.05555 (.0224)	.09308 (.0342)	-.01182 (-.0040)	.07388 (.0287)	.30237 (.1325)	183 (.2656)	99	162	163	106	106	106	116	118	123	183	147	31	26	26	27
M_{R3}	.38040 (.2113)	.45207 (.3036)	.35518 (.2179)	.00557 (.0031)	.09680 (.0628)	.15556 (.1137)	.09408 (.0417)	105 (.7391)	104	104	52	52	52	57	58	59	105	91	13	11	11	12
M_{A3}	.40061 (.1529)	.37199 (.1716)	.33114 (.1396)	.11397 (.0442)	.02372 (.0106)	.13762 (.0691)	.00311 (.0009)	.43728 (.2221)	173 (.3489)	173	101	101	101	110	113	115	173	152	26	23	23	24
M_{C3}	.33661 (.1246)	.34592 (.1548)	.31432 (.1285)	.24409 (.0917)	.10204 (.0441)	.00515 (.0025)	.18449 (.0545)	.22375 (.1102)	.20570 (.0696)	174 (.3283)	101	101	101	110	113	115	174	152	26	23	23	24
E_{R2}	-.03346 (-.0172)	.19755 (.1224)	.20813 (.1179)	.01598 (.0083)	.07170 (.0429)	.13425 (.0906)	.06435 (.0263)	.07525 (.0513)	.05503 (.0258)	-.13468 (-.0612)	191 (.6296)	191	191	165	165	172	191	101	77	72	71	73
E_{A2}	.21536 (.1168)	.18324 (.1201)	.06201 (.0371)	.07271 (.0400)	.12094 (.0766)	.15750 (.1124)	.05711 (.0247)	.04738 (.0342)	.07533 (.0373)	.01698 (.0082)	.03190 (.0212)	191 (.7046)	191	165	165	172	191	101	77	72	71	73
E_{C2}	-.02689 (-.0095)	-.04587 (-.0195)	-.02959 (-.0115)	-.06352 (-.0227)	.01397 (.0057)	.17743 (.0822)	.27301 (.0767)	.31962 (.1497)	.10700 (.0344)	.08155 (.0255)	.12946 (.0560)	.18832 (.0861)	191 (.2968)	165	165	172	191	101	77	72	71	73
M_{R2}	.26183 (.1319)	.45642 (.2781)	.13144 (.0732)	.17441 (.0892)	.14378 (.0846)	.06191 (.0411)	.00803 (.0032)	.35253 (.2364)	.44827 (.2065)	.11372 (.0508)	.12326 (.0763)	.19030 (.1246)	.19142 (.0813)	239 (.6084)	234	238	239	111	70	66	65	67
M_{A2}	.23347 (.1402)	.32165 (.2335)	.11698 (.0776)	.03387 (.0206)	.03806 (.0267)	.06482 (.0512)	-.02977 (-.0143)	.40308 (.3221)	.46430 (.2549)	.14000 (.0746)	.04234 (.0312)	.19540 (.1525)	.12190 (.0617)	.69147 (.5013)	250 (.8640)	249	250	113	72	68	67	69
M_{C2}	.11315 (.0527)	.32282 (.1818)	.26869 (.1382)	.17427 (.0824)	.12076 (.0657)	.09379 (.0575)	.10454 (.0388)	-.00101 (-.0006)	.10218 (.0435)	.43261 (.1787)	.12191 (.0697)	.08990 (.0544)	-.03253 (-.0128)	.31881 (.1792)	.37729 (.2528)	262 (.5196)	262	116	78	74	72	75
SEX	-.31551 (-.1016)	-.29713 (-.1157)	-.31752 (-.1130)	-.05562 (-.0182)	-.07028 (-.0264)	-.01558 (-.0066)	-.04349 (-.0112)	-.23219 (-.0995)	-.14075 (-.0415)	-.12391 (-.0354)	-.10601 (-.0419)	-.07720 (-.0323)	.04087 (.0111)	-.18011 (-.0700)	-.14273 (-.0661)	-.18691 (-.0672)	406 (.2486)	187	96	90	88	92
IQ	-.30740 (-2.8608)	-.18803 (-2.1158)	-.17394 (-1.7882)	-.00495 (-.0468)	.00359 (.0390)	-.07397 (-.9059)	.01137 (.0845)	-.43931 (-5.4409)	-.30095 (-2.5609)	-.19587 (-1.6168)	-.03619 (-.4137)	-.05925 (-.7164)	-.05657 (-.4440)	-.58668 (-6.5923)	-.57388 (-7.6845)	-.20213 (-2.0989)	-.03740 (-.2687)	187 (207.5357)	30	26	26	27
$ABIL_1$	.47376 (.2293)	.53786 (.3148)	.05537 (.0296)	-.01042 (-.0051)	-.30750 (-.1739)	-.15873 (-.1011)	-.23957 (-.0925)	-.11573 (-.0745)	.16885 (.0747)	.14747 (.0633)	-.05387 (-.0320)	-.07703 (-.0484)	-.21057 (-.0860)	.22774 (.1331)	.25706 (.1790)	.30613 (.1653)	-.11269 (-.0421)	-.27055 (-2.9204)	96 (.5615)	89	87	91
PE_{R1}	.03642 (.0182)	.31468 (.1904)	-.19167 (-.1059)	-.06579 (-.0334)	.04119 (.0241)	-.42852 (-.2821)	-.54412 (-.2172)	-.04348 (-.0289)	-.02829 (-.0129)	.08802 (.0391)	.04979 (.0306)	.01100 (.0072)	-.15006 (-.0633)	.35857 (.2166)	.35887 (.2584)	.29627 (.1654)	-.17953 (-.0693)	-.10618 (-1.1847)	.47157 (.2737)	90 (.5999)	88	90
PE_{A1}	.02453 (.0111)	.46744 (.2563)	.06699 (.0336)	-.09773 (-.0450)	.08487 (.0450)	-.30778 (-.1836)	-.49271 (-.1782)	.02786 (.0168)	-.01997 (-.0083)	-.09664 (-.0389)	.20023 (.1115)	.00710 (.0042)	-.17277 (-.0661)	.16975 (.0929)	.24859 (.1622)	.26789 (.1355)	-.23167 (-.0811)	-.03681 (-.3722)	.36718 (.1931)	.70009 (.3806)	88 (.4927)	88
PE_{C1}	-.29280 (-.1425)	-.07304 (-.0430)	-.29669 (-.1595)	.18621 (.0920)	.00000 (.0000)	-.39081 (-.2503)	-.28031 (-.1088)	-.14552 (-.0943)	.00000 (.0000)	.03288 (.0142)	-.02308 (-.0138)	-.00369 (-.0023)	.09795 (.0402)	.06450 (.0379)	.10972 (.0768)	.31549 (.1713)	-.17765 (-.0667)	.15774 (1.7120)	.26633 (.1503)	.39078 (.2280)	.32844 (.1737)	92 (.5676)

[a]Covariances in parentheses.

[b]Variances on diagonal.

Table D.16

Correlations, Covariances[a], Variances[b], and Number of Pairwise Present Observations for Cycle 4, Black Lower-Class School (Corresponding to Model in Figures 5.6 and 6.4B)

	E_{A4}	E_{C4}	M_{R4}	M_{A4}	M_{C4}	E_{R3}	E_{A3}	E_{C3}	M_{R3}	M_{A3}	M_{C3}	PE_{R3}	PE_{A3}	PE_{C3}	$ABIL_3$	$PEER_4$	ABS_4
E_{A4}	126 (.7343)	126	90	116	115	119	119	119	71	119	120	65	65	65	69	125	125
E_{C4}	.22627 (.1058)	126 (.2977)	90	116	115	119	119	119	71	119	120	65	65	65	69	125	125
M_{R4}	.07356 (.0544)	.14553 (.0685)	129 (.7443)	129	128	116	116	116	75	123	123	54	54	53	55	112	129
M_{A4}	.17662 (.1126)	.20497 (.0832)	.77535 (.4977)	178 (.5535)	176	159	159	159	102	168	169	70	70	70	73	149	178
M_{C4}	.09031 (.0488)	.33263 (.1144)	.35069 (.1907)	.31923 (.1497)	177 (.3972)	158	158	158	100	167	168	71	71	71	74	148	177
E_{R3}	.04640 (.0300)	.10203 (.0420)	.00879 (.0057)	.02120 (.0119)	-.06209 (-.0295)	183 (.5694)	183	183	99	162	163	74	74	74	77	147	170
E_{A3}	.04081 (.0297)	.10751 (.0499)	.01885 (.0138)	.18823 (.1191)	.06516 (.0349)	-.14056 (-.0902)	183 (.7227)	183	99	162	163	74	74	74	77	147	170
E_{C3}	.13137 (.0580)	.30109 (.0847)	-.13879 (-.0617)	.01059 (.0041)	.15302 (.0497)	.07388 (.0287)	.30237 (.1325)	183 (.2656)	99	162	163	74	74	74	77	147	170
M_{R3}	.03792 (.0279)	.23058 (.1082)	.55343 (.4105)	.58824 (.3762)	.31634 (.1714)	.09680 (.0628)	.15556 (.1137)	.09408 (.0417)	105 (.7391)	104	104	40	40	40	44	91	105
M_{A3}	.07255 (.0367)	.10073 (.0325)	.50746 (.2586)	.71082 (.3124)	.19019 (.0708)	.02372 (.0106)	.13762 (.0691)	.00311 (.0009)	.43728 (.2221)	173 (.3489)	173	71	71	71	74	148	173
M_{C3}	.24178 (.1187)	.31965 (.0999)	.32144 (.1589)	.23431 (.0999)	.63964 (.2310)	.10204 (.0441)	.00515 (.0025)	.18449 (.0545)	.22375 (.1102)	.20570 (.0696)	174 (.3283)	72	72	72	75	149	174
PE_{R3}	.07541 (.0505)	.08013 (.0341)	.38328 (.2583)	.38748 (.2252)	.25958 (.1278)	-.03008 (-.0177)	.09049 (.0601)	.05555 (.0224)	.45207 (.3036)	.37199 (.1716)	.34592 (.1548)	79 (.6101)	79	78	77	70	74
PE_{A3}	.23295 (.1424)	.02423 (.0094)	.15328 (.0944)	.28515 (.1514)	.15205 (.0684)	.18202 (.0980)	.03323 (.0202)	.09308 (.0342)	.35518 (.2179)	.33114 (.1396)	.31432 (.1285)	.69724 (.3886)	79 (.5092)	78	77	70	74
PE_{C3}	.16182 (.0909)	.13120 (.0469)	.10945 (.0619)	.18141 (.0885)	.14240 (.0589)	.02139 (.0106)	-.11049 (-.0616)	-.01182 (-.0040)	.00557 (.0031)	.11397 (.0442)	.24409 (.0917)	.30308 (.1553)	.31914 (.1494)	79 (.4301)	77	70	74
$ABIL_3$	.06865 (.0380)	.05664 (.0200)	.56871 (.3169)	.45273 (.2176)	.23001 (.0936)	-.01069 (-.0052)	.07438 (.0408)	.03600 (.0120)	.38040 (.2113)	.40061 (.1529)	.33661 (.1246)	.55389 (.2795)	.48463 (.2234)	.17426 (.0738)	82 (.4173)	74	77
$PEER_4$	.02589 (.0067	.15181 (.0248)	.40449 (.1047)	.24374 (.0544)	.13979 (.0264)	.12711 (.0288)	.15652 (.0399)	.05603 (.0087)	-.08087 (-.0208)	.27808 (.0493)	.16129 (.0277)	-.04315 (-.0101)	-.01195 (-.0026)	-.12914 (-.0254)	.08714 (.0169)	160 (.0899)	159
ABS_4	.06951 (.8838)	.02790 (.2259)	.17589 (2.2518)	.16096 (1.7771)	.05474 (.5120)	.11930 (1.3360)	.08322 (1.0498)	.11227 (.8586)	.29233 (3.7295)	.05953 (.5218)	.10977 (.9334)	.17124 (1.9849)	.11562 (1.2244)	.05920 (.5761)	.06371 (.6108)	.04878 (.6405)	125 (220.2167)

[a]Covariances in parentheses.

[b]Variances on diagonal.

Table D.17

Correlations, Covariances[a], Variances[b], and Number of Pairwise Present Observations for Cycle 5, Black Lower-Class School (Corresponding to Model in Figures 5.7 and 6.5B)

	$ABIL_5$	PE_{R5}	PE_{A5}	PE_{C5}	E_{R5}	E_{A5}	E_{C5}	M_{R5}	M_{A5}	M_{C5}	E_{R4}	E_{A4}	E_{C4}	M_{R4}	M_{A4}	M_{C4}	SEX	IQ	$ABIL_3$	PE_{R3}	PE_{A3}	PE_{C3}
$ABIL_5$	117 (.6406)	112	111	112	111	111	111	73	108	109	73	73	73	66	89	87	117	94	50	49	49	48
PE_{R5}	.55040 (.3894)	114 (.7813)	113	114	108	108	108	71	104	105	73	73	73	65	89	87	114	93	50	49	49	48
PE_{A5}	.41635 (.2484)	.53099 (.3498)	113 (.5556)	113	107	107	107	70	103	104	72	72	72	65	88	86	113	92	50	49	49	48
PE_{C5}	.31322 (.1582)	.42189 (.2354)	.31059 (.1461)	114 (.3984)	108	108	108	71	104	105	73	73	73	65	89	87	114	93	50	49	49	48
E_{R5}	.11076 (.0651)	.23115 (.1499)	.08848 (.0484)	.22250 (.1031)	158 (.5385)	158	158	94	149	150	89	89	89	94	124	122	158	128	56	54	54	54
E_{A5}	.03613 (.0236)	.06025 (.0435)	.11880 (.0723)	.07142 (.0368)	-.04092 (-.0245)	158 (.6663)	158	94	149	150	89	89	89	94	124	122	158	128	56	54	54	54
E_{C5}	.06360 (.0272)	.12327 (.0582)	-.06145 (-.0245)	.17389 (.0587)	.24798 (.0973)	.13266 (.0579)	158 (.2858)	94	149	150	89	89	89	94	124	122	158	128	56	54	54	54
M_{R5}	.40626 (.1982)	.36436 (.1963)	.27769 (.1261)	.10564 (.0406)	.27963 (.1250)	-.12659 (-.0630)	.10552 (.0344)	105 (.3714)	105	105	57	57	57	59	76	76	105	84	39	36	36	35
M_{A5}	.35679 (.1878)	.42554 (.2474)	.28609 (.1403)	.23171 (.0962)	.08428 (.0407)	.10451 (.0561)	.06276 (.0221)	.47511 (.1904)	165 (.4326)	165	89	89	89	95	122	120	165	133	54	51	51	51
M_{C5}	.10885 (.0590)	.07840 (.0469)	.13049 (.0658)	.11359 (.0485)	-.06058 (-.0301)	-.07249 (-.0401)	.13720 (.0497)	.28900 (.1192)	.07378 (.0329)	166 (.4583)	89	89	89	95	123	121	166	133	54	51	51	51
E_{R4}	.07158 (.0426)	.05548 (.0365)	-.08635 (-.0479)	.01253 (.0059)	.31817 (.1737)	.06747 (.0410)	.06896 (.0274)	.07328 (.0332)	.04397 (.0215)	.09438 (.0475)	126 (.5537)	126	126	90	116	115	126	111	69	65	65	65
E_{A4}	.09510 (.0652)	.09089 (.0688)	.20407 (.1303)	.01768 (.0096)	.04206 (.0264)	.21949 (.1535)	.14798 (.0678)	-.04836 (-.0253)	.07200 (.0406)	-.05683 (-.0330)	-.07807 (-.0498)	126 (.7343)	126	90	116	115	126	111	69	65	65	65
E_{C4}	.17486 (.0764)	.19414 (.0936)	.27299 (.1110)	.15690 (.0540)	.28143 (.1127)	.20175 (.0899)	.21997 (.0642)	.28725 (.0955)	.03412 (.0122)	.07507 (.0277)	.01564 (.0063)	.22627 (.1058)	126 (.2977)	90	116	115	126	111	69	65	65	65
M_{R4}	.17963 (.1240)	.30307 (.2311)	.35056 (.2254)	.22758 (.1239)	.24171 (.1530)	.00878 (.0062)	.07946 (.0366)	.45280 (.2380)	.59807 (.3393)	.29453 (.1720)	-.04790 (-.0307)	.07356 (.0544)	.14553 (.0685)	129 (.7443)	129	128	129	115	55	54	54	53
M_{A4}	.21675 (.1291)	.41787 (.2748)	.48577 (.2694)	.25375 (.1192)	.15711 (.0858)	.12930 (.0785)	-.01121 (-.0045)	.37239 (.1688)	.47657 (.2332)	.20285 (.1022)	.03634 (.0201)	.17662 (.1126)	.20497 (.0832)	.77536 (.4977)	178 (.5535)	176	178	151	73	70	70	70
M_{C4}	.38836 (.1959)	.35432 (.1974)	.37325 (.1753)	.31553 (.1255)	.31575 (.1460)	.01634 (.0084)	.11573 (.0390)	.30260 (.1162)	.18466 (.0765)	.10238 (.0437)	.00790 (.0037)	.09031 (.0488)	.33263 (.1144)	.35069 (.1907)	.31923 (.1497)	177 (.3972)	177	150	74	71	71	71
SEX	-.15965 (-.0637)	-.20575 (-.0907)	-.00424 (-.0016)	-.10343 (-.0326)	-.14059 (-.0514)	-.00515 (-.0021)	-.11954 (-.0319)	.04331 (.0132)	-.03113 (-.0102)	-.16875 (-.0570)	-.11973 (-.0444)	-.02911 (-.0124)	-.16002 (-.0435)	-.15231 (-.0655)	-.19648 (-.0729)	-.24449 (-.0768)	(.2486)	187	82	79	79	79
IQ	.16845 (1.9424)	.27858 (3.5473)	.18141 (1.9480)	.33441 (3.0408)	.07346 (.7765)	.08904 (1.0471)	.06974 (.5371)	.34626 (3.0399)	.42197 (3.9981)	.01378 (.1344)	-.14751 (-1.5812)	.06200 (.7653)	.09556 (.7511)	.52717 (6.5517)	.39894 (4.2759)	.22409 (2.0345)	.03740 (.2687)	187 (207.5357)	68	65	65	65
$ABIL_3$	.56575 (.2925)	.41595 (.2375)	.35553 (.1712)	.29554 (.1205)	.35750 (.1695)	-.09116 (-.0481)	.06514 (.0225)	.42890 (.1688)	.44025 (.1870)	.27532 (.1204)	.09520 (.0458)	.06865 (.0380)	.05664 (.0200)	.56871 (.3169)	.45273 (.2176)	.23001 (.0936)	-.31551 (-.1016)	.30740 (2.8608)	82 (.4173)	77	77	77
PE_{R3}	.31379 (.1962)	.50088 (.3458)	.40985 (.2386)	.21864 (.1078)	.13324 (.0764)	.18846 (.1202)	-.01718 (-.0072)	.36105 (.1719)	.30087 (.1546)	.06784 (.0359)	-.06493 (-.0377)	.07541 (.0505)	.08013 (.0341)	.38328 (.2583)	.38748 (.2252)	.25958 (.1278)	-.29713 (-.1157)	.18803 (2.1158)	.55389 (.2795)	79 (.6101)	79	78
PE_{A3}	.28447 (.1625)	.40135 (.2532)	.47683 (.2536)	.16947 (.0763)	.01657 (.0087)	.19597 (.1142)	-.11432 (-.0436)	.44185 (.1921)	.27139 (.1274)	.11355 (.0549)	-.14045 (-.0746)	.23295 (.1424)	.02423 (.0094)	.15328 (.0944)	.28515 (.1514)	.15205 (.0684)	-.31752 (-.1130)	.17394 (1.7882)	.48463 (.2234)	.69724 (.3886)	79 (.5092)	78
PE_{C3}	.20702 (.1087)	.17762 (.1030)	.06344 (.0310)	.05573 (.0231)	.01748 (.0084)	-.08945 (-.0479)	.12714 (.0446)	.27215 (.1088)	.05445 (.0235)	.04240 (.0188)	-.08715 (-.0425)	.16182 (.0909)	.13120 (.0469)	.10945 (.0619)	.18141 (.0885)	.14240 (.0589)	-.05562 (-.0182)	.00495 (.0468)	.17426 (.0738)	.30308 (.1553)	.31914 (.1494)	79 (.4301)

[a]Covariances in parentheses.

[b]Variances on diagonal.

Table D.18

Correlations, Covariances[a], Variances[b], and Number of Pairwise Present Observations for Cycle 6, Black Lower-Class School (Corresponding to Model in Figures 5.8 and 6.6B)

	E_{R6}	E_{A6}	E_{C6}	M_{R6}	M_{A6}	M_{C6}	E_{R5}	E_{A5}	E_{C5}	M_{R5}	M_{A5}	M_{C5}	PE_{R5}	PE_{A5}	PE_{C5}	$ABIL_5$	$PEER_6$	ABS_6
E_{R6}	130 (.5177)	130	130	121	125	126	121	121	121	81	123	124	104	103	104	108	127	127
E_{A6}	.00029 (.0002)	130 (.7315)	130	121	125	126	121	121	121	81	123	124	104	103	104	108	127	127
E_{C6}	.26117 (.1045)	.09981 (.0475)	130 (.3091)	121	125	126	121	121	121	81	123	124	104	103	104	108	127	127
M_{R6}	.24205 (.1360)	.16902 (.1129)	.14326 (.0622)	166 (.6098)	164	165	143	143	143	103	158	158	99	98	99	103	141	163
M_{A6}	.18251 (.1083)	.35851 (.2529)	.19918 (.0913)	.64269 (.4139)	171 (.6803)	170	148	148	148	103	163	163	103	102	103	107	145	168
M_{C6}	-.03084 (-.0158)	.04739 (.0289)	.13596 (.0539)	-.08028 (-.0447)	.06968 (.0410)	172 (.5089)	148	148	148	105	164	164	104	103	104	108	145	169
E_{R5}	.22988 (.1214)	.01547 (.0097)	.23376 (.0954)	.24856 (.1424)	.15262 (.0924)	-.02067 (-.0108)	158 (.5385)	158	158	94	149	150	108	107	108	111	140	149
E_{A5}	.05352 (.0314)	.28871 (.2016)	.01634 (.0074)	.04609 (.0294)	.21692 (.1460)	.08429 (.0491)	-.04092 (-.0245)	158 (.6663)	158	94	149	150	108	107	108	111	140	149
E_{C5}	.31213 (.1201)	-.02419 (-.0111)	.34261 (.1018)	.12889 (.0538)	.06532 (.0288)	.18280 (.0697)	.24798 (.0973)	.13266 (.0579)	158 (.2858)	94	149	150	108	107	108	111	140	149
M_{R5}	.17018 (.0746)	.18142 (.0946)	.20246 (.0686)	.69714 (.3318)	.42690 (.2146)	.06107 (.0265)	.27963 (.1250)	-.12659 -.0630)	.10552 (.0344)	105 (.3714)	105	105	71	70	71	73	90	104
M_{A5}	.26530 (.1255)	.21980 (.1236)	.14505 (.0530)	.59462 (.3054)	.73346 (.3979)	-.01215 (-.0057)	.08428 (.0407)	.10451 (.0561)	.06276 (.0221)	.47511 (.1904)	165 (.4326)	165	104	103	104	108	142	162
M_{C5}	.02537 (.0124)	.06259 (.0362)	.13016 (.0490)	.00624 (.0033)	.03838 (.0214)	.70492 (.3405)	-.06058 (-.0301)	-.07249 (-.0401)	.13720 (.0497)	.28900 (.1192)	.07378 (.0329)	166 (.4583)	105	104	105	109	143	163
PE_{R5}	.29052 (.1848)	.12220 (.0924)	.28296 (.1391)	.39732 (.2742)	.46513 (.3391)	.10984 (.0693)	.23115 (.1499)	.06025 (.0435)	.12327 (.0582)	.36436 (.1963)	.42554 (.2474)	.07840 (.0469)	114 (.7813)	113	114	112	104	104
PE_{A5}	.11945 (.0641)	.23962 (.1528)	.09079 (.0376)	.26727 (.1556)	.35926 (.2209)	.16445 (.0875)	.08848 (.0484)	.11880 (.0723)	-.06145 (-.0245)	.27769 (.1261)	.28609 (.1403)	.13049 (.0658)	.53099 (.3498)	113 (.5556)	113	111	103	103
PE_{C5}	.10723 (.0487)	.03723 (.0201)	.22167 (.0778)	.19059 (.0939)	.31809 (.1656)	.18555 (.0836)	.22250 (.1031)	.07142 (.0368)	.17389 (.0587)	.10564 (.0406)	.23171 (.0962)	.11359 (.0485)	.42189 (.2354)	.31059 (.1461)	114 (.3984)	112	104	104
$ABIL_5$	.22968 (.1323)	.01751 (.0120)	.27945 (.1244)	.24515 (.1532)	.40779 (.2692)	.11440 (.0653)	.11076 (.0651)	.03613 (.0236)	.06360 (.0272)	.40626 (.1982)	.35679 (.1878)	.10885 (.0590)	.55040 (.3894)	.41635 (.2484)	.31322 (.1582)	117 (.6406)	108	108
$PEER_6$	-.00806 (-.0018)	.15187 (.0400)	.04753 (.0081)	.25227 (.0606)	.35422 (.0899)	.09834 (.0216)	.03440 (.0078)	.15334 (.0385)	.09610 (.0158)	.17749 (.0333)	.32594 (.0660)	.10045 (.0209)	.30331 (.0825)	.30474 (.0699)	.18759 (.0364)	.13378 (.0329)	150 (.0947)	148
ABS_6	.13974 (1.3910)	.25198 (2.9818)	.00470 (.0361)	.22019 (2.3789)	.21632 (2.4684)	-.14986 (-1.4791)	.04579 (.4649)	.13472 (1.5214)	-.01249 (-.0924)	.11166 (.9414)	.22843 (2.0786)	-.20491 (-1.9193)	.22112 (2.7041)	.35338 (3.6444)	.12723 (1.1111)	.12806 (1.4181)	.10211 (.4347)	175 (191.4153)

[a]Covariances in parentheses.

[b]Variances on diagonal.

References

Adelman, H. S. 1969. Reinforcing effects of adult non-reaction on expectancy of underachieving boys. *Child Development* 40:111–22.

Alberti, J. M. 1971. Correlates of Self-Perception-In-School. Paper presented at annual meeting of American Educational Research Association, New York.

Alexander, K., and Eckland, B. K. 1975. Contextual effects in the high school attainment process. *American Sociological Review* 40:402–16.

Alexander, K., McPartland, J. M., and Cook, M. A. 1981. Using standardized test performance in school effects research. *Research in Sociology of Education and Socialization* 2:1–33.

Alwin, D. F., and Hauser, R. M. 1975. The decomposition of effects in path analysis. *American Sociological Review* 40:37–47.

Alwin, D. F., and Otto, L. B. 1977. High school effects on aspirations. *Sociology of Education* 50:259–73.

Ambron, S. R., and Rogosa, D. R. 1975. Structural Equation Models and Causal Inference in Child Development Research. Paper presented at meetings of the American Educational Research Association, Washington, D.C.

Anderson, J. G. 1978. Causal models in educational research: Non-recursive models. *American Educational Research Journal* 15:81–98.

Ausubel, D. P., DeWit, F., Goldens, B., and Welkowitz, J. 1954. Perceived parent attitudes as determinants of children's ego structure. *Child Development* 25:173–83.

Averch, H. A., Carroll, S. J., Donaldson, T. S., Kiesling, H. J., and Pincus, J. 1972. *How effective is schooling? A critical review and synthesis of research findings.* Report prepared for President's Commission on School Finance. Santa Monica: Rand Corporation.

Bachman, J. G., O'Malley, P. M., and Johnston, J. 1978. *Adolescence to adulthood: Change and stability in the lives of young men.* Ann Arbor: University of Michigan, Institute for Social Research.

Baker, J., and Crist, J. 1971. Teacher expectancies: A review of the literature. In *Pygmalion reconsidered*, ed. J. Elashoff and R. Snow. Worthington, Ohio: Charles A. Jones.

Bandura, A. 1973. *Aggression, a social learning analysis.* Englewood Cliffs, N.J.: Prentice-Hall.

Bandura, A. 1977. *Social learning theory.* Englewood Cliffs, N.J.: Prentice-Hall.

Baratz, J. C. 1970. Educational considerations for teaching standard English to Negro children. In *Teaching standard English in the inner city,* ed. R. W. Fasold and R. W. Shuy. Washington, D.C.: Center for Applied Linguistics.

Beady, C. H., Jr., and Hansell, S. 1981. Teacher race and expectations for student achievement. *American Educational Research Journal* 18:191–206.

Becher, R. M. 1978. Teacher Behaviors Related to the Mathematical Achievement of Young Children. Paper presented at the meetings of the American Educational Research Association, Toronto, Canada.

Beers, J. S. 1973. Self-Esteem of Black and White Fifth Grade Pupils as a Function of Demographic Categorization. Paper presented at meetings of the American Educational Research Association, New Orleans.

Bell, R. R. 1975. Lower class Negro mothers' aspirations for their children. In *The sociology of education: A sourcebook,* ed. H. R. Stub. Homewood, Ill.: Dorsey Press.

Benbow, C. P., and Stanley, J. C. 1980. Sex differences in mathematic ability: Fact or artifact. *Science* 210:1262.

Berger, J., Conner, T. L., and Fisek, M. H., eds. 1974. *Expectation states theory: A theoretical research program.* Cambridge, Mass.: Winthrop.

Berger, J., Fisek, M. H., Norman, R. Z., and Zelditch, M. 1977. *Status characteristics and social interaction.* New York: Elsevier.

Berger, J., Rosenholtz, S. J., and Zelditch, M. 1980. Social processes. In *Annual review of sociology,* Vol. 6, eds. A. Inkeles, N. J. Smelser, and R. H. Turner. Palo Alto: Annual Reviews, Inc.

Berkeley, M. V. 1978. Inside Kindergarten. Ph.D. dissertation, The Johns Hopkins University.

Bernstein, B. 1970. A socio-linguistic approach to socialization: With some reference to educability. In *Directions in sociolinguistics,* eds. J. Gumperz and D. Hymes. New York: Holt, Rinehart, and Winston.

Bilby, R. W., Brookover, W. B., and Erickson, E. L. 1972. Characterizations of self and student decision making. *Review of Educational Research* 42:505–24.

Blau, P., and Duncan, O. D. 1967. *American occupational structure.* New York: Wiley.

Bloom, B. S. 1964. *Stability and change in human characteristics.* New York: Wiley.

Blyth, D. A., Simmons, R., and Bush, D. 1978. The transition into early adolescence: A longitudinal comparison of youth in two educational contexts. *Sociology of Education* 51:149–62.

Bohrnstedt, G. W., and Carter, T. M. 1971. Robustness in

regression analysis. In *Sociological Methodology.* San Francisco: Jossey-Bass.

Bossert, S. T. 1978. Activity Structures and Student Outcomes. NIE Conference on School Organizations, San Diego, January.

Braun, C. 1976. Teacher expectation: Sociopsychological dynamics. *Review of Educational Research* 46:185–213.

Breland, N. S. 1970. Expectations for Achievement: A Basic Model. Unpublished manuscript, State University of New York at Buffalo.

Brim, O. G. 1976. Life-span development for the theory of oneself: Implications for child development. In *Advances in child development and behavior,* Vol. II, ed. H. W. Reese. New York: Academic Press.

Brookover, W. B., Erickson, E. L., and Joiner, L. M. 1967. Self-Concept of Ability and School Achievement, III. U.S. Office of Education Cooperative Research Project No. 2831. East Lansing: Office of Research and Publications, Michigan State University.

Brookover, W. B., Gigliotti, R. J., Henderson, R. D., and Schneider, J. M. 1973. Elementary School Social Environment and School Achievement. Final Report, U.S. Office of Education Cooperative Research Project No. 1-E-107. East Lansing: College of Urban Development, Michigan State University.

Brookover, W. B., LePere, J., Hamachek, D., Thomas, S., and Erickson, E. 1965. Self-Concept of Ability and School Achievement, II. U.S. Office of Education Cooperative Project No. 1636. East Lansing: Office of Research and Publications, Michigan State University.

Brookover, W. B., Patterson, A., and Shailer, J. 1962. Self-Concept of Ability and School Achievement. U.S. Office of Education Cooperative Research Project No. 845. East Lansing: Office of Research and Publications, Michigan State University.

Brookover, W. B., and Schneider, J. M. 1975. Academic environments and elementary school achievement. *Journal of Research and Development in Education* 9:83–91.

Brookover, W. B., Schweitzer, J. H., Schneider, J. M., Beady, C. H., Flood, P. K., and Wisenbaker, J. M. 1978. Elementary school social climate and school achievement. *American Educational Research Journal* 15:301–18.

Brookover, W. B., Thomas, S., and Patterson, A. 1964. Self-concept of ability and school achievement. *Sociology of Education* 37:271–78.

Brophy, J. E., and Good, T. L. 1970. Teachers' communication of differential expectations for children's classroom performance. *Journal of Educational Psychology* 61:367–74.

Brophy, J., and Good, T. 1974. *Teacher-student relationships.* New York: Holt, Rinehart, and Winston.

Campbell, B. P. 1965. Self-Concept and Academic Achievement in Middle Grade Public School Children. Ph.D. dissertation, Wayne State University. *Dissertation Abstracts* 27:1535A–36A.

Caplin, M. D. 1966. The Relationship between Self-Concept and Academic Achievement and between Level of Aspiration and Academic Achievement. Ph.D. dissertation, Columbia University. *Dissertation Abstracts* 27: 979–80A.

Carpenter, T. R., and Busse, T. B. 1969. Development of self-concept in Negro and white children. *Child Development* 40:935–39.

Claiborn, W. L. 1969. Expectancy effects in the classroom: A failure to replicate. *Journal of Educational Psychology* 60:377–83.

Clark, B. B., and Trowbridge, N. T. 1971. Encouraging creativity through inservice teacher education. *Journal of Research and Development in Education* 4:87–94.

Clark, K. B. 1963. Educational stimulation of racially disadvantaged children. In *Education in depressed areas,* ed. H. A. Passow. New York: Bureau of Publications, Teachers College, Columbia University.

Clifton, R. A. 1980. Ethnicity, Teachers' Expectations and the Academic Achievement Process. Unpublished manuscript, University of Manitoba.

Cohen, E. G. 1968. Interracial Interaction Disability. Technical Report No. 1. Stanford University, School of Education.

Cohen, E. G., Lohmann, M., Hall, K., Lucero, D., and Roper, S. 1970. Expectation Training I: Altering the Effects of a Racial Status Characteristic. Technical Report No. 2. Stanford University, School of Education.

Cohen, E. G., and Roper, S. S. 1971. Expectation Training II: Modification of Interracial Interaction Disability. Technical Report No. 7. Stanford University, School of Education.

Cohen, E. G., and Roper, S. 1972. Modification of interracial interaction disability. *American Sociological Review* 37:643–57.

Coleman, J. S. 1961. *The adolescent society.* Glencoe, Ill.: Free Press.

Coleman, J. S., Campbell, E. Q., Hobson, C. J., McPartland, J., Mood, A., Weinfeld, F. D., and York, R. L. 1966. *Equality of educational opportunity.* Washington, D.C.: U.S. Government Printing Office.

Cook, M. A., and Alexander, K. L. 1980. Design and substance in educational research: Adolescent attainments, a case in point. *Sociology of Education* 53:187–202.

Cooley, C. H. 1922. *Human nature and the social order.* New York: Scribner.

Cooper, H. M., Baron, R. M., and Lowe, C. A. 1975. The importance of race and social class information in the formation of expectancies about academic performance. *Journal of Educational Psychology* 67:312–19.

Cooper, H. M., and Lowe, C. A. 1977. Task information and attributions for academic performance by professional teachers and role players. *Journal of Personality* 45:469–83.

Coopersmith, S. 1959. A method for determining types of self-esteem. *Journal of Abnormal and Social Psychology* 59:87–94.

Crandall, V. 1969. Sex differences in expectancy of intellectual and academic reinforcement. In *Achievement related motives in children,* ed. C. P. Smith. New York: Russell Sage.

Crano, W. D., and Mellon, P. M. 1978. Causal influence of teachers' expectations on children's academic performance: A cross-lagged panel analysis. *Journal of Educational Psychology* 70:39–49.

Darley, J. M., and Fazio, R. H. 1980. Expectancy confirmation process arising in the social interaction sequence. *American Psychologist* 35:867–81.

Davis, J. A. 1966. The campus as a frog pond: An application of the theory of relative deprivation to career decisions of college men. *American Journal of Sociology* 72:17–31.

DeBlaissie, R. R., and Healy, G. W. 1970. *Self-concept: A comparison of Spanish-American, Negro, and Anglo adolescents across ethnic, sex, and socioeconomic variables.* Las Cruces, N.M.: ERIC Clearinghouse on Rural Education and Small Schools.

DeBord, L. L., Griffin, L. J., and Clark, M. 1977. Race, sex, and schooling: Insights from the Wisconsin model of the early achievement process. *Sociology of Education* 50:85–102.

Denzin, N. K. 1972. The genesis of self in early childhood. *The Sociological Quarterly* 13:291–314.

Deutsch, M. 1960. *Minority groups and class status as related to social and personality factors in scholastic achievement.* Ithaca, N.Y.: Cornell University Press.

Dickstein, E. 1972. The Development of Self-Esteem: Theory and Measurement. Ph.D. dissertation, The Johns Hopkins University.

Doma, cited by Finn, J. D. 1972. Expectations and the educational environment. *Review of Educational Research* 42:387–409.

Dornbusch, S. M., and Scott, W. R. 1975. *Evaluation and the exercize of authority.* San Francisco: Jossey-Bass.

Duncan, O. D. 1975. *Introduction to structural equation models.* New York: Academic Press.

Durkheim, E. 1961. *Moral Education.* New York: Free Press.

Dwyer, C. A. 1973. Sex differences in reading. *Review of Educational Research* 43:455–60.

Echelberger, E. 1959. Relationships between Personality Traits and Peer Status. Ph.D. dissertation, University of Michigan.

Eder, D. 1981. Ability grouping as a self-fulfilling prophecy: A micro-analysis of teacher-student interaction. *Sociology of Education* 54:151–62.

Elder, G. H. 1968. *Adolescent socialization and personality development.* Chicago: Rand McNally.

Engel, M. 1959. The stability of the self-concept in adolescence. *Journal of Abnormal and Social Psychology* 58:211–15.

Entwisle, D. R., and Baker, D. P. Young children's expectations for performance in arithmetic, forthcoming.

Entwisle, D. R., Cornell, E., and Epstein, J. 1972. Effect of a principal's expectations on test performance of elementary-school children. *Psychological Reports* 31:551–56.

Entwisle, D. R., and Doering, S. G. 1981. *The first birth: A family turning point.* Baltimore: Johns Hopkins University Press.

Entwisle, D. R., and Hayduk, L. A. 1978a. *Too great expectations: The academic outlook of young children.* Baltimore: Johns Hopkins University Press.

Entwisle, D. R., and Hayduk, L. A. 1978b. Schooling of Young Children: Cognitive and Affective Outcomes. Final Report Project No. NIE-G-74-0029. Department of Social Relations, The Johns Hopkins University.

Entwisle, D. R., and Hayduk, L. A. 1981. Academic expectations and the school attainment of young children. *Sociology of Education* 54:34–50.

Entwisle, D. R., and Webster, M. 1972. Raising children's performance expectations. *Social Science Research* 1:147–58.

Entwisle, D. R., and Webster, M. 1973. Research notes: Status factors in expectations raising. *Sociology of Education* 46:115–26.

Entwisle, D. R., and Webster, M. 1974a. Raising children's expectations for their own performance: A classroom application. In *Expectation states theory: A theoretical research program,* eds. J. Berger, T. Conner, and M. H. Fisek. Cambridge: Winthrop.

Entwisle, D. R., and Webster, M. 1974b. Expectations in mixed racial groups. *Sociology of Education* 47:301–18.

Entwisle, D. R., and Webster, M. 1978. Raising expectations indirectly. *Social Forces* 57:257–64.

Epps, E. G. 1969. Correlates of academic achievement among northern and southern urban Negro students. *Journal of Social Issues* 25:55–70.

Epstein, J. L. 1980. *A longitudinal study of school and family effects on student development.* Report No. 301, Baltimore: Center for Social Organization of Schools, The Johns Hopkins University.

Epstein, S. 1967. Toward a unified theory of anxiety. In *Progress in experimental personality research,* ed. B. A. Maker, Vol. 4. New York: Academic Press.

Epstein, S. 1973. The self-concept revisited. *American Psychologist* 28:404–16.

Erickson, E. H. 1950. *Childhood and society.* New York: W. W. Norton.

Estes, W. K. 1970. *Learning theory and mental development.* New York: Academic Press.

Felsenthal, H. 1971. Pupil Sex as a Variable in Teacher Perception of Classroom. Paper presented at meetings of American Educational Research Association, New York.

Finifter, B. M. 1972. The generation of confidence: Evaluating research findings by random subsample replication. In *Sociological methodology.* San Francisco: Jossey-Bass.

Finn, J. D. 1970. The Educational Environment: Expectations. Paper presented at meetings of American Educational Research Association, Minneapolis.

Finn, J. D. 1972. Expectations and the educational environment. *Review of Educational Research* 42:387–409.

Firkowska, A., Ostrowska, A., Sokolowska, M., Stein, Z., Susser, M., and Wald, I. 1978. Cognitive development and social policy. *Science* 200:1357–62.

Fishman, J. R. 1964. Guidelines for testing minority group children. *Journal of Social Issues* 20:127–45.

Fleming, E. S., and Anttonen, R. G. 1970. Teacher Expectancy or My Fair Lady. Paper presented at meetings of American Educational Research Association, Minneapolis, Minnesota.

Frerichs, A. H. 1970. Relationship of Self-Esteem of the Disadvantaged to School Success. Paper presented at meetings of American Educational Research Association, Minneapolis. ERIC: ED 040223.

Gibby, R. G., and Gabler, R. 1967. The self-concept of Negro and white children. *Journal of Clinical Psychology* 23:144–48.

Goldsmith, J. S. 1970. The Effect of a High Expectancy Prediction on Reading Achievement and IQ of Students in Grade 10. M.Ed. thesis, Rutgers University.

Gottfredson, D. C. 1980. Personality and Persistence in Education: A Longitudinal Study. Paper presented at the annual meeting of the American Psychological Association.

Green, B. F., Jr. 1977. Parameter sensitivity in multivariate methods. *Multivariate Behavioral Research* 12:263–88.

Green, R. B., and Rohwer, W. D. 1971. SES differences on learning and ability tests in black children. *American Educational Research Journal* 8:601–9.

Gustafson, R. A., and Owens, T. 1971. Children's Perceptions of Themselves and Their Teacher's Feelings Toward Them Related to Actual Teacher Perceptions and Social Achievement. Paper presented at meetings of Western Psychological Association, San Francisco.

Haller, E. J., and Davis, S. A. 1981. Teacher perceptions, parental social status and grouping for reading instruction. *Sociology of Education* 54:162–74.

Hanushek, E. A. 1972. *Education and race.* Lexington, Mass.: D. C. Heath.

Harari, H. 1973. Specialist: Name can hinder child. *The Minneapolis Star,* June 2, p. 1. Cited by Braun, 1976.

Harcourt, Brace & World, Inc. Test Department. 1961. *Report No. 4 Otis quick-scoring mental ability tests: Correlations of IQ's with IQ's from two other mental ability tests.*

Harcourt, Brace & World, Inc. Test Department. 1968. *Report of Otis quick-scoring mental ability test and Otis-Lennon mental ability test equivalence study.*

Hauser, R. M. 1971. *Socioeconomic background and educational performance.* Washington, D.C.: American Sociological Association Rose Monograph Series.

Hauser, R. M. 1978. On "a reconceptualization of school effects." *Sociology of Education* 51:68–72.

Hauser, R. M., and Goldberger, A. S. 1971. The treatment of unobservable variables in path analysis. In *Sociological methodology.* San Francisco: Jossey-Bass.

Hauser, R. M., Sewell, W. H., and Alwin, D. F. 1976. High school effects on achievement. In *Schooling and achievement in American society,* eds. W. H. Sewell, R. M. Hauser, and D. L. Featherman. New York: Academic Press.

Havighurst, R. J. 1970. Minority subcultures and the law of effect. *American Psychologist* 25:313–22.

Henderson, G. 1967. Beyond poverty of income. *Journal of Negro Education* 36:42–50.

Henderson, N. B., Goffeney, B., and Butler, B. V. 1969. Do Negro children project a self-image of helplessness and inadequacy in drawing a person? In *Proceedings of the 77th Annual Convention of the American Psychological Association.* ERIC: ED-036-329.

Hess, R. D. 1970. Class and ethnic influences upon socialization. In *Carmichael's manual of child psychology,* ed. P. H. Mussen. New York: Wiley.

Hess, R. D., and Shipman, V. 1965. Early experience and socialization of cognitive models in children. *Child Development* 36:869–86.

Heyns, B. 1978. *Summer learning.* New York: Academic Press.

Hieronymus, A. N., and Stroud, J. B. 1969. Comparability of IQ scores on five widely used intelligence tests. *Measurement and Evaluation in Guidance* 2:135–40.

Hirsch, J. G., and Costello, J. 1970. School achievement and under-achievers in an urban ghetto. *Elementary School Journal* 71:78–85.

Hodgkins, B. J., and Stakenas, R. G. 1969. A study of self-concepts of Negro and white youths in segregated environments. *Journal of Negro Education* 38:370–77.

Hoffman, L. W., and Hoffman, M. L. eds. 1966. *Review of child developmental research.* New York: Russell Sage.

Honzig, M. P., MacFarlane, J. W., and Allen, L. 1948. The stability of mental test performances between two and eighteen years. *Journal of Experimental Education* 17:309–24.

Horowitz, F. D. 1962. The relationship of anxiety, self-concept, and sociometric status among fourth, fifth, and sixth grade children. *Journal of Abnormal and Social Psychology* 65:212–14.

Hunt, D. E., and Hardt, R. H. 1969. The effect of Upward Bound programs on the attitudes, motivation, and academic achievement of Negro students. *Journal of Social Issues* 25:117–29.

Husen, T. 1969. *Talent, opportunity and career.* Stockholm: Almqvist and Wiksell.

Janis, I. L. 1958. *Psychological stress.* New York: Wiley.

Jencks, C. S., Smith, M., Acland, H., Bane, M. J., Cohen, D., Gintis, H., Heyns, B., and Michelson, S. 1972. *Inequality: A reassessment of the effect of family and schooling in America.* New York: Basic Books.

Jöreskog, K. G. 1970. A general method for analysis of covariance structures. *Biometrika* 57:239–51.

Jöreskog, K. G., and Sörbom, D. 1976. *LISREL III: Estimation of linear structural equation systems by maximum likelihood methods. A FORTRAN IV program.* Chicago: National Educational Resources, Inc.

Jöreskog, K. G., and Sörbom, D. 1978. *LISREL: Version IV.* Chicago: National Educational Resources, Inc.

Jose, J., and Cody, J. 1971. Teacher-pupil interaction as it related to attempted changes in teacher expectancy of academic ability and achievement. *American Educational Research Journal* 8:49–59.

Jourard, S. M., and Remy, R. M. 1955. Perceived parental attitudes, the self, and security. *Journal of Consulting Psychology* 19:361–66.

Kagan, J. 1980. Perspectives on continuity. In *Constancy and change in human development,* eds. O. G. Brim and J. Kagan. Cambridge, Mass.: Harvard.

Kagan, J., and Moss, H. A. 1962. *Birth to maturity.* New York: Wiley.

Kahn, R. L. 1978. Foreword. In *Youth in transition,* eds. J. O. Bachman, P. M. O'Malley, and J. Johnston. Ann Arbor: University of Michigan.

Kaminski, D. M., Erickson, E. L., Ross, M., and Bradfield, L. 1976. Why Females Don't Like Mathematics: The Effect of Parental Expectations. Paper presented at the 1976 American Sociological Association meeting in New York.

Kashinsky, M., and Wiener, M. 1969. Tone in communication and the performance of children from 2 socioeconomic groups. *Child Development* 40:1193–1202.

Keller, S. 1963. The social world of the urban slum child:

Some preliminary findings. *American Journal of Orthopsychiatry* 33:823-31.

Kerckhoff, A. C., and Campbell, R. T. 1977. Black-white differences in the educational attainment process. *Sociology of Education* 50:15-27.

Kinch, J. W. 1960. A formalized theory of the self-concept. *American Journal of Sociology* 68:481-86.

Klitgaard, R. E., and Hall, G. R. 1977. A statistical search for unusually effective schools. In *Statistics and public policy,* eds. W. Fairley and F. Mosteller. Reading, Mass.: Addison-Wesley.

Kohn, M. L. 1969. *Class and conformity.* Homewood, Ill.: Dorsey Press.

Kranz, P. L., Weber, W. A., and Fishell, K. N. 1970. The Relationships Between Teacher Perception of Pupils and Teacher Behavior Toward Those Pupils. Paper presented at meetings of American Educational Research Association, Minneapolis.

Kraus, P. E. 1973. *Yesterday's children.* New York: Wiley.

Lambert, W. E., and MacNamara, J. 1969. Some cognitive consequences of following a first-grade curriculum in a second language. *Journal of Educational Psychology* 60:86-96.

Lamy, N. W. 1965. Relation of self-perceptions of early primary children to achievement in reading. In *Human development readings in research,* ed. J. J. Gordon. Chicago: Scott, Foresman.

Lazarus, A. S. 1966. *Psychological stress and coping process.* New York: McGraw Hill.

Lippitt, R., and Gold, M. 1959. Classroom social structure as a mental health problem. *Journal of Social Issues* 15:40-49.

Lockheed, M. E. 1976. *Some determinants and consequences of teacher expectations concerning pupil performance.* Princeton, N.J.: Educational Testing Service.

Lockheed, M. E., and Morgan, W. R. 1979. *A causal mode of teachers' expectations in elementary classrooms.* Research Report 79-12. Princeton, N.J.: Educational Testing Service.

Luecke, D. F., and McGinn, N. F. 1975. Regression analyses and education production functions: Can they be trusted? *Harvard Educational Review* 45:325-50.

Maccoby, E. E., and Jacklin, C. N. 1980. Sex differences in aggression: A rejoinder and reprise. *Child Development* 51:964-80.

Marjoribanks, K. 1979. *Families and their learning environments.* London: Routledge and Kegan Paul.

Marks, R. W. 1951. The effect of probability, desirability and privilege upon the stated expectations of children. *Journal of Personality* 19:332-51.

Massey, G. C., Scott, V. S., and Dornbusch, S. M. 1975. Racism without racists: Institutional racism in urban schools. *The Black Scholar* (November):10-19.

McCarthy, P. J. 1976. The use of balanced half-sample replication in cross-validation studies. *Journal of American Statistical Association* 71:596-604.

McDaniel, E. L. 1967. Relationships between Self-Concept and Specific Variables in a Low-Income Culturally Different Population. Final Report of Head Start Evaluation and Research to the Institute for Educational Development, Section VIII.

McDermott, R. P. 1977. Social relations as contexts for learning in school. *Harvard Educational Review* 47:198-213.

McPartland, J. 1968. *The segregated student in desegregated schools, sources of influence on negro secondary students. Final Report.* Report No. 21. Baltimore: Center for the Social Organization of Schools, The Johns Hopkins University.

McPartland, J. M., and Karweit, N. L. 1978. *Methodological issues in school effects research.* Report No. 245. Baltimore: Center for the Social Organization of Schools, The Johns Hopkins University.

Mead, G. H. 1934. *Mind, self, and society from the standpoint of a social behaviorist.* Chicago: University of Chicago Press.

Mendels, G. E., and Flanders, J. P. 1973. Teachers' expectations and pupil performance. *American Educational Research Journal* 10:203-12.

Meyer, W. J., and Thompson, G. G. 1956. Sex differences in the distribution of teacher approval and disapproval among sixth-grade children. *Journal of Educational Psychology* 47:385-96.

Meyers, E. 1966. Self-Concept, Family Structure and School Achievement. Ph.D. dissertation, Columbia University. *Dissertation Abstracts* (1967) 27:3960A.

Miller, D. T., and Ross, M. 1975. Self-serving biases in the attribution of causality: Fact or fiction? *Psychological Bulletin* 82:213-25.

Morse, W. C. 1964. Self-concept in the school setting. *Childhood Education* 41:195-98.

Morse, R. 1967. Self-concept of ability and school achievement: A comparative study of Negro and Caucasian students. In Self-Concept of Ability and School Achievement, III, W. B. Brookover, E. L. Erickson, and L. M. Joiner, pp. 205-209. U.S. Office of Education Cooperative Research Project No. 2831. East Lansing: Office of Research and Publications, Michigan State University.

Mosteller, F., and Moynihan, D. P., eds. 1972. *On equality of educational opportunity.* New York: Vintage Books.

Murnane, R. J. 1975. *The impact of school resources on the learning of inner city children.* Cambridge: Ballinger.

Nicholls, J. G. 1979. Development of perception of own attainment and causal attributions for success and failure in reading. *Journal of Educational Psychology* 71:94-99.

Otto, L. B. 1976. Social integration and the status-attainment process. *American Journal of Sociology* 81:1360-83.

Page, E. B. 1958. Teacher comments and student performance: A seventy-four classroom experiment in school motivation. *Journal of Educational Psychology* 49:173-81.

Palardy, J. M. 1969. What teachers believe—what children achieve. *Elementary School Journal* 69:370-74.

Parsons, J. E., and Ruble, D. N. 1977. The development of achievement related expectancies. *Child Development* 48:1075-79.

Parsons, T. 1955. Family structure and the socialization of the child. In *Family socialization and interaction process,* eds. T. Parsons and R. F. Bales. New York: Free Press.

Paschal, B. J. 1968. The role of self-concept in achievement. *Journal of Negro Education* 37:392-96.

Pedersen, E., Faucher, T. A., and Eaton, W. W. 1978. A new perspective on the effects of first-grade teachers on children's subsequent adult status. *Harvard Educational Review* 48:1–31.

Perry, E. 1975. Communication of Teacher Expectations Over Time. Paper presented at meetings of the American Psychological Association, Chicago.

Phillips, B. N. 1972. School-related aspirations of children with different socio-cultural backgrounds. *Journal of Negro Education* 41:48–52.

Portes, A., and Wilson, K. L. 1976. Black-white differences in educational attainment. *American Sociological Review* 41:414–31.

Pouissant, A. F., and Atkinson, C. O. 1968. Negro youth and psychological motivation. *Journal of Negro Education* 37:241–51.

Pouissant, A. F., and Atkinson, C. O. 1970. Negro youth and psychological motivation. In *Educating the disadvantaged: School year 1968–1969,* ed. A. C. Ornstein, New York: AMS Press.

Radke-Yarrow, M., Trager, H., and Davis, H. 1965. Social perceptions and attitudes of children. In *The self in growth teaching and learning,* ed. D. E. Hamachek. Englewood Cliffs, N.J.: Prentice Hall.

Rahe, D. F., and Blaess, D. A. 1975. Effects of Feedback on Children's Expectations. Paper presented at meetings of American Educational Research Association, Washington, D.C.

Reeder, T. A. 1955. A study of some relationships between level of self-concept, academic achievement and classroom adjustment. *Dissertation Abstracts* (1955):2472.

Reese, H. W. 1961. Relationships between self-acceptance and sociometric choices. *Journal of Abnormal and Social Psychology* 62:472–74.

Reschly, D. J., and Lamprecht, M. J. 1979. Expectancy effects of labels: Fact or artifact? *Exceptional Children* 46:55–58.

Riley, M. W., Johnson, M., and Foner, A. 1972. *Aging and society.* New York: Russell Sage.

Rist, R. C. 1970. Student social class and teacher expectations: the self-fulfilling prophecy in ghetto education. *Harvard Educational Review* 40:411–51.

Rist, R. C. 1973. *The urban school: A factory for failure.* Cambridge, Mass.: MIT Press.

Rosenberg, M. 1965. *Society and the adolescent self-image.* Princeton, N.J.: Princeton University Press.

Rosenberg, L. A., and Adcock, E. P. 1979. The effectiveness of early childhood education: Third grade reading levels. Interim Report, December, 1979. ESEA, Title IV C Longitudinal Evaluation Project for Selected Early Childhood Educational Programs, Maryland State Department of Education.

Rosenberg, M., and Simmons, R. A. 1971. *Black and white self-esteem.* Washington, D.C.: American Sociological Association Rose Monograph Series.

Rosenthal, R. 1972. *On the social psychology of the self-fulfilling prophecy: Further evidence for Pygmalion effects and mediating mechanisms.* New York: MSS Modular Publications.

Rosenthal, R., and Jacobson, L. 1968. *Pygmalion in the classroom.* New York: Holt, Rinehart and Winston.

Rubin, R. A., Maruyama, G., and Kingsbury, G. G. 1979. Self-Esteem and Educational Achievement: A Causal-Model Analysis. Paper presented at the Annual Meeting of the American Psychological Association, New York, September.

Ruble, D. N., Boggiano, D. K., Feldman, N. S., and Loebl, J. H. 1980. Developmental analysis of the role of social comparison in self-evaluation. *Developmental Psychology* 16:105–15.

Rubovits, P. C., and Maehr, M. L. 1970. The Effect of the Labels Gifted and Nongifted on Teacher's Interaction with Black and White Students. Working Paper, Center for Instructional Research and Curriculum Evaluation, University of Illinois.

Rubovits, P. C., and Maehr, M. L. 1973. Pygmalion black and white. *Journal of Personality and Social Psychology* 25:210–18.

Sarason, S. B., and Gladwin, T. 1958. Psychological and cultural problems in mental subnormality: A review of research. *American Journal of Mental Deficiency* 62:115–137.

Sattler, J. M. 1970. Racial "experimenter effects" in experimentation, testing, interviewing, and psychotherapy. *Psychological Bulletin* 73:137–60.

Scarr, S. W. 1980. "Commentary" pp. 76–83 in Early Patterns of Cognitive Development. *Monographs of the Society for Research in Child Development* 45:No. 2.

Scheirer, M. A., and Kraut, R. E. 1979. Increasing educational achievement via self-concept change. *Review of Educational Research* 49:131–50.

Schmuck, R. 1962. Sociometric status and utilization of academic abilities. *Merrill Palmer Quarterly* 8:165–72.

Schmuck, R. 1963. Some relationships of peer liking patterns in the classroom to pupil attitudes and achievement. *School Review* 71:337–59.

Schneider, B. L. 1980. Production Analysis of Gains in Achievement. Paper presented at meetings of the American Educational Research Association, Boston.

Scott, L. J. 1969. An Analysis of the Self-Concept of Seventh-Grade Students in Segregated-Desegregated Schools of Oklahoma City. Ph.D. dissertation, University of Oklahoma.

Seaver, W. B. 1973. Effects of naturally-induced teacher expectancies. *Journal of Personality and Social Psychology* 28:333–42.

Sewell, W. H., and Armer, J. M. 1966. Neighborhood context and college plans. *American Sociological Review* 31:159–68.

Sewell, W. H., Haller, A. O., and Portes, A. 1969. The educational and early occupational attainment process. *American Sociological Review* 34:82–92.

Sewell, W. H., Haller, A. O., and Straus, M. 1959. Social status and educational and occupational aspirations. *American Sociological Review* 22:67–76.

Sewell, W. H., and Hauser, R. M. 1972. Causes and consequences of higher education: Models of the status attainment process. *American Journal of Agricultural Economics* 54:851–61.

Sewell, W. H., and Hauser, R. M. 1975. *Education, occupation, and earnings: Achievement in the early career.* New York: Academic Press.

Sewell, W. H., and Hauser, R. M. 1976. Causes and consequences of higher education: Models of the status attainment process. In *Schooling and achievement in American society,* eds. W. H. Sewell, R. M. Hauser, and D. L. Featherman. New York: Academic Press.

Silberman, M. L. 1969. Behavioral expression of teachers' attitudes toward elementary school students. *Journal of Educational Psychology* 60:402–7.

Silverstein, B., and Krate, R. 1975. *Children of the dark ghetto: A developmental psychology.* New York: Praeger.

Smith, M. S. 1972. Equality of educational opportunity: The basic findings reconsidered. In *On equality of educational opportunity,* eds. F. Mosteller and D. P. Moynihan. New York: Vintage.

Soares, A. T., and Soares, L. M. 1969a. Self-perceptions of culturally disadvantaged children. *American Educational Research Journal* 6:31–45.

Soares, A. T., and Soares, L. M. 1969b. A comparative study of the self-perceptions of disadvantaged children in elementary and secondary schools. *Proceedings of 77th Annual APA Convention* 4:659–60.

Soares, A. T., and Soares, L. M. 1970a. Differences in Self-Perceptions of Disadvantaged Students. Paper presented at meetings of the American Educational Research Association, Minneapolis, March.

Soares, A. T., and Soares, L. M. 1970b. Interpersonal and self-perceptions of advantaged and disadvantaged high school students. *Proceedings of 78th Annual APA Convention* 5:457–58.

Soares, A. T., and Soares, L. M. 1970c. Self-concepts of disadvantaged and advantaged students. *Proceedings of 78th Annual APA Convention* 5:655–56.

Sorensen, A. B., and Hallinan, M. T. 1977. A reconceptualization of school effects. *Sociology of Education* 50:273–89.

Spady, W. G. 1970. Lament for the letterman: Effects of peer status and extracurricular activities on goals and achievement. *American Journal of Sociology* 75:680–702.

Spady, W. G. 1976. The impact of school resources on students. In *Schooling and achievement in American society,* eds. W. H. Sewell, R. M. Hauser, and D. L. Featherman. New York: Academic Press.

St. John, N. H. 1975. *School desegregation.* New York: Wiley.

Stanley, J. C. 1976. Use of tests to discover talent. In *Intellectual talent: Research and development,* ed. D. P. Keating. Baltimore: The Johns Hopkins University Press.

Stendler, C. B. 1951. Social class differences in parental attitude toward school at Grade 1 level. *Child Development* 22:37–46.

Stephens, J. M. 1967. *The process of schooling.* New York: Holt, Rinehart & Winston.

Stephens, J. M. 1956. *Educational psychology.* New York: Holt, Rinehart, and Winston.

Stevens, P. H. 1956. An investigation of the relationship between certain aspects of self-concept behavior and students' academic achievement. *Dissertation Abstracts* (1956):2531–32.

Stevenson, H. W., Hale, G. A., Hill, K. T., and Moely, B. E. 1967. Determinants of children's preferences for adults. *Child Development* 38:1–14.

Stinchcombe, A. L. 1964. *Rebellion in a high school.* Chicago: Quadrangle.

Sullivan, E. T., Clark, W. W., and Tiegs, E. W. 1974. *Short form test of academic attitude. Technical report.* Monterey, Calif.: CTB/McGraw Hill.

Sullivan, H. S. 1947. *Conception of modern psychiatry.* Washington, D.C.: William Alanson White Psychiatric Foundation.

Summers, A. A., and Wolfe, B. L. 1977. Do schools make a difference? *American Economic Review* 65(4):639–52.

Thorndike, R. L., and Hagen, E. 1971. *Examiners manual. Cognitive abilities test.* Boston: Houghton Mifflin.

Thorndike, R. L., Hagen, E., and Lorge, I. 1974. *Cognitive abilities test.* Boston: Houghton Mifflin.

Thurstone, L. L., and Thurstone, T. G. 1965. *Primary mental abilities technical report No. 7-1806.* Chicago: Science Research Associates.

Trowbridge, N. T. 1969. Project IMPACT Research Report 1968–1969. U.S. Office of Education Cooperative Research Report, May.

Trowbridge, N. T. 1970a. The measurement. In *IMPACT 70,* ed. J. P. Rowson. Des Moines, Iowa: Polk County Education Services.

Trowbridge, N. T. 1970b. Self-concept and socio-economic class. *Psychology in the Schools* 7:3.

Trowbridge, N. T. 1972. Self-concept and socio-economic status in elementary school children. *American Educational Research Journal* 9:525–37.

Van Egmond, E. 1960. Social Interrelationship Skills and Effective Use of Intelligence in the Classroom. Ph.D. dissertation, University of Michigan.

Walberg, H. J., and Marjoribanks, K. 1976. Family environment and cognitive development: Twelve analytic models. *Review of Educational Research* 46:527–51.

Wattenberg, W. W., and Clifford, C. 1964. Relation of self-concepts to beginning achievement in reading. *Child Development* 35:461–67.

Wax, M. L. 1969. *Indian education in Eastern Oklahoma.* Research Contract Report No. O.E. 6-10-260 and BIA No. 5-0565-2-12-1. Washington, D.C.: U.S. Office of Education.

Webster, M., and Entwisle, D. R. 1976. Expectation effects on performance evaluations. *Social Forces* 55:493–502.

Weikart, D. P., Bond, J. T., and McNeil, J. T. 1978. The *Ypsilanti Perry preschool project: Preschool years and longitudinal results through fourth grade.* Ypsilanti, Michigan: High/Scope Educational Research Foundation.

West, C., and Anderson, T. 1974. A Review of the Teacher Expectancy Effect: The Question of Preponderant Causation. Multilith, University of Illinois.

West, C. K., and Anderson, T. H. 1976. The question of preponderant causation in teacher expectancy research. *Review of Educational Research* 46:613–30.

Whiting, B. 1975. The problem of the packaged variable. In *The developing individual in a changing world,* eds. K. F. Reigel and J. A. Meacham. Historical and Culture Issues, Vol. 1, The Hague: Mouton.

Wiley, D. E. 1973. The identification problem for structural equation models with unmeasured variables. In *Structural equation models in the social sciences,* eds. A. S. Goldberger and O. D. Duncan. New York: Seminar.

Williams, T. 1976. Teacher prophecies and the inheritance of inequality. *Sociology of Education* 49:223–36.

Wilson, A. B. 1959. Residential segregation of social classes and aspirations of high school boys. *American Sociological Review* 24:836–45.

Wilson, A. B. 1967. Educational consequences of segregation in a California community. *Racial isolation in the public schools.* Washington, D.C.: Government Printing Office.

Wilson, K. L., and Portes, A. 1975. The educational attainment process: Results from a national sample. *American Journal of Sociology* 81:343–63.

Winkler, D. R. 1972. The Production of Human Capital: A Study of Minority Achievement. Ph.D. dissertation, University of California, Berkeley.

Wylie, R. C. 1963. Children's estimates of their schoolwork ability as a function of sex, race, and socioeconomic level. *Journal of Personality* 31:204–24.

Yeatts, P. P. 1967. An Analysis of Developmental Changes in the Self-Report of Negro and White Children, Grades Three Through Twelve. Ph.D. dissertation, University of Florida.

Zigler, E., and Delabry, J. 1962. Concept-switching in middle-class, lower-class, and retarded children. *Journal of Abnormal and Social Psychology* 65:267–73.

Zirkel, P. A., and Moses, E. G. 1971. Self-concept and ethnic group membership among public school students. *American Educational Research Journal* 8:253–66.

Zuckerman, M. 1979. Attribution of success and failure revisited, or: The motivational bias is alive and well in attribution theory. *Journal of Personality* 47:245–87.

Index

The Johns Hopkins University Press

Early Schooling: Cognitive and Affective Outcomes

This book was composed in Times Roman text and display type by Action Comp Co. Inc. from a design by Alan Carter. It was printed on 60-lb. Decision Opaque Smooth paper and bound in Holliston Roxite A cloth by the Maple Press Company.